ITALIAN NATIONALISM
and ENGLISH LETTERS

ITALIAN NATIONALISM and ENGLISH LETTERS

Figures of the Risorgimento and Victorian Men of Letters

By HARRY W. RUDMAN

AMS PRESS, INC.
NEW YORK
1966

AMS PRESS, INC.
NEW YORK, N.Y. 10003
1966

Manufactured in the United States of America

Acknowledgments

I SHOULD like to thank the staffs of the British Museum, the New York Public Library, the Columbia University Library, the City College Library, and the Reform Club in London, who made available to me the resources of these collections.

I am indebted to Columbia University for a University Fellowship, 1934–35, which enabled me to carry on researches in England, and to The City College for a grant from the Samuel Greenbaum Scholarship Fund.

At Columbia University, Professor Emery E. Neff has been chiefly helpful, but I have also profited by the suggestions of others, particularly of Dr. Roderick Marshall, Professors Oscar James Campbell, Jefferson B. Fletcher, and Susanne Howe Nobbe.

My friends and colleagues at The City College, Professor Arthur Dickson, Professor Ralph Gordon, Mr. Seymour Copstein, Mr. Milton Millhauser, Mr. Warren B. Austin, Mr. Edgar Johnson, and Dr. John C. Thirlwall, Jr., have all aided me to improve the accuracy and the wording of my manuscript. Similarly, I have gained much from the criticism of Dr. Leo J. Henkin of Brooklyn College.

I remember gratefully the unselfish services of my sister, Miss Annie Rudman.

Contents

PART III

Introduction

There is in Machiavelli's *The Prince*, written in 1513, a famous description of his fatherland: "enslaved . . . oppressed . . . scattered . . . ; without a head, without order, beaten, despoiled, lacerated, and overrun. . . ." Some three centuries later, when the Hundred Days of the first Napoleon were over, Italy was still a dismembered land: here ruled by Austria, and there divided into her spheres of influence; elsewhere dominated by petty tyrants; and everywhere terrorized by a close surveillance over all opinion.

In the early decades of the nineteenth century, the idea of a united Italy was not uppermost in the minds of most Italians. True, desperate and inspired by the dynamic slogans of the French Revolution, a few patriots did revolt. As the century grew older, intermittent outbursts became more frequent and no longer resembled so much the puffs of a mud geyser on uncertain schedule as rather a volcano steadily aflame through a funnel-like pillar of cloud. Ultimately, the unity of Italy was achieved—by a diplomacy unscrupulous and temporizing, by heroism and by opportunism, with the aid of French and Prussian arms.

Patriotic Italians were divided on the method of uniting their country. Mazzini and his party of *Young Italy* favoured a unitarian republican programme. Cavour gave his adherence to the notion of a centralized state representing a swollen kingdom of Piedmont. This the Mazzinians abhorred as if it were a python, gorged and distended. Of those who inclined to a federal government, some would have given its leadership to the Pope; others, to the sovereign of Piedmont.

From different points of view, Italy was to the British both of the Romantic Period and of the Victorian Age a land of, and under, enchantment. Many, under the powerful spell of a kind of nostalgia for an ancient civilization, of which the modern Italians were the titular heirs, regarded her as the theatre of the Roman world, the centre of culture during times past. A second group travelled in Italy and was moved to indignation by the Shelleyan vision of Victorious Wrong, whose vulture scream saluted the rising sun and pursued the flying day. Above all, the contemporaneous struggles of the Italians against their oppressors and the personal magnetism of exiles like Mazzini were sources of superb literary material. It is therefore not astonishing that the *Risorgimento*, the "resurrection "of Italian nationalism from 1815 to 1870 (when Rome at long last became again the capital of Italy), should be reflected in the work of a great many British writers. Of those who readily occur to one's mind, Wordsworth, Byron, Shelley, Thomas Moore, Landor, Hazlitt, Clough, Elizabeth Barrett and Robert Browning, Arnold, Meredith, and Swinburne, are only a few; and pamphlets, novels, poems, plays, travel accounts, etc., are numerous indeed.

Only one satisfactory account of how the politics of nineteenth-century Italy influenced contemporary English writers has been published, Dr. Margaret C. W. Wicks's *The Italian Exiles in London, 1816–1848* (Manchester, 1937); and that does not extend beyond 1848. *Italian Nationalism and English Letters* is intended to serve only as a cross section of British and Italian intellectual relationships during the *Risorgimento*, particularly those which were expressed in literature; for the theme is enormous, and one must be content with sampling in the manner of a geologist. Though my study will include some of the exiles treated by Dr. Wicks, the point of view is different in that my emphasis is placed as much as possible on literary aspects rather than on biographical details for their own sake. I have added sketches of patriots like Saffi, Orsini, and those prisoners of King Ferdinand of Naples whose innocence Gladstone championed; but the important *rôles* can be played only by the leaders of the Italian national revival, Mazzini, Cavour, and Garibaldi, the currents of whose lives mingled with the mighty torrent of English life and letters. One could even maintain, and with more than a show of reason, that Italian exiles like Foscolo and Mazzini were really English literary figures. In any case, as Bertrand Russell once remarked, to the nineteenth century the patriot of an oppressed country was as attractive as the idealized noble savage had been to the eighteenth.

Latterly, there have appeared competent English monographs on Gabriele Rossetti, Sir Anthony Panizzi of the British Museum, and Joseph Mazzini, which, together with Dr. Wicks's book, reveal a continued interest in nineteenth-century Italian themes and serve as evidence that the Italian patriots whom the Victorians knew are not forgotten.

BRITISH POLICY AND THE *RISORGIMENTO*

§ 1. *The British Attitude towards the* Risorgimento *in Italy*

The official British attitude toward Italy's aspirations for national unity was, on the whole, limited to wishing her well. To be sure, the traditional policy of Downing Street was in harmony with the ideals of the *Risorgimento*. An independent and unified Italy would aid England in maintaining the balance of power on the Continent and would doubtless promote and extend English trade. Yet the Foreign Office avoided the risks of any overt acts in the interest of Italian revolution.

It is true that the English general, Lord William Bentinck, in command of forces garrisoned in Sicily, there proclaimed a constitution in 1812—a statement of fundamental law influenced by English political usages. It is also true that Bentinck, landing at Leghorn two years later with an Anglo-Sicilian force, exhorted the Italians to rise for their freedom. But both steps were taken only as important tactics in the general English programme of encouraging as many of

Napoleon's potential enemies as possible. Indeed, since Napoleon had founded the Kingdom of Italy in the north and subsequently the Kingdom of Naples, it is to him as much as to anybody else that the Italians were indebted for awareness of their national identity. As Giusti's famous poem, "The Boot," inspired by the physical appearance of the Italian peninsula, indicated, the Corsican had come closest to uniting all Italy.

The English, after Waterloo resolute for peace that their trade might flourish, did very little at the Congress of Vienna to moderate the pious whims of the autocrats who subdivided the Italian peninsula according to the principle of "legitimacy." To restore the *status quo*, the Holy Alliance equated the making of peace with the treatment of peoples as pawns in a game of dynastic aggrandizement. English influence did not oppose attaching Genoa to Piedmont in order to strengthen the latter for its function as a buffer state between French and Austrian interests. The result of this process was that Austria became the dominant Italian power—with Hapsburg princes in the duchies of Tuscany, Parma, and Modena, through direct control over Lombardy and Venetia, and in accordance with the secret clause in a treaty of 1815 by which Ferdinand of the Two Sicilies bound himself not to introduce methods of government incompatible with those of Austrian Italy. Croatian soldiery, stationed at strategic places, menaced Italian patriotism, similarly, Italians garrisoned Austrian Poland, for the Hapsburg policy was to separate the different ethnic groups and thus rule a conglomerate empire.

In 1820, a Carbonarist mutiny in the Neapolitan army compelled King Ferdinand to assent to a constitutional government. But at Rieti, the Austrians ignominiously routed the Neapolitan forces under General Gugliemo Pepe*

* Pepe's historical writings and memoirs are devoted to vindicating the courage of Neapolitans in particular and of Italians in general. *The English in Italy*, 1825, a series of tales by the Marquess of Normanby,

and crushed for the time being the moderate hopes of the southern Italians. In Piedmont also, there was a Carbonarist rising in the army, which resulted in the granting of a constitution in 1821 by Prince Charles Albert in the absence of King Charles Felix. On the King's return, the document was withdrawn, and the Prince was exiled. In Lombardy, there was mild plotting against Austria, and many of the revolutionary leaders, like the enlightened Count Federico Confalonieri and the poet, Silvio Pellico, were imprisoned in the Spielberg. Here Pellico experienced the agonies recorded in his *Le mie prigioni.*

Now all these revolts of 1820–21 were defeated by Austrian intervention in one form or another. More intent upon aiding English trade with the new South American republics than upon assisting the Italian liberals, George Canning, successor to Castlereagh in the post of British Foreign Secretary, urged on the international congress assembled at Verona a policy of non-interference. In short, Canning declared his country no friend of revolution but in favour of the proposition that peoples had the right to select their own governments and to manage their own affairs. Canning's statement did not materially help the Italians.

The July Revolution in Paris in 1830 was followed by Italian risings the next year in the papal territories of Romagna and the March and in Parma and Modena. Again the Austrian bayonets dispersed the insurgents, but it is noteworthy that the great powers recommended a policy of reform to Pope Gregory XVI. England, in particular, favoured a gradual amelioration of Italian grievances for the purpose of maintaining European tranquillity. But when a new and liberal pope, Pius IX, did attempt to institute administrative reforms in his temporal possessions and even

writing anonymously, contains a tart sketch of Pepe: very handsome, exceedingly good-natured, but devoid of brains. Alexander Nelson Hood's *Adria: a Tale of Venice*, published almost eighty years later (1904), treats Pepe much more indulgently.

proclaimed an amnesty in behalf of political prisoners, the Austrians reoccupied Ferrara as a concrete sign that they would not tolerate elsewhere in Italy conditions in glaring contrast to their own rule. The English passed over this flouting of their programme of peaceful improvement.

The mission of Lord Minto to recommend reforms to the Italian rulers, motivated by the English desire to forestall the expected revolution of 1848, failed. At Palermo, there was a rising accompanied with a renewed demand for a constitution; everywhere was political convulsion; and, eventually, King Charles Albert of Piedmont declared war on Austria. The Hapsburgs, profiting by Italian disunion and the prowess of old Marshal Radetzky, preserved their hegemony. At one critical moment in 1848, it looked as if Austria were beaten; and at that time England counselled her to quit the peninsula for the sake of permanent peace.

During the Crimean War, England subsidized a large Piedmontese contingent, which fought gallantly. On King Victor Emmanuel's subsequent visit to London, Victoria honoured him with the Order of the Garter. The English, at the peace congress which closed the war, helped Piedmont obtain a hearing by means of which the civilized world was informed of Italian grievances against Austria. In a word, Great Britain had aided Piedmont in becoming the recognized champion of Italian nationalism. England, after Gladstone's sensational exposure of Neapolitan tyranny, continued to be the leader of that humanitarian opinion which was in 1860 to applaud Garibaldi's Redshirts.

Prior to the war (1859) of Piedmont and France against Austria, the English offered to mediate on a basis of liberal reforms in Lombardy and Venetia and of Austrian renunciation of all intervention in central Italy. At the conclusion of the war, Palmerston encouraged the union of the central Italian provinces with Piedmont. He was more interested in preventing the establishment of a French puppet state than in strengthening the new Kingdom of Italy.

In 1860, Lord John Russell's firm stand enabled Garibaldi to cross the Straits of Messina and so complete the conquest of southern Italy. In effect, Russell said that no foreign power, that is, the government of Napoleon III, could interfere in any part of Italy, but that any Italian or Italian state might. Again, Lord John Russell was acting more to thwart the French (against whom the voluntary riflemen movement in Great Britain was directed) than to assist the unification of Italy.

Such is the sketch of England's realistic Italian policy. In fine, the British favoured the *status quo* only as long as it was beneficial to their commercial interests. For the most part an agricultural country during the nineteenth century, Italy was potentially an excellent market for British manufactures, provided that the customs barriers erected by disunion were broken down. Eventually, it was the British opinion that Italian unification would promote trade. Moreover, the anticlerical policies of Piedmont earned wide approbation in Protestant England, where some wanted to believe that a new religious reformation was in process in Italy.

§ 2. *British Treatment of Italian Exiles*

The attitude of Great Britain towards nationalism in the Italian peninsula has been described. There now remains the question, "How, in general, did Italian political refugees fare in their English exile?" In other words, what was England's solution to the problem of Italian patriotism unreconciled to Continental tyranny?

The Holy Alliance, a collective entity for the suppression of liberalism, refused to countenance the plotting of exiles, who dared think of undermining from afar the buttresses of the *status quo*. Hence, it brought pressure to bear on small countries like Belgium and Switzerland not to shelter refugees. Thus, the nineteenth century witnessed the concentration in England of militant opposition to European reaction. Those exiles who emigrated to America indicated by their destination that they had given up the fight. On the other hand, London could be utilized as a base for plots against the system of Metternich, who consequently maintained there numerous spies and *agents provocateurs*.

In the course of time, the number of refugees clustering around Leicester Square in London grew fairly large. Here these Italian patriots lived and dreamed their dreams, of revolution, of remittances from relations, and, infrequently, of obtaining money without working. Many were men of singularly attractive personalities and wide culture, which gained for them entry to homes of refinement and means. It should be remembered that, before Mazzini's great work of propaganda, the Italian nationalistic movement was essentially a manifestation of the nobility and the upper middle class, strata of society likely to produce individuals able to fit readily into polite circles. Exiles of this type not only advanced the Italian cause indirectly, since enlightened Englishmen were moved to a natural abhorrence of the despotism that endangered a Lacaita or a Panizzi, but they also propagandized actively in behalf of their fatherland. Some became British subjects, married into wealthy families, and attained to positions of affluence and prestige, both of which they did not fail to use in the service of Italian patriotism.

When an Italian exile came to London, he would, of course, seek out such of his countrymen as he knew were from his own district. Milanese called upon Milanese, and recently exiled Neapolitans gravitated towards their forerunners from southern Italy. Often, a refugee who prospered became the centre of a group of his compatriots, who would then constitute a coterie devoted to the interminable rehearsing of political woes and antipathies. Eventually, a body of information essential to the expatriated accumulated. One soon learned that certain English people were well disposed towards nationalistic Italians. In this way, a William Roscoe, a Joseph Cowen, a William Shaen would be approached by refugees and asked to furnish aid or legal advice; a Carlyle might be importuned to obtain employment for some poor wretch escaped from Italian or Austrian secret police. After all, the English propertied classes had secured their position against a narrow oligarchy by the Reform Bill of 1832 and could safely indulge in liberalism, especially when it was directed in anticlerical and antidespotic ways. Helping Italians in England was a kind of rebuke to the Pope—an affirmation in its way of "No Popery." Moreover, the Irish did not like the idea of assistance to anti-Catholic Italian refugees; and what an Irishman disliked was naturally the delight of an Englishman. Then, too, the property-conscious British public loathed the Austrian policy after 1853 of sequestrating the estates of exiles and even of voluntary emigrants. Whatever the reason—religious prejudice, distress at the mistreatment of men of talent, the belief in the sacredness of property, the natural indignation of liberals—Italian expatriates found in England their kindest European haven.[1]

After a revolt in Italy, committees of Englishmen and Italians would be formed to assist the new harvest of refugees by raising money through various methods—balls, bazaars, benefit musical and dramatic entertainments, concerts. On the Continent, English diplomatic agents, acting on their own initiative, often interceded in behalf of distressed Italians. Indeed, it was not unusual for unsucessful patriots to escape under the protection of British passports. The governors of British possessions in the Mediterranean were expected to grant the mercy of asylum to political fugitives. That is why a More O'Ferrall, Governor of Malta, who refused to allow the refugees of Mazzini's Roman Republic to land could arouse the anger of a Landor[2] and be subjected to the investigation of a committee of liberal members of Parliament.[3]

What has been so far described has been mostly the general

relations of Englishmen and Italians as individuals. The British government itself rarely attempted to coerce the exiles who flocked to its domains, but sometimes an unfriendly policy towards liberal refugees was manifest during a Tory *régime*. On the whole, the various "Acts for the Registration of Aliens, and Naturalisation and Denization" were temperately administered. It is true that the Alien Office, which ceased to exist in 1836, kept its eye on politically active refugees like General Pepe; that the great poet, critic, and patriot, Foscolo, was fearful lest the particular Aliens Act * in force in 1816 restrict his freedom to travel about in Great Britain; that some Italians like Pecchio likened restriction on the movements of foreigners to a sword of Damocles; that information gathered from Mazzini's letters, opened in secret, was transmitted to an interested Continental power by a Tory government: yet England merited the complaints of Prince Carini,[4] envoy to London of the Neapolitan Bourbons, and of the Austrians, Count Nesselrode[5] and the influential Prince Schwarzenberg.[6] More or less freely, the Italian expatriates, organized in associations, inundated the Continent from London with incendiary proclamations and even issued loans and subscriptions in order to expend the receipts for the purchase of arms and ammunition.

Sometimes, the English government regretted the presence of certain exiles within its territories. There was, for example, the Italian who in 1857, at Panton Street, Haymarket, in London, stabbed four spies supposed to be in the pay of Napoleon III.[7] There was also the notorious case of Felice Orsini, who plotted in London the assassination of the same French emperor, used bombs manufactured in Birmingham,

* To it were subject all aliens except (after an amendment introduced by Sir Robert Peel) those continually resident for seven years. This Act was repealed in May 1836, and replaced by one reducing the period of supervision to three years. The Secretary of State had power to deport any alien. See Margaret C. W. Wicks's *The Italian Exiles in London*, 1816–48, pp. 50, 70, and 79. The revolutionary year of 1848 was marked by a new Bill for the Registration of Aliens, which was put into effect in 1849.

and availed himself of a forged English passport to go to Paris in 1858 as Mr. Allsop. After Orsini's desperate attempt, Palmerston yielded to French pressure and introduced a Bill directed against the Italian political refugees. But the measure failed to become a statute because the liberals defeated it and overthrew Palmerston's cabinet in their resentment at his succumbing to foreign displeasure. In a genuine sense, men like Stansfeld gloried in the presence of exiles and regarded them as concrete evidence of the superiority of free England to the despotic Continent. It was the liberal English element which fervidly welcomed the sixty-six released political prisoners, the victims of Ferdinand II of Naples. To a Poerio, a Settembrini, a Castromediano, the homes of important men of state like Gladstone were freely open.

We may rightly conclude that official British practice, if not so generous as the conduct of individual English citizens, was both humane and considerate of the right of political asylum. We have still to inquire how certain of the more noteworthy Italian patriots actually fared in Great Britain.

PART I

The Exile *Par Excellence:* Mazzini's English Life

CHAPTER I

Doctrine and Personality

ITALY of the last century, said Richard Garnett,[1] was the princess of the legend—she that was carried off by a dragon and kept on a desert island in the most remote recesses of the ocean until her three brothers rescued her. One of them, an astrologer, found where she was; the second, a mechanician, built a winged horse; the third, a soldier, mounted on this horse, reached the island, slew the dragon, and rescued the distressed damsel. The astrologer was Mazzini, the mechanician was Cavour, the soldier was Garibaldi. Such a presentment in little omits a host of considerable figures: where is Manin? where is Ricasoli? where is Crispi? where are many others? Were not these also brothers of the princess? And those who assert that Mazzini originated the idea of a united Italy are mistaken. Present-day Italian historians very correctly deny this[2] and attack those who tend to exaggerate Mazzini's importance.[3] What then was his mission? What did he accomplish more notably and more single-heartedly than any other man? He spread the idea of Italy a nation; he quickened what had in Gallic derision been called the land of the dead. Carducci summarized Mazzini's lifework, the resurrection of Italy, in these lines:[4]

e con le luci fise
A lei trasse per mezzo un cimitero
*E un popol morto dietro a lui si mise.**

So glazed was Mazzini's look as he sought freedom for his country that his later career has been called blind fanaticism.[5]

* "His eyes fixed on that goal, moved onward through
A graveyard, with a nation dead behind."—G. L. Bickersteth.

The Mazzinian policy of frequent *émeutes* has been compared to "the uprising of bad gases upon the surface of a stagnant pool."[6] Apparently, those who adulate Cavour, the man of practical politics and carefully weighed expediency, cannot take kindly to a graduate of hazard and emergency, to a preparer of failures. But his writings caused the English to sympathize so strongly with Italy as to aid powerfully her unification.[7]

Mazzini was a man of only a few constantly reiterated ideas. Hence, a presentation of the doctrines which the English gathered from his pages or heard from his lips or from those of his disciples is not especially difficult or singularly long. An Italian exile[8] of our own day has described Mazzini's profound revulsion against the classicism, materialism, irreligion, rationalism, and individualism of the eighteenth century. Between the ages of fifteen and thirty, he was susceptible to the influences both of the French romantics and of mysticism, and came to believe that truth was hidden in an intuition inaccessible for analysis. Yet he had bases of faith, apothegms which he accepted as working principles. With Kant, he said not only that God exists and need not be proved, but also that He was the source of the true, the good, and the beautiful. Under the influence of the Saint-Simonians* and of Condorcet, he maintained that humanity is a unity, and that, in accordance with God's law, mankind was progressing indefinitely. Progress was merely the evolution of the thought of God, and made itself manifest only as it passed through stages, each marked by the revelation of a fragment of truth. According to Mazzini, the next stage was the social epoch[9] when, by doing one's duty to humanity, one could collaborate with the Deity[10] and help achieve the perfection of the world. Thus was the Mazzinian concept of

* Afterwards, Mazzini rejected both Saint-Simonianism and the system of Louis Blanc. See Pia Onnis, "*Battaglie democratiche e Risorgimento in un carteggio inedito di Giuseppe Mazzini e George Jacob Holyoake*," *Rassegna Storica del Risorgimento*, December 1935, p. 927.

democracy given religious sanction. In other words, the method of progress, especially in the light of the oneness of humanity, was co-operation or association. And making meaningful and viable the Great Society of Man was a dynamic principle, a new morality, stressing duties[11] to be performed rather than rights to be won. Indeed, Mazzini had an apocalyptic vision, long before Woodrow Wilson, of the concatenation of the peoples into a confederated and beneficent entity. Such was God's purpose[12]—the Universal Republic.[13]

To attain this goal, Mazzini believed, it was necessary to establish a universal church, centering in Rome, the purpose of which was to be the control of education. Since he disliked all unorthodoxy except his own, this church was to be an agent for *Gleichschaltung*—a process not remarkably tolerant of heresies. (Yet, so inconsistent was his mind that he had been able to include individual freedom and political equality elsewhere in his programme.) He thought Christianity obsolete and felt that, particularly in its Roman Catholic form, it was an obstacle to be overthrown and then to be replaced by his new faith—the cult of humanity, subsumed under units of like nationality. For no state, he argued, could be well governed unless it consisted of a homogeneous nation. Besides, did not the existing correspondence of racial uniformities to geographical facts imply that nationality was God's method of arranging humanity? The divinely indicated nation was therefore an intermediate term between the individual man and the unimaginable multitude of the human race—"Nations are the citizens of humanity as individuals are the citizens of the nation." Appropriately, his slogan was God and the People; or, restated, Mankind divided into nations and led by Duty towards co-operation. But what did Mazzini really mean by Duty? To whom was it to be owed? And for what ends? The answers are either vague or vacuous. One thing is clear: by God, Mazzini did not mean the deity of Christianity but rather a symbol of a faith in the law of progress, which is the manifestation of the Godhead.[14] In the England of the last century, Mazzini's undefined theism was elastic enough not only to satisfy the spiritual doubts of Low and Broad Churchmen, to answer the questionings of Nonconformists in almost all their gradations, but also to harmonize with the doctrine of the state Church of England.[15] In point of fact, his religion had only a few adherents, mostly Englishwomen, but these, significantly, were, by birth, of various creeds.

This advocate of a universal republic and of a generous utopianism, this believer in politics as religion* in action, included first on his agenda a unified, republican Italy to be organized on the principle of universal suffrage (for Rousseau had made him a democrat) and to be accomplished by revolution, in which the lower classes were to be summoned to the struggle. What made Mazzini a republican? The answer, it has been pointed out,[16] lay in the nature of Italy before its unification. In a particular sense, he was a republican because he was a patriotic Italian who wished to surmount the contradictory interests of the Italian princes. Yet the history of Italy in the nineteenth century is one of unity under the aegis of the House of Savoy. The course of events has proved the plan of an Italian republic chimerical. But Mazzini never accepted the idea of monarchy because he thought that in monarchies, the bureaucracy, the police, the nobility, and the clergy would oppose constitutional liberties. The error in his reasoning lies in the absence of a realization that constitutional liberties are not of any necessity discrete from monarchy and are not of any necessity conjoined with a republic. Besides, a man who did not believe in doctrines different from those of his own universal church and who did not accept any guardianship for dissidence—what did he have to do with constitutional liberties?

Yet the English working class saw in Mazzini a champion

* To Mazzini, his proposed capital of the world (once the earth had been reorganized according to his ideas), *Roma*, was mystically identical with its palindrome, *Amor*.

of European democracy.[17] It has even been asserted[18] that he taught statesmen like Gladstone to regard great nations as having missions which rendered a selfish isolation unworthy. But nobody who is a prophet of a genuine democracy could see, as Mazzini did, in the imperialism of the great powers the apostleship of civilization for savages and barbarians.

Mazzini's economic programme has been definitely formulated by Bolton King.[19] According to his exposition, the Mazzinian state is to make its attitude of good will toward the masses effective by social legislation, which is to include the elimination of economic inequality by a severely graduated income tax. In opposition to socialism on the ground that it is anti-religious and anti-nationalistic, Mazzini, nevertheless, aims to cause the decay of capitalism and *laissez faire* by encouraging the growth of workmen's voluntary co-operative associations. These societies (the productive capital of which is to be indivisible but the profits from which are to be distributed according to the work done by the members) are to be aided by a national fund to be derived from the nationalization of church lands, mines, railways, and certain great industrial enterprises. Mazzini does not indicate how this nationalization is to be carried out. Is the method to be expropriation or compensation? If it is compensation, the funds necessary for any peaceful procedure are so great as to render it unlikely that much would be left for the co-operative societies. If it is expropriation, then it cannot be gradual. It must succeed at once or be bloodily defeated. For, as Machiavelli observed,[20] men forget more readily the deaths of their relatives than the loss of their relatives' property. To round out his scheme, Mazzini provides for special local banks to lend money on easy terms to the co-operative societies.

Mazzini profoundly impressed those who knew him. From the portraits thay have handed down, one gathers that he possessed that indefinable personality which evokes respect and an acknowledgment of greatness, even of moral grandeur. It was all this that moved John Morley[21] to note that one could not resist a feeling of awe in the presence of certain revolutionists whom he had known, like Gambetta or Mazzini. "But then they cherished moral ideals and had an eye for moral forces." Morley went on to add[22] that Mazzini was two distinct beings. On the one hand, he was the tireless organizer, the disseminator, the plotter in behalf of an idea he had invented and made viable—the idea of a unified Italy. And over and above his never-ending toil as a man of action, he had a moral genius that spiritualized politics and

> gave a new soul to public duty in citizens and nations. As practical statesmen, when we have applauded him for the exalting political conception which his energy, ardour, and fire forced upon Italy and Europe, we have perhaps said all.

Morley deplored Mazzini's disbelief in compromise and his lack of patience.[23] But the Italian did represent a valuable point of view, for he

> stood for the voice of conscience in modern democracy. Of all the democratic gospellers of that epoch between 1848 and 1870, when Europe swarmed with them—they were so prolific, so ingenious, in schemes and doctrines, political, economic, and religious—it was Mazzini who went nearest to the heart and true significance of democracy. He had a moral glow, and the light of large historic and literary comprehension, that stretched it into the foremost place in the minds of men with social imagination enough to look for new ideals, and courage enough to resist the sluggard's dread of new illusions. He pressed his finger on the People's intellectual pulse and warned them against the feverish beats that came from words and phrases passed off as ideas, or, still more dangerous, from fragments of an idea treated as if they were the idea whole.* He warned them that

* Mazzini knew German philosophy and literature; and while he lived, he kept in his heart this noble sentiment from Goethe:

> "*Sich vom Halben zu entwöhnen*
> *Und im Ganzen, Vollen, Schönen*
> *Resolut zu leben.*"

See *Märchenfrau und Malerdichter: Malwida von Meysenbug und Ludwig Sigismund Ruhl*, ed. Berta Schleicher, Munich, 1929, p. 205.

> human history is not a thing of disconnected fragments, and that recollection of great moves and great men in the past is needed to keep us safe on the heights of future and present. He did more; though figuring as restorer of a single nation, he was as earnest as Kant himself in urging the moral relations between different States, and the supremacy and over-lordship of cosmopolitan humanity.[24]

Similarly, William Roscoe Thayer,[25] praising Mazzini, affirmed that his conspiracies were only the transient part of him. His greatness lay in his obedience to ideals. Indeed, by preaching the Duties of Man he quickened conspiracy with moral aspirations. To this writer,

> it is as plain now that Mazzini was the greatest individual moral force in Europe during the nineteenth century, as that the world has scarcely begun to draw from him the benefits which he has to bestow.[26]

Frederic Harrison acknowledged[27] that Mazzini was one of several influences which had made his orthodoxy melt away, and along with Comte had impressed him most for his personality and genius.

Many, like Tennyson,[28] admired from afar Mazzini's keen intellectual face, but others who knew him at closer hand stressed rather his charm and his excellent conversation. David Masson, the great Milton scholar, paying Mazzini tribute for his genius in propaganda in behalf of the unity of Italy, testified to his versatility and wide culture.[29] Of one conversation with the exile, Masson wrote:

> One such occasion I particularly remember, on which for two hours there was a discussion . . . so intimate and so eager that, though I went away unconvinced on the main point, it was with a sense that I had never before been engaged in such an exercise of give and take, or had my mind so raked and refreshed by the encounter. Few such conversations do men's habits of intercourse now allow; and more is the pity! Let it not be supposed, however, that an evening with Mazzini was always, or often, so severe a matter. Varied and interesting chat, with only the due dash

> of the very seriously Mazzinian, was the general rule; and you might light a second or a third cigar. It was late before you went away. . . .[30]

In a similar vein, another writer observed that it was impossible to resist Mazzini's personality, for even his accent added to the charm of his conversation.[31] Clearly, Mazzini was a host in himself in behalf of the Italian cause; and his effectiveness as a propagandist was enhanced by the fact, said George Jacob Holyoake,[32] that he knew the English people more than any other foreigner. For he had said, exile though he was, "Italy is my country, but England is my real* home, if I have any."[33]

The spectacle of unconquerable courage, reluctant to submit or yield and for ever nursing a hope that always eludes and always beckons, is not lightly to be dismissed. Such was the career of Joseph Mazzini. Indeed, it is unfair to depreciate what he did: the preparation in Italy of the 'Forty-eight (which he was unfit, says G. M. Trevelyan,[34] to direct) and the energizing of her middle class, assisted from the outside, to assume the revolutionary task of overthrowing both native despotism and the Hapsburg colonial, military, and feudal ascendancy. What he failed to achieve was the Universal Republic, based more on directed Duty than creative Right, in which was to flourish the Great Society of good men able to do what they ought.

* When Mazzini was in Genoa in May 1857, plotting the Pisacane *émeute*, he confessed that he no longer liked the voices of Italian women, but only those of Englishwomen. See the *Edizione nazionale degli scritti di Giuseppe Mazzini*, LVIII, 123.

CHAPTER II

Mazzini's Early Career, 1805-36

THE middle-class family into which Mazzini had been born in 1805 at Genoa was one above the average in culture, for his father, Giacomo, was a physician and professor of anatomy at the University.[1] Such was Giacomo's eminence that he had once had as a patient the Duke of Kent, the father of Queen Victoria.[2] From an early age, Mazzini revealed sympathy for the poor and the suffering. As a child, he is said to have embraced an old beggar, who told his mother: "Love him well, lady; he is one who will love the people."[3] His development in an Italy where freedom was merely a word was in line with the bent of his character, and he became a Carbonaro though he thought the ritual comical. He had been enrolled by a spy who afterwards betrayed him.[4]

In April 1821 occurred an event which changed the course of his life and gave him his mission—the accomplishment of Italian national unity. He had been walking in Genoa with his mother and a family friend. The Piedmontese insurrection, fathered by similar risings in Spain and Naples, had just been crushed with methods both undiscriminating and ferocious.

Presently we were stopped and addressed

> by a tall black-bearded man, with a severe and energetic countenance, and a fiery glance that I have never since forgotten. He held out a white handkerchief towards us, merely saying, *For the refugees of Italy.* My mother and friend dropped some money into the handkerchief. . . . I afterwards learned his name. He was one Rini, a captain in the National Guard. . . .

> That day was the first in which a confused idea presented itself to my mind—I will not say of country or of liberty—but an idea that we Italians *could* and therefore *ought* to struggle for the liberty of our country.[5]

Thereafter, at the University of Genoa, he dressed in black—"in mourning for my country."[6] Perhaps he felt as did the mother of the hero in Bulwer-Lytton's novel *Pelham* when she told her son:

> *A propos* of the complexion; I did not like that blue coat you wore when I last saw you. You look best in black, which is a great compliment, for people must be very distinguished in appearance to do so.*

By 1827 he was a Carbonaro,[7] in popular parlance a Good Cousin. Within the next few years, although he did somehow find time to do literary reviewing,† he had so involved himself in theatrical, ritualized conspiracies that in November 1830 he was arrested[8] on the usual charge of having initiated a new member. Because of a juridical system eager to apprehend and to condemn, he was imprisoned for several months in the Ligurian fortress of Savona while awaiting trial.[9] In February 1831 he was released and went to Switzerland. One of his activities as a conspirator had been his participation in a midnight parade, held at the old Carignano bridge at the orders of one Doria, who was betraying his fellow Carbonari.[10]

At the time of Mazzini's arrest, Venanson, the Governor of Genoa, told Dr. Mazzini that his son was gifted with some talent but was too fond of walking by himself, absorbed in thought, at night on the outskirts of the city. At his age, what on earth did he have to think about? The authorities preferred to know what young people had in their thoughts.[11] It has been asserted that, when Mazzini was in jail, he was

* After all, Pelham and Mazzini were contemporary romanticists!

† Mazzini reviewed favourably Sir Walter Scott's *The Fair Maid of Perth*, and also his *Essays* (which had first appeared in the *Encyclopaedia Britannica* and had been reprinted by Galignani of Paris).

allowed to render his stay less arduous by reading the Bible, Tacitus, and Byron.* And out of these and Dante sprang (in 1831) *Young Italy*.[12]

What manner of person was the creator of this new instrument for the glory of a greater Italy, who discarded the paraphernalia of the Good Cousins for less histrionic trappings? We have a description of Mazzini about the year 1831, said to have been left to us by Enrico Mayer, the Tuscan educator:

> He was about 5 feet 8 inches high and slightly made; he was dressed in black Genoa velvet, with a large "republican" hat; his long, curling black hair, which fell upon his shoulders, the extreme freshness of his clear olive complexion, the chiselled delicacy of his regular and beautiful features, aided by his very youthful look and sweetness and openness of expression, would have made his appearance almost too feminine, if it had not been for his noble forehead, the power of firmness and decision that was mingled with their gaiety and sweetness in the bright flashes of his dark eyes and in the varying expression of his mouth, together with his small and beautiful moustachios and beard. Altogether he was at that time the most beautiful being, male or female, that I had ever seen, and I have not since seen his equal.[13]

Such was the young David destined to bruise the Hapsburg Goliath, and others even more monstrous. His sling was *Young Italy*,† a new revolutionary organization. In his native Genoa, its chiefs were the brothers Ruffini, Dr. Iacopo and Giovanni,[14] numbered among his closest friends.

The existence of *Young Italy* was a declaration that the Carbonari had failed; [15] and, thought Mazzini, had failed because its members had become engrossed in their own mummery. Perhaps a sketch of this secret, terroristic order

* In 1828, Mazzini had said that a translation of Byron was for Italy a literary and political necessity. Byron's poems, letters, and journals, are highly sympathetic with Italian national aspirations.

† *Cf.* Disraeli's *Young England* party with Mazzini's *Young Italy*. Only the names are similar, for *Young Italy* was the epitome of liberalism and *Young England* its antithesis. By 1833, *Young Italy* had 60,000 members.

may be useful. There were in the Carbonari two grades of members: apprentices and masters. The initiated were called "Good Cousins," and outsiders were termed "Pagans"; at the head were Grand Masters.[16] So carefully was everything worked out that even a patron saint was included in the apparatus of conspiracy—St. Theobald.[17] Opposed to the Carbonari (charcoal-burners) were the Calderari (braziers), a reactionary organization;[18] and affiliated were the Guelphs and the Freemasons.[19] Other offshoots were the Philadelphians, the Reformed European Patriots, and the Decisi—the last being very desperate men.[20] Still other branches were the Adelphi[21] and the Italian Federati.[22] We have then a revolutionary organization divided so as to render co-operation unlikely and distracted by an elaborate ritual which preoccupied its members to the loss of any effective action.

On the other hand, *Young Italy* had a definite objective, a united republican Italy, and a practical form of organization. There were two classes of members, the "Initiated" and "Initiators." Dues were made as low as possible, fifty centimes a month. A section of *Young Italy* was called a "congregation" and was composed of groups of "Initiated" headed by an "Initiator." Their flag was the present-day Italian tricolour—red, white, and green; and on one side of their banner was the glamorous slogan of "Liberty, Equality, Humanity." On the other side flamed the words, "Unity, Independence." Their symbol was a cypress branch in memory of the martyrs of Italian liberty; and their motto, "Now and for ever."[23] Mazzini had retained enough of the mysterious to attract the former Carbonari to whom the melodramatic was irresistible, and had even included an oath[24] impressive even from the point of view of the American "joiner." To publicize his society, he founded a journal, *La Giovine Italia*, to which distinguished Italian patriots contributed.[25] As a necessary precaution, it was understood that members were to be at least pseudonymous. For example, Garibaldi was Joseph Borel;[26] Mazzini, Filippo Strozzi.[27] Plotters had good need of *noms de guerre*, for theirs was a liberation warfare driven underground.

Arrived at Marseilles* from Switzerland, Mazzini continued his "business of that general conspiracy against social order."† In 1831, he issued a famous manifesto to *Young Italy*, which was later to be a recurrent motif in Swinburne's *Songs before Sunrise*.[28] During the next year, he first encountered the slander that *Young Italy* fostered assassination,[29] and energetically repudiated statements originating in France that his was an organization of which he was the Old Man of the Mountain. His devotion to literature was not wholly eclipsed by conspiracy, for, as he wrote to Emilie Venturi in 1869 when *Lady Byron Vindicated* was creating a sensation, he had guessed the truth in 1832, "when I had nothing but Byron's works to judge from."[30] At that time he had written an article[31] in ecstatic praise of the English poet and had emphasized the peer's belief in a universal republic and his noble conduct in fighting for the freedom of Greece. Finding his own ideas in Byron's writings was, however, a secondary interest. All his energies were devoted to *Young Italy*, which was growing so formidable that the young Bulwer, occupied in Naples with his *The Last Days of Pompeii*, expressed in that novel sentiments opposed to the unification of Italy, and extolled a revival of its city-states:

> Italy, Italy, while I write, your skies are over me, your seas flow beneath my feet. Listen not to the blind policy which would unite all your crested cities, mourning for their republics, into one empire; false, pernicious delusion! Your only hope of regeneration is in division. Florence, Milan, Venice, Genoa, may be free once more, if each is free. But dream not of freedom for the whole while you enslave the parts; the heart must be the centre of the system, the blood

* There is an interesting portrait of Mazzini at this stage of his career in the late Mr. John Drinkwater's play, *Garibaldi* (1936).

† So the Tory *Quarterly Review* said years later (July 1853, XCIII, 125) of his career in Marseilles and elsewhere.

> must circulate freely everywhere; and in vast communities you behold but a bloated and feeble giant, whose brain is imbecile, whose limbs are dead; and who pays in disease and weakness the penalty of transcending the natural proportions of health and vigour.[32]

The year 1833 was eventful in Mazzini's life. He was exceedingly disquieted because the *Moniteur*, a French publication, had printed forged documents to show him involved in assassination.[33] (This fabrication was fated in the letter-opening case of 1844 to be cited as a justification of Lord Aberdeen's secret surveillance over Mazzini's mail.)[34] But righteous anger due to malignant slander was soon to be replaced by the *lacrimae rerum* which accompanied his failures whenever he assumed an active revolutionary *rôle*. The rising he had planned for Piedmont was cruelly suppressed by Charles Albert; a description of Mazzini* was broadcast by the police; and hundreds of arrests were made,[35] including that of his friend Dr. Iacopo Ruffini. Years later, it was discovered that a certain Dr. Castagnino had betrayed the plot; but those who held Dr. Ruffini tried to break his indomitable courage by telling him that Mazzini had played the traitor. Afraid lest in a moment of weakness under torture he disclose his accomplices, Ruffini committed suicide.[36] Mazzini always thought of him, and his memory has been preserved in a considerable body of English literature of the nineteenth century. Into his own literary work Mazzini was, characteristically, introducing propaganda. When he reviewed[37] John Bowring's study of Bohemian poetry, Mazzini stressed the idea of Bohemian nationality, which was thwarted by Austria. In this same tragic year of

* One police circular read thus:

> "Of medium stature, thin features, olive complexion, with a longish face, black hair, brilliant black eyes, a handsome forehead, small black moustache, an attractive, sonorous voice, a ready speaker, noble carriage, and energetic in all his actions."

See Alessandro Luzio, "Mazzini's Metamorphoses," *The Living Age*, October 1, 1921, p. 45.

1833, he first met Garibaldi, whom he enrolled at Marseilles in *Young Italy* and assigned to organize a mutiny in the Piedmontese navy. There is evidence that Mazzini planned also to stage an *émeute* in Naples.

The astute Metternich, whose mission it was to be the head of a general staff for the great reactionary powers, had early become aware of the disruptive influence of *Young Italy*.[38] Very soon, Mazzini made it clear how inimical he was to the European *status quo* (best pictured as Metternich in the act of stamping on a lighted fuse leading to barrels of gunpowder labelled *Nationalism*) by heading a republican incursion into Savoy from Switzerland.[39] As usual, it failed.

Indisposed to surrender to discouragement, Mazzini maintained the revolutionary mood; and in 1835, published in French an essay since translated as "Faith and the Future." It contains a picture of a Promethean captive, Italy incarcerated by reaction:

> Look at Italy!
>
> In her there is neither progress, nor any chance of progress, save by revolution. Tyranny has raised an impenetrable wall along her frontier. A triple army of spies, of customs-officers, and of constabulary, holds nightly and daily vigil to prevent the circulation of thought. Mutual instruction [the Bell-Lancaster monitorial system of teaching] is proscribed. The universities are closed or enslaved. The penalty of death hangs not only over those who print clandestinely, but over those who possess or read the forbidden book.
>
> The introduction of independent foreign newspapers is forbidden. Intelligence perishes in infancy for lack of nourishment. Young men sell their faith for self-indulgence, or waste their strength in fits of barren cynicism.[40]

A mind disposed to order things terrestrial into a Universal Republic had very evidently much to do. Soon, his coign of vantage was to be England; the blurred sun by day and the red haze of the London sky at night were to replace the clearer atmosphere of Continental Europe.

CHAPTER III

First Years in London

As if in anticipation of the long years which he was henceforward to pass within the British Isles, Mazzini had begun on the Continent to acquaint himself with English life and culture. He knew the works of Byron, Scott, and Macpherson (of Ossianic fame). He had translated into Italian Alfred de Vigny's play, *Chatterton.* He was not only aware of influential British periodicals like *The Edinburgh*, *The Quarterly*, *The Westminster*, *The European*, *The British and Foreign*, *The Foreign Quarterly*, and *The Foreign* reviews, but could also definitely say what policies these magazines urged. His idea of British political affairs had already been formulated in a short and excellent analysis (1834) of the principles of Whigs, Tories, and Radicals. He had termed Wellington the representative of a brutal military despotism. Regarding Ireland as an oppressed land, he had followed closely both the career and the speeches of Daniel O'Connell, who, at that time, held the parliamentary balance of power. Manifestly, it was no ordinary foreigner, bewildered with new sights and alien customs, who was on this twelfth day of January 1837* setting his feet on English shores.

In a short while, Mazzini found lodgings† at 24, Goodge Street, Tottenham Court Road, London, and mingled in the pulsating life of the enormous city. He had a letter of introduction to Thomas Campbell, and was able to count on the assistance of Dr. John Bowring, Member of Parliament and

* The only source for the statement that Mazzini first came to England in 1836 is a note in William Allingham's diary.

† These he shared with Giovanni and Agostino Ruffini.

backer of the Anti-Corn Law League. Naturally, he was interested in the local political situation, and even paid a visit to the House of Commons (where he was scandalized by the manner in which the members took their seats). To his mother, he wrote[1] concerning the Scottish Highlands that one fifth of the people lived on the charity of others and that property and money were in the hands of a few. He predicted for the United Kingdom a great crisis marked by social convulsions.

Early in the autumn, he met John Stuart Mill, who asked him to write some articles for *The Westminster Review** on contemporary or recent Italian politics. This journalistic connection Mazzini intended to utilize (despite the fact that he could criticize the *Review* for being materialistic) as a medium of propaganda for his idea of an association of Europe. Meanwhile, an editor of one London review refused an article praising Byron on the ground that the latter was immoral.† A rejection was no light matter to Mazzini, harassed as he was at this time by debts, his own and those of others. That is why he asked, late in November, whether *Tait's Edinburgh Magazine* not only accepted articles but also paid for them.

On November 12, 1837, Mazzini made the acquaintance of Carlyle. Of this first meeting, Mazzini wrote [2] two years later:

> I, not much after my arrival in England, met him through an Englishman [the husband of John Stuart Mill's Mrs.

* *The Westminster Review* printed, in October 1837 Mazzini's essay, "On Italian Literature since 1830," in which he praised (characteristically) those authors whose *political* ideas agreed with his own. For this reason, he depreciated Vincenzo Monti, in whom he saw the trimmer, and lauded Foscolo as a patriot poet and Guerrazzi as a novelist. What was especially notable in Foscolo was that he had recognized in Dante the prophet of Italian nationality. Mazzini did not care for Botta as a historian because the latter was something of a Tory. Finally, he pointed out how much of Italian literature since 1830 was the work of exiled or imprisoned writers.

† Not much later, Mazzini was amazed at the rejection, by the Dean of Westminster Abbey, of Thorwaldsen's statue of Byron.

> Taylor[3]]: I got on well with him; when we were on the point of leaving each other, he asked me where I was living. I replied that it did not really matter, that I would come back and see him; and at that moment I meant it.

Carlyle even told him the time he usually had tea. They did not meet again for two years. Carlyle, it seemed, lived too far (four or five miles) from Mazzini's lodgings, the weather was bad, and Mazzini was too inert to bother. Moreover, it was expensive going to the Carlyles' by coach. The upshot of it all was that, since he had delayed so long in seeing them again, the Italian thought it would have been strange if he had paid a sudden visit. Another new and important acquaintance was W. J. Linton, English artist, notable wood engraver, Chartist, and ardent republican.

Perhaps the best account that we have of Mazzini at this time (1837) is Mrs. Eliza Fletcher's.[4] She met him in April and found him young, slim, dark, and of very prepossessing appearance. He wanted to obtain access to some public library through the facilities of which he might carry on literary studies, for he had discovered in London (to his dismay) a swarm of competing Italian teachers.[5] She thought he looked so despondent as to be contemplating suicide; and to prevent such a calamity, she wrote him a letter, when he left, to cheer his flagging spirits. In reply, Mazzini sent a noble answer denying any despair. To him life was a series of duties, and its aim was virtue. Thus, early in his career he had formulated his doctrine and had strengthened his soul against the sadness of the Horatian tag, "*post equitem sedet atra Cura.*"

From 1838 to 1840, Mazzini augmented his income somewhat by contributions to *The Westminster Review*, *The Monthly Chronicle*, *Tait's Edinburgh Magazine*, and *The British and Foreign Review*.[6] In the last, he published an article (January 1838) on Victor Hugo, whom he considered a poet on the decline. He contemplated writing for *The Athenaeum* and *The Examiner*. The latter magazine, he observed to a friend, was

Whig in politics, and said little of literature in general, and nothing of foreign letters.[7]

Mazzini's miscellaneous writings clearly indicate that he could not omit political considerations. His *Westminster Review* article (April 1838) on Fra Paolo Sarpi laid especial emphasis on the fact that this friend of Galileo, this anticipator of Newton and of Harvey, had been an enemy of the political power of Rome and of the Jesuits. Similarly, when Mazzini reviewed a treatise by Sismondi in *Tait's* (August 1838), he took the occasion to restate his own theories of humanity and nationality, his belief in universal suffrage, and his faith in the right of the people to rule themselves directly or indirectly.

In addition to literary work, he kept his eyes focused on public affairs. Republican though he was, he described to his mother in great and vivid detail the coronation of Queen Victoria. Moreover, he was very much interested in a mass meeting of 200,000 workers at Birmingham (August 1838), for the purpose of presenting a petition to Parliament, in which they demanded universal suffrage and the secret ballot. A foreign political figure, whom Mazzini was destined after 1851 to loathe with all his soul, was the subject of friendly comment in an article in *The Westminster Review* (December 1838). At this time, Mazzini could say that Prince Louis Napoleon Bonaparte was a man of courage and capacity. Yet it was evident that if the reviewer was in no manner personally hostile to the Prince, he detested Bonapartism.*

To supplement his magazine work and to recall the memory of Iacopo Ruffini, Mazzini projected (*c.* 1838) an autobiographical novel to be called *Benoni*.[8] It was actually written by Iacopo's brother, Giovanni. When it appeared, in

* In July 1865 Mazzini published an article (*Macmillan's Magazine*, XII, 259–66), "On Caesarism," in essence both an attack on authority based upon force and a plea for collective life or association. He was reviewing Napoleon III's book on Julius Caesar and had in mind its imperial author.

1853, Mazzini wondered[9] which Ruffini had written it—Agostino or Giovanni, surviving brothers of the martyred Iacopo, who had come to England with him. And at that time he added:

> The name, Benoni, is, strange to say, of my creation. It means in Hebrew, "the son of my grief"; and I mentioned it to them some fifteen years ago as the title of a hypothetical novel I was proposing to write.

Earning a living by the pen was such a precarious venture that Mazzini was constrained to think now of entering the wine-importing business.[10] His other ventures in commerce had included the selling of wine and sausages.[11] Nevertheless, he was properly included by a fellow exile, Pepoli, in a list of important contemporary Italian writers.[12]

Mazzini continued in 1839 to write reviews for English periodicals, especially for *The Monthly Chronicle*. His article in the March issue, "The Present State of French Literature," gave much praise to Lamennais and George Sand. Though Mazzini acknowledged that Alfred de Musset had some talent, he could not refrain from attacking this poet's servility before royalty. In general, it was Mazzini's thesis that poetry lives on liberty. Hence, he was on the whole unfavourable to contemporaneous French letters. It may be added that Mazzini's essay revealed a considerable familiarity with Wordsworth's writings. In the next issue of *The Monthly Chronicle* appeared Mazzini's superb article on Lamennais, the author of *Words of a Believer* and perhaps the man who most influenced the exile's thought. In this essay, Mazzini repeated his belief in the inevitable progress of mankind.

Thereafter, he wrote for the magazine a series of papers (May to September 1839) entitled "Letters on the State and Prospects of Italy." One passage, on English travellers in Italy, is very interesting:

> There are the sons of noble families, or others, who travel in Italy merely because it is the fashion, and who see

> nothing except the main roads, the principal hotels, the chief theatres, and perhaps some large parties—the directions given to their tutors are confined to these. Then we have the amateurs—a useless race, but very inoffensive—for whom all that Italy contains of value are paintings which they criticise very ill, operas which they criticise still worse, and sherbet which they are able properly to appreciate. There are the poets for whom Italy is altogether dead, because the corpse of a nation is a beautiful image—and dead for ever, because eternity adds to the effect of the image: they would be in despair if a spark of its third life [after the Rome of the Caesars and of the Popes] were visible. . . . There are the consumptive travellers, who only see the sun—the tourists, the most traditional and tenacious of races, who, even in 1839, after having traversed Italy very comfortably stage by stage, talk still as in the good old time of brigands and of the stiletto—good people who study Italy in the romances of Mrs. Radcliffe, and sometimes in the memoirs of Casanova.

In ringing tones, Mazzini declared that there had been a Rome of the Caesars and a Rome of the Popes. There would yet be a Rome of the Italian people, despite the opposition of the clergy of the upper ranks, and it would be the offspring of the republican and not of the monarchical principle. Next. he issued his famous challenge to the Italians: "Do not think to avoid or to defer the struggle against Austria; it is inevitable: provoke it: the offensive is the war of revolution: attack. . . ." There in brief was the genesis of the numerous Mazzinian *émeutes* and of that continuous guerrilla warfare which the chief of *Young Italy* was to wage against the Hapsburgs and the native rulers of his fatherland.

Other articles in *The Monthly Chronicle* by Mazzini during 1839 included one in appreciation of the life and work of George Sand, whom he ranked only after Lamennais in contemporary French literature, and another on Thiers—a brilliant and bitter invective against a person whom he called trimmer and ingrate and sensualist in power. Similarly, he had excoriated Guizot (in *Tait's Edinburgh Magazine*, 1839) as the representative of the middle-class plutocracy and as the promoter of a paternal despotism; and he had attacked Lamartine in a paper in *The British and Foreign Review*. In the last, he had affirmed that poetry is not art for art's sake but should be social and prophetic. Did he equate *prophetic* with *propagandistic*? At any rate, very few have equalled Mazzini's talent for verbal vivisection.

Little by little, the English were getting to know him. In August 1839 no less a person than Wordsworth was aware of Mazzini and thought highly of his character. Indeed, the elderly poet even grew angry enough to denounce Austrian despotism in Italy,[13] for it did not fit in with his belief in the principle of nationalism which he shared with Mazzini and in the utterance of which he had been his precursor.*

Of all the Britons known to Mazzini Carlyle was the most notable. It was with the volcanic Scottish prophet, jetting up thousands of burning words dedicated to, among other things, the proposition that Silence was part of greatness, that the Genoese renewed his acquaintance in November 1839. A few days before their second meeting, Mazzini had

* In the tract (1809) "Concerning . . . the Convention of Cintra," and in the "Letter to Captain Pasley . . ." (1811). On March 16, [1815], Wordsworth wrote to Sara Hutchinson a letter in which appears the following:

> "If Buonaparte were a man of genuine talents, such is the present state of Italy [?] I am persuaded he might yet atchieve a noble work, which would almost redeem him in my estimation; I mean the making and consolidating the several states of that divided Kingdom into one; and if this were done the independence [of] that people would be established—one of the most desirable political events that could possibly take place. The Italians have been abominably used, in being transferred to Austria, to the King of Sardinia and the rest of those vile Tyrants."

See *The Letters of William and Dorothy Wordsworth: The Middle Years*' ed. Ernest De Selincourt, Oxford, 1937, II, 649–50. Note should be made of a collection of poems by Wordsworth entitled "Memorials of a Tour Through Italy in 1837," the last including several sonnets highly in sympathy with Italian national aspirations.

thus described Carlyle to his mother: "This Mr. Carlyle is a man of great talent, and of the highest goodness according to what people say."[14] When he dined at the Carlyles', they exacted from him a promise to see them again in the near future. However, he was uneasy because he was resolved, despite his liking for Carlyle, to give his honest (and hostile) opinion of *The French Revolution* in a forthcoming review in *The Monthly Chroncile*—"Fiat justitia, ruat coelum." A little afterwards, Carlyle returned his visit; and at this point, Mazzini wrote to his mother that he would strengthen this new friendship since Carlyle was "a man of heart, of conscience and of genius." Mazzini also included in his letter biographical details about the Scot, such as his struggles to gain fame.[15] On December 11th, exactly a week later, Mazzini paid tribute to Carlyle's genius, but said ominously: "two thirds of our opinions differ without any hope of my converting him or his changing me." Oppressed with apprehension, he concluded that his article on *The French Revolution* would decide the great question: could one tell the truth* to a man of merit and remain friends?[16] In the interim, Mazzini followed with eager attention the fate of John Frost, chief of the Newport Chartists, whose death sentence was eventually commuted to transportation to an Australian convict settlement. When Carlyle did read Mazzini's review, his reaction proved that he was a man far above all manner of pettiness. In the friendliest spirit, he wrote Mazzini an invitation to pay him an early visit.[17]

By the commencement of 1840 and even a little before, Mazzini was seen pretty regularly at the Carlyles'. From February 1840 to about eight years later, he dined almost every Friday at Cheyne Row.[18] Yet, from the beginning, Carlyle and he were poles apart in their ideas.[19] Indeed, a

* Mazzini was of the opinion that Carlyle's *French Revolution* recognized only individuals, not humanity; that it contained wrong views and lacked aim; that it neglected the causal and emphasized the fortuitous; and that it was influenced by Goethe's "evil genius."

second article by Mazzini in *The Monthly Chronicle*, "Byron and Goethe," was really an answer to Carlyle, who had ranked the German ahead of the English poet. Mazzini expressed his dislike for Goethe's Olympian calm and his annoyance with those who, to elevate Shelley and Scott, depreciated Byron.* What evoked the most enthusiasm in Mazzini was the fact that Byron had fought for Greek liberty and had thereby joined thought and action. Characteristically, the review was lyrical criticism.[20]

Steadily, Mazzini's esteem for the Carlyles grew.[21] On one occasion, he informed his mother, Maria, that Mrs. Carlyle was "an exceptional woman" and that he contemplated moving to Chelsea, especially since it was quiet there, the air was good, and the countryside pleasant. The Carlyles were always exhorting him to be their neighbour.[22] On another occasion, he wrote to his mother that his friendship for Carlyle was sound in that it was based on respect and absolute frankness. Regarding Mrs. Carlyle, he acknowledged that he liked her sympathetic nature. When she read items like these in his letters, Maria Mazzini grew so alarmed that her son had to reassure her: his country was not England, and he had no intention at all of dying there.[23]

During May 1840 Mazzini went to hear Carlyle's lectures on heroes. He thought the speaker in the habit of telling his auditors the boldest things. Yet somehow, declared Mazzini, the Scot spoke with such genius that they were obliged to listen patiently. By this time, the exile had fallen into the habit (so a letter to his mother went) of consecrating to Carlyle one day of every week. Sometimes he would go to a concert; and once, thanks to a complimentary ticket, he heard the great Liszt play the piano. He found time even to accompany Mrs. Carlyle to the top of St. Paul's, from which

* Mazzini was always vexed at the fact that people in England treated Byron with what he considered ingratitude. At this time, too, the exile believed that his own ideas were saner and more advanced than Goethe's. See the *Edizione nazionale degli scritti di Giuseppe Mazzini*, XVIII, 184.

he could see the panorama of London. Carlyle, it was evident, had no time for diversions like these. During July, the Carlyles helped him find quarters in Chelsea only two blocks from their home, and Mazzini was now no more under the necessity of returning to his lodgings on foot in order to save coach fare.

Meanwhile, he was studying English politics and reading as many magazines as he could lay his hands on. So discerning was he that he was able (late in August) to tell a friend that *Fraser's* and *Blackwood's* were Tory in sympathies, that *The Quarterly* was hostile to every revolutionary writer, that *Tait's* was Radical, and that the Whigs and the Tories contended for power, not for principles.[24] At the moment, the Chartists occupied his thought, and it was on them that he wrote for *Tait's Edinburgh Magazine* the sagacious article entitled "Is It Revolt or a Revolution?" To the English ruling caste he said in effect: do not get a constabulary and five thousand more soldiers to overawe the Chartists; instead, work with the lower classes and lead them; make concessions now in order to avoid reaping a future whirlwind; Chartism is no dread portent but rather a sign of the times. Was the last phrase of his message an echoing of Carlyle?

With Mrs. Carlyle he was on excellent terms. By September, she had begun to write letters in Italian to Maria Mazzini, to whom the son was soon compelled to send a quieting statement: Mrs. Carlyle had the affection only of a sister for him. Unfortunately, this served only to strengthen his mother's curiosity, for Mazzini had, shortly, to describe for her benefit Mrs. Carlyle's slender frame and black eyes, to say that she was neither beautiful nor ugly, and to add that she was vivacious in spite of poor health marked by severe headaches. He concluded his account by affirming energetically that he loved her in a brotherly way because she had a good heart and sympathized with his country and his ideas in its behalf. One wonders whether Signora Mazzini's fears were allayed by her son's picture of himself as the brother of a Scottish sister.

Besides carrying on a tremendous correspondence,* Mazzini was working with might and main to further his programme of a united republican Italy. To this end, he founded (November 10, 1840) the *Apostolato Popolare*, a journal of propaganda, which appeared irregularly from London. By such endeavours for the Italian cause, Mazzini provoked very late in the year a Carlylese outburst so characteristic as to be worth repetition:

> Carlyle walked up and down the room like a raging lion in a cage, shaking his forest of grey hair. "Happiness! Happiness! The fools ought to be chained up! Man is born to work, not to enjoy! The ideal is within us, the ideal lies in the present moment; work with all your might, and to the best of your abilities. Work, and produce even the least atom. Every kind of work, whether intellectual or manual, is sacred and gives peace to the human soul. Be silent and work—these are the cardinal virtues of humanity. Silence! Yes, only Silence is grand; we live suspended between two silences: the silence of the stars and the silence of the grave. Nations, too, should be silent until genius speaks for them—genius is their voice and interpretation. How great was the silence of the ancient Romans! The Middle Ages too had a solemn silence, which was broken by the sublimest song, human or divine, ever sung—the poem of Dante. These are the true voices of the nations, and when one of them is heard, the nation for which he spoke is a consecrated nation; it is redeemable even if oppressed, divided, humiliated. Your Italy, oppressed as it is by Austria, is actually a great nation, because Italy has Dante. One day she, too, will be allowed to speak, and will be listened to.
>
> "The great *blagueurs* made a loud noise*'* but renewed nothing, created nothing, exploded like cannon loaded only with powder, and a simple breath of wind swept all their smoke away."
>
> Then, looking at Mazzini, Carlyle with his imperial, scrutinizing smile, slowly added: "You, you have not suc-

* Mazzini's letters are easily among the noblest and most interesting ever written.

ceeded yet, because you have talked too much: the fundamental preparation is wanting!"[25]

A tirade like this must move the reader of the present day to hilarity: the advocate of Silence scolding with many, many words the prophet of Italy a nation! Indeed, what *did* Carlyle mean by "fundamental preparation"?

All the time, Mazzini read widely in the British Museum in order better to equip himself for his political tasks.[26] He would take an occasional holiday (in the spring of 1841 he watched the Oxford and Cambridge crews racing on the Thames), but on the whole he was an assiduous worker. For example, he published an interesting article in *The Westminster Review* (April 1841) on "Modern Italian Painters," which revealed his theory of art as a social manifestation and as an element of collective development. To demonstrate the correctness of this point of view, he maintained that contemporaneous Italian painting was thwarted by political oppression and by a want of all avowed national inspiration.

By this time, his friendships had grown both in strength and in number, for his letters show how powerfully he was drawn to Carlyle;[27] John Stuart Mill had come to admire him;[28] and Harriet Martineau was favourably impressed when they met.[29] With Carlyle there were, to be sure, points of disagreement—the Scot thinking Italy would be made by "some God-sent Cromwell," and Mazzini reposing his faith in the people.[30] Socially, he was treated so very well by the Carlyles (*e.g.* in July 1841 Carlyle invited him to see them in Scotland where they were going) that Mazzini's father, unsuccessfully attempting to read between the lines of his son's letters (in a very Latin spirit), was worried lest there be an entanglement between Mrs. Carlyle and his Joseph. His mother now had a greater insight, no doubt, into Platonic considerations and sent Mrs. Carlyle a ring as a gift and also a bouquet. To these tenders of esteem Jane Carlyle wrote in Italian a letter of thanks,[31] and eventually dispatched a small pocketbook to Maria Mazzini in Genoa.

But Mazzini's mind was, in line with his character, elsewhere directed. We find him describing (October 15, 1841) Communism as bad because it

> would substitute the idea of a certain material well-being for any idea of moral progress, would paralyse society, and would reduce us to the level of bees or beavers, performing a certain series of acts necessary for our physical life, and nothing more.[32]

This somewhat distorted account, which sounds almost like Aldous Huxley's *Brave New World*, explains why Mazzini later opposed Karl Marx and the International. Unceasingly, the Genoese tried to enroll prominent Italian residents of London in the ranks of *Young Italy*.[33] The cause to which he had dedicated himself always outweighed all things else.

Nevertheless, if his life was essentially an attempt to realize the ideal, "Italy for the Italians," Mazzini did not forget the needs of Italians in London. For them he organized on November 10, 1841 an Italian Free School,* which was primarily intended to meet the needs of working men. By Christmas, it had 150 pupils. He attracted sympathy for his project by stressing the condition of *small boys* exploited in London streets as organ-grinders and as hawkers of white mice. These children had been sent out of Italy into a kind of slavery by their parents, deceived by glowing promises of lying *padroni*. Mrs. Carlyle donated an atlas to the School, Mario and Grisi sang in benefit concerts, and Lady Byron sent an initial gift of £3,[34] for she was possibly moved by Mazzini's appreciative essay on Byron.[35] Others who helped towards the support of this free night school were Gabriele Rossetti, Thomas Campbell (who became a trustee), Harriet Martineau, John Stuart Mill, Joseph Toynbee, the Bullers, Lord Ashley, the Barings, and Mrs. Macready.†

* A similar school was established in October 1842 by the New York colony of Italians. At the beginning, it had forty pupils. See the *Edizione nazionale degli scritti di Giuseppe Mazzini*, XXIII, 380.

† Her husband, the actor, had been the friend of Foscolo.

At this time, Mazzini was affording Jane Welsh Carlyle a great deal of amusement, mostly good-natured. For example, she had a habit of noting and quoting foreign idioms* and pet phrases in his English: "improved physically at least," "strange, upon my honour," "Thanks God," "an English," "a scissor," "here down," etc. These she would repeat in her letters with a prefatory remark: "as Mazzini would call it," "to use Mazzini's words," and other introductory or explanatory material.

In Mazzini's opinion, Mrs. Carlyle was an object of respect and compassion. On one occasion, he denied to his mother, with a fervid "God forbid it!" that there was any coldness between himself and Mrs. Carlyle. Later, he wrote of her that, since her mother had died and because she had no children, she felt herself alone. Her husband was a good man, Mazzini said, but he lived not so much in the heart as in thought, in books, and in brain. For this reason her sadness was growing, deepened in her case by the fact that she was a person of exquisite feeling.[36] Naturally, Maria Mazzini became eager to know more about Mrs. Carlyle. Thereupon, the exile added that Mrs. Carlyle was a Protestant by education, but in fact neither Protestant nor Catholic although she did believe firmly in God and in the immortality of the soul.[37]

Mrs. Carlyle had a kindly disposition which did not diminish her genuine sense of humour. She could and did give Mazzini a donation for his school;[38] she could also ridicule his extraordinary and bizarre scheme for invading Italy in balloons.† He had proposed to avail himself of the

* His letters to George Jacob Holyoake, written a *score* of years later, abound in forms like *safed*, *costed*, etc., not to say anything about numerous errors in spelling. On the other hand, Mazzini once commented on the mistakes Mrs. Carlyle made whenever she wrote him messages in Italian.

† Garibaldi too harboured extraordinary opinions concerning feasible revolutionary tactics. His favourite ambition was to embark the *émigrés* of 'Forty-eight on several ships by means of which they might be able to land wherever freedom was fighting against tyranny. (See *Rebel in Bombazine: Memoirs of Malwida von Meysenbug*, New York, 1936, p. 194, for this notion of the floating republic.)

invention of an Italian named Mussi to descend on the Austrians from the sky.[39] There is, however, nothing cruel about her account of this scene, which occurred at the Carlyle home:

> Darwin [Erasmus Alvey, brother of Charles] and Mazzini met here the other day and the three of us sat with our feet on the fender. . . . Mazzini said that Sismondi had at one time been "nearly *lapidated*." "Nonsense," said I, "you should say *stoned*, there is no such word as lapidated in that sense." "Let him alone," said Darwin, "he is quite right, *lapidated* is an excellent word." "Do not mind him," said I to M., "he only wants to lead you into making a mistake." "But are you sure?" asked M. with the greatest simplicity—"in the Bible, for instance, does not *She call it lapidated* in speaking of St. Stephen?" This femalizing of the Bible so delighted Darwin that he gave a sovereign to the school![40]

By November 1842 Mazzini had begun to feel the economic pincers, for his compatriots took so much advantage of his kindness that he had to resort to the moneylenders. Once, with a bitter smile, he remarked[41] to Mrs. Carlyle: "I am fortunate, you see!—I have always credit." Then too, his school drained away much of his own resources, though he counted on the generosity of people like Harriet Martineau and Lady Byron (who gave a second donation of £5) to cancel its current deficit of £50. By this time, Mrs. Carlyle recognized fully Mazzini's worth. She noted with appreciation the modesty with which he received the honours paid him on the occasion of the first anniversary of his school.[42] If she acknowledged Mazzini's quality, her formidable husband often gave vent to contrary sentiments, for he regarded the exile's unsuccessful cause as a kind of "sick Sentimentalism."[43]

In 1843, Mazzini was closer than ever to genuine want, for he was now indebted to an English usurer for about £200.[44] To profit by Carlyle's successful example and to settle his finances, he thought of giving a comprehensive series of five public lectures in English on the Spirit of the

Age as expressed in its literature, politics, society, philosophy, and religion; and hopefully fixed on a charge of a guinea for tickets to the course.[45] It was, perhaps, in preparation for these talks that he read Carlyle's *Past and Present*, of which he declared that it told the hard truth to the aristocracy of birth. So far as is known, his lectures were never delivered. More promising of remuneration was an invitation from Lady Baring to tutor her in Italian literature. Since she was a woman of spirit and culture, he did not, in her case, resent giving private instruction. At this time, his other teaching project, the Italian free school,* was being harassed by toughs hired by the Sardinian embassy.[46]

At heart a man of letters, Mazzini again considered Carlyle's literary significance and arranged his judgments in a superb† essay, "On the Genius and Tendency of the Writings‡ of Thomas Carlyle," which he published in *The British and Foreign Review* for October 1843. It marked a definite breach between his thought and Carlyle's. On the credit side, he acknowledged Carlyle's sincerity, his spiritual emphasis and antimaterialism, his humanitarianism, his artistry, and his humour. But once more he indicated what was to him bad in Carlyle: the fact that the latter saw individuals and not humanity. The democratic Mazzini took the occasion to denounce Carlyle's theory of heroes, his ready applause for mere success, and his identification of might with right. Mazzini granted that what the Scottish *vates* combated was false, and none the less asserted that what he taught was not always true. In short, Carlyle liked "progress," but disliked progressives.[47]

Mazzini still visited the Carlyles once a week. There is, however, a hint of exasperation with him in a letter of Mrs.

* At Mazzini's school, teaching geography involved teaching a united Italian republic.

† It made, said Mazzini (November 1843), a good impression. However, he had difficulty in securing payment for it even if, as a result, some ladies requested his autograph!

‡ *Sartor Resartus*, the lectures on *Heroes*, *Past and Present*.

Carlyle's: "I never saw a mortal man who so completely made himself into 'minced meat' for the universe."[48] Nevertheless, she esteemed him as a genuine and unaffected friend.* When he was made ill by an abscess on one cheek, she lamented his self-neglect and thought even of nursing him, only to relinquish the idea.[49] This was, after all, the age of Victoria Regina. All the while, Mazzini and Carlyle grew farther apart, for the Scot thought (1843) his friend's opinions incredible, not to say tragically and comically impracticable. His wife too came gradually to share this view, though to the last she retained her liking for the dreamer in exile.[50] She did not think much of Mazzini as a *practical* conspirator and said so to her spouse.

> He a conspirator chief! I should make an infinitely better one myself. What, for instance, can be more out of the *rôle* of conspirator than his telling me all his secret operations, even to the names of places where conspiracy is breaking out, and the names of people who are organising it? *Me*, who do not even ever ask him a question on such matters; who on the contrary evade them as much as possible! A man has a right to put his own life and safety at the mercy of whom he will, but no amount of confidence in a friend can justify him for making such dangerous disclosures concerning others. What would there have been very unnatural, for example, in my sending a few words to the Austrian Government, warning them of the projected outbreaks, merely for the purpose of having them prevented, so as to save Mazzini's head and the heads of the greater number, at the sacrifice of a few?[51]

Obviously, there was nobody to lead a party driven underground by repression.

Though the Italian republic remained his preoccupation, Mazzini continued to manifest a strong interest in British affairs. In reference to Lord Ashley's Bill (1844) reducing

* When thieves visited the Carlyles late in September, 1842, Mazzini, in all seriousness, gave Mrs. Carlyle a beautiful dagger to keep under her pillow and promised to teach them how to shoot a pistol. See the *Edizione nazionale degli scritti di Giuseppe Mazzini*, XXIII, 282.

women's hours in factories from twelve to ten, he was of the opinion that Ashley was a good man but that his proposals did not adequately meet the situation, for, if women worked less, they got less.[52] To be sure, a more typical example of Mazzini's thinking is the article on Dante (*The Foreign Quarterly Review*, April 1844), in which he extolled the poet as the patriotic prophet of national unity.

Surely, the summer of 1844 must have been stamped in Mazzini's memory to his dying day, since it marked a turning point in his relations with the English. Henceforth, he was to be known to all on account of the notorious post office espionage case, which made liberal spirits rally round him, evoked the fulgurous tones of Carlyle, and almost brought about the fall of a culpable ministry.

CHAPTER IV

Lord Aberdeen Spies on Mazzini's Letters

In the martyrology of the *Risorgimento*, the brothers Bandiera are not the least important names. Though their father was an officer in the Austrian navy, they remembered their origin and plotted in behalf of Italy unredeemed. The outcome of their plans was disaster. When they landed in Calabria, they were captured, and were shot by a weeping firing squad.[1] Mazzini had advised against their attempt and had seen his counsel rejected for the weasel words of *agents provocateurs*. Invoking their *manes* to advance the Italian cause, he disclosed that his mail had been opened by the Home Secretary, Sir James Graham, at the prompting of the Earl of Aberdeen, its contents read, and its information transmitted to the despotic rulers of the Italian peninsula. Seemingly, an English government had blood on its hands. But if the English Foreign Office did send enough information to the Bourbon government to enable it to be prepared for an attack, it had other and earlier sources of information.

Mazzini's discovery that his letters were being opened was the result of an ingenious process of deduction. He observed that they were doubly stamped—having, for instance, the stamp of two o'clock in the afternoon over that of twelve noon. He had read in an Austrian newspaper that the English authorities had undertaken to watch the movements of the Italian refugees in Great Britain; he surmised that his letters might be opened. His fears he communicated to an Italian friend who held the private character of the Foreign Secretary, Lord Aberdeen, in such esteem that he strongly dissuaded Mazzini from judging him capable of being a party to so dishonourable a procedure as that of opening letters, and playing the spy to a foreign government. Mazzini was of a different opinion and therefore sent off, in the presence of witnesses, letters addressed to himself and to others. They found that the self-addressed letters were delayed. To make a confirmatory test, he sealed his letters with wax, placing the impression in a particular position. The seals on his letters were not only moved from their original locations but even altered in form. In his next few letters he enclosed grains of sand which safely reached other persons but were missing in the letters directed to himself. Then he was sure that an English Secretary of State might also play the spy.

In Parliament, a tremendous row ensued, into which the Duke of Wellington was drawn. Sir James Graham evasively defended his conduct against Sheil, Macaulay, Monckton Milnes, Thomas Duncombe, and Sir John Bowring. *Punch* caricatured Graham as Paul Pry at the Post Office, printed the contents of his imaginary letters (which it pretended to have acquired by espionage), and nicknamed him Fouché. Later, it published a cartoon showing Graham reviewing the London postmen in this manner:

> Present letters!
> Feel for seal!
> Thumb on seal!
> Open letters!
> Read letters!
> Re-fold letters!
> Re-seal letters!
> Pocket letters!

In addition, the following squib circulated:

NOTICE

EMPERORS, Kings, Princes, Grand Dukes, Viceroys, Popes, Potentates, Infants, Regents, Barons, and Foreign Noblemen in general, are respectfully announced that, on and after the present month, the following alterations will take place in the opening of letters:—

Letters posted at	*Opened at*
9 A.M.	10 A.M.
12	2 P.M.
2 P.M.	4 P.M.

Copies of letters opened will be despatched the same evening, and every information afforded as to the address of suspected parties.

A Polish and Italian* translator is now permanently engaged, and a choice assortment of foreign seals has lately been added to the extensive collection.

Great dexterity practised since the recent disclosures.

*** *No increase in the prices.*[2]

Naturally citizens marked their mail, "Not to be Grahamed."[3]

In the whole affair, W. J. Linton acted as one of Mazzini's most active partisans.[4] The notoriety brought them so closely together that Linton now became a supporter of Mazzini's night school and wrote in its behalf a pamphlet called *Address and Rules of the Society for the Protection and Education of the Poor Italian Boys.*†

The censorship controversy gave Mazzini tremendous publicity and access to many English periodicals,[5] and added to the number of his influential friends, who were soon to include Charles Buller, Joseph Toynbee, J. S. Mill, William Shaen, Joseph Cowen, Peter Taylor, M.P., the Courtaulds, the Mallesons, Dickens, and the Ashurst-Stansfeld clan. William Henry Ashurst, the head of this family, was notable for favouring women's rights and for having conceived the idea of the penny post.[6] Shaen was later to help Italian

* Poland and Italy were at this time more revolutionary than the rest of Europe.

† In 1846, Linton wrote an article on "The Italian Gratuitous School," which appeared in *The People's Journal*, II, 147–48.

refugees* by legal advice and in other ways (so that they called him *l'angelo salvatore*), and to give financial aid to the insurrections initiated by Mazzini. Cowen, the future orator and political power of Newcastle, was in attendance in 1844 at Edinburgh University, where at the Debating Society he denounced Graham. Thereafter, Cowen's home was open to political outlaws—Kossuth, Orsini, and others; and he used to forward revolutionary Mazzinian propaganda in the merchandise which his father's firm shipped to Continental ports.[7]

On Saturday, June 15, 1844, the London *Times* printed a long report of the House of Commons debate on the letter-opening case, which had been started by Duncombe's petition in behalf of Linton and Mazzini.† On the following Monday, June 17, 1844, *The Times* published an editorial, or leading article, on the ministerial responsibility involved:

> . . . they were the first Ministry of late years that had resorted to the meanness of espionage, and condescended to pursue a policy at once unconstitutional, un-English, and ungenerous. . . .
>
> Hitherto, it has been the peculiar boast of England that she is not as other countries, that her citizens are not liable to the same petty persecution, the same rigorous police, the same insidious and incessant watching, the same dogging of their footsteps, opening of their letters, and prying into cabinets as harass the subjects of continental states. But this boast cannot now be uttered with justice. The national *prestige* has gone.

* Mazzini used to send these refugees to Shaen. For example, in February 1855, Shaen received a note from Mazzini to the effect that it was all right to give Francesco Crispi £3. (But the Genoese told Shaen not to inform Crispi of his address—otherwise, if he had seen every Italian who came to England for political reasons, he would never have been able to carry on his plots.) See the *Edizione nazionale degli scritti di Giuseppe Mazzini*, LIV, 50–51.

† Mazzini had been in close touch with Duncombe and had informed him that, since March, sixty or seventy of his letters had been intercepted by the postal authorities. Duncombe is to be remembered as the defender of Chartist prisoners like Thomas Cooper.

In regard to Mazzini, the leader went on to say:

> . . . Mr. Mazzini's character and habits and society are nothing to the point, unless connected with some certain or probable evidence of evil intentions or treasonable plots. We know nothing, and care nothing about him. He may be the most worthless and the most vicious creature in the world. But this is no reason of itself why his letters should be detained and opened.

At these words which seemed to insinuate a sneer at Mazzini under the guise of standing by principles, Carlyle was stirred to write a letter, printed in *The Times* for Wednesday, June 19, 1844. It was this which Mrs. Carlyle* described as "a glorious letter . . . on the subject":

> Sir,—In your observations in yesterday's *Times* on the late disgraceful affair of Mr. Mazzini's letters and the Secretary of State, you mention that Mr. Mazzini is entirely unknown to you, entirely indifferent to you; and add, very justly, that if he were the most contemptible of mankind, it would not affect your argument on the subject.
>
> It may tend to throw further light on this matter if I now certify you, which I in some sort feel called upon to do, that Mr. Mazzini is not unknown to various competent persons in this country; and that he is very far indeed from being contemptible—none farther, or very few of living men.

Then Carlyle continued:

> I have had the honour to know Mr. Mazzini for a series of years, and whatever I may think of his practical skill in worldly affairs, I can with great freedom testify to all men that he, if I have ever seen one such, is a man of genius and virtue, a man of sterling veracity, humanity, and nobleness of mind, one of those rare men numerable, unfortunately, but as units in this world, who are worthy to be called martyr souls, who in silence piously in their daily life, understand and practise what is meant by that.

He went on to disclaim any interest in *Young Italy*, the pope,

* Months before the scandal was exposed, Mrs. Carlyle knew that Mazzini's letters were being opened.

or the Austrian emperor; but he vented his wrath on the following account:

> But it is a question vital to us that sealed letters in an English Post Office be, as we all fancied they were, respected as things sacred; that opening men's letters, a practice near of kin to picking men's pockets, and to other still viler and fataler forms of scoundrelism, be not resorted to in England except in cases of the very last extremity.[8]

When next he wrote to his mother, Mazzini translated into Italian the letter to *The Times*; and subsequently informed Carlyle of the fact and of her heartfelt gratitude.[9] Very shortly, the Scot was again to exercise his indignation in defence of the exile. The formidable Lord Brougham had privately said in the House of Lords that Mazzini was a scamp who had once kept a gaming house in the East End. Arthur Penrhyn Stanley reported the remark at a dinner at the Barings'* at Addiscombe (July 6, 1844). Carlyle, present, defended Mazzini, declaring him far above dishonourable conduct.[10] Naturally, Lord Aberdeen never forgave Carlyle for his letter to *The Times*, and as Prime Minister prevented, in 1853, his obtaining a pension. The honour had been suggested by Prince Albert, and the excuse for not granting it was "heterodoxy."[11]

The ripples of the stone dropped into the Parliamentary pond because of Duncombe's petition spread farther and farther. Secret committees were appointed by both Houses of Parliament to investigate.[12] In debate, it was disclosed that the practice of opening letters was of long standing. When Radnor, in the House of Lords, proposed a Bill to prevent such espionage, he did not succeed in getting it past the first reading.[13] Moreover, the published *Report from the Secret Committee (of the House of Lords) relative to the Post Office* was in

* Lord Ashburton, father of Lady Baring, reproved her for associating with revolutionaries like Mazzini. But she was not affected and is said to have disliked Lord Brougham's attitude so much that she swore she would never see him again.

essence a feeble attempt at easing out of an awkward situation. It admitted that since 1626 mail had been pried into, and that the power had been exercised from the earliest period and had been recognized by several Acts of Parliament. Complacently, it observed that the issue of six or seven warrants upon a circulation of 220,000,000 letters was not to be regarded as materially interfering with the sanctity of private correspondence, which, with few exceptions, there was not the slightest ground to believe had been ever invaded. It acknowledged that Mazzini's letters had been for about four months stopped and opened, under the warrant of the Home Secretary, and inspected by the Foreign Secretary. But this had been done only upon an apprehension that the exile was engaged in a correspondence having for its object designs which might injure the tranquillity of Europe. And it confessed that certain parts of the information thus obtained had been communicated to a foreign government, in so far as such a communication appeared to be warranted, but without the names or details that might expose to danger any person then residing in the foreign country to which the information had been transmitted. In conclusion, the Committee declared the practice of surveillance over letters to have been sparingly exercised and to have been motivated by an earnest and faithful desire to adopt that course which appeared to be necessary, either to promote the ends of justice or to prevent a disturbance of the public tranquillity, or otherwise to promote the best interests of thc British people.

In the November *North British Review*, Panizzi denounced this *Report* as whitewashing,[14] and called Lord Aberdeen a liar for denying (July 4, 1844, in the Lords) that Mazzini's letters had been communicated to a foreign government.[15] In discreet terms, he commended Mazzini:

> Although Sir J. Graham refused all information, it was well known that the correspondence which had excited his particular curiosity was that of Mr. Mazzini, a Genoese

gentleman of considerable talents and extreme democratic opinions, who has lived in England universally respected for several years, and whose letters had been regularly opened for months previous to his complaining. It was also well known that Mr. Mazzini is a political refugee, who has taken shelter in England from the persecution of his political enemies—the usurpers of his once free country—and who is looked upon as a leader by those Italians who, entertaining the same political opinions with himself, were anxious to free it from the iron rule of ecclesiastical as well as civil—foreign as well as native—despots.[16]

The next person in this *cause célèbre* of 1844 to fire a shot was Mazzini himself,[17] lurking, however, in the shadow of an anonymous article, "Mazzini and the Ethics of Politicians," which appeared in the September *Westminster Review*. He described the opening of his correspondence not only as a formal recognition of petty larceny, which had now become a fundamental maxim of state policy, but also as an example of the commission of felony and acts of dirty meanness. Those who defended opening letters reasoned in a utilitarian fashion—"after the practical philosophy, not of Locke, but of Sheppard [the highwayman]." He went on to summarize the moral creed of English statesmen in the nineteenth century. Theft was permissible when information important to the public interest could be obtained only by stealing it from a letter. In the tacit form of resealing a letter in order that the fact of its having been opened might never be detected, lying to conceal theft was also allowable. And for the same object, so was forgery—in the form of counterfeiting seals and imitating post office stamps. Treachery too was permissible in cases of emergency. The servant might betray his master for the "public good," and the confidential agent might play the secret spy. The bearer of a written communication, compromising, perhaps, the lives and fortunes of individuals, might carry it direct to their bitterest enemies and be honourably praised for a breach of trust. Moreover, rogue-making was also permissible, for the arts of knavery were somewhat distasteful to honest men. In particular, forgery was a skilled profession not to be thoroughly acquired without many opportunities of practice. In short, the code of such statesmen included tyrannous injustice in the form of secret accusations and secret tribunals for trying a man in the dark upon the evidence of stolen documents. Apparently, it was a duty of a minister to steal, to lie, to commit forgery, treachery, and injustice, and to keep in training a staff of rogues fit for similar acts of public service. The anonymous reviewer then spoke of "the open, candid character of the man"—meaning Mazzini himself; and reprinted Carlyle's letter to *The Times*.

George Meredith, who long held Mazzini a hero, was possibly first drawn to the *Chief* (whom he portrayed in *Vittoria*) by reading Carlyle's defence of the Italian patriot.[18] Another man of letters, Richard Monckton Milnes,[19] had joined against Sir James Graham in the debate in the Commons. Late in June 1844, Charles Dickens, having written a short note to an old friend, Thomas Beard, added, on the back of the envelope, this comment: "It is particularly requested that if Sir James Graham should open this, he will not trouble himself to seal it"![20] Previously, Dickens had read Carlyle's letter to *The Times* about Mazzini and had thought it noble.[21] In 1855, Giovanni Ruffini's novel, *Dr. Antonio*, alluded to Mazzini and post office surveillance. A character who represents that formidable creature, the Victorian *paterfamilias*, becomes indignant because his letters are opened in Italy. Ruffini remarked in an *obiter dictum*:

> We suppose that he knew nothing at that time of a certain English statute which made it legal in certain circumstances, and under certain regulations, to break the seal of private letters and pry into their contents, even in his constitutional and free country. . . .[22]

The *affaire Mazzini* was not allowed to die down. The Methodists condemned the members of the Cabinet responsible for the opening of the letters, and Duncombe later brought the subject up again. In February 1845, the rising Disraeli, supporting him, mocked at Peel and Graham.[23] Sir James then ventured to repeat the slander that the exile was an Old Man of the Mountain and was forced to ask Mazzini's pardon.[24]

Now Mazzini had the ear of the English public. He was determined to take advantage of all the publicity which Graham and Aberdeen had brought him. Accordingly, he wrote a steady stream of letters to *The Times* and to *The Morning Chronicle* from January to April; and eventually published in May 1845 his long and stirring pamphlet in which he pleaded the Italian cause: *Italy, Austria, and the Pope. A Letter to Sir James Graham.* The Home Secretary had termed the actions of Italian patriots in exile *Conspiracy*. Mazzini called it *Duty* and went on to say in the most fiery language that Graham, by his opening of letters, had ranged England on the side of the oppressors against the oppressed, with the executioner and against the victim. The pamphleteer, describing the hegemony of Austria in Italy, asserted that Lombardo-Venetia possessed no autonomy but was governed from Vienna. To him Austria represented in Europe "the Chinese principle of immobility" and was, therefore, an obstacle to progress. He drew a horrible picture of Austrian-controlled education in Italy, the details including an account of ignorant teachers who spied on their pupils and reported to the government their conduct. Then he quoted from the Austrian catechism for Italian children in asylums and in schools:

> Question: How ought Subjects to conduct themselves towards their Sovereign?
>
> Answer: Subjects ought to behave towards their Sovereign like faithful *slaves* towards their *master*.
>
> Question: Why ought they to behave like *slaves*?
>
> Answer: Because the Sovereign is their *master* and his power extends *over their property, as over their persons*.
>
> Question: Is it a blessing that God bestows in giving us good and Christian Kings and Superiors?

> Answer: Yes, it is one of the greatest blessings the Deity can bestow when he gives us good and Christian Kings and Superiors, such as those under whom we have the happiness to dwell. We ought to pray that God will grant a long life and a long reign to our beloved Monarch.

Mazzini added that 2,721 copies of this catechism were distributed annually to the schools in Lombardy, but that the students had no textbooks dealing with Italian history. He pictured the curricula of the secondary schools and the universities as a jumble of subjects taught servilely and with no logical order. Students might not wear moustaches, for these were signs of liberalism. Censorship extended to everything printed and included plays. Literary men were subjected to persecution. Had not Foscolo died in exile? Had not Berchet, Pellico, Melchior Gioja, Romagnosi been exposed to ill-usage?

Very clearly, Mazzini disclosed why Vienna held so tightly to Lombardo-Venetia—that province was a goodly milch cow, yielding 60,277,000 lire annually. Yet Austria impeded trade, appointed to the higher judicial posts Germans ignorant of Italian, whereas a minute knowledge of even the Italian dialects was necessary, and played the tyrant in ways for more heinous. There was, for example, the treatment of political offenders who were confined in dungeons, secluded from all communication, with only so much light and space as was necessary to sustain life. These unfortunates were constantly loaded with heavy fetters on hands and feet; were never, except during the hours of labour, without chains attached to circles of iron round their bodies; and their diet was bread and water, a hot ration every second day, but never any animal food. Their beds were naked planks. Of course, no visitors were permitted. The hot ration (*cibo caldo*) previously mentioned consisted of slices of bread steeped in hot water and flavoured with tallow. It was a common thing for those condemned to the *carcere duro* to wear twenty pounds weight of chains. They had neither light nor paper nor books and were worked like galley slaves.

This was not all. Mazzini supplied a moving account of Austrian tyranny maintained by an arbitrary police, a practice of restrictions on passports for abroad and for the Italian hinterland, espionage, and *agents provocateurs*. An army of 80,000 foreigners was kept at Italian expense in Lombardy. Similarly, Italians were employed to overawe Hungary, Bohemia, and Galicia. In a word, central despotism was the character of the Austrian government.

The Papal States* constituted an organized anarchy, which imposed heavy taxes and shackled industry. The moral Mazzini asked: "Who at Rome but can point out the mistresses of the cardinals?" To Mazzini, the Pope was the cross, the pommel of a sword, of which Austria was the point; and this sword hung over all Italy. The Pope clutched the soul of the Italian nation; and Austria, the body—whenever it showed signs of life. On every member of that body was seated a petty absolute prince, viceroy in turn under either potentate—Pope or Emperor.

Italy itself was divided into eight states (Lombardy, Parma, Tuscany, Modena, Lucca, the Popedom, Piedmont, the Kingdom of Naples), a fact which meant eight systems of custom houses, of currency, of weights and measures, of civil, commercial, and penal legislation, besides other results of lack of unity. Mazzini rehearsed the history of those times when these eight states could have perhaps been made one. For example, in 1809, the Archduke John of Austria spoke of Italy free and constitutional; the Austrian General Nugent in 1813 pronounced for an independent Kingdom of Italy; and Lord William Bentinck gave a constitution to Sicily in 1812 and proclaimed two years later the liberty and independence of the Italian people. But when Napoleon

* Mazzini wrote an article on "The Papal States" for *The Westminster Review*, December 1845, and said that popes were "all-powerful for evil, absolutely impotent for good," and usually old imbeciles! In this essay, he repeated scandal about the Roman clergy, and condemned the graft, corruption, and nepotism prevalent in the papal domains.

fell and the Italians were no longer to be considered as his potential enemies, then these promises were forgotten; and Austrian arms were to foil in 1820, 1821, and 1831 all attempts at achieving independence.

Italian disaffection was not fomented by irresponsible agitators. Rather, said Mazzini, it was caused by the fact that Italy was a vast prison, guarded by jailers and gendarmes, who were supported in case of need by the bayonets of foreign soldiery. If the Italians spoke out, they were gagged; and if they acted, they were shot. Any petition signed *collectively* constituted a crime against the state. Nothing was left but the endeavour to conspire in secret, to wrench the bars from the doors and windows of their prison.

Mazzini then went on to defend the right of revolution where there was a chance for success—not for a weak minority but for the majority. Peaceful agitation was so miserable a failure that even men like Silvio Pellico turned conspirators and ended in the Spielberg. Peaceful and legal means had failed—only force was left. Striving to win English sympathy, he suggested an analogy between Italy and England:

> Imagine eighty thousand French soldiers stationed in Ireland or Scotland; imagine that, whenever the people in that portion of the English territory remaining free called for improvement, advancement, or change in their internal laws, the eighty thousand foreigners should intrude the points of their bayonets, and say, "In the name of brute force, stir not"; what would you do?

Then Mazzini sketched examples of cruelty in putting down supposed revolts, told of the harshness of sentences, and of the use of reformers. Eloquently, he concluded his pamphlet with a plea to England. She had abolished Negro slavery. Would she permit the enslavement of white men in Italy?

In this same year of 1845, Robert Browning published his remarkable poem, "The Italian in England." Surely, he must have read Carlyle's letter to *The Times*; and certain it is that his poem was suggested by the life and personality of Mazzini, who was "the Italian in England" *par excellence.*[25] Then, too, Browning had been in Naples in 1844, the year of the Bandiera tragedy and of the letter-opening case. Mazzini translated* the poem into Italian and is said to have told Browning that he used to read it aloud to his fellow exiles to show how an Englishman could sympathize with their struggles for liberty and their sorrows.[26] In the dramatic monologue, the Italian in hiding says to the peasant girl:

I am that man upon whose head
They fix the price, because I hate
The Austrians over us: the State
Will give you gold—oh, gold so much!—
If you betray me to their clutch,
And be your death, for aught I know,
If once they find you saved their foe.
Now, you must bring me food and drink,
And also paper, pen and ink,
And carry safe what I shall write
To Padua, which you'll reach at night
Before the duomo shuts; go in,
And wait till Tenebrae begin;
Walk to the third confessional,
Between the pillar and the wall,
And kneeling whisper, *Whence comes peace?*
Say it a second time, then cease;
And if the voice inside returns,
From Christ and Freedom; what concerns
The cause of Peace?—for answer, slip
My letter where you placed your lip;
Then come back happy we have done
Our mother service—I, the son,
As you the daughter of our land!

So must *Young Italy* have conspired—with passwords and the furtiveness of secrecy. So, too, must it have wished:

* During 1846, Mazzini sent his mother bit by bit a translation, which is said still to exist in Florence in his autograph.

However, if I pleased to spend
Real wishes on myself—say, three—
I know at least what one should be.
I would grasp Metternich until
I felt his red wet throat distil
In blood through these two hands.

The Italian in England is of course an exile who recalls an episode in his career, how near Padua he hid in an old aqueduct for some six days from the Austrians hot on his trail, how a peasant girl did not betray him but brought him aid. He would like to see her again, learn her fate—children, husband, etc. But he says:

So much for idle wishing—how
It steals the time! To business now.

So also Mazzini never rested and always planned and conspired. To have inspired a piece of poetry so eloquent and so fine in picturing Italy after 1831 and *Giovine Italia*—that was pleasing indeed.

With the years, Mazzini acquired more English friends, such as Dickens,* Douglas Jerrold, John Cam Hobhouse (the friend of Byron), and many others; and he became a vice-president (1847) of Jerrold's Whittington Club, where he used to play chess.[27] Of this game he was very fond,† along with cards, cigars, and the guitar—a rather necessary

* A swindler, using Mazzini's name, obtained £2 from Dickens. Eventually (February 1846), the impostor was caught, but he had been the means of bringing the exile and the novelist together. Dickens's *Pictures from Italy*, 1846, is very sympathetic towards the Italians. [For another Victorian novelist, Thackeray, Mazzini had (1857) little liking—not so much for any lack of appreciation of the skill of the writer as for the character of the man.]

† In February 1848, Mazzini derided a proposal designed to forbid the playing of chess on Sundays. Indeed, his tactics were Swiftian, for he suggested drastic "blue laws" in order to make the chess ruling appear silly; *e.g.* members of the Whittington Club were to be compelled to listen to a public reading of "a chapter from the second volume of [Disraeli's] *Tancred.*" See the *Edizione nazionale degli scritti di Giuseppe Mazzini*, XXXV, 10–12.

vice for a conspirator. Even in England one might find substitutes for the *caffè* life of Genoa. Living among a people which in the course of trade had assembled an empire, he even fell into their point of view. And so he wrote his mother a letter in which he expressed an interesting judgment, an opinion which a Mussolini might use: the imperialistic expansion of France, Russia, and England made them missionaries of civilization to backward peoples.[28] But Austria was no missionary of civilization to Italy.

Occasionally, the Genoese was discovered in the company of Samuel Rogers, the banker-poet, who had him "for breakfast" as he had had many another celebrity. And if Mazzini could relish a Lucullan feast from one poet, he was, on the other hand, unable to appreciate Shelley despite the fact that the latter had also disliked the Austrian "anarchs."* Meanwhile, since he was ever on the alert for an Italian capable as Machiavelli's Prince of patching the Italian boot, Mazzini was broadcasting† the deeds of his old comrade, Garibaldi, now playing the revolutionary *condottiere* in South America.[29]

Mazzini had so quickly grown into the circle of the Ashurst family of Muswell Hill that by 1846 they had invited him (in vain) to live with them[30] and were accustomed to call him *Mazz* or the *Angel.*[31] For him they created a new and English home,‡ where he would spend his evenings in a delightful and interesting society without stiffness§ or constraint; and he entered into their discussions and thoughts. Presently, he was so much at ease as to jest

* See Shelley's *Ode to Naples* (1820).

† *E.g.* Mazzini's letter to *The Times*, January 30, 1846. See the *Edizione nazionale degli scritti di Giuseppe Mazzini*, XXVIII, 277–83.

‡ It was quite different from his own small room, with the sofa that at night became his bed.

§ Mazzini told his mother that the Ashursts were a "strange and excellent family": three sisters smoked; the fourth brought him flowers and took tea in his house—"all capital crimes against English *mores*"! See the *Edizione nazionale degli scritti di Giuseppe Mazzini*, XXX, 91.

to a daughter, Emilie Ashurst, then* married to Sydney Hawkes, on her utilitarianism (which she soon abandoned). On another occasion, he spoke derisively of the notion of the soul as a pleasure-pain engine.[32]

With the Carlyles he remained on familiar terms. Early in the year (1846), Mrs. Carlyle had written that Mazzini had not gone mad as yet—

> but I do not know whether it would not be better for him if he could—these long many years of failed hopes and destroyed illusions seem to be taking effect on him—not on his health—or sanity—but on his *temper*—he is grown so *captious* and *silently irritable.*

But not always was he a subject of anxiety to her. He could afford amusement by, let us say, his notions of English law: "I thought perhaps by your laws *poligamy* [sic] might be allowed to a Mad"![33] And when that bitter couple quarrelled some time in July, it was to Mazzini that Mrs. Carlyle turned for advice. He did not fail her, as the following very noble letter shows:

> My dear Friend,—I was yesterday almost the whole day out, and did not receive your notes, except in the evening, when it was too late to answer them. Your few words sound sad, deeply, I will not say irreparably sad; and the worst of it is that none can help you but yourself. It is only you who can, by a calm, dispassionate, fair re-examination of the past, send back to nothingness the ghosts and phantoms that you have been conjuring up. It is only you who can teach yourself that, whatever the *present* may be, you must front it with dignity, with a clear perception of all your duties, with a due reverence to your immortal soul, with a religious faith in times yet to come, that are to dawn under the approach of other cloudless suns. I could only point out to you the fulfilment of duties which can make life—not happy—what can?—but earnest, sacred, and resignated [sic]; but I would make you frown or scorn. We have a different conception of life, and are condemned here down [sic] to walk on two parallels. Still it is the feeling of those

* Later, after her divorce, she married an Italian named Venturi.

duties that saves me from the atheism of despair, and leads me through a life every day more barren and burdensome, in a sort of calm composed manner—such, I repeat, as the consciousness of something everlasting within us claims from every living mortal. For I now most coolly and deliberately do declare to you, that partly through what is known to you, partly through things that will never be known, I am carrying a burden even heavier than you, and have undergone even bitterer deceptions than you have. . . .[34]

What the burden was, we may only guess: the memory of Iacopo Ruffini and others like him? or the weight of Italy a Nation to be made? Later in the month, he wrote her, apparently in answer to her next plaintive communication, another letter of sympathy and tender wisdom.[35] The following excerpt is particularly of interest:

You have affection for me, as I have for you; you would not shake mine? You would not add yourself to the temptations haunting me to wreck and despair? You would not make me worse than I am by your example, by your showing yourself selfish and materialist? You believe in God. Don't you think, after all, that this* is nothing but an ephemeral trial. . . .[36]

When in October of the same year Carlyle was "fluent in invectives 'on rosewater imbecilities,' " meaning Mazzini's ideas on progress and on other things, Mrs. Carlyle loyally said:

These are but opinions to Carlyle; but to Mazzini, who has given his all, and helped to bring his friends to the scaffold in pursuit of such objects, it is matter of life and death.[37]

It is interesting to note that Mazzini had earlier in the year contributed a series of papers to *The People's Journal* on the martyrs for Italian liberty, like the brothers Bandiera and Iacopo Ruffini. For the same periodical he had also written an essay (April 21, 1846) on Poland, in which he prophesied that, Prometheus-like, she would cast off her chains. Probably, what Carlyle had termed impractical nonsense was

* Her difficulties with her husband.

that remarkable sequence of articles, the "Thoughts Upon Democracy in Europe,"* which ran in *The People's Journal* from August 29, 1846 to April 17, 1847. In them he had emphasized the religious character of the European democratic movement; had defined democracy as "the progress of all through all under the leading of the best and wisest"; had again attacked model republics "of beavers or of bees" for human beings; and had favoured universal suffrage, progress of industry, increase of comfort, and co-partnership of labour with intelligence and capital. Furthermore, he had added that democracy was "not the liberty of all, but *government freely consented to by all, and acting for all*"; and he had assailed, with dignified warmth, Bentham and the utilitarians, *laissez-faire*, Saint-Simonianism, Fourierism and its "phalansterian world," and Communism. What was necessary, he had said, was not the greatest happiness for all but the highest nobleness possible. He had criticized both Saint-Simonianism and Communism on the ground that these destroyed individuality; and had asserted that "Communism [could not] reckon a single vigorous thinker in its ranks," that it undermined the family, that it meant "a government, at once proprietor, possessor, and distributor of all that exists." Instead, he believed "property, as the sign and fruit of labour, to be good and useful," and saw in it "the representation of human individuality in the material world." Whether or not one regards these views as correct, one can justly say that Mazzini's writing was not merely extraordinary for its fusion of passion and austerity, but was also on a very high moral and literary plane.

At the commencement of 1847, Mazzini wrote two articles for *The People's Journal*. The first, "Cracow," dealt with the recent action on the part of Austria by which the ancient city was formally absorbed into her domains and which marked the official disappearance of Poland as a country.

* From this work, it is clear that Mazzini was thoroughly acquainted with Shakespeare and could quote him with readiness.

Yet, said Mazzini, the Polish people remained and would arise. A week later (January 9th), a second article, entitled "The European Question," appeared; essentially it was an appeal for English sympathy with European nationalism, but it also prophesied the revolutions of 1848. In March, he published a third paper in *The People's Journal*, on his friend, George Sand, whose cult in England he did as much as anybody else to foster.

Additional essays by Mazzini during 1847 included one on "The National Question in Switzerland" (*Lowe's Edinburgh Magazine*, May), in which he favoured a strong, central government, a uniform coinage system, etc.; another on "Nationality and Cosmopolitanism" (*The People's Journal*, May 8th), in which he defined nationality as meaning not kings but rather the people; and also his interesting reply to attacks by the radicals, Doherty and Goodwyn Barmby, on the "Thoughts upon Democracy in Europe." Ideologically, "A Last Word upon Fourierism and Communism . . ." (*The People's Journal*, June 19, 1847) contains nothing new, for Mazzini merely repeated his objections to both systems of collectivism; but it is exceedingly worth while from the literary point of view. However, his most important article (to people living to-day) was the extraordinary "On the Slavonian National Movement" (*Lowe's Edinburgh Magazine*, July and September 1847). Besides revealing an excellent knowledge of Slavic literatures, Mazzini predicted a resurrected Poland, declared that Russia's mission of civilization lay only to the East, and foretold the end of the Hapsburg Empire and of European Turkey.

To promote the point of view indicated in these writings, Mazzini found expedient the establishment, April 28, 1847, of The People's International League,* members of which

* Mazzini's article, "The People's International League" (*Lowe's Edinburgh Magazine*, April 1847), publicized the League and advocated England's giving up her policy of isolation in behalf of the struggling nationalities. In addition, W. J. Linton wrote a manifesto, or outline, of the League's aims.

included Thornton Hunt; William Henry Ashurst; Peter A. Taylor, radical member of Parliament for Leicester and known for his opposition to the Corn Laws; Henry Vincent, Chartist orator; W. J. Fox, a leading orator of the Manchester School; and Joseph Toynbee, the aurist. The purpose of its existence was propaganda—the enlightenment of the British people as to the political condition and relations of foreign countries, the dissemination of principles of national freedom and progress, the fostering of efficient public opinion in their favour, and the promotion of a good understanding between the peoples of all countries.[38] Such was its general programme, but its particular object was the Italian cause as interpreted by Mazzini. Thomas Cooper, the Chartist poet, joined the League, which usually met weekly at the home of its secretary, W. J. Linton. Cooper, whose verses repeated the still cries of the disinherited, early manifested an admiration for Mazzini's personality and for his ability to foresee impending political upheavals. For example, in September 1847, the Italian repeated his prediction of the 'Forty-eight which was to overthrow Louis Philippe;[39] and from Paris, two months later, he wrote to Mrs. Carlyle of projected risings in Italy.[40] Others who attached themselves to his League were Charles Dickens* (as a member of its Council), Dr. Bowring, Duncombe, Douglas Jerrold, Shaen, and James Stansfeld.† Such were the friends of European nationalism who meant to enlist English sympathy for Italy.[41] At this time also David Masson became acquainted with Mazzini.

Not all saw in Mazzini Italy's Perseus. In August 1847,

* About this time, Mazzini was reading Dickens's *Dombey and Son* as the parts came out. See the *Edizione nazionale degli scritti di Giuseppe Mazzini*, XXXII, 263.

† Stansfeld was in future years a noted champion of women's rights. He also sympathized with the Chartists, though once Feargus O'Connor denounced him as "a capitalist wolf in sheep's clothing." When Stansfeld was elected to Parliament, he generally co-operated with Liberals like Bright and Forster.

one John Frederick Stanford wrote a pamphlet wholly in favour of Italy and against the Austrian policy of intervention for the purpose of stamping out the embers of Italian nationalism. Nevertheless, Stanford termed Mazzini's *Young Italy* visionary.[42] And Charles Lever, writing of the new pope, Pius IX,* called him an ass for making even moderate concessions to "a mob, who only look for a new constitution as an occasion for general pillage." The Pope should merely sweep the Church free of abuses, not go on "fraternising with Mazzini & Co."[43] To Tories like the Irish novelist, the Genoese was not to be tolerated.

But Mazzini regarded himself as affianced to his country,[44] and once had a dream[45] of having been sent as its ambassador to the Court of St James's. Did not this vision symbolize the character of his career and his hopes? For after all, it would have been fitting had the "Italian in England," his ambition of the Republic of Italy attained, come to London as its envoy. And when Paris ejected Louis Philippe, Mazzini hastened to the Continent in his eagerness to change shadows into substance. The 'Forty-eight had begun in earnest.

* Mazzini had written on Pio Nono in *Lowe's Edinburgh Magazine* (November 1846, and January 1847). His articles, "The Pope and the Italian Question," maintained that Pius IX had good intentions of reforms, but that papal government was anarchy. In short, the world should have no faith in popes; instead, it ought to trust the Italian people to unify Italy. See the *Edizione nazionale degli scritti di Giuseppe Mazzini*, XXXIV, 249–91.

CHAPTER V

The Sunset of the 'Forty-eight

THE lid placed over Europe after Waterloo by the allied powers never fitted tightly. There were always rumblings of revolutionary significance, but the military would come and restore the *status quo*. Finally, the accumulated lava burst out in a remarkable sequence of popular risings—the 'Forty-eight (the *quarantotto* as the Italians called it). Primarily democratic and nationalistic in character, it began in January in Sicily, whence it spread to France; eventually, all Europe was affected except Russia, Spain, and the Scandinavian peninsula. In Great Britain, it was marked by Chartist demonstrations and an Irish republican agitation; in Denmark and in the Low Countries, it showed itself in the form of peaceful reforms. There were barricades in the streets of Paris, Vienna, and Berlin; but the movement was successful only in France, where the republic was proclaimed and universal suffrage instituted. Elsewhere, the armies extinguished the rebellious ardour of the populace; and the governments, in alliance with the upper classes and the clergy (both terrified by socialistic proposals), strengthened the police and persecuted the press and liberal associations. The gains that were retained were few: universal suffrage in France, and constitutions in Prussia and in Sardinia.

Mazzini, whom Mrs. Fletcher [1] at this time reckoned the master spirit destined to save his country, arrived* in Italy,

* W. J. Linton published a poem (*The Reasoner*, June 14, 1848, V, 62) on "Mazzini's Return to Italy" and in it exulted at the Italian revolutions and the apparent disintegration of the Austrian empire.

firm in his resolution to make the revolution republican in nature. Thomas Adolphus Trollope,* describing what took place in Tuscany in 1848, asserted that the Mazzinian propaganda had spoiled the effectiveness of the Tuscan allies of Piedmont, for it had made them detest an alliance with a *royal* army, that of Charles Albert, the unfortunate King Shilly-Shally, who was trying to expel the Austrians from Italy.[2] Antonio Gallenga portrayed the republican conspirator as uniting the boldest ambition to the highest capacities; but significantly, he pointed out that Mazzini was widening the breach† between himself and those moderates who desired a united Italy but did not mind if a king accomplished it.[3] Another contemporary writer, Charles MacFarlane, denounced Mazzini as the visionary republican rhetorician accountable for the troubles in Italy.[4] MacFarlane ventured to utter the slander that Mazzini sent men to death without daring to risk himself.[5] Anathematizing all popular disturbances of established things, this publicist declared:

> Giuseppe Mazzini has told us that there was a Rome of a bloody aristocratic republic, a Rome of the Caesars, a Rome of the Popes, and that all this Rome was bad and damnable; but that the Rome of the people was yet to come. It is come! and about the worst wish that an enemy could bestow upon this demagogue is that he should be condemned to live in it.[6]

Soon enough, Mazzini went to the newly established Roman Republic whence Pius IX had fled; and thenceforth, the European stage was to resound with the clamour of men and the clangour of trumpets, in the midst of which he assumed a directive *rôle*.

* Brother of Anthony and almost as prolific a novelist.

† *E.g.* Mazzini's three articles in *The Spectator* (December 2, 1848 to March 3, 1849), which compose the long essay, "Parties and Affairs in Italy," confirmed Gallenga's opinion. Mazzini attacked the notion of uniting Italy from above, and said that not the King of Piedmont but the Italian people would accomplish the unification of his fatherland.

Emilio Dandolo has given to posterity a fine account of the siege of the Roman Republic, which expired violently under the assaults of the French under Oudinot. Our chronicler was no Mazzinian and censured the leading triumvir, to whom he allowed a misguided sincerity, for having desired to prolong the siege uselessly.[7] The remarkable master of guerrilla warfare, Garibaldi, who defended the beleaguered city on behalf of its ruling triumvirate, Aurelio Saffi, Armellini, and Mazzini, blamed the last for his mistakes as dictator of the Roman Republic.[8] But in English eyes the conspirator, now turned from the secret preparations of exile to the open hazards of revolution, had grown enormously. People like Mrs. Fletcher[9] followed the fortunes of the short-lived Roman Republic with great interest. *Punch*[10] paid tribute to Mazzini's conduct thus:

> Though brutish force the game has won,
> Triumvir, thou hast nobly done;
> Calm courage in a rightful cause
> Gains thee a loftier world's applause;
> And Rome's old heroes from their spheres
> Shout, chiming in with British cheers,
> Bravo, Mazzini!

Before this, when the fate of the Republic was wavering in the balance, the magazine had published an "Ode to Louis Napoleon":

> The Romans may be right or wrong,
> I don't care which, in turning Pius out
> And sending all the Cardinals along
> With that good Pontiff to the right about;
> But let them choose their form of government,
> And what's the odds, so long as they're content?
> Are you to cram down their reluctant gullets
> The kind of Constitution you think best,
> By means of swords and bayonets and bullets?
> Against such tyranny I must protest.[11]

Such was a British middle-class reaction to the presence of Oudinot's army before Rome.

Writing in February 1849 from Florence whence she beheld the course of things in the Papal States, Mrs. Browning said: ". . . though Mazzini is virtuous and heroic, he is indiscreet and mistakes the stuff of which the people is made, if he thinks to find a great nation in the heart of it."[12] In May, as she considered the spectacle of one republic, France, putting down another to save it from Austria, she was unable to refrain from calling Mazzini the truest hero and patriot Italy had to boast of. Yet even he, she thought, could merely die for his fatherland but never would cause it to live.[13] In London, Mrs. Carlyle eagerly followed the march of events on the Tiber and thought more tenderly of

> poor dear Mazzini—all my affection for him has waked up since I knew him in jeopardy and so gallantly fulfilling his destiny—and not mine only—the public sympathy is fast going over to his side—under the atrocious injustice of the French, who one year ago loudly invited all nations to form republics and now proceed to shoot lead into the only one that has obeyed the call.[14]

But later, when Mazzini seemed to be too obdurate against the remorselessness of Gallic bayonets, she commented more acidly that he was born to make a martyr of himself.[15] In his journal, her husband made a long entry (May 17,1849), characterized by a caustic kindness:

> Mazzini busy at Rome resisting the French, resisting all people that attack his "Repubblica Romana," standing on his guard against all the world. Poor Mazzini! If he *could* stand there in Rome, in sight of all Italy, and practically defy the whole world for a while, and fight till Rome was ashes and ruin, and end by blowing himself and his assailants up in the last strong post, and so yielding only with life, he might rouse the whole Italian nation into such a rage as it has not known for many centuries; and this might be the means of shaking out of the Italian mind a very foul precipitate indeed. Perhaps that is really what he was worth in this world. Strange, providential-looking, and leading to many thoughts—how, of all the immense nonsense that lay in this brave man, the one element of noble perennial truth

> that pervaded him wholly withal is at length laid hold of by the upper powers of this universe, and turned to the use that was in it. Whatsoever good we have, the gods know it well, and will know what to make of it in due season. Mazzini came much about us here for many years, patronised by my wife; to me very wearisome, with his incoherent Jacobinisms, George-Sandisms,* in spite of all my love and regard for him; a beautiful little man, full of sensibilities, of melodies, of clear intelligence, and noble virtues. . . . What *will* become of him? we ask daily with a real interest. A small, square-headed, bright-eyed, swift, yet still, Ligurian figure; beautiful, and merciful, and fierce; as pretty a little man when I first saw him, eight or nine years ago,† as had ever come before me. True as steel, the word, the thought of him pure and limpid as water; by nature a little lyrical poet; plenty of quiet fun in him, too, and wild emotion, rising to the *shrill* key. . . .[16]

Meanwhile, a man of letters whose muse was elegiac rather than fulgurous was travelling in Italy as tourists do—with an eye for the blue Latin sky and for classic marbles and Renaissance art. From Liverpool in February he had indicated his awareness that the great powers meant to restore the Pope and to crush the renascent Roman republic of which Joseph Mazzini had just been declared a citizen.[17] However, Arthur Hugh Clough was at the beginning of his tour more concerned, republican though he was, with his disappointment at St. Peter's than with arms and the man. And since this was the current thing to do, he visited Mazzini and found that a French envoy was with him. The Italian was so available to all that he wondered at his not being assassinated by some Jesuit—it would be so easy.[18] Clough acknowledged the triumviral dignity by waiting almost an hour in an antechamber and was rewarded with a half-hour's interview with the dictator, whom he thought less fanatical and less single-minded than he had expected—

* Mazzini was capable of weeping over George Sand's novels! See the *Edizione nazionale degli scritti di Giuseppe Mazzini*, LVI, 50.

† Carlyle was mistaken about the date, for he first met Mazzini in 1837.

nay, was led to judge him even "shifty, and practical enough." Mazzini seemed in excellent spirits—confident and at ease, and made inquiries whether the Englishman had seen anything of the pillaging which the English papers were describing. English residents, said Mazzini, could bear witness to the prevailing tranquillity. And Clough himself saw nothing to the contrary so that he thought "S.P.Q.R." merited a defence in *The Globe*, for it was a "most *respectable*" republic.[19] Late in May, he was uncertain whether it would stand, but he was moved to declare to Thomas Arnold that under Mazzini's inspiration it had shown "a wonderful courage and a glorious generosity."[20] When he was in Geneva in August, he expressed to Palgrave, of *Golden Treasury* fame, his admiration for Mazzini and then alluded to his own disgust with the overthrow of the Republic by saying, "Farewell, politics, utterly!"[21]

The gallant struggles of the Romans, led by Garibaldi and animated by Mazzini, to preserve their commonwealth, have been commemorated by Gerald Massey in *Cries of 'Forty-Eight*, a collection of fervid verse of ballad heartiness, and by Clough in his long poem, *Amours de Voyage*. The futilitarian hero of the second, Claude, is made to lapse out of his attitude of jaded indifference, to shed a tear for the poor little Roman Republic, to denounce France, and to scold England for not interfering. Naturally, Claude was unable to endure the restoration of the Bourbons and the Hapsburgs to their Italian possessions. He observed that the Romans did not find it too sweet and decorous to die for their country and was pleased with Mazzini's government, which was keeping order despite slanders to the contrary by the English conservative press:

> Meantime, notwithstanding all journals,
> Honour for once to the tongue and the pen of
> the eloquent writer!
> Honour to speech! and all honour to thee,
> thou noble Mazzini![22]

For Clough's fairness and love for verity had made him rise above his own feeling of superiority to the Roman republicans; and it was for them that he, very possibly,* intended his best-known poem:

Say not the struggle nought availeth,
  The labour and the wounds are vain,
The enemy faints not, nor faileth,
  And as things have been they remain.

If hopes were dupes, fears may be liars;
  It may be, in yon smoke concealed,
Your comrades chase e'en now the fliers,
  And, but for you, possess the field.

For while the tired waves, vainly breaking,
  Seem here no painful inch to gain,
Far back, through creeks and inlets making,
  Comes silent, flooding in, the main.

And not by eastern windows only,
  When daylight comes, comes in the light,
In front, the sun climbs slow, how slowly,
  But westward, look, the land is bright.

Under similar circumstances, more than a score of years before, Pushkin had written his noble "Message to Siberia," on the Decembrists who had revolted against Czar Nicholas I for the sake of constitutional government.

That was one side of it—the good opinion which the aged Leigh Hunt,† Clough, and Margaret Fuller (then in Rome) had of the Republic. Miss Fuller was moved at the sight of the wounded, whom she nursed in the hospitals as a volunteer, and brought them books and flowers. Emily Winkworth,

* "Say Not the Struggle Nought Availeth" immediately follows two other poems on the Italian revolution, "Peschiera" and "Alteram Partem," also written in 1849 and both emphasizing that

" ''Tis better to have fought and lost,
Than never to have fought at all.' "

† Hunt, though he preferred a limited monarchy, wished success for the Roman Republic, and was bitter against the French for their intervention. See his *Autobiography*, ed. Roger Ingpen, New York, 1903, II, 179–80.

the future Mrs. William Shaen, wrote, while the siege of Rome was in progress, that Mazzini was not a mere ideal but an honest and noble man.[23] *The Illustrated London News* gave the Italians a good press, but *The Quarterly Review*, always anti-Jacobin, praised the good old days of the reactionary Gregory XVI and compared Mazzini to Robespierre. *The Times* also favoured the Italian rulers against their rebellious subjects,[24] as did the future Cardinal Newman in a vivid description of the armed soldiers of Mazzini at war with the spiritual power of the papacy in 1848–49:

> Punctual in its movements, precise in its operations, imposing in its equipments, with its spirit high and its step firm, with its haughty clarion and its black artillery, behold the mighty world is gone forth to war—with what? With an unknown something, which it feels but cannot see; which flits around it, which flaps against its cheek, with the air, with the wind. It charges and it slashes, and it fires its volleys, and it bayonets, and it is mocked by a foe who dwells in another sphere, and is far beyond the force of its analysis, or the capacities of its calculus.[25]

It is apparent that Newman had omitted a simple fact. Mazzini had been vanquished only by superior physical force.

Mazzini's defence of the Roman Republic renewed English interest in the letter-opening case of 1844. For example, an anonymous writer, identified as one Hamilton Geale, composed in 1849 a novel, *Ernesto di Ripalta*, dealing with the very recent Italian revolutions. The letters of one character in this tedious narrative having been opened, Geale uttered the following *obiter dictum*: "England—free England—under the congenial sway of Toryism, consented to play the eavesdropper, and break the seals of unhappy refugees, to furnish his Holiness with intelligence of the earliest designs of his enemies."[26]

The siege of Rome had been a period of such high excitement and feverish thought* that it left Mazzini (so Margaret

* Mazzini had written to Mrs. Ashurst: "I am living as if in a whirlwind." See the *Edizione nazionale degli scritti di Giuseppe Mazzini*, XL, 30.

Fuller sorrowfully recorded)[27] an old man with grey-streaked hair, a beard almost white, bloodshot eyes, and a jaundiced skin. It has been maintained that it would have been better for his political reputation had he died at this time; but the literary world would have suffered by his passing. He had to share his grief; and so, when Oudinot took Rome, he reported, briefly and superbly, to Emilie Hawkes, his favourite in the Ashurst clan, the overthrow of his Republic.[28] After all, it had also been their republic, since Messrs. Ashurst and Stansfeld are said to have financed it.[29] The manner of his escape from Rome paralleled in hazard and in *élan* anything in the annals of history. He boarded a vessel about to sail from Civitavecchia and disclosed his identity to the Corsican captain named Cambiaso with the admission that he possessed no passport. The Captain agreed, nevertheless, to take him. At Leghorn, the Austrians searched the ship, and Mazzini merely went to the steward's galley, got a cap, pulled it down, and washed glasses![30]

After the defence of Rome, Mazzini became one of Walter Savage Landor's heroes.[31] The versatile W. J. Linton wrote a few sonnets in requiem for the murdered republic.[32] Henry Lushington, then Chief Secretary to the Maltese Government, defended Mazzini for relying on the military prowess of Garibaldi, "the condottiere," as he had been maliciously called by Gallenga. After all, said Lushington, the unspeakable king of Naples had Swiss mercenaries.[33] At this time also another enthusiast for Mazzini and Garibaldi was by his own confession Bulwer-Lytton,[34] he who, many years before, had praised the city-state as ideal for Italy. But the most singular product of the unfortunate republic was the number of English children christened Mazzini!*

* *E.g.* George Jacob Holyoake named (November 11, 1849) a new-born baby boy Mazzini Trulove, and took the occasion to eulogize the conspirator. See *The Reasoner*, VII, 305. *Cf.* also Mazzini Dunn, a character in George Bernard Shaw's play, *Heartbreak House*. (By September 1851, there was at least one British yacht called the *Mazzini*.)

The sad aftermath saw the refugees from Rome fleeing everywhere—to Malta, to England, to any haven from immediate peril. In their behalf, Dickens wrote (August 1849) an address asking for help and praising the Roman Republic. It was printed in the English papers and may have been inspired by a letter (afterwards published in *Royalty and Republicanism in Italy*) which Mazzini wrote from Geneva on August 6, 1849, to an English friend. In it, he told of the reaction in Rome after the fall of the Republic, when brute force was enthroned and the prisons were filled with men arrested and held without trial.[35]

In Paris, Alexander Herzen, the Russian revolutionist, saw Mazzini, again in exile, and left a memorable record:

> Even in Italy a head so severely classical, so elegant in its gravity, is rarely to be met with. At moments the expression of his face was harshly austere, but it quickly grew soft and serene. An active, concentrated intelligence sparkled in his melancholy eyes; there was an infinity of persistence and strength of will in them and in the lines on his brow. All his features showed traces of long years of anxiety, of sleepless nights, of past storms, of powerful passions, or rather of one powerful passion, and also some element of fanaticism—perhaps of asceticism.[36]

Apparently, the Italian was not fundamentally changed, for he had in no way abandoned his calling. At Lausanne he bought a steam press from Germany in order to print literature, and was ready to resume the burrowing work of the revolutionary mole as busily as Hamlet's ghost—*hic et ubique*. Indeed, his aspirations led him now to propose a Holy Alliance of Peoples.

The German patriot and poet, Moritz Hartmann, has described how warmly the Carlyles welcomed Mazzini back to London in 1850:

> Suddenly Mrs. Carlyle started: a voice in the hall had reached her ear, stirring her like an electric shock. Her eyes sparkled, and opening the door she grasped the hands of

> the visitor in such a transport of joy that it seemed almost an embrace.

She was sad because his beard had turned white. He was only forty-five. He was thin and pale; his complexion was still olive-tinted; his frame remained well knit and slight; and he was dressed with extreme simplicity. As ever, the majestic forehead and the form of his head were beautiful indeed. Had one met him in the street with his brow concealed, one would scarcely have noticed him. But when one saw his eyes, a sense of pleasure mixed with veneration possessed one. When he spoke, the music of his voice conquered. So Hartmann wrote.[37] Ironically enough, Carlyle was defending Russian despotism at the moment of Mazzini's entrance.[38] His return was marked by a pilgrimage to Byron's grave.[39] To a cousin, Mrs. Carlyle repeated some of Mazzini's interesting yarns: he had lived in a Marseilles madhouse to avoid arrest while waiting for a false passport; in Geneva* he had lodged in the same house with the magistrate assigned to discover him![40]

In Florence, Charles Eliot Norton, visiting (November 1850) the Brownings, in whose estimation Mazzini had grown, received from them the loan of a book by the titular chief of *Young Italy*.[41] There were other echoes. Landor's incoherent letter to *The Examiner* (August 3, 1850) called Mazzini "the defender of Rome and of liberty" and summoned liberals to come forward "in the only feasible defence of Italy's defenders." Apparently, Landor desired the giving of financial support to the refugees. John Nichol, destined to have a great influence on Swinburne, met the Italian in London and learned to worship him.[42] Perhaps the greatest enthusiast of all was Emily Winkworth, who had

* Emilie Ashurst Hawkes sent him at Geneva a false passport in her husband's name. He asked her to insert in *The Times* or other newspapers a rumour of his being in England, in order to throw the Swiss police off his trail. See the *Edizione nazionale degli scritti di Giuseppe Mazzini*, XL, 281; XLII, 125.

just seen the returned exile. A letter to her sisters reveals Mazzini's overpowering personality*:

> Well, altogether he is simply the most wonderful-looking man I ever saw in my life. He may be any height he likes, he is so thoroughly manly-looking, you do not think of it. Forehead high and cliff-like, with caverns underneath for his eyes; great round temples, with a little scanty black hair straying over them. Altogether a perfectly straight face; straight nose; straight lines across; strong chin; erect-set head; looks like the sort of man that everybody round him can't help obeying; strange colour over his face, sort of grey ashy halo, not like the white or yellow paleness one sees always. Then his eyes you know about; the only ones I ever saw that looked like flames. Well, you have seen his portrait, and there is no other face I can compare him with. All that I can think of have something heavy in them beside his. There are signs of struggle on all the grand English faces I know. He is vehement in his ways rather; at least foreign and quick; very foreign accent; full of fun. All the talk nearly about the concert, except at last a few words he said to me about national feeling in Italy. It's because I've heard

* Similarly, George Gilfillan, the critic, wrote to Sydney Dobell (February 13, 1852) his impressions on first meeting Mazzini:

> "What a white capacious forehead! What a mass of blackness opens like a dark star in his eye, what firmness in his mouth, and how his words came forth from his lips through that grizzly beard, like sharp cutting winds from a forest! His talk is clear, strong, practical, choked almost at times with its earnestness, and the emphasis which his confused English sometimes fails to give is always supplied by his eye."

See R. A. and E. S. Watson, *George Gilfillan: Letters and Journals, with Memoir*, London, 1892, p. 158.

Compare also the account (1853) of Mazzini recorded by Malwida von Meysenbug, *Gesammelte Werke*, ed. Berta Schleicher, Leipzig, 1922, I, 363:

> "Mazzini was of middle height, delicately and slenderly built, rather thin than strong, no imposing figure—only his head expressed the impression which people got of him; and when one saw the noble features, the brow on which thought was enthroned, the dark eyes, from which at the same time the fire of the fanatic and the mildness of the saint spoke, then one felt himself immediately held in the magic circle of this man. . . ."

> so much about him beforehand, I dare say, but his eyes made me fairly shiver when he came and sat beside me and looked at me. I was certain before that I had seen finer faces than his, and yet I couldn't help feeling as if I had never seen genius before. In English grand faces it is intellect and thought, the faces seem to stand between you and the soul, and the feeling only comes out sideways. In him it's spirituality and passion that you see. I don't mean that there's not strength too—he looks strong enough for anything—but that's not the thing you notice.[43]

Surely, it is plain why Englishwomen like Jessie Meriton White, Linda White,* and Emilie Ashurst Hawkes were drawn to proselytize in the United Kingdom for the Italian cause.

Mazzini's friends were warm enough, but in the same London lived a fellow exile who had become a deadly enemy. One of Gallenga's collection of anecdotes, *Scenes from Italian Life*, deals with Iacopo Ruffini. He has been arrested for treason; and to make him break down into indiscretions, his jailers in the Forte Diamante of Genoa have shown him the signed confessions of his companions. Ruffini resolves on suicide rather than that he should in a moment of weakness betray his fellow plotters. If he confesses, he will become an exile,

> an Italian master to the daughters of London shop-keepers! to listen to all their twaddle about Italy! to undergo all their sympathy for its sacred cause; and, under that thin veil of pity, to see their sovereign contempt for the faintheartedness of its vindicators. . . .

Instead, he stabs himself with a piece of iron wrenched from the lining of his dungeon door of oak. As he bleeds to death, his thoughts revolve about the Italian woe. Then Gallenga launches into an attack on Mazzini, the friend of Iacopo Ruffini. He was not the only foe to express himself in print. Alexander Baillie Cochrane's *Young Italy* (1850) was a defence

* She first married a certain Mazini, and then Villari. Occasionally, she employed the pseudonym, M. Dalin.

of Austrian rule in Italy and a mocking of all Italian aspirations. Cochrane* charged Mazzini's Roman Republic with having harboured assassins who had accounted for two hundred and fifty murdered priests. Mazzini and the Italian revolutionists were merely fanatics and firebrands.

In 1850, Mazzini had a threefold task: to offset the harmful influence of writers like the foregoing, to help the starving refugees from Italy, and to vindicate in England the conduct of the republicans in the 'Forty-eight in such a wise as to show that the Piedmontese party (composed of the Moderates who favoured Italian unity under the House of Savoy) was not to be entrusted with the Italian cause. Specifically, he proposed public meetings at Manchester, Leeds, and other manufacturing towns; organized benefit concerts; and published the programmatic *Royalty and Republicanism in Italy*. In this long pamphlet, he maintained that union among Italian princes had proved impossible, that there was no single prince able to lead the Italian cause, that the only course left was a republic. He asserted that Charles Albert had attacked the Austrians only because of dread of a republic in Piedmont if he had failed to act. Mazzini urged upon the Italians a definite programme: independence from the foreigner, unity of the country, a republic. But he put this republican notion last; and if the others came, he would not be intolerant about it. The pamphlet was hostilely criticized in *The Edinburgh Review*, January 1851.

Mazzini's return to England may have occasioned the appearance of a volume of anonymous poetry called *For Rome: Ora e Sempre*—a phrase used by *Young Italy*. Whoever the author may have been, he was clearly a Mazzinian republican and the possessor of a vein of genuine poetic talent and a Shelleylike music—passionate, angry, harmonious, rapid. There was first a sonnet called "June 1849," in which Oudinot's French soldiers were properly

* He was a member of Parliament.

and poetically scourged for their infamy. Then followed a longer poem, "To the Future (April 1848)," which was in essence the ecstasy of a republican beholding a freed Europe. In form an irregular Pindaric ode, it sang the overcoming of the reactionary Sonderbund in Switzerland and the expulsion of Louis Philippe, and awaited with optimism a French republic. It hailed the democratic movements in Prussia and rejoiced that the double-headed vulture of Austria was drooping his feathers, for the execrable Metternich had been expelled from Vienna. It summoned the Spielberg prison to open its gates, and it encouraged the Italian martyr, Silvio Pellico. It greeted Sicily, first to rise in Italy, and then the rest of the roll of honour of the valiant patriot cities—Venice, Milan, Genoa, Rome. The unknown poet expressed distrust of Charles Albert, for he had once played the traitor, and recalled the martyred Bandieras. He hoped for a Poland free from the knouts of the Cossacks, and said England too should be free, for her people would triumph over feudal reaction. Thrones were crashing, and the nations were rushing on with the might of mightiest hurricanes.

More sombre was a third poem, "The Dirge of the Nations (November 1848)," a threnody for the freedom-seeking nations, defeated in their aspirations. The Republic had been overcome by Hypocrisy calling itself Order—the French against Mazzini's Rome. Again the Bourbon throttled Naples, again was Charles Albert a traitor. Jellachich and his Croats had restored the "idiot Kaiser," and Poland was a new Prometheus bound. In Ireland there was famine, and in England there was peace—because the slaves did not feel their thraldom. The nations were king-stricken, for the Croat and the Cossack made their lair in Europe's palace-dens; and Metternich, like a ghoul, revelled. The indignant poet presented Mazzini as ever hopeful, since these things, he believed, would also pass. A concluding sonnet, "June 1849," sings the fallen Roman Republic whose cause was Man and the People. *For Rome* was destined to be not the only poetry which Mazzini could evoke from his disciples.

During the next year, 1851, there was voiced with a persistent frequency in England and elsewhere the statement that Mazzini had now become a hindrance to his own cause. For example, Gabriele Rossetti said[44] that it was the fate of Italy that those of her sons who loved her most should do her most harm:

> To you, Mazzini, first I turn my gaze
> Who for your land would give a hundred lives;
> For her you faced swift death in perilous ways;
> In you the former ardour still survives.
> But to what end? Your country in distress
> Not more would have you undertake but less.*

The Earl of Ellesmere translated an account[45] of the military history of the Italian revolutions in which the Genoese was dubbed "the notorious Mazzini." Pseudonymously unfriendly despite a fanfare of respect, Gallenga accused him of having divided the Italians, and thus of being responsible for the failure of the 'Forty-eight (because the Lombards had remained aloof from Charles Albert on account of Mazzini's propaganda). The conspirator was "the most unmanageable, the most unconquerable, the most fatal specimen of *one-sidedness* the world ever witnessed."[46] In Paris, Nassau Senior conversed, late in December, with the distinguished patriot, the Abbé Gioberti, now an exile, and was amused to hear him say that Mazzini and Kossuth had been the most mischievous men of the century; and that if liberty was to be destroyed, no one did the work better than a demagogue.[47] To this maxim the economist gave assent. Another hostile writer was the historian, Luigi Carlo Farini, whose long *The Roman State* Gladstone had largely translated; in it, Farini said Mazzini was mystical and without common sense.[48]

* Englished by Mrs. R. D. Waller.

Moreover, the more extreme radicals regarded Mazzini with mixed emotions. With typical irony, Marx dubbed him "the Pope of the Democratic Church *in partibus*";* and Engels, though he respected Mazzini's disinterested nature, thought that the Italian had a pointless, silly, and abstract passion for revolution.[49] On the other hand, Mazzini once said of Marx that he was "a man of penetrating but corrupting intelligence, imperious, jealous of the influence of others," that he lacked "strong philosophic [sic] or religious convictions," and that he possessed "more hatred, if righteous hatred, in his heart than love."[50] Mazzini even complained[51] to George Sand about the German Communists, who called republicans like himself aristocrats. For anarchists too he had no use; and for Louis Blanc, the Socialist, he abandoned[52] *all* hope because the Frenchman was repeating (November 1851) the Marxian slogan: "From each according to his capacity; to each according to his needs."

* On another occasion Marx said:

> "Mazzini knows only the towns with their liberal aristocracy and their enlightened citizens. The material needs of the Italian agricultural population—as exploited and as systematically emasculated and held in stupidity as the Irish—are naturally too low for the phraseological heaven of his cosmopolitan, neo-Catholic, ideological manifestos. It needs courage, however, to inform the bourgeoisie and the aristocracy that the first step towards the independence of Italy is the complete emancipation of the peasants and the transformation of their semi-tenant system into free bourgeois property."

See Franz Mehring's *Karl Marx: The Story of His Life*, tr. Edward Fitzgerald, New York, 1935, p. 269.

CHAPTER VI

The Ebbing of the Mazzinian Tide

AGAINST the cacophony of dissent, a new organization devoted to the Mazzinian programme was formed in England. It called itself The Society of the Friends of Italy; and its object was, by public meetings, lectures, the press, and especially by promoting the publication of works on the history of the Italian national movement, to foster a correct appreciation of the Italian question in England.* It promised to use every available constitutional method of furthering in Parliament and elsewhere the cause of Italian independence. The membership fee was small—only half a crown—and its council included among others W. H. Ashurst, of Muswell Hill; W. H. Ashurst, junior; Cowen; Duncombe; John Forster; J. A. Froude; G. J. Holyoake; Edward Miall; Leigh Hunt; Douglas Jerrold; Walter Savage Landor; G. H. Lewes; W. J. Linton; W. C. Macready; David Masson (secretary); Professor Francis Newman; Professor J. P. Nichol† (the father of Swinburne's friend); William Shaen; the important brewer, James Stansfeld, junior; P. A. Taylor (treasurer); and Arthur Trevelyan. Its announcement of aims attained a circulation of more than five thousand. It also printed a refutation of the charge of terrorism in Rome during the republic, which was docu-

* *E.g.*, Sydney Dobell belonged to these Friends of Italy; and his popular poem, "The Roman," is Mazzinian in its Italian politics. Indeed, Mazzini, to whom Dobell had sent a copy of the poem (together with a hero-worshipping letter), praised "The Roman."

† The elder Nichol, in the fall of 1857, wanted Emilie Ashurst Hawkes to write accounts of the more noted Italian patriots for an English biographical dictionary. See the *Edizione nazionale degli scritti di Giuseppe Mazzini*, LVIII, 308.

mented by Mazzini. The Society concluded that the Roman republic was during its short existence the best government that central Italy had known for ages; nay, "a spectacle for the whole of Europe to be proud of." Indeed, it was described as "the highest example of ability and virtue which modern democracy [had] yet exhibited, and a phenomenon of all but unparalleled interest and promise in modern political history."[1]

By 1851, Mazzini was less intimate with the Carlyles. It is true that Mrs. Carlyle obtained employment for Aurelio Saffi, Mazzini's dear friend. It is also true that Carlyle suggested to Robert Browning, then in Paris, that Mazzini could give the Brownings an introduction to George Sand.[2] Moreover, one knows that Mazzini used to discuss Dante* with John Carlyle, the great Thomas's brother, who was translating *The Divine Comedy*; and one acknowledges the loyalty with which Carlyle defended Mazzini in 1853 against the aspersions of D'Azeglio, the Piedmontese minister. "Sir, you do not know Mazzini at all, not at all," he had angrily said, and had turned away and sat down to a newspaper. Yet the fact remains that these two prophets of dissimilar hopes had drifted apart. Though they respected each other's character,† they detested each other's opinions;[3] indeed, Mazzini loathed Carlyle's reactionary *Latter-Day Pamphlets*. Nothing makes the Scot's attitude clearer than his letter to Emerson‡ (July 8, 1851):

> Mazzini, as you perhaps know, is with us this summer; comes across once in the week or so, and tells me, or at least

* Mazzini had completed Foscolo's unfinished edition of Dante in the early 'forties, and had been praised for this by a writer in *Fraser's Magazine* (April 1845).

† Carlyle once told Sir Charles Gavan Duffy (*Conversations with Carlyle*, New York, 1892, p. 109) that Mazzini was "a perfectly honourable and true man, but possessed by wild and fanciful theories borrowed from the French Republicans."

‡ In 1861, Mazzini called Emerson an idiot! *i.e.*, philosophically. See the *Edizione nazionale degli scritti di Giuseppe Mazzini*, LXX, 245.

> my Wife, all his news. The Roman revolution has made a man of him,—quite brightened up ever since;—and the best friend *he* ever saw, I believe, was the same Quack-President of France [later Napoleon III], who relieved him while it was still time.[4]

With Elizabeth Barrett Browning, Mazzini was at the zenith of esteem, as she indicated in her *Casa Guidi Windows.* In part, the poem reveals her disillusionment with Pius IX, which she told Mazzini to record as a gain. But he must realize, she wrote, that if the people no longer trusted in the Pope, yet they lacked valour and faith, and were divided. These things too he should record:

> Yes, but first
> Set down thy people's faults; set down the want
> Of soul-conviction; set down aims dispersed,
> And incoherent means, and valour scant
> Because of scanty faith, and schism accursed
> That wrench these brother-hearts from covenant
> With freedom and each other. Set down this,
> And this, and see to overcome it when
> The seasons bring the fruits thou will not miss
> If wary. Let no cry of patriot men
> Distract thee from the stern analysis
> Of masses who cry only!

Praising Mazzini's defence of Rome, she did not fail to urge on him the necessity for uniting the land, though in him she saw an extreme theorist. Perhaps men would not follow him to the limit.[5] She was right—Italy was to be united, but not republican.

Mazzini did not neglect to spread propaganda in America. For example, Colonel Hugh Forbes, an English army officer, came in 1851 to the United States to preach Mazzinian ideas. Forbes, who had been intimately associated with revolutionary movements in Venetia, Palermo, and Rome in 1848–49, delivered four lectures at New York University on the 'Forty-eight in Italy.[6] His apostleship is only one example of the enormous influence exerted by Mazzini over his disciples. And it was even greater with women. Indirectly, Forbes's mission suggests Mazzini's tireless and fertile energy, concerning the nature of which the Genoese himself had once remarked:

> My life is nothing but one thought and an unceasing activity for it; an activity, however, which, a few instances excepted, has consisted of one or two millions of letters, notes, instructions, forgotten, lost, burnt. And the correspondence of others with me, which could give a clue to many things, has been burnt too.[7]

Thanks to a letter of introduction which Carlyle had obtained for them from Mazzini, the Brownings, early in 1852, met George Sand in Paris. When they returned to London, they were anxious to make the acquaintance of the conspirator, who had been so useful to them. Perhaps Mrs. Carlyle's own words best describe what took place when she introduced Mazzini to the couple: "Oh, such a fuss the Brownings made over Mazzini this day." It may be added that Mrs. Carlyle did not take to Robert but liked his wife.[8] Very shortly, Mazzini called on the poets. This visit was recorded in Mrs. Browning's letter (July 31, 1852) to Miss Mitford:

> Mazzini came to see us the other day, with that pale spiritual face of his, and those intense eyes full of melancholy illusions. I was thinking, while he sate there, on what Italian turf he would lie at last with a bullet in his heart, or perhaps with a knife in his back, for to one of these ends it will surely come.[9]

It was certainly a dolorous prophecy, in which Mrs. Carlyle could have concurred—but with a tart kindness. He had visited her on one Sunday morning early in August and had made her hair stand on end with his projects. If within a month he was not shot or in an Austrian fortress, it would be, she thought, more by good luck than good guiding. But she took consolation in the promise that "God is kind to women, fools, and drunk people."[10]

What frightened both Mrs. Carlyle and Mrs. Browning was the political side of Mazzini's character. On the other hand, nothing is more engaging than one particular instance (1852) of Mazzini's social behaviour. It happened that Emily Shaen and he had a serious dispute about the highest motives in life. He championed morals, and she defended the doctrine of art for art's sake. At this, he became so eager that he forgot his dinner; and, when urged by William Shaen, her husband, to eat, replied: "No; I have something else to do; here is Mrs. Shaen travelling to perdition as fast as she can, and I must save her soul!"[11] Rather soon, Emily Shaen receded from her stand in favour of the sterile doctrine which had made Mazzini forbear eating: "Oh dear, I wish I had six thousand pounds! That is exactly what Mazzini wants and that would be enough." So she wrote to her sister early in November. Enough for what? To buy English muskets and other such equipment! However, her husband was not hopeful of Mazzini's success.[12]

Mazzini was also trying in other ways to raise money.* In June, the radical publisher, George Jacob Holyoake, printed as a broadside an appeal[13] from Mazzini for shilling subscriptions in aid of Italian freedom. Deliberately, the limit was set at a shilling in order that working-class sympathy could be readily and concretely manifested. Reprinting the pamphlet in Holyoake's magazines, *The Reasoner* and *The Leader*, effected the raising of £450 in *shilling* gifts[14] (9,000 shillings). It is Holyoake† who casts a vivid light on Mazzini's life in London: his pseudonym of Mr. Flower or Mr. Silva;[15] his secrecy (the Englishman admitted to having seen only one letter from him bearing

* The Mazzinian *Comitato Nazionale Italiano* issued bonds, in various denominations, to be sold in Italy after being smuggled in by English travellers. For this body, James Stansfeld was the London agent.

† Mazzini disliked Holyoake's secularism, a variety of atheism. Holyoake was a pioneer in co-operative activities and was associated with the Rochdale movement. He once asserted that he was the first to use the expression *jingo* for a chauvinist.

an address and date);[16] and his frugality, so marked as to have inspired these lines:

> A cheaper world no one can know,
> Where he who laughs grows fat;
> Man wants but little here below—
> Mazzini less than that.[17]

Incidentally, Landor, W. E. Forster, George Lewes, and W. J. Linton wrote for *The Leader*; W. H. Ashurst helped to finance it; and it offered Mazzini and others* a free place to publish propaganda. It had been founded in 1850 on the model of *Galignani's Messenger*.[18]

For *The Westminster Review*, the future George Eliot† was trying to induce Mazzini to write on "Freedom *v.* Despotism."[19] In March 1852, she even attended a *conversazione*, which caused her to observe ruefully that Mazzini's speeches were "better read than heard."[20] Nevertheless, she always esteemed him. The indefatigable Mazzini went on writing, from nine o'clock in the morning to ten at night, his countless letters in that minute script which graced the collections of the secret police of Italy and Central Europe, and yet made time to carry on his agitation in England. Yielding at last to George Eliot's requests, he published, in her *Westminster Review* (April 1852), an article of genuine eloquence. Primarily, *Europe: its Condition and Prospects* was written to oppose the demands of European despots that political refugees be expelled from London and sent to America. These rulers, he said, falsely maintained that a single country, France, popularized the revolutionary ideas of four or five agitators, who alone were responsible for every disturbance on the Continent; the truth was that subversive movements originated among the masses. Consequently Mazzini again urged the reorganization of Europe by

* In January 1850, Mazzini asked his close friend, George Sand, to write something for the magazine. See the *Edizione nazionale degli scritti di Giuseppe Mazzini*, XLII, 91.

† She was then known as Mary Ann Evans.

nationalities, in whose favour England ought, for her own advantage, actively to intervene. Furthermore, he insisted that the European problem involved social as well as national questions. But he attacked, in veiled though discernible terms, the famous *Communist Manifesto* of Marx and Engels (1848). Yet he did admit to a desire for a greater spread of income. According to Mazzini, Socialism would not do tactically, for it had alienated the petty *bourgeoisie* and had moved to reaction the *bourgeoisie*. As for Communism, he mistakenly asserted that,

> with the exception of Marx, who was desirous of being the chief of a school at any price, there is not a single man of any intelligence who has given in to the notion that [it] can be established by enactment.

In fine, for scientific analyses, Mazzini, in his characteristic manner, had substituted other considerations.

Political methods were never neglected by Mazzini and his partisans. His instrument, The Society of the Friends of Italy, adopted a petition (November 10th) to be presented to the House of Commons as a protest against the continued occupation of Rome by French and Austrian troops.[21] Nothing came of it. A pamphlet by Lord Beaumont denounced Napoleon III's interference with the Roman Republic of Mazzini and Garibaldi.[22] A certain Dr. Julius Casto published another eloquent pamphlet in behalf of the Mazzinian ideas as expressed by *Young Italy*.[23] After Professor Newman lectured before The Society of the Friends of Italy on *The Place and Duty of England in Europe*—in brief, her sin in failing to help Italy and Hungary during the 'Forty-eight, Mazzini himself addressed the meeting to rehearse the Italian cause:

> Do you know that in a country where nothing is done by government to diminish poverty, a government decree shuts out of the elementary schools all rag-wearing children? . . . Do you know that, whilst mutual tuition [the Bell-Lancaster

> monitorial method] is proscribed, *espionnage* is inculcated between the pupils? etc.[24]

The result of his multifarious efforts in England in behalf of the idea of Italy a Nation was that Mazzini won a grudging recognition from a most high source. None other than Carl Ludwig von Ficquelmont, peer of the Holy Roman Empire and Austrian Foreign Minister, asked Viscount Palmerston why England harboured people like Mazzini if the noble lord called her (June 17, 1851) the Temple of the Peace of the World.[25] Whom Prince Metternich had previously feared,* Count Ficquelmont also judged dangerous. By the trepidation of his enemies in high places, one must consider Mazzini no failure. Indeed, there is a tacit acknowledgment of the conspirator's European renown in a German traveller's description of customs delays experienced at Civitavecchia in the Papal States:

> There were, perhaps, two hundred packages, and they were all searched as if it had been thought that a Mazzini would be found hidden in every carpet-bag. Each stocking was viewed with distrust; every shirt regarded as suspicious; and, as for a bit of written or printed paper, it was treated at once as a probable criminal.[26]

For the proverbial devil, the forces of reaction had substituted a little man with burning eyes and an ardent faith.

On February 6, 1853, Mazzini emerged from the shadows of conspiracy to abet an insurrection in Milan so poorly planned and so ferociously terminated that thereafter in Italy his prestige waned. The Austrians hanged sixteen for their parts in the insurrection, the only definite result of

* Metternich once said: "I had soldiers to fight with the greatest, I succeeded in uniting emperors and kings, the Czar, the Sultan, and the Pope; but nobody on earth has given me more difficulties than a brigand of an Italian, thin, pale, shabby, yet as eloquent as the storm, as shining as an apostle, as cunning as a thief, as impudent as a comedian, as indefatigable as a lover—and his name was Joseph Mazzini!" (Translated from Adolf Saager's *Giuseppe Mazzini. Die Tragödie eines Idealisten*, Zürich, 1935, p. 236.)

which was an ever-growing feeling that *Young Italy* was not the agency to unite the Italians.[27] Both Sydney Dobell[28] and John Bright[29] were worried lest Mazzini had been apprehended, but *The Chronicler* damned him very simply by calling him a marplot.[30] Similarly, Carlyle pronounced the *émeute* insane and yet was glad the Austrians had not caught him, for Mrs. Carlyle had been quite anxious.[31] When Mazzini returned to England early in the summer, the Scot found him cheerful, gay, and amusing, and not in the least conscious of "what a poor figure he had cut in the eyes of all rational onlookers, or how much he had lost in men's esteem by such a pitiful 'Revolution' *à la Donnybrook.*" And Carlyle noted that the Italian was a happier and pleasanter, but by no means wiser man.[32] What would he have said had he known that Mazzini borrowed from Peter Taylor, in August, £400 to be used by Kossuth for some desperate project?[33]

In a larger sense, Mazzini's failure in Milan did not injure the attainment of Italian unity, for the blood of martyrs and the confiscation of property* (by way of Austrian reprisal) helped the cause. Every one in Italy learned how Antonio Sciesa, on being offered pardon at the gallows if he would disclose his confederates, boldly commanded the executioner to go on; and all revered Father Grioli who, similarly tempted, asked to be shown where to kneel and a moment later was a riddled corpse—the heroic victim of a firing squad.[34]

There were some in England who regretted Mazzini's escape. The conservative Earl of Malmesbury, third of that title, thought the conspirator's always eluding the foreign police very suspicious. If he credited Mazzini with great cleverness at disguises, he could hardly understand how one so terribly marked with smallpox and with such piercing black eyes could uniformly evade arrest.[35] The noble lord

* Bulwer-Lytton's *My Novel* (1853) refers to this politically inspired sequestration of estates.

would have been angrier if he had known that, not content with his Milanese adventure, Mazzini had ordered Felice Orsini to leave England (March 1853) in order to organize a new Italian outbreak.[36]

Unlike Malmesbury, Mrs. Browning was relieved by Mazzini's escape from Italy. For a time, she had been fearful lest he be taken and shot. To her, his was a noble character, though incompetent to effect his purposes. He always had her sympathies as a person if not her admiration as a wise man.[37] Mrs. Carlyle too was getting impatient with Mazzini's tactics of irritating the Austrians by the pin-pricks of sporadic outbursts. In September 1853, she wrote to Dr. John Carlyle that

> Mazzini is in hopes of kicking up another shine almost immediately. He told me when I last saw him, he might go off again within ten days. I am out of all patience at his reckless folly. If one did not hear every day of new arrests and executions, one might let him scheme and talk, hoping it might all end in smoke; but it ends in blood, and that is horrible. Thirteen hundred arrests made in the Papal States within a week![38]

Mazzini must have undergone agony whenever he thought of the long roll of those imprisoned or executed in the furtherance of his projects. Mrs. Carlyle had denounced "his reckless folly." Perhaps this was rather a ruthless anxiety for his country so strong that it had driven him demoniacally to feverish plotting and to exile far from his people and his kin.

The death of his mother* in 1852 and his subsequent feeling that now he had nothing but graves to visit in Italy,[39] did not in any wise lessen his political activity. Fifteen thousand, including Americans and Englishmen, had followed in Maria Mazzini's *cortège*; and for her the flags of

* Maria Mazzini's last words were: "My son, my son." She left him an income of £120 a year, making sure that he could not touch the principal. She had always feared for him a life of poverty.

foreign ships, American, Danish, Dutch, English, and Swedish, had flown at half-mast in the harbour of Genoa.[40]

There was one feeble literary echo, during 1853, of the heroic Roman Republic, Walter Savage Landor's imaginary conversation entitled *Garibaldi and Mazzini.*[41] The latter is represented as having wanted to bar the French from landing at Civitavecchia, but unfortunately Garibaldi* has trusted to their honour. Though one assault has been repelled, daily the besieged Romans grew weaker in numbers since the French have superior weapons. Mazzini repeats his lack of faith in French honour. Garibaldi casts doubt (uncharacteristic of the Italian but not of Landor!) on the legitimacy of the perfidious Napoleon's birth. The Roman triumvir is made to say that Napoleon has ambitions to be an emperor and counsels a determined resistance in the streets of Rome. If Landor's sketch is by no means very important, nevertheless it is an indication of the increasing English Italomania.

More worthily in verse did Landor celebrate the Roman Republic. The following poem (1853) is a message of hope to Mazzini:

In summer when the sun's mad horses pass
  Thro' more than half the heavens, we sink to rest
In Italy, nor tread the crackling grass,
  But wait until they plunge into the west:
And could not you, Mazzini! wait awhile?
  The grass is wither'd, but shall spring again;
The Gods, who frown on Italy, will smile
  As in old times, and men once more be men.[42]

Perhaps the most important appearance of Mazzini in literature during 1853 was in an English novel, Giovanni Ruffini's *Lorenzo Benoni.* It contains a notable portrait of

* In reality, it was Garibaldi who had urged preparations for repelling the French; and it was Mazzini who had reposed his trust in the idea that a French republic could not conceivably attack the Roman Republic.

Mazzini—faithful and luminous and tender. Lorenzo [Giovanni Ruffini] has just made friends with Fantasio [Mazzini]:

> He was certainly the most fascinating little fellow I ever knew.
>
> Fantasio was my elder by one year. He had a finely-shaped head, the forehead spacious and prominent, and eyes black as jet, at times darting lightning. His complexion was a pale olive, and his features, remarkably striking altogether, were set, so to speak, in a profusion of flowing black hair, which he wore rather long. The expression of his countenance, grave and almost severe, was softened by a smile of great sweetness, mingled with a certain shrewdness, betraying a rich comic vein. He spoke well and fluently, and when he warmed upon a subject, there was a fascinating power in his eyes, his gestures, his voice, his whole bearing, that was quite irresistible. His life was one of retirement and study; the amusements common with young men of his age had no attraction for him. His library, his cigar, his coffee; some occasional walks, rarely in the day time, and always in solitary places, more frequently in the evening and by moonlight—such were his only pleasures. His morals were irreproachable, his conversation was always chaste. If any of the young companions he gathered round him occasionally indulged in some wanton jest, or expression of double meaning, Fantasio—God bless him!—would put an immediate stop to it by some one word, which never failed of its effect. Such was the influence that the purity of his life, and his incontestable superiority, gave to him.
>
> Fantasio was well versed in history, and in the literature, not only of his own but of foreign countries. Shakespeare, Byron, Goethe, Schiller, were as familiar to him as Dante and Alfieri. Spare and thin in body, he had an indefatigably active mind; he wrote much and well both in prose and verse, and there was hardly a subject he had not attempted, historical essays, literary criticisms, tragedies, etc., etc. A passionate lover of liberty under every shape, there breathed in his fiery soul an indomitable spirit of revolt against tyranny and oppression of every sort. Kind, feeling, generous, never did he refuse advice or service, and his library, amply furnished, as well as his well-filled purse, were always at

> the command of his friends. Perhaps he was rather fond of displaying the brilliancy of his dialectic powers at the expense of good sense, by maintaining occasionally strange paradoxes. Perhaps there was a slight touch of affectation in his invariably black dress; and his horror of apparent shirt-collars was certainly somewhat exaggerated; but, take him all in all, he was a noble lad.[43]

Fantasio was a romanticist, who published articles in a Florentine periodical.[44] Ruffini narrated Mazzini's taking an LL.D. degree; his founding a literary journal, which the censor ended at the tenth number; his failure to obtain a passport to go to Tuscany; his dislike of the play-acting, or ritualistic mummery, of the Carbonari; his project of a new political organization; and his arrest by the police, who found on his desk a volume of Byron.

Though Mrs. Carlyle granted Mazzini a generous and self-devoted character, she thought it marred by a spirit not above unscrupulous intrigue. For example, she asserted that when Saunders, the American consul, invited Mazzini alone to a dinner[45] given on the eve of Washington's birthday, February 21, 1854, the Italian manœuvred the consul into inviting Kinkel, Herzen, Kossuth,* Ledru-Rollin,* Louis Blanc, Orsini, and Garibaldi also, for he wanted it to seem that these European revolutionists had American approval. The only result was that the American ambassador got into trouble.†

The Crimean War was not marked by the appearance of great literature in England. But Gerald Massey's "War-Waits" contains a long and fairly good poem on Mazzini, who, it is known, welcomed the war as a chance to strike at

* Mazzini did not care too much for Kossuth but thought him useful. In fact, the Italian used facetiously to call conspirators like the Hungarian aristocrat and Ledru-Rollin the "great men." See the *Edizione nazionale degli scritti di Giuseppe Mazzini*, LIII, 46, and LXIII, 38.

† Since Mazzini sympathized with those Americans who opposed Negro slavery, he was an especially unsafe person then for an American politician to know on terms of friendship or even of mere acquaintance.

Russian despotism. In "New Year's Eve in Exile," Massey thus[46] portrayed the Italian among his fellow patriots:

> Dilating as the prophet's soul of flame
> Lightened within him, all his aspect burned
> With an unearthly fire: he was caught up
> The Mount Transfiguration, with eyes fixed
> Far-off, intense as though he talked with God,
> He stood there gazing down the unseen time
> Like some hoar Hill that loftily o'erlooks
> The mists of night, and rises with bare brow
> To catch the unrisen Morn.

Thereupon, the poet had Mazzini deliver a long and stirring rhapsody, the message of which was that England ought to rouse herself against Russia.

Mazzini took advantage of the Crimean situation to abet another insurrection directed against Austrian dominance in Italy. Again Peter A. Taylor[47] lent him £400 for revolutionary purposes, but the rising in Parma (July 1854) was a total failure. Tragically, the conspirator then wrote to Emilie Ashurst Hawkes that he had dreamed

> that I was the leader of an immense procession of coffins. I went to take them from all sorts of churches and chapels; Mrs. Carlyle was there fulfilling some sort of function too.[48]

He was compelled to seek refuge in Switzerland, where the police hunted him closely and even arrested him on one occasion. With his usual adroitness, he convinced them that they were mistaken, but on September 5th he wrote an indignant and excellent letter* to the members of the Helvetic Federal Council on their refusal to give him the privilege of asylum.

By 1855 there had already developed in England a very important section of public opinion which looked to the unification of Italy as the task of the House of Savoy, not of Mazzini. It was Harriet Martineau[49] who best voiced this

* Reprinted by Holyoake's *Reasoner*, XVII, 229–32.

judgment. She had met Mazzini at the Carlyles' at the time when he was working for the education of the Italians in London and "before he entered openly on the career of insurrection by which he has since become the most notorious man in Europe." She expressed herself as entirely believing in all that his adorers said of the noble qualities of his heart and temper. She could quite understand how it was that some of those who knew him best believed him to be the best man in existence. There was, she declared, no doubt whatever of his devotedness, his magnanimity, his absolute disinterestedness. But the more, and not the less, for all this did his career seem to her almost the saddest spectacle of the times. He was merely an ideologist who would preach for ever in a mood of exaltation and a style of fustian, without being listened to by any but those who did not need his incitements. She thought that insurrection was too serious a matter to be stirred up by turgid appeals like his, vague and irreducible to the concrete. She reproved him for having aggravated the tyranny of Austria "with his perfect plots, his occult armies, his buried arms and ammunition, his own sufferings and dangers, and his holocaust of victims." She could now wish that his devotedness had met with acceptance and that the early sacrifice of his life had spared the hundreds of his followers who were wept by thousands more. In a word, his was a *vie manquée*. For analogous reasons, Garibaldi no longer saw eye to eye with Mazzini on politics. A contemporary historian, Richard Heber Wrightson,[50] called Mazzini the sectarian conspirator of absurd and pernicious combinations, and affirmed that his *émeutes* were criminal and cold-blooded, serving to compromise as many victims as possible, and, by multiplying suffering, to aggravate discontent. Moreover, Wrightson blamed *Young Italy* for the frustration of the 'Forty-eight, since it had caused disunion; and he pronounced Mazzini's doctrines misty and speculative. To this agreement of condemnation Disraeli's weekly organ, *The Press*, assented; on December 1, 1855, it described

Mazzini's tactics as mere "ensanguined practices."[51] But the faithful Landor's incoherent letter to *The Atlas*, March 31, 1855, pictured Mazzini as both valiant and wise, and recalled the martyred brothers Bandiera—theirs was "one sudden flash of fire, and everlasting glory."

Robert Browning was another who then found occasion to refer, even if indirectly, to Mazzini. In his poem, "Old Pictures in Florence," 1855, he wonders whether he shall be alive to see a more successful Tuscan revolution than the one his wife beheld from Casa Guidi, and whether the banner with "God and the People" as its motto will anew be unfurled. "God and the People" was a Mazzinian slogan.

In Mazzini the revolutionary fervour could grow ardent quickly enough, as when he heard that Mrs. Milner-Gibson, a benefactress of his school, had inherited £12,000 a year. The truth turned out to be that she had been disinherited, and so Europe was fortunately spared a sequence of bloody and futile risings.[52] Again, Mazzini did attend the great mass meeting (February 27, 1855) arranged by leading refugees (Stanislas Worcell,* the Polish patriot, Ledru-Rollin, etc.) in memory of the 'Forty-eight. Several radical poets—Gerald Massey, Thomas Cooper, and Ernest Jones—were present, but Karl Marx was unable to come.[53]

To an astonishing degree by now, Mazzini had intimately associated himself with English life and thought; and nothing demonstrates this better than a long letter to Francesco Crispi, who was eager to know the British scene. Mazzini told[54] Crispi (April 25, 1855) to read *The Westminster Review*, *The North British Review*, and *The Athenaeum* if he wished to find out what was vital in contemporary Anglo-Saxon thinking. He also advised Crispi to study Carlyle's works, for the latter, as the antagonist of "democracy and of aristocracy at the same time," was a significant figure, the head of an important school adoring both the individual (or the hero)

* His death in 1857, when with his last words he told Mazzini not to forget the Poles, deeply affected the Italian.

and fact, force, and success. Crispi was also to acquaint himself with the work of John Stuart Mill, Tennyson* (in whom Mazzini saw distinction combined with enervation), and Mr. and Mrs. Browning. "All the other poets are mediocre." For religious ideas, Crispi was to ascertain the opinions of Kingsley and Professor Francis Newman; in art, he was to consider Edwin Landseer, Ruskin, and the Pre-Raphaelites like Dante Gabriel Rossetti. In a word, Mazzini's epistle had sounded important currents of English literary, religious, artistic, and philosophic life. Incidentally, he now no longer saw the Carlyles with any regularity, for even Mrs. Carlyle considered him inflexibly intolerant. In a subsequent letter[55] to Crispi (May 25, 1855), he summarized Carlyle's ideas in greater detail: the Scot saw in Chartism a symptom of the ills of the times and would treat them by a hero-dictator who would overthrow lies and hypocrisies and worship truth. Carlyle, said Mazzini, asked for his hero a blind obedience, since he hated democracy and scorned the common people. Mazzini also recommended to Crispi a reading of Mrs. Browning's *Casa Guidi Windows*.

Practically no year now passed without Mazzini's being the centre of a controversy, and 1855 was not an exception. This time a Mr. David Urquhart (of Turkish bath fame) went around asserting that the Italian was a spy in the service of Russia.† Of course, the accusation was denied by Mazzini, in an excellent letter which appeared (September) in the Sheffield *Free Press*. However, the London *Times* urged the English government to put into effect the stringent provisions of the Alien Bill; and consequently, Mazzini, late

* Mazzini disliked Tennyson's "Maud" on the ground that it was "too Tennysonian."

† Since Mazzini used London as a base for plotting against Austria, he jeopardized diplomatic relations between England and the Hapsburgs. Furthermore, the Crimean War, then in progress, saw Austria neutral but under a debt of gratitude to Russia for having crushed the Hungarians in the 'Forty-eight. It follows that Urquhart thought that Mazzini's actions might put Austria on the side of Russia.

in October, planned meetings at London and Newcastle (the seat of his friend Joseph Cowen's industrial activities) to discourage the Cabinet from alien-baiting. As a matter of record, a pamphlet by Mazzini, *Two Letters to the People of England on the War* (1855), was definitely anti-Russian.

The next year witnessed another unedifying controversy—between Daniel Manin, the heroic defender of Venice in 1849, and Mazzini. It seemed that Manin had written a letter to a foreign newspaper in which he asserted that the Italian republican party would never succeed if it did not renounce the "theory of the dagger." In other words, that section of Italian political belief headed by Mazzini was now being called the faction of assassins. *The Times* of London reprinted Manin's statement, and it was this which provoked Mazzini's hot denial (in his *Letters to D. Manin . . .*) that he countenanced assassination. Moreover, he took the occasion offered by the notoriety of the discussion to affirm again his distrust of monarchs and his faith in the people of Italy. It is true that Manin had not mentioned Mazzini by name, but everybody knew that the Venetian, one of the founders of the new Italian National Society (with a unitarian but *royalist* programme), had meant Mazzini. In the bickering that ensued Landor joined, contributing a letter to *The Examiner*, July 26, 1856, in which he hinted at tyrannicide and said that to the destroyer of a despot "the cup and the symbolic bunch of myrtle would have been presented" even in preference to Manin, Garibaldi, or Mazzini. What is more amazing and monetarily more substantial, he wrote[56] to one of Mazzini's friends and unhopefully promised £95 for the *family* "of the first patriot, who asserts the dignity and fulfils the duty of tyrannicide." Also to the defence of Mazzini came the interesting traveller and novelist, Bayle St. John (1822–1859), who called Mazzini the great Italian of the century[57] and denounced Manin as a libeller.[58]

Very clearly, Mazzini was becoming more and more the subject of differing opinions. For example, Lord Clarendon wrote to E. d'Azeglio (June 21, 1856) that the Italians in England did not like Mazzini,[59] but it should be remembered that this Tory peer would be inclined to know only Italians of a similar stamp. Likewise, an anonymous historian[60] of Italian affairs, evidently an exile and patriot, said of Mazzini that he was chimerically visionary. The most virulent attack on Mazzini, however, appeared in a poor novel (1856) by J. R. Digby Beste. *Modern Society in Rome*, more of a sketch of political events than of human beings in dramatic propinquity, drearily rehearsed the happenings of the 'Forty-eight. It ascribed their failure to Giuseppe Mazzini—a deviser of mad and wicked schemes,[61] a charlatan and weak-minded dreamer,[62] but more the high priest than the politician. In his conduct of the Roman Republic, Mazzini is represented as duping the Roman National Assembly with grandiloquent phrases disguising a proud and selfish spirit and the soul of a mere mountebank. Furthermore, Beste denominated Mazzini a mystic deist talking a "classic rodomontade" and blinded by egotism, pride, and fanatical republicanism. There is violent prejudice even in the physical description of the Roman triumvir:

> his fine forehead rose high and bare; and his bushy eyebrows, bent over his full sleepy eyes, wore not yet the ominous expression of one who was to approve partial risings or tumultuary assassination.

Beste's aversion represents only one aspect of anti-Mazzinianism. On the Continent, some hated Great Britain for its sheltering of Mazzini, Kossuth, and others; for example, when Felice Orsini was in jail, his keeper, a Signor Casati, expressed the fiercest dislike of England for its having become the refuge of radicals.[63]

In spite of unfriendly opinions, Mazzini still possessed a magical ability to gain new adherents to the Italian cause as he interpreted it. It was in 1856 that one of the most remarkable of the women of the last century made Mazzini's acquaintance and was so profoundly affected that she went to Genoa to help him organize the unfortunate Pisacane's expedition against the Kingdom of Naples. Jessie Meriton White* has left us some of the most vivid reminiscences of Mazzini: his room with birds flying around, books and papers every where, and

> there, writing on his knee on the smallest fragment of the thinnest imaginable paper, sat Mazzini. He rose at once: his hand-grasp and luminous eyes fascinated and encouraged you, yet filled you with momentary awe.[64]

Then was won not the least of the Mazzinian disciples in personality and sheer intellect. If he has gained a valuable associate, he retained his old friends: The Society of the Friends of Italy which had suspended with the Crimean War began its activities anew.[65]

The Westminster Review was exceedingly sympathetic to the Italian cause. At the beginning, it championed Mazzini's idea of a *republican* united Italy, but later it changed its mind. The January 1857 issue had an article on the "State of Parties in Italy since 1848" which favoured English intervention in behalf of the Italians and called the Austrian rule an ascendancy of brute force countenanced by the evil of the pope's infallible spiritual authority. It concluded that the Mazzinian or National Party was the sole hope of Italy. If this was a friendly voice, not such was Felice Orsini's, who now described Mazzini as a "man of theories, and only fit to dictate Protocols and Proclamations from his Cabinet and to act the diplomatist, as time has since proved."[66]

Matters were now coming to a head, and Mazzini got ready to resume the *rôle* of the man of action. So sanguine was he of a favourable outcome that he discussed[67] with Jessie White his programme† for Italy: a tax on surplus

* Mazzini used to call her *Cara Bianca* and send her cigars.

† Though Mazzini regularly attacked socialism and its leaders like Louis Blanc (Mrs. Carlyle once told Malwida von Meysenbug that on this score many people thought him intolerant), he considered that he had the socialist idea in a practical way. See Malwida von Meysenbug, *Gesammelte Werke*, II, 92–93.

income; public works of all kinds; a gigantic national fund (derived from the taking over of the property of the Church, the Austrians, and the native rulers) to finance a credit establishment for *voluntary* industrial and agricultural societies of working men, at an interest rate of one half of one per cent. To this English girl he also communicated[68] his scheme for altering the map of Europe: Spain and Portugal were to be united; likewise, the Scandinavian countries; similarly, the British Isles would be one unit; and Italy another. In addition, he prophesied a Confederation of the Alps composed of Switzerland, Savoy, and the German Tyrol; a Magna Graecia in the Balkans; the disappearance of Austria to be replaced by a Danubian Confederation (Hungarians, Rumanians, Czechs, etc.); a greater Germany to include Holland and the Flemish part of Belgium; a greater France with the absorption of the Belgian Walloons; and finally, Russia with only Russians, and Poland with only Poles.

But for the time being he needed funds* to buy muskets, and so Miss White, a very capable and personable speaker,† and Aurelio Saffi went, under the sponsorship of a London philo-Italian committee, on a lecture tour to raise money in Scotland, where sentiment was warmly Mazzinian. Miss White also tried to influence British opinion by her pro-Italian articles in the London *Daily News*. Soon, in his native Genoa, Mazzini flashed the signal for revolt; but his plan to seize the city as a base for Carlo Pisacane's descent on

* In January 1857, Mazzini was eager to borrow £1,000 at 7 per cent interest.

† In 1858, she delivered a second series of lectures at Newcastle (where Joseph Cowen introduced her to the audience), at Manchester, at Rochdale, etc. In September, Mazzini asked her to go to America for the purpose of explaining the Italian cause from his point of view. Her talks in the United States (1858–59) were an artistic success, for she was glowingly praised by the New York *Herald*, and Horace Greeley once appeared on the platform with her, but a financial failure. It may be of some interest to add that the Brownings and she had a dispute about her American speaking tour.

the Kingdom of the Two Sicilies miscarried, and Pisacane* himself was slain in Sicily. Miss White was arrested and kept in a Piedmontese jail,[69] where her flaming red hair and her long cigars, in contrast with her fine, intellectual cast of features, must have mildly amazed† her keepers. In William Michael Rossetti's presence,Mrs. Browning had pleaded with her not to go to the Continent on her mission.[70] Yet she had gone anyway, for the Mazzinian fervour was always more eloquent than a sober mind commending caution. Indeed, to Jessie White, Mazzini was the Christ of his century[71]— and Mrs. Browning only a good friend.

After the Genoese fiasco, Mazzini made good a curiously hilarious and dangerous escape from an implacable and thwarted government, which sentenced him to death in his absence and in its chagrin. His saviour from detection was Ernesto Pareto,[72] who had married an Englishwoman devoted to the Italian cause. When the police came, Signora Pareto hid Mazzini's tiny missives in her bodice and him in a mattress, where he almost suffocated. The officers came back again and did not find him; presently, he shaved off his beard and left the house. Dall'Ongaro, a popular poet, derided[73] the attempts to apprehend the elusive Mazzini:

> "Where is Mazzini?" hear them cry! We answer with disdain
> "Some say he is in Germany, or in England once again,
> Some swear he's in Geneva, some are certain he's in Spain.
> Some place him on an altar, some wish him underground,
> But none amongst his hunters know where he can be found.
> Oh stupid men who seek him, once more look wildly round!
> There is only one Mazzini, and can he not be found?"

* Pisacane had been in London in 1850 under the passport name of Stansfeld. See the *Edizione nazionale degli scritti di Giuseppe Mazzini*, XLIV, 30.

† In November 1857, the authorities tried to have her declared insane and freed as such. Perhaps the only mental aberration that could be imputed to her was her sudden falling in love with Alberto Mario, another political prisoner.

Where is Mazzini? Ask it of the pine
That guards the slope of Alp and Apennine.
In every spot where trembling tyrants fear
The dawn of freedom, seek Mazzini there!
And where Italia's sons' supreme desire
To die that she may live flames ever higher,
Go, find him there—he lit, he guards, that fire.

Its flames had only been temporarily dimmed, for Pisacane's martyrdom was after all a prophecy[74] of the expedition of Garibaldi's amazing Thousand, who were very soon to set out from Genoa and win the south of Italy.

About this time the young Swinburne[75] was following with ardent sympathy the propaganda of The Society of the Friends of Italy, at the head of whose executive council stood the inspiring name of Walter Savage Landor. The Italian press was attacking Austrian rule in Lombardy as tyranny; and so, on March 16, 1857, the Austrian ambassador was withdrawn from Turin. Thereupon Mazzini felt that the hour was at hand to leave London for Italy, and at this stage Swinburne composed his "Ode to Mazzini"—that is, just before the insurrections at Genoa, June 1857, and Leghorn; and Pisacane's misadventure. Hence, the poem was written between March and June 1857; but because certain following events dated its wild and vague aspirations, he did not publish it. And since it was an irregular Pindaric ode—that is, a false poetic form—, for that reason also, the maturing Swinburne was led to abandon it. In the Ode we are told that the world awaits Mazzini, for too long has murder ruled in Italy, and the life of freedom bled away. The slain lie forgotten and bleach in sun and rain while priests and kings defile the Italian skies. The stench of venomous injustice pollutes the air, and above hovers the double-headed carrion eagle of Austria. A slow curse stains all; from the Italians there leaps a sullen flame into the sunless air. Smitten by "brute-handed Austria," Italy is downtrodden; but God hears her groans antiphonally mingling with the Austrian lies and echoing to the listening sky. In Italy's final triumph over wrong, Mazzini's memory shall be the first kept since he is dear to liberty

> In peril, banishment, and blame,
> And all the loud blind world calls shame,

and because at his name priests look pale. Then Swinburne addresses him:

> O brother, crownèd among men, O chief
> In glory as in grief!
> O throned by sorrow over time and fate
> And the blind strength of hate!

Wildly, incoherently, rhapsodically, the poem draws to a close.

John Nicol,* Swinburne's closest friend at Oxford, had a marked influence on the panegyric for Mazzini. Indeed, Nichol had once contributed an essay on the conspirator to the *Undergraduate Papers* and was reputed to nourish a violent dislike for Napoleon III[76] matched only by Swinburne's own sentiments regarding the Emperor. Swinburne himself had not yet made Mazzini's acquaintance, and therefore dared call him "O brother, crownèd among men. . . . " Thereafter, he was solely and reverently the *Chief* or the *Master*.[77] About 1857, Lord Sheffield remembered[78] seeing in Swinburne's Oxford chambers a portrait of Mazzini in the place of honour in the sitting-room. Before this icon, the poet would declaim verses "with gestures of adoring supplication." Were the lines he intoned the Shelleyan "Ode to Mazzini"—found incomplete in his papers and printed in 1909?

* Years later, Nichol wrote the *English Men of Letters* critical biography of Carlyle, in which he censured his subject for having acted patronizingly towards Mazzini, "the inspired Italian, pure patriot and Stoic moralist." In 1860, two and thirty years earlier, Nichol had said of Mazzini:

> "Right or wrong in his views, he is one of the purest, most upright, and most fascinating men I have ever met. His fault is that he is more of a poet than a statesmen. . . ."

See W. A. Wright, *Memoir of John Nichol* . . ., Glasgow, 1896, p. 168.

For the Newdigate Prize (March 1857), Swinburne wrote "The Temple of Janus,"[79] notable on account of a portrait of Mazzini in verse. With a vaguely pantheistic invocation the poem opens; and then follows an intoning of a eulogy of Liberty, identified with the Roman Republic. Before Swinburne's eyes rises the vision of Rome in its heyday when the Temple of Janus was outstanding. All around are grouped its poets and great men. A spirit appears by the side of our poet and summons the Hours; and at Janus's command, the last of these speaks and describes the greatness of Rome from Tarquin's flight until the Decii and the two Brutuses. This Hour neglects the emperors and the barbarian invaders; but exalts Rienzi. Kings, emperors, priests, from Caesar to Romulus the Little, from the Visconti to the Ezzelini to Ferdinand II, "crowned snake of Naples"—all are damnable. After this, appears a splendid form, prophecy of "the visioned Rome that nobler hours shall bring."

Now Janus turns to the future—the new Rome with liberty alone crowned. And very soon we know again that freedom and the Roman Republic are one and the same thing. Such is Swinburne's love of Italy. The great years of ancient Rome are those of the republic, and in spite of Cannae and Trasimene and Carthage, she triumphed. Swinburne exalts the second Brutus, for he was a tyrannicide. Next comes the present in Italy—the unspeakable *Bomba*,* nothing but a monarch-criminal. And then he sees Mazzini, whom he does not name:

> I turned; beside me One stood silent there,
> Whose face, but for the sad eyes' onward strain
> And the grey look of immemorial pain,
> Were godlike; for no human hopes or fears
> Trouble the calm it keeps thro' sunless years;

* Ferdinand II of Naples, called *Bomba* for having Messina (1848) and Palermo (1849) bombarded hour after hour even when there was no more resistance. He ceased firing on account of the protests of foreign naval officers.

His hair is whiter than wind-sifted snow,
And calm as death the regal brows below;
Strange memories sadden o'er his dim deep eyes;
On his closed lips a changeless sorrow lies,
As one scarce risen above the clouds of care
Above the starless gloom those spirits wear
Who face to face have known a hideous thing
And felt a snake-like thought round hope and memory
cling.

At his vision's call (Mazzini's), there appears as with the splendour of sunrise the new Italy; "The visioned Rome that nobler hours shall bring." And the man Mazzini beholds her and is hushed and fair with pride.

Perhaps Swinburne was not proud, for "The Temple of Janus" failed to win the Newdigate award. But then it lacked sincerity of inspiration and was too reminiscent of Dryden, Shelley, and Keats both in vocabulary and in style. Even worse, it made Italian independence an abstract thing.

In a minor way, Mazzini made another, if indirect, appearance in literature during this same year of 1857. A Mrs. Hamilton wrote a jejune novel called *The Exiles of Italy*—the sort of dreadful thing that is shackled by footnotes and a discouraging adherence to other factual apparatus. The hero is a member of The Society of the Friends of Italy whose propaganda our novelist has relished. Calmly considered by one trying to forget its dullness, it is a straightforward and pathetic presentment of Mazzinian propaganda in the guise of fiction.

Returned to London by August, Mazzini took up his quarters in the vicinity of Portman Square, where he managed to live on £80 a year, endured neuralgia and lumbago, and was known[80] to the uninformed merely as Mr. Flower. As usual, he was devoting himself to a pamphlet, which was published by Holyoake under the title of *The Late Genoese Insurrection Defended.** This *apologia* for the fiasco of the preceding year denied that Mazzini had destroyed the

* It was addressed to Joseph Cowen of Newcastle.

peaceful liberty of Piedmont. Rather had the rising been an attempt to achieve the unity of Italy to which Piedmont, satisfied with its own prosperity and freedom, was not devoted. By way of a final word, Mazzini repeated that the hope of Italy lay in the aspirations of the Italian republicans. It was soon apparent that he was in no wise deterred by his critics. If Pisacane had died in vain, that did not prevent his abetting Bentivegna's similar venture, which also ended in failure.[81] Would such always be the case? At any rate, Mazzini now urged[82] on Francesco Crispi the necessity for propaganda of all kinds. His, then, was a voice that would never cease clamouring in the wilderness as long as the Italians were straying. Indeed, within a few months after the untoward Genoese rising, he had cherished a dream of getting £6,000 somewhere for another go at the Austrians.

Consequently, he resolved on a new publication to be printed in Italian and to be circulated clandestinely from London. When this paper, *Pensiero ed Azione* ("Thought and Action"), appeared, it rapidly attained an immense, if surreptitious, reading public, which it amazed by a correct prediction in 1858 of the terms of the Treaty of Villafranca.[83]

Early in that year, the *affaire Orsini* glanced at Mazzini, since the French, through Lord Palmerston, tried to induce the English government to enact a law for the extradition of political refugees. It was against this proposal that Mazzini wrote a fiery pamphlet, *To Louis Napoleon.** As has already been seen, the failure of the Conspiracy Bill put the complaisant ministry out of office; thus had Mazzini twice been connected in some fashion with a Cabinet crisis. He himself was enduring at this time a species of domestic crisis. It seemed that Saffi and his wife were staying with Mazzini; and Saffi could not write a letter or translate an article without interrupting him and then reading it to him.

* Louis Napoleon, as an exile in England, had himself plotted against the French king. Now, as Napoleon III, he wished the English to break their tradition of asylum.

Besides, the couple had an immense dog with them: "... the dog overturns my coals and sweeps away my papers with his tail."[84] Yet Mazzini was very fond of his guests, and in September was extremely happy when they were blessed with a son.

Indirectly, Mazzini was the cause of another tempest in an international teapot. When Swinburne went during the Easter Vacation to Paris, having given his word not to undermine the authority of Napoleon III, a very ludicrous incident took place. Admiral and Lady Jane Swinburne, riding with their Algernon in an open carriage, chanced to meet Napoleon ("the Accursèd") in the Champs-Elysées. His parents bowed, the Emperor politely raised his hat, but Swinburne kept his very determinedly on.

On his return to Balliol in the same year, his incantations before Mazzini's portrait and a recently purchased one of the executed Orsini became more ridiculous than ever. In these rites of submissive adoration, he was humorously supported by T. H. Green; but the other students thought them silly and blasphemous.

Mazzini still took an interest in Carlyle—at least sufficiently to write[85] to Emilie Ashurst Hawkes (November 3, 1858) that the latest work of the talkative Champion of Silence, his painful history of Frederick the Great, was

> unredeemably bad and immoral. It is *feudalism*: worship of force, intellectual or brutal. Friedrich Wilhelm, the father [of Frederick the Great], made into a hero, "c'est trop fort." Besides . . . the *people* does not exist for [Carlyle]; kings, margraffs and burgraffs are all Humanity to him: any corporal, drilling man, is a remarkable phenomenon, etc.

But of Byron, his idol, Mazzini had recently said[86] that "Don Juan" was "a crusade against Cant in all things, fought by Irony. . . ."

In the next year, Mazzini was himself vigorously denounced by Mrs. A. L. V. Gretton, an historian[87] of Italian affairs, who, when she turned her notice to *Young Italy*, was constrained to call its actions a succession of desperate and foolhardy expeditions, ill-conceived and rashly executed, invariably leading to the axe, the bullet, or the dungeon, and yet fruitless in teaching a lesson of wisdom to their originator, or in shaking the blind confidence of his followers. Whenever he failed, he dismissed the fact by describing it as the sowing of the seeds of future successes; and at his bidding, undaunted by the fate of their predecessors, ardent and dedicated men were never lacking to go forth and offer themselves as victims to the oppression they were powerless to subvert. Meanwhile, Mazzini, she said, ran no personal risk—a charge which another woman historian repeated[88] during this same year of 1859 in an account of Italian affairs written for children. Even *The Westminster Review*, which hitherto had supported Mazzini, now in April came out with a long article ("The Italian Question") that declared him, genius of conspiracy as he admittedly was, nothing but an infallible pontiff of inflexible recklessness, and cited the abortive rising in Genoa. Liberal English opinion had switched bets; and Cavour, not Mazzini, was the favourite to unite Italy.

Napoleon III had been won by the diplomacy of Cavour and the detonation of Orsini's bomb to the resolution of "doing something for Italy." The outcome of this sentiment was the war of 1859, which led Mrs. Browning to call[89] the Emperor "the very angel of the resurrection." But when Jessie Meriton White, now the wife of Alberto Mario, belittled Napoleon, Mrs. Browning had to find an explanation. Very simply, Mme Mario was too much influenced "by that man of a narrow head and unscrupulous conscience, Mazzini." After the Treaty of Villafranca, our Italomaniac poet was in terror lest the Mazzinians should come to Italy and spoil everything.[90] But if she implicitly reposed her confidence in the French sovereign, not so Swinburne. At the Oxford Union early in 1859, Lord Sheffield heard[91] him launch an excited but ineffective tirade of great length against Napoleon and in favour of Mazzini. Even poets were disagreeing about the exile. Nevertheless, when H. F. Chorley, the music critic of *The Athenaeum*, an influential weekly magazine, published a novel, *Roccabella*, unfriendly to the Italians, both Mrs. Browning and Dickens chided him. One notes with interest that the leading character, Roccabella, speaks in Italianate idioms very much like those Mrs. Carlyle used to repeat with amusement in her letters. For example, Chorley has his hero say: "She is a mad, my dear, we laugh at her."[92] Mazzini also used to say *a mad*. Had Chorley known him? Chorley had no high opinion of revolutionary conspirators:

> What a revelation of want of faith and high motive—of the martyr spirit snatched up as a theatrical inspiration, and a masquerade dress—of reform, more stupid in its proceedings than repression—of advanced intelligence, falling back on every exploded desire of ancient barbarism—of disunion, impatience, mistrust![93]

Meantime, Mazzini was corresponding with Capell Lofft, the old Chartist poet, and was publishing *Pensiero ed Azione*, being now financially and otherwise aided in this venture by Susanna and Catherine Winkworth,[94] two interesting Victorian ladies of the Stansfeld-Shaen-Ashurst circle of Muswell Hill and London.

In November 1860 a magazine writer[95] paid tribute to Mazzini's courage, firmness, and tact, called him a gentleman without ostentation, and affably described his person. Opposed to Mazzini were spies and *agents provocateurs* like the extraordinary villain of Wilkie Collins's *The Woman in White* (1860), Count Fosco, whose task it was to keep a watch in England over the Italian expatriates. A man like Fosco led a life which was "one long assertion of the rights of the aristocracy, and the sacred principles of Order." After 1860, secret agents on the order of the sinister Fosco would have little need to watch Mazzini's activities, for the unification of Italy had been largely accomplished.

CHAPTER VII

Mazzini's Last Years

EIGHTEEN Fifty-nine and Eighteen Sixty were the epochal years of the Italian *Risorgimento*. The armies of Piedmont and of France humiliated Austria, the central Italian provinces voted for annexation to the new Kingdom of Italy, and Garibaldi led his Thousand in their red shirts on to Sicily.

These Italian crises having placed Mazzini somewhat in the British limelight, the usual charge of abetting assassination appeared in a reverend gentleman's account[1] (1860) of the late Italian war against Austria. Charles Dickens also wrote most bitterly in condemnation of

> these unavailing risings; my blood runs hotter . . . at the thought of the leaders safe, and the instruments perishing by hundreds; yet what is to be done? Their wrongs are so great that they *will* rise from time to time somehow. . . . Unavailing struggles against a dominant tyranny precede all successful turnings against it.[2]

Simultaneously in 1860, two women novelists published dull and stodgy works of fiction—in tone friendly to Italy but hostile to Mazzini. One of them, a certain Kate Crichton, who had witnessed the Mazzinian rising of February 6, 1853, in Milan, called that abortive insurrection a series of stupidly fanatical assassinations.[3] A character in her novel, *Before the Dawn*, exhibits a picture in the National Gallery, London. Symbolically, Italy is shown as striving to touch the tree of liberty just above her reach. There are a few broken steps before her, but she hesitates to attempt them, for they are, in many places, covered with blood. Close at hand are some wildly ferocious spirits (Mazzinians) who urge her to mount them. On the other side, a cherub is drawing her away and is pointing to a path longer, yet more secure and free from stains. So Miss Crichton represented the two causes—the republican and the monarchical. Likewise hostile to Mazzini was Margaret Roberts in her poor novel, *Mademoiselle Mori*. In a third novel, *Angelo Sanmartino: a Tale of Lombardy in 1859*, anonymous and fairly good, there is mention of an *unsuccessful* Mazzinian *émeute*. It can be rather assuredly said that by 1860 most of the English were for Italy but not for Mazzini's programme in behalf of his fatherland.

Certainly, Harriet Martineau was merely expressing[4] the feelings of the more influential English classes when she now called Mazzini an enemy of his country. True, he had kept alive his countrymen's hopes but now he was "the most dangerous obstruction in the path of free Italy." She maintained that it would have been indeed better for his reputation if he had not survived the siege of Rome in 1849.

In spite of frequent dejection, due in part to opinions like the foregoing, Mazzini continued his agitation by writing a fiery pamphlet, which was essentially a summons to the Italians to expel the Austrians from Venetia. *The Italian Question and the Republicans*, 1861, attacked the policy of Count Cavour as Sardinian, not Italian; pleaded for European non-intervention in Italy; termed Cavour merely a man of tactics, not principles; denounced the French alliance; and called Napoleon III a "foreign Brennus" using Cavour as a servile tool. If she read this, Miss Martineau must have had rather sombre thoughts about Mazzini. At any rate, having probably acquainted herself with his latest effusion, Mrs. Browning actually uttered[5] what others also felt: "Mazzini deserves what I should be sorry to inflict. He is a man without conscience." It is not surprising that when Cavour died in 1861, Mazzini drew some unfavourable comparisons[6] in *The Times* and in *The Morning Chronicle* of London.

A contemporary biographer of Cavour, Sir Edward Dicey,[7] also disparaged Mazzini and his faction; and so did the Swedish writer, Fredrika Bremer, whose travels[8] were translated in 1861. More and more, people were saying that Mazzini by his attempts was discrediting the Italian hope of freedom. Indeed, Isabella Blagden, Mrs. Browning's friend and confidante,* wrote a novel, *Agnes Tremorne* (1861), which among other things showed by a specific example that *Young Italy* did not hesitate to avenge itself by assassination.

If Miss Blagden's novel was worthless, what should be said of Antonio Bresciani's *The Jew of Verona: an Historical Tale of the Italian Revolutions of 1846–9*? The author had published in 1854 an American edition, which was now reprinted in England. Bresciani's intention was "to expose the wicked tendency and the treacherous designs of the secret societies" like that of *Young Italy*, led by Mazzini. Such societies were calculated to force back civilization into a state of barbarism, and were composed of the dregs of Italy—ruffians, desperadoes, and murderers who worshipped Satan by an adoration similar to that paid to a supreme deity; who gave the devil homage in the form of incense, tremendous vows, obscene sacrifices, and execrable offerings; who established altars round which twelve infamous females danced every night and as priestesses celebrated filthy rites; who cut out the hearts of Roman Catholics. And their Old Man of the Mountain, their King of Assassins, was Joseph Mazzini—a monster of crime, who, however, even Bresciani conceded, had committed no murders himself. Yet he rendered his followers inhuman and imparted to them a thirst for blood by his perfidious and seductive words like liberty, patriotism, and Italian independence. Nay, they were transformed by him into fiends capable of blowing up St. Peter's and the Vatican and committed to even greater blasphemies. The

* Both Miss Blagden and Mrs. Browning believed in spiritism as manifested in the form of mesmerism, which they called animal magnetism.

answer to this type of vilification is Mazzini's own statement of his creed (which he wrote, early in 1861, to a member of Parliament who had asked only for his autograph):

> God, sole Ruler in Heaven, the People sole interpreter of his law on Earth, Genius and Virtue sole guides, the progress of all by means of the work of all—this is the Future. On this path Italy will do her duty.[9]

An Englishman who had joined Garibaldi's Redshirts and had participated in the exploits of the Thousand, one W. B. Brooke, recorded his experiences in the form of a novel. Like most stories concerned with contemporary Italian events, it was remarkably bad. Yet it was somehow different from others in that it was kind to Mazzini and said he had idealism and courage.[10] But, in 1861, the man who most generously considered Italy newly risen from the ashes was Frederic Harrison. He allotted credit for the resurrection to all three, Cavour, Garibaldi, and Mazzini—the last being that "thinker, poet, preacher, or agitator" to whom was "due in this generation the strength of that principle which is the very life of Italy at this day," that is, the principle of national unity.[11] Yet even Harrison reproached Mazzini for a long series of disastrous insurrections.

By 1862 London was the place of refuge for most of the ardent radicals of Europe, who were very naturally objects of curiosity. People knew where* these expatriates could be found—to be sure, always furiously discussing some point of revolutionary tactics or subversive gossip over their black coffee. The satiric poet, John Waters, in a volume entitled *The Refugees, and Other Poems*—trifling things in Hudibrastic lines, Spenserian stanzas, and heroic couplets—told how in the evening he had had an extra glass of wine at the "Cock

* In 1853, George Jacob Holyoake established in Fleet Street "The British Secular Institute of Communism [in the Owenite sense] and Propagandism," popularly called the "Political Exchange," where exiles like Orsini, Herzen, Bakunin, Ledru-Rollin, Louis Blanc, etc. might be seen. Naturally, there were always spies on the alert.

and Bull," a tavern where these exiles revived the *café* life of the Continent. He represented himself as listening to their rant:

> Here are encounter'd men of sense,
> Some Monarchs in the future tense;
> Some have been Kings, great heroes all,
> But every one has had a fall,
> And now is strictly radical.

And thus he drew Mazzini:

> Another, of a smaller size,
> Propounds, in manner wondrous wise,
> The doctrine, savouring of divinity,
> Contain'd in the republic's trinity;

and put into his mouth these words:

> The cause of freedom calls us; to obey
> Is but the duty of her every child. . . .

Women, however, never took Mazzini lightly or in jest. Now Harriet Eleanor Baillie Hamilton joined herself to that remarkable group of women who were his disciples. Previously, she had read Rogers's *Italy*, had sympathized with Silvio Pellico in the Spielberg prison, had paid her shilling to see a picture of Felice Orsini in a Regent Street shop, and had been so deeply impressed with that tyrannicide's career as to have composed a powerful and genuinely poetic narrative of his execution. When, in 1859 on Midsummer Day, the battle of Solferino was won, she had been listening at the Crystal Palace to Handel's "Israel in Egypt" and had been thinking only of Italy. In 1860, she had wanted to join Jessie White Mario as a nurse to Garibaldi's Redshirts. On August 16, 1862, she wrote her first letter to Mazzini, one phrase of which went thus: "I have worshipped you, reverenced you so long." Then she asked Mazzini to enlist her as a nurse to Garibaldi's men. This was before the Aspromonte fiasco. On August 19th, Mazzini replied that he would enrol her if her conscience called her to the cause. But her parents immediately intervened and dragged her off to northern Scotland to cure her of Mazzinianism.[12] When the news became known that Garibaldi had been wounded at Aspromonte by Italian troops sent to prevent his march on Rome, Miss Hamilton mourned the sad event in a poem.

There was a growing disposition among some, now that Italy had been practically united by the diplomacy of Cavour and the swords of Garibaldi and the third Napoleon, to regard Mazzini very indulgently and to give him a measure of credit in proportion as the influence of *Young Italy* diminished. For example, Count Carlo Arrivabene, a friend of Cavour, admitted that "the thought and the desire of a united Italy only began to grow in the minds of the Italians after the publication of the Mazzinian paper, *La Giovine Italia*."[13]

In August 1862 David Masson, reviewing Clough's poems, pronounced

> the most remarkable thing about [the "Amours de Voyage"] . . . the testimony borne all through it to the nobleness of that Mazzinian defence of Rome, and to the fine behaviour of the people in those last days of their brief Republic.[14]

Nevertheless, if Masson still was at heart the lover of Italy, if he still was the same man as he who had been secretary of The Society of the Friends of Italy, there was a certain justness to the complaint in Mazzini's letter early in 1863 to W. J. Linton that Masson had become conservative and was "shunning every political question."[15] Perhaps his having become in 1852 professor of English literature at University College, London, had sobered him.*

* In January 1860, Mazzini met Masson at the Peter Taylors', and remarked more with sorrow than with satire:

> ". . . the fiery, political, philo-italian [sic] Masson, transformed now into a contemplative book-worm, devoting days of enquiries to ascertain what shape the knockers on the right side of the street through which Milton happened, once, to walk, had."

See the *Edizione nazionale degli scritti di Giuseppe Mazzini*, LXVII, 69.

More staunch in his allegiance to Mazzini was James Stansfeld, member of Parliament, who had married a daughter of the Ashurst clan. Stansfeld's pamphlet (March 1862), *The Italian Movement and Italian Parties*, recalled the Italian martyrs—Ugo Bassi, Pellico, Pisacane, the brothers Bandiera, and defended the party of *Young Italy*.

Another loyal friend was Miss Hamilton, whom we have last seen in Scotland. Mazzini had read her lines on the wounded Garibaldi (*The Observer*, November 15, 1862), and had received a copy of her poem on the late Orsini. Praising these verses, he offered to help her (January 1863) with biographical material on the tyrannicide. "Only," he declared, "there are shadows in his conduct which a biographer cannot overlook, and which might be left instead to sleep in his grave." Consequently, she abandoned her projected biography. When a bazaar was to be held in London for the "Venice and Rome Emancipation Fund,"* Mazzini wrote to her: "Can you work some little thing for it? or send something belonging to you?—autographs, sketches, any small embroidery, or whatever other little thing will do." In May, her parents forbade her to correspond with Mazzini, who sadly told her: "Evidently the members of your family know nothing of me, and, in common with many others, choose to judge me from *The Times*."[16] She was released[17] from her parents' vigilance when she married Henry King, of Smith, Elder, and Company, the publishers.

In 1862, Emilie Ashurst, another of Mazzini's disciples, translated into English his important ethical study, *The Duties of Man*. This work, influenced by Lamennais's *Words of a Believer*, was meant for working men. Mazzini reminded them of their duties before he considered their rights, for these, when gained, had not improved the condition of the

* For this fund Mazzini, a year earlier, had thought of getting Jenny Lind to sing at a concert. See the *Edizione nazionale degli scritti di Giuseppe Mazzini*, LXXII, 259.

people. He said that the upper classes had been conscious only of their rights, not their duties; and hence, there had been no sharing of material things with the depressed masses. True, he was for the economic improvement of the condition of workers, but the elevation of men's natures should precede their material enhancement. "A change of social organisation is of little moment, while you yourselves remain with your present passions and egotism." He restated his belief in God, who was the source of Duty; and he manœuvred between the devil-take-the-hindmost of *laissez-faire* and the "denial" of individual initiative of Communism. The *moral or ethical* man, led by duty, would lead the way to the better society of the future. And since he was, in a special sense, an internationalist believing in the interdependence of all nations, he repeated that one had duties to Humanity. In one's own country, he urged a ceaseless striving against privilege and inequality. He also affirmed a belief in free speech and a free press, which were important, since they concerned education and instruction. The first addressed itself to the moral faculties and led men to a knowledge of their duties. Instruction developed the intellect of mankind and gave it a capacity for achieving them. He recorded himself a believer in the Principle of Property and as usual called Communism "the existence of the Beaver, not the life of a Man." As concrete proposals, he suggested voluntary profit-sharing associations and by way of example mentioned the American whalers; also, he again proved himself a single-taxer—in favour of an income tax.

Although Mazzini retained the friendship of various English sympathizers with Italy, he gradually lost his control over his fellow expatriates. For example, Giovanni Ruffini's *Vincenzo* (1863) was evidence that the author now believed in a unitarian and *monarchical* solution to the Italian problem. Mazzini's influence had been undermined by the march of events on the Continent. Now, more than ever, he was almost alone.

Since the affair of 1844, Mazzini did not trust the Post Office to handle letters marked under his own name. At the beginning of 1864, the French government discovered a plot against Napoleon III and tried to link Mazzini with it. Now Stansfeld had become a Junior Lord of the Admiralty in the Palmerston *régime*, a circumstance which made politically unwise Mazzini's habit of receiving letters, addressed to him under a feigned name, at Stansfeld's London house. This connection came out; *The Times* printed long and hostile editorials; and to save Palmerston embarrassment, Stansfeld resigned after a narrow escape from a vote of censure. During a bitter debate in the Commons, Disraeli severely castigated Stansfeld for his friendship with Mazzini and for his defence of the Italian's character. As was to be expected, Disraeli repeated a story that Mazzini believed in tyrannicide—that he had approved a plot against the life of King Charles Albert of Piedmont. John Bright* asked Disraeli whether he had not himself praised tryannicide. Disraeli said no. Then Bright referred to some lines from Disraeli's early *A Revolutionary Epick* (1834). Disraeli denied that these lines or such lines occurred in his poem, and Bright accepted this statement. Nevertheless, the lines are there, but Disraeli took advantage of the advertising to issue a new edition dedicated to Lord Stanley.[18] When the public examined (in the British Museum) the old version and compared it with the new, it discovered that Disraeli had omitted the lines on tyrannicide:

> And blessed be the hand that dares to wave
> The regicidal steel that shall redeem
> A nation's sorrow with a tyrant's blood.[19]

* Later, Stansfeld thanked Bright for parrying Disraeli's attack. In July 1864, Bright again met Mazzini and observed "the same intelligent, thoughtful and kind expression of countenance." The orator respected the Italian very much and always referred to him as Mr. Mazzini. See *The Diaries of John Bright*, ed. R. A. J. Walling, London, 1930, pp. 273 and 282.

In any case, for a third time Mazzini had been the cause of a Cabinet crisis. One pungent comment on the whole matter (from the Tory point of view) is not to be overlooked. Charles Lever, the Irish novelist, summed up his own reaction by calling Stansfeld an ass![20] On the other hand, both George Meredith and W. E. Forster defended him; and Henry Crabb Robinson, the diarist, thought that Stansfeld had gained in public esteem by his manful demeanour and by his loyalty to his friend Mazzini, devotion so great as to overleap ignominious careerism.

The most notable event during 1864, of all that concerned the relations of Italy and England, was of course Garibaldi's visit to London, when the hero of the Thousand was lionized by the mighty and cheered by hundreds of thousands of the populace. At a banquet, the idol of the hour proposed a toast to Mazzini:

> To-day I have a duty to fulfil, which I ought to have fulfilled long ago. Here, in the midst of us to-day, is a man who has rendered both my country and the ideals of freedom the greatest service of all. When I was a young man and guided only by vague impulses, I looked for a man to be my leader and the counsellor of my youth. I sought him as a thirsty man seeks water. . . . I found him. He alone was on guard, he watched alone, when everyone around him was still sleeping. He became my friend, and will always be my friend. In him the sacred flame of love for our Fatherland and for Freedom has never been extinguished. This man is Giuseppe Mazzini, my friend and my master—I drink to him.

One of those present, Alexander Herzen, heard Mazzini, very much moved, whisper: "It is too much!"[21]

Perhaps as a result of Garibaldi's visit and his noble praise of Mazzini, more and more people began to write in amiable accents about the great exile. It might be too, that, now that Italian unity was practically attained, they thought the cause of Italy immune from his good intentions. A typical statement of this kindly feeling towards Mazzini was that of John Sale Barker in a pamphlet of lectures,[22] ably summarizing the history of the *Risorgimento* from a Mazzinian standpoint. Similarly, the Reverend Gavin Carlyle gave credit to Mazzini for maintaining the spirit of the Italians;[23] and a certain E. H. Nolan, who took advantage of the Italomania aroused by Garibaldi's visit to write a popular history[24] of Italian liberation, pronounced Mazzini to be a man of sincerity.

Interest in Mazzini had grown sufficiently to warrant an English edition of his works.* Printing was begun in 1864, and the sixth and last volume appeared in 1870 under the auspices of Smith, Elder, and Company of London. For this project, George Meredith read proof in the spring of 1864.[25] It was to Henry King, husband of the former Harriet Eleanor Baillie Hamilton, that Mazzini owed the gratification of seeing a collected edition of his writings. Unfortunately, so Mrs. Hamilton King disclosed, it did not pay the publishers;[26] nevertheless, the Kings and Mazzini maintained the most happy relations.

When Garibaldi came to London, the impressionable Mrs. King was one of the vast throng that watched him pass. On April 14th, he went in state to the Italian opera, where Bellini's *Norma*† was being given. She "sat entranced, gazing fixedly at Garibaldi the whole time. He sat well in front of the principal box, and full in view. . . . [She] drank it all in, in a long unforgettable impression." Now she was resolved to meet the hero. On April 19th, armed with a note from Mazzini, she went with her husband to the William Ashursts'; was presented to the great man; and, to her embarrassment, was seated next to him on the right hand.[27] Such was the Italomania of the 'sixties which Mazzini, more than anybody else, had nurtured.

* Excellently and favourably reviewed in *Macmillan's Magazine*, XVI, 54–61 (May 1867).

† The libretto was by the refugee, Carlo Pepoli, who succeeded Panizzi as professor of Italian at the University of London. Pepoli's inaugural lecture (1838), *On the Language and Literature of Italy*, contains an interesting digression on the misery of exile.

On the other hand, Robert Browning now called the Mazzinian party "too contemptible!"[28] George Eliot,* having received a very vaguely written circular for a Mazzini fund, declared herself unable to subscribe because she had no faith in *hopeless* conspiracy. She did, however, believe in revolutionary activity when it was feasible. Significantly, she said that since Lewes and she had "a real reverence for Mazzini," she thought necessary an explanation for her refusal to give money.[29]

Just before the Austro-Prussian war, W. J. Linton published a spirited poem, "To Victor Emmanuel," calling on that monarch to go forth to win Venice and Rome for Italy. Let him, however, show that he was not a king bent on conquest for power but dedicated to Italy. Hence, let him recall Mazzini from exile:

And now thy greatest son,
The *Man Italian*, he whose high design
And never-wearying pertinacity
Did even create thy patriot energy,
Whose life has been thy banner and the sign
In which thou conquerest, whose very name
Means Italy,—must bear an exile's shame
And sit far from thy festival, beside
A stranger's hearth. O king who would be king!
Freed Italy waits her lover. . . .

Call back Mazzini! Place him by thy side. . . .[30]

It is in George Meredith's *Vittoria*, written in 1864 and 1865 as a sequel to *Sandra Belloni*, that Mazzini makes his most lasting appearance. While the novel was in progress, George Lewes expressed his liking for it. In December 1865, Meredith told Lewes that he had read a great deal of the story to Mme Venturi† "the other day, who says the Italian

* Mazzini had read and admired George Eliot's novel, *Romola*.

† It has been maintained that Emilie Ashurst Venturi was the original of Meredith's charming heroine, Sandra Belloni. See René Galland's *George Meredith* . . ., p. 232.

colouring is correct."[31] She was, of course, the disciple of Mazzini. If one also remembers that Meredith had been reading proof for the collected edition of Mazzini's works in 1864, one may realize how much the novelist had saturated himself in the very spirit of that glamorous figure known to lovers of *Vittoria* as the Chief.

Undeniably, the serial which ran in *The Fortnightly Review* during 1866, *Vittoria*, represents the high-water mark of Mazzini's influence on English letters. With skill and drama, the novel describes the Chief—Mazzini—as he surveys the waveless Lombard plain from Monto Motterone, on which he meets his fellow conspirators of the 'Forty-eight:

> He was a man of middle stature, thin, and even frail, as he stood defined against the sky; with the complexion of the student, and the student's aspect. The attentive droop of his shoulders and head, the straining of the buttoned coat across his chest, the air as of one who waited and listened, which distinguished his figure, detracted from the promise of other than contemplative energy, until his eyes were fairly seen and felt. That is, until the observer became aware that those soft and large dark meditative eyes had taken hold of him. In them lay no abstracted student's languor, no reflex burning of a solitary lamp; but a quiet grappling force engaged the penetrating look. Gazing upon them, you were drawn in suddenly among the thousand whirring wheels of a capacious and a vigorous mind, that was both reasoning and prompt, keen of intellect, acting throughout all its machinery, and having all under full command: an orbed mind, supplying its own philosophy, and arriving at the sword-stroke by logical steps,—a mind much less supple than a soldier's; anything but the mind of a Hamlet. The eyes were dark as the forest's border is dark; not as night is dark. Under favourable lights their colour was seen to be a deep rich brown, like the chestnut, or more like the hazel-edged sunset brown which lies upon our western rivers in the winter floods, when night begins to shadow them.
>
> The side-view of his face was an expression of classic beauty rarely now to be beheld, either in classic lands or elsewhere. It was severe; the tender serenity of the full bow

> of the eyes relieved it. In profile they showed little of their intellectual quality, but what some might have thought a playful luminousness, and some a quick pulse of feeling. The chin was firm; on it, and on the upper lip, there was a clipped growth of black hair. The whole visage widened upward from the chin, though not very markedly before it reached the broad-lying brows. The temples were strongly indented by the swelling of the forehead above them: and on both sides of the head there ran a pregnant ridge, such as will sometimes lift men a deplorable half inch above the earth we tread. If this man was a problem to others, he was none to himself; and when others called him an idealist, he accepted the title, reading himself, notwithstanding, as one who was less flighty than many philosophers and professedly practical teachers of his generation. He saw far, and he grasped ends beyond obstacles: he was nourished by sovereign principles; he despised material present interests; and, as I have said, he was less supple than a soldier. If the title of idealist belonged to him, we will not immediately decide that it was opprobrious. The idealized conception of stern truths played about his head certainly for those who knew and who loved it. Such a man, perceiving a devout end to be reached, might prove less scrupulous in his course, possibly, and less remorseful, than revolutionary Generals. His smile was quite unclouded, and came softly as a curve in water. It seemed to flow with, and to pass in and out of, his thoughts,—to be a part of his emotion and his meaning when it shone transiently full. For as he had an orbed mind, so had he an orbed nature. The passions were absolutely in harmony with the intelligence. He had the English manner; a remarkable simplicity contrasting with the demonstrative outcries and gesticulations of his friends when they joined him on the height.[32]

One notices in Meredith's delineation of the Chief, notable as it is since nobody else ever drew him so well or so greatly,* the immense concession that Mazzini could be lacking in scruples sufficiently to abet assassination. What such a judg-

* *E.g.*, in Amelia Blandford Edwards's novel, *Half a Million of Money* (London, 1865), there is a slightly earlier portrait of Mazzini. One character, Giulio Colonna, is presented as constantly writing manifestoes and pamphlets, and conspiring ruthlessly and indefatigably for a

ment reveals is this, that Meredith never met Mazzini. In *Vittoria*, the fence-straddling Count Serabiglione recognizes the woes of Italy but charges the professional doctrinaire [Mazzini] with originating them.

> He was, the count declared in answer, a born intriguer, a lover of blood, mad for the smell of it! an Old Man of the Mountain; a sheaf of assassins; and more—the curse of Italy! There should be extradition treaties all over the world to bring this arch-conspirator to justice, [for] England nourished the wretch that she might undermine the peace of the Continent.[33]

In the course of the novel, one learns that the heroine, Vittoria, is to sing the *rôle* of Camilla in an opera of that name. The most dramatic scene occurs not within the libretto itself but as a result of the fact that a song added after the end is to serve as the lighting of the fuse of the 'Forty-eight—more exactly of the famous *Cinque Giornate*, or Five Days, when the Milanese rose up, erected barricades, and expelled an Austrian army led by the redoubtable Radetzky. The dying Camilla (Vittoria) sings at the close:

> Our life is but a little holding, lent
> To do a mighty labour: we are one
> With heaven and the stars when it is spent
> To serve God's aim: else die we with the sun.[34]

Thus, in that superb scene in La Scala where the opera *Camilla* rehearses the Italian wrongs and appeals to revolution as the means of redress, even the song which Vittoria interpolates as the final call to arms follows a restatement of Mazzini's doctrines of the religion of humanity and its duties.*

republican united Italy. In one episode, Colonna is almost apprehended by a Neapolitan searching party but escapes through sheer nerve. However, Miss Edwards's protagonist can in no way compare with Meredith's superb delineation of the Chief.

* On the headstone of Meredith's grave appear the lines:

> "Life is but a little holding,
> Lent to do a mighty labour."

One thing else is of interest. Mrs. Carlyle, we know, thought Mazzini dangerously careless as a plotter. It is significant that the Chief is made to trust Vittoria despite the uneasiness of the other conspirators met on the heights, and it is she who justifies their fears by an indiscretion, innocent as it is in motive. Meredith had rightly read Mazzini's character and knew it was not cased in the triple bronze of a great leader of forces subversive of established things.

Nobody, however, has—if we omit one poem by Carducci and one by Swinburne—so grandly as Meredith set forth how Mazzini revived Italy during those years of preparation from 1831 to 1848:

> Watching over his Italy; her wrist in his meditative clasp year by year; he stood like a mystic leech by the couch of a fair and hopeless frame, pledged to revive it by the inspired assurance, shared by none, that life had not forsaken it. A body given over to death and vultures—he stood by it in the desert. Is it a marvel to you that when the carrion-wings swooped low, and the claws fixed, and the beak plucked and savoured its morsel, he raised his arm, and urged the half-resuscitated frame to some vindicating show of existence? Arise! he said, even in what appeared most fatal hours of darkness. The slack limbs moved; the body rose and fell. The cost of the effort was the breaking out of innumerable wounds, old and new; the gain was the display of the miracle that Italy lived. She tasted her own blood, and herself knew that she lived.[35]

When Venice was freed from Austrian rule in 1866, Meredith's friend, Swinburne, thought it good, for to him liberty was an end, not a means. (But Mazzini found the event repugnant in that Italy was being further unified under monarchical auspices.) Thus it was that Swinburne resolved, after many months of inaction through worry and weariness, to write a song of congratulation for Venice. He had once spoken of his poem as little; but under the influence of a verbose Muse, it became the long "A Song of Italy."

He hoped to include in his poem an adequate expression of reverence for Mazzini:

> I have already touched on most others of the later patriots and martyrs—I am half afraid and half desirous to touch on him—*i.e.*, to lay my lips on his feet. If I do finish this poem at all to my satisfaction, there will be a bit of enthusiasm in verse for once—*rather*.

He told W. M. Rossetti that it was pleasant to love and believe in Italy. It was only Dante Gabriel Rossetti and those other preachers of art for art's sake who had turned him aside from singing the cause of Italy. But "ever since I was fifteen I have been equally and unalterably mad . . . about *this* article of faith; you may ask any tutor or schoolfellow." He knew that the outcome would be a poem more rhetorical than imaginative; but then he preferred being an Italian stump-orator to an English prophet; and he

> meant to make it acceptable to you [W. M. Rossetti] and a few others of our sort. As far as I can judge, I think it contains already some of my best verses. Only, just as one hears that intense desire has made men impotent at the right (or wrong) minute, my passionate wish to express myself in part, for a little, about this matter, has twice and thrice left me exhausted and incompetent; unable to write, or to decide if what has been written is or is not good. I never felt this about my poems on other subjects; and I'd give a year of my life to accomplish the writing of a really great song on this one.[36]

As the intermediary of poetic parturition, Mazzini very evidently made it difficult for Swinburne to have an easy delivery. After all, his was a moral force and perhaps not too well adapted to the nourishing of Swinburne's genius.

About 1866 also, Swinburne was working on that section of *Lesbia Brandon*,[37] a novel, which includes a portrait of a certain political exile named Attilo Mariani. Of course, it was Mazzini, who is here presented as the symbol of republican nationalism of a narrow sort. Newspapers are described as calling Mariani assassin and plotter. *Lesbia Brandon* was left unfinished, probably having been abandoned on account of Mazzini's influence.

Yet Mazzini (*c.* January 1867) feared that his ascendancy over the erratic poet would be feeble from its inception:

> [Swinburne] might be transformed as far as direction goes, but only by some man or woman—better a woman, of course —who would love him very much and assert at the same time a moral superiority on him.

However, between blind adulators and blind revilers, Mazzini believed Swinburne would remain as he was.[38]

In *The Fortnightly Review* (March 1, 1867), Swinburne published[39] his "Ode on the Insurrection in Candia," a fine performance, learnedly constructed, but dull, so that in later years he hated to hear it mentioned.[40] It is Sir Edmund Gosse who tells[41] us the following anecdote, which, if it were true, were very attractive. Certain friends of Swinburne met at George Howard's [later Earl of Carlisle], where Benjamin Jowett used to come; and there held a council of war to discuss what could be done *with* and *for* the erring Algernon. In this great consult, the leading figures, we are given to believe, were Jowett and Mazzini, the latter having been summoned by Karl Blind, a German refugee poet. The next pretty little fiction is that Mazzini, previously unacquainted with Swinburne, was told of the promise and situation of the poet (too much Priapus and Cotytto and Astarte!), and was led, by the perusal of a copy of the ode for the freedom of the Cretan (Candiote) Greeks, to take intellectual charge of him. The only trouble about Gosse's great literary conspiracy story is that it is not true, even if so pleasantly conceived as to make one wish it were authentic; for we know[42] that Jowett first met Mazzini in the spring of 1871. Moreover, the truth seems to be that Mazzini had often seen

Swinburne during 1858.* Seven years later, the poet dispatched a copy of his *Atalanta in Calydon* to the Italian. Having received no answer, he sent a second arrow after the first, the ode on the Candiote outbreak. On March 10, 1867, Mazzini finally replied. The conspirator apologized for his neglect to acknowledge "the gift of your beautiful 'Atalanta' " by pleading ignorance of Swinburne's address! "From the reading of your masterly Ode on Greece," he ventured to infer that Swinburne's art had found its true direction—"to transform *us*, to rouse the sleeping, to compel thought to embody itself into Action. That is the mission of Art; and yours." Mazzini was repeating his own slogan of *Pensiero ed Azione*, restated by the Marxists—art is a weapon. What should a poet do? As long as the immense heroic Titanic battle was being fought between the dual forces of the world—Right and Wrong, Truth and Lie, God and the Devil; as long as crowned reaction throttled freedom, then, said Mazzini, a poet should be "the apostle of a crusade, his word the watchword of the fighting nations and the dirge of the oppressors." Therefore Swinburne was not to lull men to sleep "with songs of egotistical love and idolatry of physical beauty"; it was rather his mission to encourage and to reproach, to salute the martyrs of liberation and to brand its cowards. Swinburne, he urged, should write a series of "Lyrics for the Crusades."[43] These were destined to be the *Songs before Sunrise*. Mazzini's long letter made Swinburne very happy.[44] Almost immediately, he began to compose pro-Italian verses of the sort which had been suggested. Naturally, the Genoese felt gratified at his disciple's progress.[45]

Swinburne and Mazzini met on March 30th at Karl Blind's through Thomas Purnell, a common friend. The

* On August 20, 1858, Mazzini wrote to a friend in Pisa:

"*Vedo sovente lo Swinburne, il cui spirito si va ottenebrando pur troppo causa l'alcool di cui abusa.*"

See the *Edizione nazionale degli scritti di Giuseppe Mazzini*, LXI, 126.

poet was full of enthusiasm; but the exile, on the other hand, was a disappointed man, for the *Risorgimento* was being realized by men and means he abhorred. Yet he was still nursing the unconquerable hope and was ready to use Swinburne for propaganda in England.[46] It is only Swinburne's words which can best describe what took place at this meeting with Mazzini:

> I unworthy spent much of last night sitting at my beloved Chief's feet. He was angelically good to me. I read him my Italian poem all through and he accepted it in words I can't trust myself to try and write down. . . . To-day I am rather exhausted and out of sorts. Il y a bien de quoi. There's a tradition in the Talmud that when Moses came down from Sinai he was drunken with the kisses of the lips of God.[47]

Perhaps Mazzini too was exhausted, for, after all, *A Song of Italy* has about one thousand verses.

Promptly Swinburne wrote to his mother and declared that he had never dreamed of such a reception as Mazzini had given him. The Italian had come forward, and had said dramatically and quietly: "I know *you*." Thereupon, Swinburne got on his knees and kissed his hand. When Mazzini asked him to read his verses, at first Swinburne read them straight through; but he confessed to feeling shy and nervous when he came to the part about Mazzini personally. However, all was well, for at that point the poet looked up at the exile and was fortified to continue. One must remember that while he read, Mazzini held his hand between his own and every now and then gave it a great pressure of reassurance. Swinburne's elation was amazing when Mazzini told him that he might visit him as he chose. And with high enthusiasm he wrote to his mother of his love for Mazzini and that the Chief had promised to take him to Rome—when the Revolution came—and to crown him with his own hands in the Capitol! "He is a born king and chief and leader of men. You never saw such a beautiful smile as his." In cast of features, Swinburne fancied a resemblance between Mazzini and his uncle Ashburnham —but with twice the life and expression.[48]

A Song of Italy (1867) was dedicated with "Devotion and Reverence to Joseph Mazzini." Swinburne presented a vision of Italy clasping the knees of Freedom, and of the Goddess of Liberty encouraging her prostrate suppliant in high dialogue. Since she would not be Freedom if Italy were not free—hitherto "abused, abased, [and] reviled," the Goddess bade the stricken land arise and weep no more. Let her array herself

> With girdles of green freedom, and with red
>   Roses, and white snow shed
> Above the flush and bondage of the hills.

And so clad in the tricolour, Italy would yet mount above the Austrian gonfalon of yellow and black death. Priest and Austrian declared her dead, but this was not so despite the words of "the herdsman of the Gadarean swine" [presumably, the pope]. Her martyrs by their deaths witnessed to her life; the brothers Bandiera, Pisacane, Felice Orsini, and others proclaimed theirs no land of the dead. Then Swinburne hailed Mazzini as Chief and prophet and priest—the man who had sustained the Italians with his propaganda:

> The milk of life on death's unnatural brink
>   Thou gavest them to drink,
> The natural milk of freedom; and again
>   They drank, and they were men,
> The wine and honey of freedom and of faith
>   They drank, and cast off death.[49]

And he urged Mazzini to bear with Italy though she had been beaten at Custoza and Lissa (1866). The memory of defeats made the poet pay tribute to Garibaldi, but presently he returned to praise of Mazzini and summoned the winds, the light of past days, storm and shore and wave, valley and alp, wisdom and love, lake and green Apennine, to sing his greatness. In the intoning of just tribute, the cities of Italy join, among them Genoa, mother of Columbus and Mazzini:

> One found a world new-born from virgin sea;
> And one found Italy. . . .

Florence, Siena, Naples, Rome—all the historic cities sing a hymn of praise to Italy's "supreme son." Then the poet, frenzied by the Mazzinian afflatus, saw a vision of a priestless Rome that was to be—the Republic,

> . . . our Republic that shalt bind in bands
> The kingdomless far lands
> And link the chainless ages. . . .

Unfortunately, the ideas of *A Song of Italy* were more appropriate to 1848 than to 1867; and very obviously, Swinburne was out of touch with the political situation in Italy. The shadow of Cavour, that man of subterfuge and expediency, who admitted that had he done for himself what he had dared for Italy, he should be compelled to acknowledge himself a great scoundrel, had eclipsed Mazzini. Rome, however, remained yet to be won, and *A Song of Italy* foretold its liberation from the papacy.

A Song of Italy did not sell well, for it was a prolix manifesto of outmoded Italian republicanism. Moreover, its truncated couplets—used previously by Ben Jonson in *The Forest*—were fatiguing for a long poem, especially one so vague and so vociferous.[50]

Lady Swinburne had become alarmed lest Mazzini send her son on a deadly errand to Rome or Paris, or lest the exile inflame him with such republican notions as laying powder-mines under Windsor Castle![51] Such thoughts were far from their minds. When Swinburne visited Mazzini on May 5, 1867, did they talk in revolutionary fervour of sudden uprisings? Merely of Prometheus and of Madame Venturi, who was, in the judgment of both, an exceptional woman; and Swinburne meant to visit her. Mazzini dwelt sadly on the fact that the *Song of Italy* was ignored in the daily press by *la conspiration du silence.*[52] It is from William Michael Rossetti that we learn how Swinburne reacted to his call on Mazzini, how he felt himself dominated by his Chief's "immense magnetic power." Apparently, Mazzini had again urged him to write poems with a directly democratic or humanitarian vein, a task the poet found difficult to shirk although he was conscious that this type of verse was not exactly his line and would not therefore "promote his true poetic development."[53]

On the same day as his conversation with William Michael Rossetti, Swinburne wrote a letter to his mother assuring her that Mazzini's influence over him was wholesome. She should be quite at rest, for though it was not to be expected that she regard the Italian with her son's eyes, his influence could lead to nothing but good. The Chief was in all ways immensely kind to her Algernon and wanted him to devote his writing power to doing right and to serving others. Alas! If her Algernon did these admirable things which his Mazzini wished, he feared he would lose his faculty of verse![54]

Yet he did persist in the channel which Mazzini had pointed out to him. Early in October, he expressed to William Michael Rossetti the diffident confidence that he would "accomplish a book of political and national poems as complete and coherent in its way as the Châtiments or Drum Taps."[55] The volume was his *Songs before Sunrise* in embryo. In November 1867, *The Fortnightly Review* printed one of these Italophil poems, "The Halt Before Rome, September 1867," which concerns the defeat of Garibaldi at Mentana by the French and papal troops and which is written as if Garibaldi were fighting for the Mazzinian republic, not irregularly for Victor Emmanuel.

Swinburne was also busy writing an "Appeal to England" against the execution of the Manchester Fenians. It was really a plea for mercy, since he did not commend the condemned patriots. For that reason the Reform League thought him a safe man and wanted him to stand for Parliament. The society was willing to pay his expenses—wasn't he a representative of advanced republican opinion? Fortunately, Swinburne turned to Mazzini for advice and was wisely and to his relief told to decline the nomination.[56] Of course, Mazzini made sure to send his difficult *protégé* a gratifying message on the poem in behalf of the Fenians.[57]

The antics of Swinburne, who thumbed his nose at Victorian proprieties, were always of great interest to Mazzini. On one occasion, the Italian wrote with astonishment to Madame Venturi that Swinburne was going on the stage. Very shortly thereafter, Mazzini informed her that he could not readily play "the part of a spiritual father" to the poet. Swinburne, it seemed, had paid him a visit, had talked of "Art and poets," and then had recited "almost unintelligibly" "Siena" and "La Via." Among other things, the poet had said that he was very much interested in Emilie Venturi,* to his mind both "a chosen sister" and "an exceptional woman."[58]

During April 1868, Swinburne worked on a poem the subject of which was Tiresias at the grave of Antigone. In reality, he meant Dante at the grave of Italy. To Swinburne, Mazzini was the successor of the great medieval poet.[59] This exalted opinion did not prevent Swinburne from interrupting his Mazzinian versifying by a prolonged drinking bout, the termination of which was marked by the following letter to the Chief: "Dr. Bird is most glad to say that for five days past Mr. Swinburne has avoided 'the perilous stuff' and is consequently much improved in body and mind."[60] In June 1868, Swinburne published in *Lippincott's Magazine* his fine elegiac poem, "Siena"—the one which he had chanted frenziedly to Mazzini a few months before. "Siena" is notable

* Swinburne had become a member of the Ashurst circle. He spent Christmas Eve in 1867 at the home of Madame Venturi's brother.

for its appreciation of the natural loveliness of Italy and for its expression of the Mazzinian doctrines of God and the People united in the image of the Republic. The other poems which comprise the *Songs before Sunrise* were practically complete by October 1868, a fact which he thought would please his Chief.[61]

If a major Victorian poet was doing his best to advance Mazzini's teachings in England, a very minor one, a certain F. W. Irby, went out of his way to address (1868) an opuscule to the Italian. Among its milder lines occur these pleasant words:

> Thou advocate of Italy,
>   From Italy depart!
> I see in thee the assassin's eye,
>   No gladiator's heart.
> Thou scum of men—beneath the shade
>   Thou lurkest like the toad,
> And sendest forth thy venom'd blade
>   From out thy dark abode.
> Who was it arm'd Orsini's hand?
>   Who sent *him* to the grave?
> 'Twas *thou*, thou recreant. . . .[62]

It is, we may suppose, some kind of distinction to attract great praise and choleric abuse. He that can lie within such limits of mankind's opinion will be known, at least more than as the shadow of a name, to posterity.

For Swinburne, Mazzini always remained the Master or the Chief; and their relations grew more and more amiable. Appropriately, the conspirator gave the poet a beautiful Angora cat, whose sad decease William Michael Rossetti recorded.[63] When Garibaldi engaged in a dispute with Mazzini in 1869, Swinburne expressed his loss of admiration for the *condottiere*. In 1861, he had thought Garibaldi the greatest man since Adam.[64] Only those who admired his master and adhered to his tenets suited his fancy. He himself believed even in the Universal Republic presently to be.[65]

Perhaps the greatest poem which Swinburne wrote under the influence of the Mazzinian muse was his "Super Flumina Babylonis," first printed in *The Fortnightly Review* for October 1869. Very admirably it described the spiritual renascence among the educated classes in Italy from 1831 to 1848 under Mazzini's political and ethical doctrine of Italy a Nation. It told how the Italians had wept by their own waters of Babylon; had been harrowed and crushed; had degenerated into riot and shame; and knowing not the great deeds of their forefathers, had sung idle songs for an empty day. From afar, the lovers of Italy beheld her tears year after year until what time a voice told her she was not dead and that her sons should not put their trust in words of kings. Thus had Mazzini prophesied that the waters of Babylon would no longer flow, fed with Italian tears. That worthless Italy which Parini's *Il Giorno* had drawn, Mazzini had quickened.

By December 1869, Swinburne had made such progress on the poems written at Mazzini's suggestion that he thought of a proper title for his forthcoming book. Not without asking the opinion of his close friend, William Michael Rossetti, did he reject Mazzini's *Songs of the Crusade* for the final *Songs before Sunrise*.[66]

Perhaps the great literary event of 1870 was the publication of Harriet Beecher Stowe's *Lady Byron Vindicated*, the contents of which had been known a year earlier. Now Mazzini had always admired Byron for having once acted in accord with Thomas Paine's noble words: "Where Liberty is not, there is my country." Hence, Mazzini was moved to defend Byron and to hope for the printing of his memoirs. For, said Mazzini,

> shall not the voice of the accused come out of his own grave and say what he may have to say in explanation, extenuation or remorse? Is it justice—should there be extenuating circumstances—to stifle them and leave the soul of a Great Poet under the stigma of baseness and hypocrisy? Is it moral, should there be only a cry of anguish and remorse,

> to suppress it and with it a warning? Can a man like Dr. Lushington persist in stealing the defence, in gagging a Soul when the accusation is hurled against the silent defenceless tomb?

To him it seemed now, more than ever,* altogether a monstrous thing. If there were true morality in England, a general outcry would compel "the thought-and-soul stealers to yield the violated deposit." He would, if only he were young again, plot to recover the defiled good name of the poet with the same activity with which he had plotted for thirty-five years to reconquer the stolen liberty of his country.[67]

But he was no more a young man. Indeed, by 1870 he was so broken in spirit that he said even Swinburne's praise made him sad, for "who am I, whom he praises?"[68] It is therefore as a disappointed man that Disraeli presents him in *Lothair*, thinly veiled under the name of Mirandola. Mirandola used sometimes to visit the drawing-room of Mrs. Putney Giles, a solicitor's wife, whose "principal mission was to destroy the Papacy and to secure Italian unity." Ordinarily, Mirandola would be feverishly writing his fiery pamphlets. It is his old age that Disraeli describes thus:

> His face was grave, not to say sad; thought, not time, had partially silvered the clustering of his raven hair; but intellectual power reigned in his wide brow, while determination was the character of the rest of his countenance under great control, yet apparently, from the dark flashing of his eye, not incompatible with fanaticism.

Of himself, Mirandola said that his health was wretched; and though writing and speaking were bad for him, yet he passed his life in writing and speaking so that towards

* In 1847, he had said that Byron was one of the most thoroughly virtuous and calumniated men of the last fifty years, and had been vexed at not knowing where to publish a long article containing this point of view. See *Mazzini's Letters to an English Family*, 1844–72, ed. E. F. Richards, London, 1920–22, I, 49. Similarly, in 1860, he expressed a desire to write a book in defence of Byron. See the *Edizione nazionale degli scritti di Giuseppe Mazzini*, LXX, 60–61.

evening he would feel utterly exhausted and become, what he had thought he could never be, the victim of despondency. Disraeli set him down for us as one unvanquished by failure and engaged at the moment in planning that march on Rome which ended in Garibaldi's defeat at Mentana in 1867 before the new French rifles. Sanguinely, Mirandola expected no foreign interference and thought that a hundred thousand men would rally to the the cause of Rome as yet unfree. And characteristically, the first thing that he would do to forward his enterprise was to write

> a manifesto addressed to the peoples. They have become absorbed in money-grubbing and what they call industry. The external life of a nation is its most important one. A nation, as an individual, has duties to fulfil appointed by God and His moral law: the individual towards his family, his town, his country; the nation towards the country of countries, humanity: the outward world.

Mirandola firmly believed that man failed and renounced the religious and divine element of his life whenever he betrayed or neglected those duties. In *Lothair*, another character pays tribute to Mazzini: he has formed the mind of their country, he has kindled and kept alive the sacred flame when everything was gloomy and all were without heart. He has shown prodigious devotion, resource and pertinacity, and patience and unbroken spirit. But now he is not the one to effect the revolution.[69] It is, as we see, with an unerring insight that Disraeli in *Lothair* portrays Mazzini. To the acute mind of the Victorian politician, the exile had had his day, and that was over—with the 'Forty-eight. Hatching Italian *émeutes* in London was now a waste of time.

Mazzini did try* again, in 1870, and was imprisoned by

* Mazzini's attempt at a republican rising in Sicily was timed to take advantage of the Franco-Prussian War. When Germany annexed Alsace-Lorraine, he said (*The War and the Commune*, London, 1871, p. 9) prophetically that this action rendered a second war inevitable; and denounced the harshness of the terms of peace as an example of Caesarism.

the Italian government in the Fortezza di Gaeta, near Naples. Here, with a fortitude that reminds one of Raleigh, he contemplated a long article on Byron, a copy of whose works had been his companion in prison. He studied the poet in the journals, letters, and works as he had never done before, for he felt that he dared not die without having been witness to the true Byron. However, writing tired him and quickly brought on threatenings of an old pain.[70] It is possible that the following sonnet by William Michael Rossetti was composed on the occasion of Mazzini's enforced stay at Gaeta:

Mazzini, greatest, purest of our time,
The future truth's proscribed interpreter;
Exiled, yet fibre of inmost chords which stir
The heart of Italy to beat its chime;
In dereliction and in want, sublime;
The pilgrim Magus bearing nard and myrrh
To Freedom's manger-cradle; Triumvir
Of Rome; for Italy's sake unscared by crime.
In Europe's sick-room thou from year to year
Wast always burning on—the single light
Never extinguished, never flickering.
To thee, and not to statesman nor to king,
Thine Italy's first debt is due, who here
Stands One, in history's and in hell's despite.[71]

A few months before his new venture into failure, Mazzini had wished to be remembered to Swinburne, to Whistler, and "—with an old affection—to Carlyle." In June, Mazzini had written to Emilie Venturi how very sorry he was, but not astonished, at a relapse by Swinburne. "I was hopeless from the beginning. He will not last more than one or two years."[72]

Swinburne continued to versify in behalf of the Mazzinian republic. One of his poems, "The Moderates" (February 1870), attacked the non-Mazzinian (or Piedmontese) party. In August, Swinburne discussed with W. M. Rossetti his lines on Tiresias, who in 1868 had stood for Dante at the grave of Italy, but who now symbolized Dante, Mazzini, and Michelangelo. The poem ends on a note of despair and doubt, for a few days before Mazzini had been arrested and shut up at Gaeta.[73] Even Swinburne's great poem, "Hertha," shows Mazzini's thought. The Earth Goddess represents the principle of growth and as such, Swinburne told W. M. Rossetti, "prefers liberty to bondage, Mazzini to Buonaparte," and is republican.[74]

Swinburne was very much relieved to learn from Mme Venturi that Mazzini, held a prisoner in Gaeta, was well; and he wrote to his mother how much the good news had comforted him.[75] One feels, however, a sense of the end of things. Mazzini who had escaped so often and so daringly to be caught at last—surely his fires were burning low, surely his genius for peril and combat was leaving him. Indeed, his release in October 1870 was only a gesture of political expediency, for the Italian government did not wish to mar the celebration occasioned by the proclamation of the new national capital, Rome.

On various occasions Mazzini had attacked Communism and other materialistic views. In 1870, he included Comtism among such philosophies, for he told John Morley that it was merely a variety of materialism. The Italian said he knew and very much lamented its spread in England, but predicted no long life for it. It was a dead voice, or like the last circle produced by a stone thrown into a clear lake. At the bottom was the stone never to reappear, and the ripple would soon die too. This judgment of Comtism by Mazzini Morley considered hasty.[76] The strange thing is that the English Comtists were drawn to Mazzini because they detected a kinship between his teachings and those of Comte. After all, both men had advocated the superiority of moral to political solutions of man's social and economic ills.

It was Morley's *Fortnightly Review* which in June 1870 published Mazzini's greatest statement of his religious beliefs, especially his faith in the doctrine of the continuity of creation. Nothing in the public eloquence of the last century, if an exception is made of Lincoln's brief speech at Gettysburg, equals the prophetic "Letter to the Members of the Oecumenical Council. *From the Council to God.*"[77] A great congress of the Roman Catholic Church had met in 1869 to proclaim the doctrine of papal infallibility. To the conclusion of this body Mazzini replied with that remarkable union of mysticism, austere magnanimity, and profoundly religious emotion which distinguished his writings. Thus, neither the materialistic views of the Marxians nor the sociological claims of the Comtists nor the spiritual assertions of the Church harmonized with his own religion of humanity. It is known that Carlyle read this latest essay by Mazzini and thought it beautiful.

Mazzini restated his faith in democracy and republicanism in another *Fortnightly Review* article entitled "Italy and the Republic"[78]—a repetition* of his beliefs concerning God, free will, duty, and the moral equality of mankind.

His Chief still followed the erratic career of Swinburne through the letters of Emilie Venturi. To her he wrote early in 1871 how glad he was that the poet showed improvement from debauchery, though his faith in its lasting was very weak.[79] On the 7th of February, Mazzini took leave of Carlyle, telling him of his intention to return permanently to Rome and there publish a newspaper.† The Scotsman had not seen him for a long time; and they talked sincerely and cordially for about an hour, even with real emotion. When they parted, neither expected to meet again in this world. In his journal, Carlyle wrote of this *ave atque vale*: "Mournfully tender, mournfully sublime even, I might call the event to me in the days that now are. Mazzini is the

* Frederic Harrison and John Morley agreed that this article was tedious. See F. W. Hirst, *Early Life and Letters of John Morley*, London, 1927, I, 180.

† He was going to edit a new republican journal, *The Rome of the People*.

most *pious* living man I now know."[80] Not long after, he called on Benjamin Jowett; and that fine Greek scholar, taking very careful notes of what Mazzini said, observed especially his opinions on the French Revolution and his anti-materialism. During their interview, Jowett did hardly any talking; Mazzini said after it: "He made me talk all the time, and I have no notion what he thought of it." The Italian had no reason for anxiety. Jowett thought a great deal of what he had heard; and though he recognized in the speaker an enthusiast and a visionary, perhaps even one who might have in early life recommended "the moral dagger," yet he judged Mazzini a very noble character, one with genius beyond that of ordinary statesmen. "Though not a statesman," commented Jowett, "his reputation will increase as time goes on, when that of most statesmen disappears."[81]

Apparently, Mazzini was unconsciously gathering up the loose ends before the final silence. Early in June, he wrote to Emilie Venturi and asked for the second time about Whistler, Swinburne, and Carlyle.[82] Mme Venturi must also have sensed the inevitable dissolution, for her long article in *The Contemporary Review* (September 1871) on Mazzini's credo included a mosaic of quotations. It was as if a disciple had recorded the words of a prophet. Since, towards the end of 1871, Mazzini was expressing anew his dislike not only of Bakunin's anarchism but also of the Marxian collectivism of the First International,* together with its doctrine of the class struggle and its materialistic philosophical foundation, from which and other influences he wished to "save" the working classes,[83] some might doubtless call his testament middle-class and unrealistic. Ultimately, of course, Bakuninism and Marxism proved

* Mazzini had dissociated himself from the First International because he had failed to win it over to his ideas. Moreover, he expressed his dislike of the Paris Commune on the ground that it was antinationalistic and materialistic. It was Bakunin who answered for the left-wing radicals.

stronger than the workers' movement* begun by Mazzini's Italian followers in the 1860's.

After much delay, the *Songs before Sunrise*, dedicated to Mazzini, appeared in 1871. The volume had been so named because Swinburne, under his Chief's influence, still hoped that a republican Rome would overthrow the Pope and King Victor Emmanuel.[84] In one poem, called "The Litany of Nations," Swinburne appealed for the world revolution, saying that Italy was destined for a *third* birth, a reference to the Mazzinian notion of the third Rome, which was to succeed the Rome of the Caesars and the Rome of the Popes. (Interestingly enough, Mussolini often has spoken of the fourth Rome, that of the totalitarian state.) The Earth-Spirit, in "Hertha," another poem, is associated with "love, the beloved Republic, that feeds upon freedom and lives," a Mazzinian idea even if strangely cast. In "Before a Crucifix," Swinburne delivered a furious invective against the Church in strident tones of antitheistic and pagan disbelief. Mazzini, however, was anti-Catholic only. "A Marching Song" merely repeats the appeal for the world revolution. It is the cry of those in the liberation war of humanity, feeding on hopeless hope; enduring derision, discord, and doubt; and cursed by "thunder-forging priests." Swinburne prophesies the bursting of the locks of the world's prisons and calls on France to rise from the dead; on Milton's England that was a republic. Princelings and kinglets buzz like flies throughout the world or curl like thin worms! England shall be perfect—but such a gift comes not from priests or kings. Therefore, in Mazzinian formula, he tells the English

* About 1858, Mazzini asked Malwida von Meysenbug to spread his ideas among German workmen in London. The Marxists in their number resisted Mazzinianism, and one of them wanted to know what would the Universal Republic do, if it came, for the labouring classes. In reply, Mazzini spoke vaguely of the task of defending the rights of workers and of the necessity of determining their duties. See Gaby Vinant, *Un Esprit Cosmopolite au XIXe Siècle, Malwida de Meysenbug* (1816–1903): *Sa Vie et Ses Amis*, Paris, 1932, pp. 168–69.

to rise and strive for the Republic of the World. In "Tiresias," Swinburne showed liberty as the new dawn. Tiresias mourning for Antigone was really Dante despairing for Italy. Unlike Antigone, Italy stirs with life; for from a third prophet [Mazzini] she has caught faith, and in him are gathered the purpose and passion of Tiresias and Dante. This poem is vague and damnably weak. "A Year's Burden, 1870," recalled that neither kings nor priests would ever slay liberty, for "the soul republican" which is "God whose name is man" would survive. Under liberty, all nations were to be one. Thus he repeats the Mazzinian idea of the Universal Republic. The "Epilogue to Songs before Sunrise" conveys the typical Swinburnian self-abasement with its overtones of algolagnia. In this poem, he lies down "at the beloved feet" [Mazzini's] and sends his songs to fly and do likewise. Furthermore, he apologizes, and properly too, for "these weak word-offerings wearisome"; and is sure the soul is republican. Of course, he must again address Mazzini as *Master* and as the man who first saw the vision of Rome, the third Rome of the Republic, inhabited by mankind, "free, boundless, fearless, perfect, one."

What he himself wrote to Thomas Purnell (March 4, 1871) is too true: the book of *Songs before Sunrise* was "infiltrated and permeated with Mazzini."[85] Swinburne considered this collection his most important work, a judgment in which Edmund Gosse concurred.[86] Compared to Carducci's *Giambi ed epodi*, written about the same time and on the same themes, Swinburne's *Songs before Sunrise* do not come off too well.[87]

On March 10, 1872, a Mr. George Brown, of London, died in Pisa. It was Mazzini *incognito* since his release from Gaeta. After a brief and terrible agony, he had uttered in a loud voice the victorious cry, "Yes! Yes! I do believe in God," and that was the end. Only a month before, he had written to Caroline Stansfeld how strange it was that so many friends younger than he was should go before him. He had known so many dying that last year in Italy too that he was always repeating to himself the lines of Goethe:

Die Vögelein schweigen im Walde.
Warte nur, balde
Ruhest du auch.[88]

There is inscribed on a stone in the Staglieno cemetery where he lies on a green hillside looking down upon his fellow Genoese a noble epitaph by Carducci:

L'UOMO
CHE TUTTO SACRIFICÒ
CHE AMÒ TANTO
E MOLTO COMPATÌ E NON ODIÒ MAI.[89]

He was that man who sacrificed everything, who loved greatly and suffered much and never hated.

CHAPTER VIII

Epilogue

When Mrs. Hamilton King heard of Mazzini's death, she put on deepest mourning and wore it for a year. She also began work on her long and impressive poem, *The Disciples*,[1] which deals with those men who had been martyred for the Christ of the nineteenth century, Joseph Mazzini. An American clergyman, Moncure D. Conway, called on Carlyle to tell him of a memorial service* in Mazzini's honour. The old man, greatly affected by the news of Mazzini's death, talked very freely of the exile:

> I remember well when he sat for the first time on that seat there. A more beautiful person I never beheld, with his soft flashing eyes and face full of intelligençe. He had great talent,—certainly the only acquaintance of mine of anything like equal intellect who ever became entangled in what seemed to me hopeless visions. He was rather silent, spoke chiefly in French, though he spoke good English even then. It was plain he might have taken a high rank in literature. He wrote well, as it was,—sometimes for the love of it, at others when he wanted a little money, but never what he might have written had he devoted himself to that kind of work. He had fine tastes, particularly in music. But he gave himself up as a martyr to his aims for Italy. He lived almost in squalor. His health was poor from the first; he took no care of it. He used to smoke a great deal, and drink coffee with bread crumbled in it; but hardly gave any attention to his food. His mother used to send him money; but he gave it away. . . . I could not have sympathy with his views and hopes. He used to come here and talk about the "solidarity of peoples"; and when he found that I was less and less interested in such things, he had yet another

* Conway held this on March 17, 1872.

attraction than myself which brought him to us. But he found that she also by no means entered into his opinions, and his visits became fewer. But we always esteemed him. He was a very religious soul. When I first knew him he reverenced Dante chiefly, if not exclusively. When his letters were opened at the post-office here, Mazzini became, for the first time, known to the English people. There was great indignation at an English government taking the side of the Austrian against Italian patriots; and Mazzini was much sought for, invited to dinners, and all that. But he did not want the dinners. He went to but few places. He formed an intimacy with the Ashursts, which did him great good,—gave him a kind of home circle for the rest of his life in England. At last it has come to an end. I went to see him just before he left London for the last time, passed an hour, and came away feeling that I should never see him again. And so it is. . . . Poor Mazzini! After all, he succeeded. He died receiving the homage of the people, and seeing Italy united, with Rome for its capital. Well, one may be glad he has succeeded. We wait to see whether Italy will make anything great out of what she has got. We wait![2]

Another to note the passing of Mazzini was William Allingham, the poet, who recorded the sad event in his diary and visited Carlyle. Like Moncure Conway, he found the Scot very talkative. Among other things, Carlyle said this time:

> Poor Mazzini! lying dead there—all done, all over. What a bright young man when he came in here in 1836 [sic] and sat on that sofa! He got into "solidarity" and all manner of absurdities. He used to trouble himself about every wretched Italian who was in any way political.

And Carlyle told a story of an Italian who fell in love with a *danseuse* and stabbed himself; Mazzini nursed him and persuaded the girl to marry him. As for Mazzini himself, he "was indolent, rose late, and smoked a good many cigars. His mother watched over him and sent him £200 a year, which he never took care of."[3] But there are too many letters of revolutionary import in police files to substantiate any notion of Mazzini's being lazy.

The day after Conway's visit to Carlyle, Swinburne wrote to his mother that he had lost the man whom he had most loved and honoured of all men on earth. Mazzini had always been "as devoted, tender, and unselfish in the details of his life as in its great things," and had "made all things great that touched him by the greatness of his own nature . . ."[4] George Eliot also recalled Mazzini sorrowfully. As she wrote to Mrs. Peter Taylor (March 17, 1872), such a man left behind a wider good than the loss of his personal presence could take away, for in her own words

> The greatest gift the hero leaves his race,
> Is to have been a hero.

She had a sense of wealth in having known him.[5] By way of memoir, as a loving tribute, and as an account of Mazzini's personality and of some of his ideas, David Masson wrote[6] in 1872 a moving essay on the exile who had returned for ever. Also, Charles Edward Mudie included in a poem[7] not without merit a eulogy on Mazzini. Mudie related the story of the Italian's life in London; his friends there; the critics who scoffed at the notion of a united Italy—it was to them only a land of art and poetry, of gentle gifts and graces; his propaganda. Now, said Mudie, his mission was fulfilled; now he was dead and to be wept and to be for ever alive in Italy. Finally, William Lloyd Garrison, the abolitionist, edited (1872) an American reprinting of his friend Mazzini's autobiography.[8]

Her year of mourning over, Mrs. Hamilton King published[9] on December 1, 1873 not the least* of the Mazzinian memorials. Her poem, *The Disciples*, went through many editions in England and in America. Cardinal Manning[10] read it and told her that it was a Catholic book, and that she was a Catholic without knowing it. So one beheld the iron-

* George Saintsbury thought *The Disciples* tedious but respectable.

ical spectacle—the singer of a heretic being won for Rome.* Mazzini had commanded her to write, and in her "Overture" she expressed a deeply religious tribute:

> I write of the Disciples, because He
> Who was their Master, having left on earth
> The memory of a face that none could paint,
> The echo of a voice that none could reach,
> Hath left his own immortal words and works
> To be a witness for him. Who should dare
> To add one line or lesson unto these?
> And in this year of loss, this first blank year
> For us whom he held near and dear to him,
> The heart is far too full to speak of thee,
> Except through speaking of thy faithful ones,
> Joseph Mazzini, Master, first of those
> The Sons of Men who are the Sons of God![11]

She added[12] that she was not proud of anything except this alone:

> That the great orb of that great human soul
> Did once deflect and draw this orb of mine,
> (In the shadow of it, not the sunward side),
> Until it touched and trembled on the line
> By which my orbit crossed the plane of his;
> And heard the music of that glorious sphere
> Resound a moment; and so passed again,
> Vibrating with it, out on its own way;
> Where, intertwined with others, it may yet
> Spin through its manifold mazes of ellipse,
> Amid the clangour of a myriad more,
> Revolving, and the dimness of the depths
> Remotest, through the shadows without shape,
> Arcs of aphelion, silences of snow. . . .

Then she told how the Holy Alliance made him outlaw in all lands except England, how he was always calumniated, and how he revived Italy when none thought her alive. Of all

* She wrote an article on "The Religion of Mazzini" (in the Catholic *Dublin Review*, CLII, January 1913), in which she tried to make the dead patriot acceptable to Catholics.

the martyrs, the most impressively celebrated is Ugo Bassi; but Iacopo Ruffini, Baron Giovanni Nicotera, and Agesilao Milano are also worthily sung. They are the disciples whom Mazzini had sent out to meet the tyrant's worst; yet he, remaining behind, had perhaps experienced greater anguish. Mrs. Hamilton King has Mazzini say as a closing word that he had seen past the agony and had beheld God in Heaven.

Miss Isabella Blagden had a poetic vision[13] of Italy winning freedom without licence and abandoning *feste* for workdays, daggers for ploughs. Hence, she bade Mazzini be hopeful—a rather inopportune exhortation to be made in a volume published as late as 1873. Linda White's novel, *Courtship and a Campaign*, 1873, reveals the singular inability of Mazzinian enthusiasts to realize that Italy was already united. Like Miss Blagden's work, it is a poor performance and of interest only for its echoes of the dead exile.

In 1875, Carlyle declared[14] Mazzini's books well worth reading. Since the old man, now in his eighth decade, had just been conversationally excoriating Garibaldi and may therefore have been in a consistently destructive mood, this was a significant tribute.

Swinburne always cherished the memory of his beloved master. The classical play, *Erechtheus*, composed during 1875, emphasized the Mazzinian idea of the sacrifice of the individual to the general good. As late as 1877, the poet considered his having met Mazzini the very highest privilege and happiness of his whole life. The exile had been to him what Christ Himself must have seemed to His very first disciples. Swinburne even declared that he would very gladly have given Mazzini all the blood of his body and all the power of his heart and mind and soul and spirit.[15] On several occasions, he repeated similar extravagant sentiments.[16]

In 1877, T. A. Trollope, now more kindly to the dead man lying under the Ligurian sky than he had been to the living conspirator, called Mazzini "that ardent patriot, sincere humanitarian, and great organiser."[17] The passing years that made green his grave had also made green his memory.

At this time, war broke out between Russia and Turkey, a circumstance which made opportune the printing of an article* in *The Fortnightly Review* (April 1877) entitled "Mazzini on the Eastern Question." It embodied translations by Emilie Ashurst Venturi of two papers by Mazzini, the first written in 1857, the second in 1871. So, in a moment of international crisis, the counsel of the dead prophet was invoked: he had said (1857) that out of the ruins of the Turkish, Russian, and Austrian domains in Europe new Slavonic nationalities would spring; and he had urged (1871) Italy to seek influence in Egypt and to seize Tunis and Tripoli. His gift of foreseeing the exigencies of militant nationalism can be properly appreciated only to-day.

In an imaginary verse conversation between "Mazzini and the Countess Ossoli," W. J. Linton recalled in 1879 the fellow radical of his youth. He presented the Countess as expostulating with Mazzini for exposing himself in the defence of the Roman Republic against the French. Mazzini is made to say that despite the slanders of some, he has not used terror in Rome; General Oudinot is called a breaker of his word; and England is denounced because it allowed French intervention. The Countess, born Margaret Fuller, consoles him, for he has done his part; thereupon, Mazzini speaks of his Faith of Humanity which he sees triumphant in the future. When he leaves, the Countess, alone, prays for him.[18]

Ernest Myers' long poem, "The Defence of Rome" (1880), is in part a tribute to Mazzini's conduct as dictator of the unfortunate republic. The lines are monotonous and cumbersome in effect, but occasionally achieve a languorous distinction.

In 1881, Arnold Toynbee, the economist, delivered a

* With a foreword by James Stansfeld.

lecture on "Industry and Democracy" to workmen and employers at various industrial towns. When he spoke on the warfare of masters and men, he said that the basis of reconciliation between the claims of employers and employees must come through Mazzini's gospel of duty—a doctrine which had made the Italian the true teacher of the age. The rights of the masses depended on their masters' assumption of duties, not defence of rights.[19] From this, one may conclude that Mazzinian tenets can become a variety of social reformism.

In James Anthony Froude's edition of Carlyle's *Reminiscences*, 1881, there is a very peculiar reference to Mazzini. Carlyle wrote that he had only once or twice talked with Mazzini—a curious understatement. With condescension, the old man said of the dead patriot:

> recognisably a most valiant, faithful, considerably gifted and noble soul, but hopelessly given up to his republicanisms, his "Progress," and other Rousseau fanaticism, for which I had at no time the least credence, or any considerable respect amid my pity.[20]

In Swinburne, however, there is no gnarled depreciation of Mazzini. His poem, "After Nine Years. To Joseph Mazzini" (1881), faithfully compares the honoured dead to Christ in soul; and, as usual, the poet humbles himself before the memory of his master. When a monument was erected in Genoa to its greatest son since Columbus, Swinburne commemorated this event in lines[21] of fervid adoration. It was as if he had trained himself to respond automatically to the mention of Mazzini with the conditioned reflex of verbose praise. Unfortunately, this reaction became with the years tediously habitual.

In the kaleidoscope of the attitudes which the English took towards the *Risorgimento*, the poems of Oscar Wilde form the most confused patterns. In one poem he mourned the pope as the prisoner of the Vatican and called the Italian tricolour a hated banner. But in a longer poem, "Humanitad," also published in 1881, he paid a most extraordinary tribute to Mazzini. "Humanitad" opens with a description of the rigours of winter and is followed by a prophecy of the expected spring. But the poet is not cheerful, nothing delights him, and love is no consolation. Apparently, he would behold a spirit in life blameless and full of actions of high courage, one who mingled love and duty.[22] At this, Wilde recalls Mazzini:

> One such indeed I saw, but, Ichabod!
>   Gone is that last dear son of Italy,
> Who being man died for the sake of God,
>   And whose un-risen bones sleep peacefully,
> O guard him, guard him well, my Giotto's tower,
> Thou marble lily of the lily town! let not the lour
>
> Of the rude tempest vex his slumber, or
>   The Arno with its tawny troubled gold
> O'er-leap its marge, no mightier conqueror
>   Clomb the high Capitol in the days of old
> When Rome was indeed Rome. . . .

Beside him, Freedom walked like a bride, and hence it is fitting that he should be mourned and that his grave be strewn with coronals of that enchanted flower which the dim woods of Vallombrosa hide. Then Wilde predicts Mazzini's apotheosis, in the manner of Shelley's "Adonais" and Milton's "Lycidas":

> He is not dead, the immemorial Fates
>   Forbid it, and the closing shears refrain,
> Lift up your heads ye everlasting gates!
>   Ye argent clarions, sound a loftier strain!

The passionate voice of Mazzini was now nought but silent dust, for the world was in its diurnal course a symbol of the triumph of wrong.[23] There are in this poem two curious things (one must first omit its effect of echoed unoriginality): did not Wilde see any contradiction in his sympathy for the self-made prisoner of the Vatican and his admiration for

F*

Mazzini? was he unaware that the Genoese was not buried in Florence?

In 1882, Genoa invited William Shaen to attend the unveiling of the Mazzini monument. His long reply included a warm tribute to Mazzini. In his old age, Shaen rejoiced at the opportunity of repeating his testimony that Mazzini was "the greatest, the wisest, and the best man" he had ever known; and he declared that he owed more to him than to any other teacher.[24]

It has usually been maintained that Thomas Purnell introduced Swinburne to Mazzini. But Aurelio Saffi's article in *La Patria* entitled "*Nota su A. C. Swinburne*" (1884) asserted that he had acquainted the poet with Mazzini: "*Conobbe per mio mezzo il Mazzini. . . .*"[25] The University of Edinburgh had in 1884 given Saffi the honorary degree of LL.D.; and on this occasion, he visited Swinburne at Putney on his way back from Edinburgh.[26] It could be that Saffi, who had taught Swinburne Italian at Oxford, was the one who had brought the Englishman and Mazzini together (perhaps in 1858), but the whole question is rather doubtful and probably can never be definitely settled.

In any case, as Swinburne's play, *Marino Faliero*, shows, Mazzini was not forgotten. Doge Marino Faliero conspires to right his own wrongs. But in prison, self-reasoning, he sees why he, led by private motives, is unfit to be the leader of a people toward liberty. In his last long speech, he prophesies the ideal leader who is to come, and thus is Mazzini anticipated:

> . . . I
> Have erred, who thought by wrong to vanquish wrong,
> To smite by violence violence, and by night
> Put out the power of darkness: time shall bring
> A better way than mine, if God's will be—
> As how should God's will be not?—to redeem
> Venice. I was not worthy—nor may man
> Till one as Christ shall come again, be found
> Worthy to think, speak, strike, foresee, foretell,

The thought, the word, the stroke, the dawn, the day,
That verily and indeed shall bid the dead
Live, and this old dear land of all men's love
Arise and shine for ever. . . .[27]

In the dedicatory verses of *Marino Faliero*, Swinburne said[28] of Mazzini that he fed the faith of the Italians because his spirit was stronger than fate; and the poet hoped for a republic in Italy and one for England too. Even in 1885, the thought of Mazzini had power to evoke the old reactions and the old watchwords.

When Ruskin was writing the first volume of his *Praeterita* during 1885 and 1886, he was proud to record[29] Mazzini's opinion* of him, given a year or so before the Italian's death, to the effect that Ruskin had "the most analytic mind in Europe." On the other hand, Lord Acton, the historian, thought[30] (1885) George Eliot's tolerance for Mazzini a criminal matter. There is also a third view, for William Morris's "The Pilgrims of Hope" (1885–86) has a vivid picture of the sort of meeting which the poet used to address for the socialist cause:

Dull and dirty the room. Just over the chairman's chair
Was a bust, a Quaker's face with nose cocked up in the air;
There were common prints on the wall of the heads of the
party fray,
And Mazzini dark and lean amidst them gone astray,
Some thirty men we were of a kind that I knew full well,
Listless, rubbed down to the type of our easy-going hell.[31]

Nevertheless, one can maintain that the democrat in Mazzini did belong here.

It is a very human thing for anybody to wish that those

* In 1857, Mazzini said that Ruskin was the best critic in Europe (at that time the Englishman had uttered some complimentary things about the exile!). But four years later, Mazzini declined to meet Ruskin on the ground that he was too busy. Nevertheless, the whole truth is that the conspirator was a great reader of Ruskin, for both believed in the moral purpose of art. See the *Edizione nazionale degli scritti di Giuseppe Mazzini*, LVIII, 143–44, and LXXI, 115.

whom he likes and admires should take to one another. When, in 1886, Swinburne wrote his *Study of Victor Hugo*, he wondered[32] why it was that Mazzini should have preferred "the pinch-beck and tinsel of Byron to the gold and ivory of Hugo"—that is, why one of his idols had not highly regarded the other. But both had hated Napoleon III—and that was a good thing, a real sign of solidarity. In 1887, Swinburne interpreted Mazzini's teachings to justify his own opposition to Irish separatism. His letters to the press show how he maintained that Mazzini, as a maker of Italian unity, would have upheld Irish union with Great Britain.[33] After all, Mazzini's dislike of Hugo was not reprehensible; Swinburne's misreading of the spirit of his master's tenets was.*

As the years after his death grow in number, literary references to Mazzini are fewer. *For Freedom*, by Tighe Hopkins, only indirectly alludes to the dead conspirator. One character in this tale (1888) of Garibaldi's Thousand is presented as distributing handbills of revolutionary doctrine in choice Mazzinian Italian. When Swinburne in 1890 recalled[34] the memory of Aurelio Saffi, he made sure to point out that his former teacher had stood beside Mazzini in the days of the Roman Republic. This fact is the basis of his lovely tribute to Saffi, praise, however, marred by a certain hysterical ranting. In 1891, John Morley[35] had after dinner a long talk with Gladstone about Mazzini. The old statesman did not think too highly of the Italian, but Morley stood up for him as one of the most morally impressive men he had ever known or that his age had known: he had breathed a soul into democracy. As late as 1903, Swinburne recalled Mazzini with the greatest admiration. Of a certain A——, he wrote[36] that he had known one other human being who always seemed to him naturally above all others "in perfect beauty and selfless nobility of character and temper and instinct." That man was Mazzini, whom in the following

* It is significant that Mazzini's friend in every need, James Stansfeld, favoured Irish Home Rule and spoke strongly for it.

year he saluted[37] as his friend and master and whose faith in republicanism he repeated in the terminology of a countenancer of dictators. But then, Swinburne was akin to these in his habitual exuberance of verbosity and had like them no mind for systematized beliefs. In the "Memorial Verses on the Death of Karl Blind" (1907), he mourned the German exile as being responsible (in part) for the meeting with Mazzini. One feels, despite this recurrent obituary adulation of Mazzini, that Swinburne never understood his Master's doctrine. Perhaps it was that Mazzini was a very confused thinker to begin with, and entirely capable of being the source of misreadings.

Of great interest is W. Hale White's* novel, *Clara Hopgood* (1896). Marshall, a Chartist, accompanied by Clara Hopgood, visits Mazzini (*c.* 1845). The exile lives in a dull, dark, little house in a shabby street of small shops and furnished apartments. White vividly describes him as

> a man, really about forty, but looking older. He had dark hair growing away from his forehead, dark moustache, dark beard and a singularly serious face. It was not the face of a conspirator, but that of a saint, although without that just perceptible touch of silliness which spoils the faces of most saints. It was the face of a saint of the Reason, of a man who could be ecstatic for rational ideals, rarest of all endowments. It was the face, too, of one who knew no fear, or, if he knew it, could crush it. He was once concealed by a poor woman whose house was surrounded by Austrian soldiers watching for him. He was determined that she should not be sacrificed, and, having disguised himself a little, walked out into the street in broad daylight, went up to the Austrian sentry, asked for a light for his cigar and escaped.[38]

To his two visitors, Mazzini preaches his doctrine of duty, as opposed to rights. When Clara Hopgood offers to help him, immediately he accepts her for the cause, as in life he had enlisted Emilie Venturi and Jessie White Mario. By having

* "Mark Rutherford."

Mazzini unhesitatingly avail himself of volunteers, White proves himself an accurate novelist. Indeed, Clara Hopgood dies for Italian freedom. Though White's story is unostentatious, it is very well written and exceedingly interesting for its own merits and because it is an example of the novel used as a forum for ideas and for discussion, neither in any way conventional.

Mrs. Voynich's novel (1897), *The Gadfly*, also has glimpses of Mazzini in his doctrines. The English hero, brought up in Italy, is exposed to the catchwords and the propaganda of *Young Italy* and is arrested as an initiate. Written with terrific bitterness against the Roman Catholic Church, this story of the Mazzinian party in Italy (1833–47) reveals exactly how Mazzini's teachings were popularized among young Italians. Unlike *The Gadfly*, George Alfred Henty's book for boys, *Out with Garibaldi* (1900), was unsympathetic with Mazzini, whom it described as a fanatical, cowardly agitator, the revolutionary scum that rises to the top.

On the other hand, George Meredith's noble poem, "The Centenary of Garibaldi," 1907, joined together the makers of Italy, those leaders

> Who blew the breath of life into her frame:
> Cavour, Mazzini, Garibaldi: Three:
> Her Brain, her Soul, her Sword; and set her free
> From ruinous discords, with one lustrous aim.

Mazzini appears in M. Hartley's *Beyond Man's Strength*, 1909, where he fascinates the hero, who meets him in London. This novel is notable for the successful creation of atmosphere, for the able presentment of a changing society, and for the sympathetic treatment of Mazzini's character. Warwick Deeping's lively novel, *The Lame Englishman*, 1910, pictures Mazzini as *tall* and noble-looking and tells how Mazzini and Garibaldi quarrelled in regard to the defence of the Roman Republic. In part, the plot revolves about the foiling of a villain who plans to murder Mazzini. Mrs. Voynich's *An Interrupted Friendship*, 1910, affords a glimpse of Mazzini.

Although she does indicate that he is a fanatical and incurable plotter, she pays tribute to the charm of his conversation. However, her novel leaves with the reader a vivid impression of his ruthlessness whenever a question of attaining his aims was concerned, his unhesitating use and sacrifice of followers, and his tireless encouragement of revolts to demonstrate that Italy was alive.

Joseph Mazzini did perhaps more than any other man to arouse the sympathy of the British for Italy in her struggles for unity. Moreover, he left such a permanent impress on English letters by the strength of his personality that literary men frequently made him their theme and repeated his doctrines. Since he stressed the moral as taking precedence over the scientific, it is possible that mankind, in need of guidance, will turn with greater confidence to other nineteenth-century thinkers. None the less, Mazzini, the exile who helped undermine tyranny and who helped solve in part the ethnic puzzle of the Hapsburg domains, had also served. Indeed, the structure of present-day Europe, in respect to the principle of nationality, is more according to his ideas than to those of any of his contemporaries.[39]

PART II

"Italy in England"

CHAPTER IX

The First Generation of Italian Exiles in Great Britain: Foscolo, Rossetti, Panizzi

THE biographies of many of the more outstanding Italians who belong to the first generation of the liberal political emigration have been adequately recorded by other authors. Nevertheless, it is proper to write selectively about a few whose careers illuminate aspects of English intellectual and literary relationships.

§ 1. Ugo Foscolo is the classic example of the Italian refugee heralded by a great literary reputation. In a genuine sense, he inaugurated in the nineteenth century a tradition of exile (which was perhaps more nobly to be maintained by certain of his fellow nationalists). He was also the first important Italian to lay the foundations of the new cultural relations between England and the fatherland.[1]

Influenced like many other men of the *Risorgimento* by the nationalism of Vittorio Alfieri,[2] Foscolo was, unlike one of these, Vincenzo Monti, a *consistent* Italian patriot. Under the spell of the French Revolution, he had in ringing verse[3] hailed Napoleon as the advent of freedom herself. But in the end, he became disillusioned, for the Corsican by the treaty of Campo Formio, October 17, 1797, gave Venice to Austria. Foscolo expressed his dejection in a famous work, *Iacopo Ortis*. When the hero of the same name destroys himself, it is the phantom of an expiring country which places the dagger in his hand. Grief for his unfortunate fatherland is as much responsible for Ortis's suicide as the melancholia of literary Wertherism, deepened in Foscolo's case by the fact that one of his favourite teachers, the Abbé Cesarotti, had cherished the lachrymose Ossianic muse.

Napoleon's star of destiny flared like a nova and then grew obscure, and the Austrians became the dominant influence in Italy. Foscolo in Milan refused to wear their uniform, and had to flee from the Hapsburg displeasure. Despite worry about English alien laws, he settled in London in September 1816, the forerunner of many another Italian in considering the British capital the only safe refuge.

Here was no unknown, this exile to whom the doors of London society were immediately opened. As early as 1810, William Stewart Rose, who in Foscolo's behalf prevented difficulties with the Alien Office, had corresponded with him.[4] Probably, Rose's article in the December 1812 issue of *The Quarterly Review* encouraged two years later a translation* of *Iacopo Ortis*. Of this English version a second edition was printed in 1818. Moreover, Rose dedicated† his unsigned rendering (1816) of Casti's *The Court of Beasts* to Foscolo in appreciation of the exile's translation of Sterne's *Sentimental Journey*. Foscolo was, said Rose, "*doctum sermones utriusque linguae*." The 1819 edition of Rose's translation also pays tribute to Foscolo's merits. It is significant that Casti's satire, *Gli Animali parlanti*, 1802, deals with the civil revolutions that took place in the animal kingdom at some time prior to the deluge, and that its darts are good-naturedly aimed at tyrants, conquerors, and cheats.

From the very beginning of his English life, Foscolo was a fashionable character, well known at Holland House, the great Whig centre. Lord John Russell,[5] to whom he later dedicated the play, *Ricciarda*, was his patron; and the

* John Murray published an edition in the original Italian in 1817. The dedication is to Samuel Rogers.

† Since Foscolo, when he lived in Zürich, had dedicated to Rose a Latin satire, this was also a repayment of literary courtesy.

Hollands* and the Dacres† also gave him aid. To Lord Holland, Foscolo was indebted for introductions to Longman and to John Murray, the publishers. Others who encouraged Foscolo were William Roscoe,[6] Liverpool banker and historian of Lorenzo the Magnificent, and John Cam Hobhouse, the friend of Byron. It was Foscolo who gave Hobhouse both the materials and the critical judgments on the six greatest Italian poets of the time, Cesarotti, Alfieri, Parini, Pindemonte, Monti, and himself, which constitute the long "Essay on the Present Literature of Italy"[7] (1818). Haydon (the painter), Thomas Campbell, Henry Hart Milman, Lady Morgan, Tom Moore, John Bowring, Samuel Rogers, Fanny Burney, Thomas Grenville, the Duke of Bedford, the Marquess of Lansdowne, John Hookham Frere, Lord Brougham, Francis Jeffrey, and Henry Hallam, were among the notables who knew the exile, in most cases as a result of his attendance at Holland House. In addition, Byron‡ mentioned Foscolo as an Italian literary man of note in the introduction to the fourth canto of *Childe Harold's Pilgrimage* (1818).

Between 1818 and 1827, Foscolo was really an English man of letters and, as such, is said to have published about twenty-four literary and historical articles in seven different magazines:[8] the *Edinburgh*, *European*, *Quarterly*,§ *Retrospective*, and *Westminster* reviews; and the *London* and *New Monthly*

* Eventually, Foscolo ceased to visit Holland House because he disliked Lady Holland. Cyrus Redding (*Fifty Years' Recollections* . . ., II, 191–92) quotes this by Foscolo: "I would not go to heaven with Lady Holland—I could go to hell with his lordship."

† Foscolo's *Essays on Petrarch* included translations by Lady Dacre from the latter poet.

‡ Some years later, Byron and Foscolo were on bad terms because the Italian, as a friend of John Murray, advised the publisher not to accept manuscripts likely to hurt his business. Foscolo meant, of course, Byron's writings. See *Fraser's Magazine*, XXXI, 412 (April 1845).

§ Foscolo once complained to Lady Dacre about John Murray's severity in editing a *Quarterly Review* article on Petrarch. See Foscolo's *Opere edite e postume*, VIII, 31.

magazines. That is to say, he had obtained access to some of the leading British periodicals of the day, in which he commented on Dante, Guido Cavalcanti, Tasso, Petrarch, Guicciardini, Michelangelo, foreign politics, translations from the Italian, works in Italian and in French, and on other matters such as Frere's *Prospectus and Specimen of an Intended National Work, by William and Robert Whistlecraft. . . .*[9] Since Frere imitated the manner of the Italian verse satirists, it was natural for Foscolo to receive the assignment for a review (1819). In regard to these critical articles, it is known[10] that more than one eminent British man of letters, *e.g.*, Jeffrey, revised Foscolo's English* or translated his Italian or French. Yet he was well versed in English literature. For example, when he reviewed Cary's translation of Dante (in *The Edinburgh Review*, February 1818), he displayed a close knowledge† of Shakespeare, Milton, Cowper, Pope, and others, to whom he referred by way of illustration of a particular idea. In other magazine essays, Foscolo revealed his staunch Italian patriotism: an instance is the article on Pius VI (*The Edinburgh Review*, March 1819). Nevertheless, only a year later, he lamented that "Italy [was] a corpse without hope of resurrection."[11]

When General Guglielmo Pepe came to England in 1821 in consequence of the unsuccessful Neapolitan rising, it was Foscolo who introduced[12] him to the poet, Thomas Campbell. A few years later, Foscolo gave assistance to Panizzi, the future librarian of the British Museum. Quite naturally, one exile made things smoother for the next.

Undoubtedly, Foscolo was at one time held in high esteem by the contemporary English. *The Quarterly Review*[13] praised his *Ricciarda* most effusively and called him a scholar in the

* Yet he could compose an ode in English as the graceful "To Callirhoe" (Caroline Russell) shows.

† Towards the end of 1817, John Murray wanted Foscolo to write a series of letters on English and Italian literature, customs, and political history. The whole was to be published in three volumes.

highest sense of the word. A poem on fallen Italy, entitled "To Ugo Foscolo," appeared in an English magazine[14] in 1821, its author having been influenced by the recent Neapolitan fiasco and by Foscolo's *I Sepolcri.* Thanks to the good offices of Lady Dacre among others, he lectured[15] in 1823 in *Italian,* to *English* audiences, on Italian literature and actually earned at least £700.

But on the whole, the infirmities of Foscolo's character created a bad impression and injured the cause of the Italian victim of depotism among the powerful Whig group of Holland House habitués. He had once described himself with a sorrowful and prophetic accuracy:

> A furrowed brow, intent and deep-sunk eyes,
> Fair hair, lean cheeks, and mind and aspect bold;
> The proud quick lip where seldom smiles arise,
> Bent head, and well-formed neck, breast rough and cold,
> Limbs well composed; simple in dress yet choice,
> Swift or to move, act, think, or thought unfold.
> Temperate, firm, kind, unused to flattering lies,
> Adverse to the world, adverse to me of old;
> Ofttimes alone and mournful: evermore
> Most pensive, all unmoved by hope or fear,
> By shame made timid, and by anger brave,
> My subtle reason speaks: but ah! I rave—
> 'Twixt vice and virtue, hardly know to steer—
> Death may for me have fame and rest in store![16]

This sonnet gives the clue to his difficulties. The shame which he experienced was due to his dread of being thought poor, for he believed that the English treated poverty and guilt alike; and therefore he played as long as he could the man of means.* The extravagant establishment which he maintained at Digamma Cottage (named after the title of one† of his erudite articles) with the ambiguous aid of a staff of

* Had he been content to live within his literary income, he would have lived rather well.

† "History of the Aeolic Digamma," *The Quarterly Review,* XXVII, 39–70.

three young maid-servants, the notorious "Three Graces," was too much for his resources. After all, the British periodicals to which he had access were not unfailing cornucopias even though at one time they had kept him so busy that he had called himself a beast of burden for Gifford and Murray. Editors were, to a man of Foscolo's temperament, an irritating lot; and he had fondly thought of freeing himself from their control by founding his own review, devoid of politics and concerned with subjects of general European interest.

He that is under the pressure of debts is also an easy victim of his own raging temper. That is why Sir Walter Scott* could record in his journal in 1825 an entry like this:

> Talking of strangers, London held, some four or five years since, one of those animals who are lions at first, but by transmutation of two seasons become in regular course Boars!—Ugo Foscolo by name, a haunter of Murray's shop and of literary parties. Ugly as a baboon, and intolerably conceited, he spluttered, blustered, and disputed, without even knowing the principles upon which men of sense render a reason, and screamed all the while like a pig when they cut its throat.[17]

Similarly, Cyrus Redding said that Foscolo looked like a monkey, and testified to his quarrelsomeness, which, on one occasion, led him to bring a court action, based on nothing but bad temper, against the Englishman. What annoyed Redding was Foscolo's habit of arguing even when he was in the wrong and knew it. Nevertheless, anybody who has examined Redding's memoirs will notice how much he respected Foscolo's talents, although he regretted the exile's loud-lunged, passionate, and overbearing manner in disputes, almost always of a trivial origin.[18] Perhaps the

* Scott in his *Life of Napoleon* had expressed the hope that Italy might before long achieve national unity. That is to say, Foscolo's manners, not his politics, had irritated the great romantic novelist. See Crane Brinton's *The Political Ideas of the English Romanticists*, London, 1926, p. 112.

following anecdote will best illustrate the pettiness of Foscolo's tantrums. In 1823, he wished his friend, the actor Macready, to deliver a challenge for him to his careless amanuensis and translator, Graham.[19]

In the end, disaster overtook Foscolo: his house was sold at auction; he was imprisoned for debt; and he died miserably in London in September 1827. He had left unfinished a critical anthology of Italian poetry in English versions. A month later, both Panizzi[20] and *The London Magazine*[21] paid him tribute in obituary memoirs. When *Blackwood's Edinburgh Magazine* (November 1827) tardily commented on *Ricciarda* with an air of beneficent malice, the reviewer testified to Foscolo's talents and honest patriotism but damned him as "prodigiously overrated." However, in 1828, Panizzi[22] praised Foscolo as a great critic of Dante; and *The Foreign Review*, later in the same year, was equally favourable and printed translated excerpts from his poetry.[23]

As Matthew Arnold's lyric (1852), "To Marguerite, in Returning a Volume of the Letters of Ortis," indicates, some English people continued to read Foscolo. *Fraser's Magazine* (April 1845) printed his biography, and Gallenga's *Present State and Prospects of Italy* (1848) contained a chapter on the dead exile's poetry. A long critical article[24] in *The Westminster Review* (1859), including translations from his work, kept his memory green. It may be added that the *Review* had thus atoned for its bitter attack on Foscolo in April 1851, when it had pronounced him "a base idol" and without either character or sincerity. In 1860, the year memorable because of Garibaldi's exploits, that remarkable little volume of poetry, a symphony on country and death, which Foscolo had called *I Sepolcri** was translated into English. In it, there

* *Cf.* the graveyard poetry of melancholy eighteenth-century English bards. But Foscolo's poem differs in tone and quality, for it does not immerse itself in tearful sentimentality and is animated by a dynamic irony.

are bitter lines on the decadence of the Italians as he knew them in 1807:

> Already are the learned, and the rich,
> And the patrician mob, the ornament
> And soul of the divine Italian realm!—
> Already are they, living, sepulchred
> Within their incense-breathing palaces,
> And their escutcheons are their only praise.

Foscolo invoked the *manes* of the mighty dead who lie in the Santa Croce in Florence, the Italian Westminster Abbey, to revive his countrymen:

> "When the dim hope
> Of freedom breaks on Italy once more,
> And on her great in soul, hence* shall we draw
> Our auspices."

In 1871, Foscolo's body was brought back to Florence and interred in the Santa Croce. He was now one of the mighty dead, of those great in soul, to whom the Italians were to turn for inspiration and hope.

On English literature Foscolo did leave a permanent impress, for, perhaps more than anybody else, he had aroused an interest in Dante and had promoted British studies of the great medieval poet. In his own right, he had been, of the Italian poets of his generation, second only to Leopardi. Above all, one may regard Foscolo as an important figure in the history of the criticism of comparative literature.

§ 2. Gabriele Rossetti is too often considered only as the father of three extraordinary children, but he deserves to be remembered in his own right. At the beginning, he was a poet of such skill as to tempt a certain Boccanera, in poetical envy and not as an act of kindness to the Muses, to hire a bravo for his assassination. Eventually, his growing reputation as an *improvvisatore*† won for him, about 1807, the post

* The Santa Croce church.

† He is said to have had a beautiful tenor voice.

of librettist to the San Carlo at Naples. Under Murat, he was for several months Secretary of Instruction and Fine Arts;[25] and for many years, he was employed as a sub-curator of the department of ancient marbles and bronzes in the Bourbonic Museum,* where he once discussed archaeological discoveries with Shelley.[26] The turning point of his career came when he, long a Freemason, devoted his poetry to the Carbonari and to the kind of political liberalism which they represented. More exactly, he adhered to the movement for securing a constitution for the Kingdom of the Two Sicilies. When Ferdinand I succumbed to the pressure of his subjects and graciously accorded them the coveted document, Gabriele Rossetti hailed the dawn of the constitution day, July 21, 1820, in his finest ode, "*Sei pur bella cogli astri sul crine*" ("Lovely indeed art thou with stars in hair"). In addition, he wrote other patriotic verses and also, at the very least, about sixty political manifestos.

On March 23, 1821, Ferdinand I returned from the Congress of Laibach at the head of an Austrian army, and inaugurated a treacherous reaction. He withdrew the constitution and instituted a systematic persecution of liberals. Since Rossetti had been prominent, it was his fate to be proscribed. For three months from March 1821, he was compelled to hide from the political police, whose present zeal for capturing him was a match for his former enthusiasm as a Carbonaro. On April 10, 1821, the Neapolitan government issued a decree of exile for Rossetti, a pronouncement which, if rightly interpreted, merely signified that he had not been caught. He never was. Fortunately for English letters, he escaped to Malta with the assistance of Admiral Sir Graham Moore, brother of Sir John Moore and chief of the Mediterranean fleet. Moore disguised him in the carlet regimentals of an English naval lieutenant and muggled him aboard the flagship *Rochfort*, which in gratitude

* Rossetti was suited to these posts, for he could draw rather well and had a scholarly disposition.

he later recalled as a wooden Albion. The Admiral had been moved to intercede for him by Lady Moore, an admirer of his poetry.

At Malta, Rossetti made friends with John Hookham Frere, the Anti-Jacobin poet. That a mild Italian revolutionary and a British Tory should take to each other was perhaps unusual but destined to become less and less uncommon. Frere helped Rossetti in a practical way, with monetary support; and the Italian never forgot his admiration for the Englishman's good heart. It was to Frere that he later dedicated his commentary on Dante.

On the island, Rossetti passed his time occasionally in extraordinary feats of improvisation and more regularly in giving Latin and Italian lessons. One event in 1822 cast a cloud over his life at Malta. On September 28th, King Ferdinand amnestied all except thirteen men, expressly named. Gabriele Rossetti was the thirteenth. Also about this time, Castlereagh ordered the expulsion of the refugees who had come to Malta, but Rossetti lingered on through English influence. When the reactionary politician committed suicide, Rossetti, a good hater, wrote:

> O Castlereagh! Thy country rightly deems
> That thy best service was thy suicide;
> But why no suicide a year before?[27]

In January 1824 Gabriele Rossetti, at Frere's suggestion and armed with letters of introduction, left Malta for England. The English ship on which he sailed anchored at Naples, where Ferdinand I demanded of Admiral Moore that Rossetti be surrendered. During the two weeks the ship lay in port, the King, his anger boiling at having been refused, assigned spies to watch near the pier. Perhaps Rossetti might be kidnapped. It was a vain hope, for on April 7, 1824 Gabriele Rossetti arrived in London and took lodgings at 37, Gerard Street, Soho.

Early in May, Lord Holland dined Rossetti at Holland

House; and Thomas Campbell not only helped him find work but also offered to introduce him to Samuel Rogers. The exile, quick to express his deep-felt gratitude, described Campbell as "the most courteous of the tuneful family." Life was not solitary, for now and then Pepe or some other compatriot would pay a welcome visit. At the moment when it was most needed, Frere had a happy way of sending Rossetti £50 or so. Frere too gave him access to Coleridge, who became angry at the tyranny of the Neapolitan government. In turn, Coleridge brought Rossetti and the Reverend Henry Francis Cary, the translator of Dante, together. Through friends like these, Rossetti found employment as an Italian coach and by the middle of 1824 had fifteen pupils.[28]

At the end of 1825, Rossetti published a work which was the fruit of long years of thought: *La Divina Commedia di Dante Alighieri con Comento Analitico*. The Freres subscribed to it, and also such men as Isaac D'Israeli, Henry Hallam, Francis Palgrave, Samuel Rogers, Lord John Russell, and Sir Walter Scott. A second volume appeared in 1827. Cary read Rossetti's *Comento* and now became the exile's friend, no longer merely an acquaintance. Gabriele Rossetti had made Dante the exclusive object of his studies, which were the expressions of a unique point of view. Wholehearted Carbonaro that he was, he passed his life in researches which sought in Dante's works proofs of that great poet's sympathy with the tenets of the Carbonari and found in them indications that Dante was a member of an occult society, similar to Freemasonry, characterized by humanitarian and secular aims, and united against political and ecclesiastical tyranny. One cannot dismiss these opinions on Dante, impossible, contradictory, and inaccurate as they often are, without pronouncing Rossetti a subtle and original, although eccentric, commentator. It is evident that he reasoned in a confused fashion and was blinded by personal considerations. He was a Freemason and Carbonaro, had been accustomed to the use of secret code languages, and had been exiled from his native land; Dante too had been exiled—by the machinations of a pope. Might not Dante have been a member of a secret society opposed to Guelphism and a supporter of Ghibellinism? Might not Dante have used a secret language? Hence Rossetti's interpretation of Dante as a political conspirator hiding behind allegory in his *Divine Comedy*; hence Rossetti's assurance of the political, and not the theological, meaning of the poem. In a word, *The Divine Comedy* described Guelphs against Ghibellines, not good and evil in conflict.[29] It may be added that Rossetti believed that the Ghibellines were the party to unite Italy.

In 1826, Gabriele Rossetti married Frances Mary Lavinia Polidori, daughter of an Englishwoman and Alfieri's secretary, Gaetano Polidri. Her brother was Byron's physician. Of the offspring of this marriage, one need list only the names to realize that this was an extraordinary family: Dante Gabriel, William Michael, and Christina. To maintain his growing family, Rossetti continued to give lessons in Italian, earning half a guinea an hour from private families and teaching sometimes forty-five lessons a week.[30] He applied for the Professorship of Italian Literature at University College, London, in 1828 but saw the post go to Antonio Panizzi, a fellow exile, whom he for ever after detested as a diabolically clever enemy. The truth is that Rossetti, even though Admiral and Lady Moore tried to use their influence in his behalf with Thomas Campbell and Lord Holland, had had very little chance, for Campbell preferred Foscolo to him and thought Foscolo a much abler man. In the end, it was Brougham who tipped the scales in Panizzi's favour[31]—Brougham and the death of poor Foscolo. Anonymously in October 1828 the successful candidate reviewed Rossetti's *Comento* in *The Foreign Review* and among other things said that he was resolved to show no mercy, "for he deserves none." He attacked Rossetti as having turned Dante into a poet of double meanings, depreciated his erudition, deplored the new interpretations and new allegories alleged by Rossetti, and scorned him for having transformed Dante into a Freemason. In its way, this review was an example of the *slashing* periodical style at its cruelest. Two years later, Rossetti learned the identity of his ruthless critic.

The Foreign Quarterly Review, February 1830, was friendlier towards Rossetti's commentary on Dante. It is true it rejected some of his views, but it appreciated his indefatigable spirit of research. At any rate, he was by now a fairly well-known man; and when he applied in 1831 for the professorship of Italian in King's College, London, he was accepted—an anti-papist was *persona grata* in those days to a Church of England enterprise. Interestingly enough, this time *he* had been selected in spite of the rival claims of Antonio Gallenga, who had been backed by Bulwer-Lytton, Disraeli, Carlyle, and Dickens.[32] The post yielded Rossetti no great income, for the most he ever made out of it was £10 a year, derived from a proportion of students' fees. But, for that matter, Panizzi at University College did not do much better. Nevertheless, Rossetti's connection with an institution of higher learning was a good thing, for it gave him professional status and was helpful, as a guarantee of respectability, in his private tutoring, now yielding him an average income of £220 to £280 a year.[33]

Meanwhile, besides adapting Byron's "Corsair" for operatic purposes, he busied himself in his Dante researches and produced in 1832 the Italian version* of his *Disquisitions on the Anti-Papal Spirit* . . ., in which he *directly* applied Masonic interpretations to Dante. This he had not done in his earlier study. *The Athenaeum* gave his new opus a very long review;[34] and though there was no agreement expressed with his conclusions, there was an acknowledgment of the merits of the work. He had repeated his notions of Dante as a kind of Freemason and had added the belief that Dante was not

* An English translation appeared in 1834.

only anti-papist but also anti-christian.[35] Incidentally Rossetti had included a very interesting biographical passage:[36]

> Was it ever reckoned a crime in the oppressed to pant for freedom? Yes; and even now it is a trespass which obliges an Italian to seek refuge in the land of the stranger. Thus was it with me. A new covenant had been made and ratified between the altar and the throne, by which every citizen was granted full liberty of speech; and I, in our short-lived hours of triumph, sang the wishes and hopes of Italy in verses which were echoed far and near by many a gladsome voice. My reward was—exile; and each revolving year speaks to me in language which will be heard, that there is no pardon for my crime.

Rossetti compared his own banishment to Dante's and pointed out that he, unlike Dante, had had no trial. So much for himself. He said that those who reproached Italy for her weakness were as unjust as the man who saw a gladiator taken in the toils and hewn to pieces with brutal violence, and who then coldly gazed on the quivering limbs and descanted on their feebleness. Thus, even in a scholarly treatise, he could not restrain the self-pity of the exile or the ardour of the patriot.

On December 22, 1832, Cyrus Redding sent a long letter to the editor of *The Athenaeum* on the subject of Rossetti's *Disquisitions*. Redding admitted Rossetti's great learning, was indeed very respectful in tone, but described his Dante theories as useless. In general, *The Athenaeum* treated Rossetti with the utmost courtesy. When it condemned, it never flogged in the manner of a Lockhart or a Gifford. In August, 1833, it published a review of a volume[37] of Italian political and religious poetry by Rossetti, which it characterized as having "lyrical sweetness." Of greater significance to this study, the *Athenaeum* writer deplored the tyranny which exiled men like Rossetti.

In contrast to Panizzi, Arthur Henry Hallam reviewed[38] very mildly Rossetti's Dante theories. He granted Rossetti's ingenuity but denied his correctness until such time as the professor adduced more proofs. On the other hand, A. W. Schlegel[39] disputed Rossetti's views much more vigorously than Hallam had. Indeed, he termed the idea that Dante was a member of a secret society a chimera. One may categorically say that no writer of any note accepted Rossetti's opinions; even his children were sceptical, and Charles Lyell,* who assisted him financially in publishing, thought he had gone too far in his point of view.

Apart from the great Dante controversy and his inclination to treat all literature, including Chaucer, Spenser, and Milton, in terms of Masonic symbolism,[40] Gabriele Rossetti led a very quiet life. Sometimes from Switzerland, sometimes from London, he published verse for which he was known in Italy, and maintained his contacts with liberalism through the visits of Italian† exiles, politicians, literary men, musicians, and others. Some of these had been fellow members of the Carbonari. His children, listening to their excited talk about Continental politics, were affected in various ways. Christina had no interest in politics, but her brother, William Michael, doubted whether she ever regarded an Austrian quite on the same footing as men of other races. Dante Gabriel eventually grew very tired of the whole subject of Italian wrongs and seldon referred to them. Indeed, William Michael Rossetti said that it was more than probable that the perpetual excited and one-sided talk about Louis Philippe and other political matters had something to do with the marked alienation from current politics which characterized his brother in his adolescent and adult years. On the other hand, William Michael himself, as the stone on his grave (in Highgate Cemetery in London) testifies, died happy at having witnessed the fact of Italian unity.

* Father of the geologist. When he died in 1849, he left the older Rossetti £50 and Dante Gabriel Rossetti £10.

† There were also exiles of other nationalities whom Rossetti knew. For example, after 1831, he was acquainted with Louis Napoleon, then in London. See E. R. Vincent's *Gabriele Rossetti in England*, p. 44.

So old Gabriele lived with his children, attracted the sympathetic notice* of an occasional English writer, and observed the passing Italian scene. He entertained respect for Mazzini, who endeavoured in 1841 to enrol him in *Young Italy* and to enlist his pen in the service of its programme. For economic reasons, Rossetti avoided all embarrassing political† connections like this, since they might have caused him to lose his pupils and hence have endangered the welfare of his family. Moreover, he was a constitutional monarchist, not a republican, and would have been satisfied with seeing a unified country under an Italian *king*. Indeed, he would have willingly returned to Naples under the *Bourbon* if King Ferdinand had invited him. When Pope Pius IX seemed anxious to introduce reforms, Rossetti hailed him with enthusiasm. But when the Pope altered his policy, the exile, who had always been a freethinker and, in England, a hater of Puseyism, became again anti-papist and anti-sacerdotal. Of the Pope, he wrote with bitter disappointment: "I hate as once I loved thee—Man of Fraud." Naturally, he favoured abolishing the secular power of Rome.

Among the visitors who sought the Rossetti home were Paganini, the violinist; Count Giuseppe Ricciardi, the revolutionary republican; Count Carlo Pepoli; and General Guglielmo Pepe. There came also as a visitor the former priest, Giuseppe Maria Campanella, who on one occasion

* As in Mrs. Gordon Smythies's anonymous novel, *Fitzherbert: or, Lovers and Fortune-Hunters*, London, 1838. *The Athenaeum*, May 19, 1838, p. 358, was not enthusiastic about this Victorian three-decker because of the surfeit of lovers and fortune-hunters!

† But Gabriele Rossetti used to grace the programme whenever Mazzini's free school for Italians in London celebrated an anniversary. On one such occasion, Mrs. Carlyle thought it amusing when Rossetti read (November 10, 1842) a *prepared* improvisation! See her *Letters to Her Family, 1839–1863*, ed. Leonard Huxley, London, 1924, pp. 51–52. Early in 1848, having resigned his university post a year before, Rossetti was serving as a vice-president of the Italian National Association at London, a Mazzinian body. See the *Edizione nazionale degli scritti di Giuseppe Mazzini*, XXXV, 51.

obtained from Rossetti a sonnet in praise of the liberal Pius IX in order to circulate it in Naples. In Italy, one must remember, Rossetti had a high reputation as a patriotic poet; and his songs were sung there up to and even including the year 1848. When Holman Hunt[41] visited (about 1848) the Rossettis in 38 Charlotte Street, he found the father among a group of exiles:

> The father arose to receive me from a group of foreigners around the fire, all escaped revolutionists from the Continent. . . . The conversation was in Italian, but occasionally merged into French, with the obvious purpose of taking into the heat of the conference refugees unfamiliar with the former language. The tragic passions of the group around the fire did not in the slightest degree involve either the mother, the daughters, or the sons, except when the latter explained that the objects of the severest denunciations were Bomba, Pio Nono, and Metternich, or, in turn, Count Rosso and his memory; with these execrated names were uttered in different tones those of Mazzini, Garibaldi, and Louis Napoleon, who had once been a visitor at the house. The hearth guests took it in turn to discourse, and no one had delivered many phrases ere the excitement of speaking made him rise from his chair, advance to the centre of the group, and there gesticulate as I had never seen people do except upon the stage. What I knew then of French was only by reading, and I was surprised to discover that it helped me scarcely at all to follow the native tongue spoken excitedly and quickly. Each orator evidently found difficulty in expressing his full anger; but when passion had done its measure in word and gesture, so that I as a stranger felt pained at not being able to join in practical sympathy, the declaimer went back to his chair, and while another was taking up the words of mourning and appeal to the too tardy heavens, the predecessor kept up the refrain of sighs and groans. When it was impossible for me to ignore the distress of the alien company, [Dante] Gabriel and William shrugged their shoulders, the latter with a languid sign of commiseration, saying it was generally so. As the dinner was being put on the table some of the strangers persisted, despite invitation, in going; some still stayed round the fire declaring solemnly that they had dined.

> It was a novelty to me to begin dinner with macaroni, and there were other dishes and dressings not usual at English tables, but in all respects we had an excellent meal. Our circle conversed in English, the father talked with his friends from the hearth, and at the end of each course he got up and joined them, until he was once more called to the head of the table by the appearance of a new dish. At the conclusion of the meal the brothers and I saw the remainder of the company established at dominoes and chess before the arrival of the other members for the P.R.B. [Pre-Raphaelite Brotherhood] meeting upstairs.

Besides these friends of old standing with whom he shared gossip about their beautiful and lost Italy, Rossetti was in the habit of seeking from any passing organ-man or plaster-cast vendor the latest news from Rome.

Meanwhile, in his exile, though he had not taste for the British leaven of social Toryism, he liked most things English—the national and individual liberty, the constitution, the people and their moral tone. Of course, as a Latin, he detested English beer and coal fires, and bemoaned the necessity of buying "his climate at the coal-merchant's."

With John Hookham Frere he maintained a correspondence until 1846. In their letters appeared not only the social side of friendship: Rossetti might receive a welcome cheque and in turn send back to Frere copious esoteric and philological notes. When Frere died in 1846, Gabriele Rossetti took it to heart. His son, William Michael, tells us how, with tears in his half-sightless* eyes and the passionate fervour of a southern Italian, his father fell on his knees and exclaimed, "*Anima bella, benedetta sii tu, dovunque sei!*" ("Noble soul, blessed be thou wherever thou art!")

When that remarkable outburst of nationalism which we call the 'Forty-eight seemed imminent, Rossetti summed up Italian sentiment in his poem, "*Canto Marziale.*" There is

* Since 1843, Gabriele Rossetti's health had been getting worse, and his eyes were now failing him. In April 1847, he resigned his professorship in King's College.

evidence that these particular verses urging Italian union and the overthrow of the papacy had a remarkable effect in Italy. By 1848, they had been translated[42] into English by the Reverend Charles Girdlestone, the first stanza of whose version is an adequate sample:

The threatening archangel of war,
Is already stalking through the realms of Italy;
  There precedes him the war trumpet,
    Which has awakened Italy from sleep;
  The Apennine resounds all along,
    And the echo goes from the Liris to the Po.
      All Italy seems as though it were
      A tumultuous sea;
    And echo goes thundering
      Through country and through towns
      "We swear, we swear, on the sword,
      Either Death or Liberty."

On other occasions, Rossetti celebrated the Milanese five days when the Lombard burgesses expelled an Austrian army after the most severe kind of street fighting. His hopes during 1848–49 were high, and his disappointment proportionately great. There was in him some inclination to put the blame for the Italian failures on Mazzini, since Rossetti had confidence only in the House of Savoy to unify the peninsula.

About 1850, old Gabriele Rossetti began to sense that his fires were burning low and therefore resolved to set down for posterity the record of his life. Because he was at heart an *improvvisatore*, he wrote his autobiography in verse, lines which formed a kind of rhymed prose. He was addicted to the less desirable Italian habits of poetic diction, that is, to the "Phoebus, Neptune, Minerva's fane" type of composition; but despite this, his autobiography is singularly attractive and very interesting. William Michael Rossetti translated it as accurately as possible into English blank verse. The son's work is pedestrian—the verse is like that of Crabbe without rhymes. Yet nothing, either in the original or in the English version, so filially written, is dull.

After Gabriele Rossetti's death in 1854, his children saw little of Italian society. Years later, his son, William Michael, recalled in a sonnet[43] the political events of the sixteen years that had intervened between his father's death and the completion of Italian unity. Link by link, freedom and union had come to Italy—did Gabriele, in the grave, know this now? For things had looked hopeless in 1854. In 1883, Gabriele's native city of Vasto celebrated his centenary with enthusiasm. At last, in the hearts of his fellow citizens, he had returned from exile.

§ 3. Sir Anthony Panizzi, like many another Italian under the influence of the ideas of the French Revolution, affiliated himself with a secret political society—the *Sublimi Maestri Perfetti*. He had denied[44] belonging to the Carbonari, but the Sublime Perfect Masters were not very different. Both organizations probably would have agreed on a programme which included the destruction of those governments the supreme power of which was not vested in the nation; the overthrow of religious imposture; and for Italy in particular, its independence under a single, but constitutional government.

People who held the views described above were not allowed to remain in Modena, and Panizzi in 1823 sought asylum in England, where he became one of the principal unofficial agents of the Italian cause. There was in him a faculty for gaining the friendship of the powerful; and Lord Brougham, Gladstone, Lord John Russell, the Marquess of Salisbury, and others helped him to advance his fortunes. On the other hand, his enemies had not enough power to delay his career. The first Lord Houghton,* Carlyle, and Gabriele Rossetti never cared much for him, and did not conceal their opinions. Nevertheless, his bust was placed near the doors of the British Museum Reading Room; for that great institution, as we of the present day know it, is the result of his labours. Justly indeed does Baron Marochetti's

* Richard Monckton Milnes.

sculpture greet whosoever enters the great room with its mighty dome, through which the sun illuminates concentric circles of black desks.

Francis IV, Duke of Modena, had thought well enough of Panizzi to make him inspector of public schools in his native Brescello; yet the servant conspired against his master in behalf of freedom. On October 22, 1822, Panizzi was placed under arrest, but made good his escape to the nearest Swiss canton through the aid of the official charged with his custody. Foreign pressure compelled Switzerland to eject him; therefore, in May of the following year, he went to London. Here he could at last breathe freely.

Such was the insolent character of Italian tyranny that he was on October 6, 1823, condemned, *in absentia*, to death. The sentence was executed on his effigy, and Duke Francis[45] sent Panizzi, in England, a bill of 225 francs 25c. for his own hanging. There was even included in this remarkable document a charge for the usual fee of the hangman. Moved to a grim humour which was in contrast to his usual quick temper, Panizzi sent back to Modena a facetious rejoinder from his departed soul, presumably now dwelling in the Elysian Fields. There was an Italian gesture which he was unable to enclose.

In comparison with Modena under despotism, London was an excellent place. Panizzi was not alone, for he knew many other exiles. At this time, the newspapers were giving much space to refugees from all lands, who were thus enabled to learn of one another. Panizzi's best friend in London was the statesman Santorre di Santa Rosa, who had been involved in the Piedmontese rising of 1821. In October of the next year, he had come to England. Of its people, Santa Rosa once said that they had received him with sincerity and kindness, that he admired their virtuous habits —but that he could not accustom himself to their singular mode of cooking. Santa Rosa left London late in 1824 and was a year later killed in Greece, for whose independence he had been fighting. Other friends of Panizzi were the brothers Ugoni, Camillo and Filippo, both men of letters, who introduced him to Foscolo.

Ugo Foscolo, telling Panizzi not to remain in London, gave him a letter of introduction to William Roscoe of Liverpool, who was the principal English patron of Italian letters. Roscoe received Panizzi very hospitably, urged him to remain in Liverpool, and assisted him in earning a living. At this time, the study of Italian was considered an essential part of an Englishman's education; and thanks to the Unitarian minister William Shepherd, as well as to Roscoe, Panizzi was soon selling verbs and articles—so he later, and not too joyously, described his private tutoring. He found the British climate detestable and perhaps laid then the foundations of his rheumatic complaints. Nevertheless, since he liked the English, he preferred living among them to dwelling under the Italian sky. At least, that is what he said in December 1823. There was no lack of pupils. He was even able to give in English a series of lectures on the Italian language. No record of these talks during 1825 was kept, but it is known that they were delivered at the Royal Institution under Roscoe's auspices. Another lifelong friend whom Panizzi made in Liverpool was Francis Haywood, the translator of Kant.

Again Foscolo proved to be of service to Panizzi by enabling him to make the acquaintance of Henry Brougham. The English barrister had come to Lancaster because of the prosecution of Edward Gibbon Wakefield, who was under charges of having kidnapped Miss Ellen Turner, a pupil of Panizzi's. The trial, one of the most celebrated of English cases during the nineteenth century, revolved about points of Continental laws of marriage. By profession an advocate, Panizzi enlightened Lord Brougham on the subject of Roman law and in other ways proved exceedingly useful. Grateful for his assistance, Brougham secured for Panizzi the not very lucrative chair of Italian literature at the newly founded

University College in London. Another powerful friend who interceded at this time in favour of his candidacy was William Roscoe.

To facilitate his teaching, Panizzi compiled an anthology[46] of Italian prose, which earned favourable comment,[47] and published an elementary Italian grammar. His students (very few, alas!) were expected to buy both, yet he never* drew much more than £10 a year from his connection with the University of London. Fortunately, Lord Brougham again manifested a proper gratitude by placing Panizzi, in 1831, as an assistant librarian, with the British Museum. The position paid £275 per annum. Henceforward, the outlines of his career are plain enough; he was resolved to throw in his destinies with the British, and to that end took out, the next year, papers of naturalization.

Panizzi seems to have cultivated a talent for attracting the acquaintance of the great. For example, when Foscolo died, Panizi bought some of the poet's books—not to keep as mementoes of his friend but to distribute among Foscolo's acquaintances so that these might perhaps know the living exile as well. Macaulay, for one, accepted a relic of Foscolo's, and thus came to know of Panizzi. Later, having prepared editions of Boiardo and Aristo, Panizzi sent copies to Macaulay, who from India expressed his thanks in 1833, and intimated a desire to review the Boiardo edition. There were other ways in which Panizzi could make himself known. From 1828 to 1830, he reviewed Italian works regularly for *The Foreign Review*. Moreover, he did not fail to cultivate people of social prestige; in particular, he had managed by 1829 to meet, through Brougham, Lady Dacre. As early as 1833, Panizzi was frequently seen at Holland House, that famous centre of London society, where he won the friendship of the Reverend Sydney Smith.

With a far greater literary personage, Carlyle, who once

* E. R. Vincent's *Gabriele Rossetti in England*, p. 23, contains a statement to the effect that Panizzi had received a guarantee of £250 a year.

called Panizzi a fat pedant, the Italian was not on good terms. It seemed that in 1834 Caryle discovered in the British Museum a great collection of printed matter, inaccessible for want of a proper catalogue. Panizzi was helpful, and the Scot acknowledged his thanks by patronizingly referring to the labours of "the respectable sublibrarian."[48] It is almost certain that from this slight to his vanity dates Panizzi's dislike for Carlyle, a feeling which naturally became mutual. Panizzi never met Gabriele Rosetti, another enemy. In 1835, he tried in vain to repair their breach by acknowledging his respect for Rossetti as a man of learning. A year before, Rossetti had expressed wonder that Panizzi did not seem to have any grudge against him.[49]

Steadily Panizzi moved towards his goal; and one is inclined to believe that few things came to him uncalculated. At last, in 1837, he was created Keeper of the Printed Books of the British Museum, despite opposition to him on two grounds: that he was a Roman Catholic and that he was a foreigner. His detractors even asserted that he had sold white mice on the streets. The candidate whom he had defeated for the post was Cary, the translator of Dante; and the rejected rival never forgave, and even wrote a letter to *The Times* in petulant exasperation. Another who felt ill will was Sir Frederick Madden, a high and disgruntled official of the Museum. To his new eminence Panizzi brought three guiding principles, the practice of which transformed the British Museum into an institution of transcendent value. The Museum was not a show, but an instrument for the diffusion of culture; not a bureau for political placemen, but a department of the civil service; not a preserve for a privileged few, but rather a means to extending the limits of knowledge.[50]

Mazzini and Panizzi were scarcely warm friends. The failure of the Modena revolt of 1831 had convinced Panizzi that plots and secret societies were useless, and he could not share Mazzini's ideas. The latter in 1839 intimated,[51] in a letter to his mother, that Panizzi, "by virtue of making himself English in opinion, in manner, in everything, is the librarian of the Public Library [British Museum], and has an excellent salary"; and that he was a sycophant—with Whigs, a Whig, and with Tories, a Tory. This opinion probably meant only that Panizzi disagreed with the *Prophet* (the title which the cohorts of *Young Italy* applied to their "mighty paramount"). That Panizzi had no sympathy with his fellow Italians was not true, for though many *soi-disant* exiles imposed on him, invariably he persisted in giving aid. But he did not believe in Mazzini's methods and looked instead to a freedom broadening down from precedent to precedent, to a constitutional monarchy for Italy similar to the government of England. At the time of the letter-opening scandal, Panizzi had brilliantly defended Mazzini. Years later, in the stage coach running between France and Italy, Panizzi saw a man[52] disguised in blue spectacles and wrapped in a long Italian cloak. "For God's sake!" said Mazzini, "be discreet." In 1860, Panizzi saw him again, near Fleet Street—"a man of very dark complexion, in a shabby black coat, with a silk kerchief wound round and round his neck, without collar, waistcoat buttoned high, and with downcast eyes." Neither gave the other any sign of recognition.[53] For contrast, one need merely recall how, fifteen years before, Panizzi had met Duke Francis IV of Modena in Vienna, and they had chatted amiably[54]—not perhaps about the unpaid bill for Panizzi's execution.

As Panizzi grew in importance, he was invited to breakfast by Samuel Rogers, who by conversation fostered the Muses and simultaneously fed their devotees. Panizzi was also a favourite guest at Holland House. Moreover, William Stewart Rose, Lady Dacre, and Thomas Grenville liked him. Indeed, Grenville, solely through Panizzi's intercession, left his magnificent library to the British Museum and not to his nephew, the Duke of Buckingham. This was a splendid acquisition, for the collection comprised 20,239 volumes, included even a first folio of Shakespeare, and had cost about £54,000. Panizzi and Grenville had been in the habit of playing whist on Sundays, and the old gentleman had evidently been impressed with the Italian's devotion to the Museum.

Hard upon this windfall, Carlyle and other men of letters joined in a complaint against Panizzi's management of the Museum. Ostensibly, the gravamen of their charges was that he had not provided the library with a proper catalogue; behind it all lay a good deal of animosity between Carlyle and the Italian. In later years, Carlyle believed that Panizzi had deliberately hindered his research on the Commonwealth under Cromwell and on Frederick the Great. Such was his antipathy that Carlyle once called the librarian "Vulture Panizzi."[55] In his neurasthenic desire for extraordinary quiet, Carlyle had once requested a private reading room in the King's Library, a department of the British Museum, but Panizzi had properly refused him any such special privilege. After all, equally great literary panjandrums had used the public reading-room. Whatever was behind the complaint, a Royal Commission investigated the British Museum in 1848, and eventually submitted a report which exculpated Panizzi.

Meanwhile, events in Italy were coming to a head. The Lombards rose against the Austrians, and the whole land resounded with the clamour of struggling men, mingling with the furious shouts of nationalism in central Europe. Though he was a Modenese, Panizzi was commissoned by the Lombards to act as their unofficial ambassador, for he was not only a British subject but an Italian patriot.

During these years, Panizzi was cementing his friendships with men of affairs influential in English politics. There was Gladstone whom he helped,[56] in 1849, to prepare an article for *The Quarterly* on Leopardi. Was it the conversations he held with Panizzi which made Gladstone write[57] that the misfortunes of Leopardi's country "have stamped their image indelibly upon his works, and may be traced, not only in the solemn and impassioned verses, or in the mournful letters, of which they are more or less directly the theme, but in the tone which pervades the whole?"

Politics, of course, never interfered with Panizzi's administrative duties. From 1850 forward, he strove to force publishers to obey the copyright law by depositing copies of their publications in the British Museum. His zeal gave him much trouble, for men like Bohn were reluctant[58] to co-operate.

Yet during those years his heart was with his fellow Italians, overcome recently by the foreign soldiery. On his own account, he went to Naples in 1851 and visited its prisons, which he found even worse than in Gladstone's report[59] of the same year. He called on Ferdinand II and spoke for twenty minutes on the famous victims of injustice, Poerio and Settembrini, and on the prisons. The Bourbon monarch closed the interview with an abrupt outburst: "*Addio, terribile Panizzi.*"[60] When he learnt that Settembrini's family was being persecuted, Panizzi was determined to aid the Neapolitan political prisoners. To that end, he carried on a surreptitious correspondence with Settembrini from 1852 to 1853; and though their communications involved the paraphernalia of invisible ink and the necessity of smuggling, Panizzi overcame all difficulties. His plans, however, did not ripen until some time later.

In England, several matters occupied Panizzi's attention. First, Cavour visited him in London in 1852, doubtless in order that they should consider together the winning of British good will. As for the Museum, Panizzi was at that very time projecting its famous Reading Room. Also, in 1853, through Mazzini's mediation, he met Felice Orsini, whom at first he liked very much. Orsini even took out, in 1856, a reader's ticket, for he was planning to write a book on military tactics. Needing money to support him in the meantime, he asked Panizzi's help in getting pupils for Italian lessons.

Panizzi turned his mind to the political prisoners kept on the Neapolitan convict-islands, and for their rescue he enlisted British ministers and members of Parliament. In particular, he plotted for the escape of Luigi Settembrini. Settembrini and the other unfortunates, including Silvio Spaventa, carried on a secret correspondence with friends and sympathizers through Sir William Temple, the British minister at Naples and Lord Palmerston's brother. Meanwhile, Panizzi persevered, collected money, and purchased a rescue ship, *The Isle of Thanet*, which none other than Garibaldi was to have commanded. Among the contributors to the mild plot were Lord Overstone; Lord Zetland; Lord and Lady Holland; Mrs. Gladstone, who gave £100; her friends, among whom she collected £200 additional; and perhaps the most generous of all, Panizzi himself. It may be that Lord and Lady Palmerston subscribed[61] anonymously. The chief plotters were, however, Temple, Sir James Hudson, English minister at Turin, and of course Panizzi. Unfortunately, in October 1855, *The Isle of Thanet* sank off Yarmouth in a storm.

In 1856, Panizzi was named Principal Librarian of the British Museum. Though his birth was held against him, he was not the first person of foreign extraction to fill the post. Among those who denounced his appointment were Carlyle, Monckton Milnes, and a Mr. Bolton Corney. On the other hand, both Lord John Russell and Benjamin Disraeli praised the choice. Macaulay too was pleased even if he did think that Panizzi cared more for books than for scientific exhibits* and "would at any time give three Mammoths for an Aldus."[62] What is of the utmost significance is this: his subordinates were glad, for Panizzi was a very fair, if stern, master. One later incident is perhaps worth noting. In 1863,

* In 1860, Corney, pronouncing Panizzi a "Dictator in literature, science, and art to this humiliated nation," maintained that the science collections of the British Museum were being neglected. See Bolton Corney's *Comments on the Evidence of Antonio Panizzi*, London, 1860, p. 2.

Disraeli had a conversation with Queen Victoria during which she expressed her wonder at Panizzi's being the head of the British Museum; but the Tory leader assured her that the Italian's colleagues esteemed him. Probably the Queen objected to Panizzi's foreign origin.[63]

Perhaps the most important event during Panizzi's administration was the ceremonial opening in 1857 of the great Reading Room, of which he had been the only begetter. David Masson, merely one of many who felt grateful for this splendid chamber, recorded in his memoirs of London this appreciative quatrain:

> Had you seen this fine hall before it was made,
> All ye London sons of the book-making trade,
> I am sure every time that your ticket admits ye,
> You would lift up your hands and bless old Panizzi.[64]

The inaugural pomp has been forgotten, but not the fact that this hall is Panizzi's monument. He is not the least among those who have laboured beneath its dome steadily and grandly. No doubt it was in recognition of this achievement that Oxford in 1859 gave Panizzi the honorary degree of D.C.L.

People of liberal sentiments did not forget the prisoners on the Neapolitan islands. The pressure of English public opinion effected the release, in 1859, of about sixty-six of them. Under dramatic circumstances, the freed men were brought to London, where they were received with overwhelming cordiality. Of the large fund raised in Great Britain to give them assistance, their steadfast champion, Antonio Panizzi, was quite justly the secretary. From 1859, Panizzi corresponded with Poerio on Italian politics. On March 14, 1859, Dickens informed Panizzi of his desire to print the story of the sufferings of Poerio and the others in his magazine, *Household Words*. The great novelist, giving every assurance that he would take pains to have their account translated in the sincerest and best manner, requested Panizzi, who had taken charge of these exiles, to fix the payment for their narrative. Panizzi replied to this offer in a very friendly manner.[65]

When in 1864 Garibaldi paid his memorable visit to London amid the cheers of the populace and the banquets of the ruling class, one of those to honour him was Panizzi, at whose home he was greeted by a throng including Gladstone and many peers. It was in Panizzi's company that this modern *condottiere* visited Foscolo's grave in April.

In autumn of the next year, Lord Palmerston died. Gladstone consoled[66] Panizzi on the passing of this friend of Italy. Panizzi himself was beginning to feel rather low in health, and consequently applied for retirement. His resignation was accepted not without protest, and Gladstone resolved to honour his friend. Taking in 1866 the same stand as in 1861, Panizzi refused knighthood. The trustees of the British Museum were more concrete in their expression of esteem, for Panizzi retired on full salary, £1,400 a year. His subordinates regretted his leaving because he had obtained in their behalf not only a pension system but also increased pay, extended vacations, and tenure.

The rest of Panizzi's life was very peaceful. Except for an illness early in 1868 which gave Gladstone much worry about "losing this very true, trusty, hearty friend,"[67] all was going well. The Italian government decorated him, and named him Senator; the English cabinet gave him a knighthood at Gladstone's instance; the future King Humbert of Italy visited him, as likewise did Napoleon III. In 1879, Sir Anthony Panizzi died, he who had been an Englishman by adoption and an Italian patriot by birth. In April 1881 *The Quarterly Review* put the conservative stamp of approval upon him in a long biographical article. So far as is known, Panizzi appears in only one English novel, Sydney Carlyon Grier's* *One Crowded Hour* (1912), where it is hinted that he helped finance Garibaldi's Sicilian expedition. Perhaps he really did.

* Hilda Caroline Gregg.

CHAPTER X

Some Italian Exiles of the 1830's: Ricciardi, the Brothers Ruffini, Gallenga

§ 1. The Paris revolution of July, 1830, which resulted in the expulsion of Charles X and in the coronation of Louis Philippe, encouraged Italian patriots in political activity. The only immediate consequence for Count Giuseppe Napoleone Ricciardi, revolutionary republican and one of the most colourful figures during the *Risorgimento*, was exile. His middle name indicated clearly from what source he drew his liberalism and how potent had been the ideas which marched with the Gallic hosts. When the Austrians entered Naples at the end of the fiascos of 1820–21, he had experienced a sense of personal grief. Later, he was confirmed in his hatred of despotism, for in 1827 his father was arbitrarily banished by Francis I of Naples. Doubtless, a parent who named a son after a Bonaparte was suspect.

Giuseppe Ricciardi very wisely made it his business to absent himself from Naples. At Milan, the capital of Lombardy, he witnessed the boycotting of the Austrians; and in Florence he met the literary coterie which assembled on Monday evenings at Vieusseux's house.[1]

In 1833, Ricciardi visited England—his mind open, his curiosity awake and strong. His sympathy for the unfortunate was especially acute, since he had just read Silvio Pellico's *Le mie prigioni*,* an account of suffering in the Spielberg

* There were numerous English translations of this work. During 1833 (January 19th to November 30th) *The Athenaeum* devoted much space to Pellico.

fortress-prison. Thanks to a letter of introduction from Pepe, Ricciardi met Gabriele Rossetti. The prevalence of vice in London astounded Ricciardi, who estimated the number of prostitutes at 80,000. He beheld riches and starvation side by side in the metropolis, and was appalled. In April, he visited Milbank Penitentiary, which impressed him as a palace in comparison with the Italian dungeons.

During 1833, Ricciardi celebrated his twenty-fifth birthday, not without bemoaning his enslaved Italy, for which he was resolved to do a great deal. Consequently, he went to Geneva in August, where he met a pseudonymous Mazzini, and was informed of an intended rising in Naples. Having hastened thither, he discovered the *émeute* had failed, and thereupon assumed the very dangerous office of Secretary of the Central Committee of the conspirators. His ardour was not dampened when he learned that Caesar Rossaroll and others, involved in plots against the King of Naples, had been tortured.

As Secretary of the Central Committee, Ricciardi carried on much revolutionary correspondence, which led to his arrest for conspiracy. The Minister of Police ordered him to cut off his whiskers, adornments then considered signs of republicanism. Perhaps in retaliation, he converted his jailer, General Ruberti, from Bourbonism to liberalism. Finally, on May 28, 1835, after an imprisonment of seven months, Count Ricciardi was free. In no wise had he altered his beliefs, which included even woman suffrage. Very soon, he was again placed under arrest, and the police committed him to a lunatic asylum for his political utterances. A month later, in October 1836, he was released for the second time, and hastened to Spain.

Of course, he continued his revolutionary activity; for example, he helped smuggle[2] to the Continent the publications of his friend, Gabriele Rossetti. There was sufficient British interest in Ricciardi to make feasible a translation[3] in 1860 of his very interesting autobiography, in which he revealed himself a curious man—of good mind, yet of no sense of dignity; indeed, a political madcap.

In December 1869 the Oecumenical Council of the Roman Catholic Church met to adopt both the dogma of papal infallibility and the famous *Syllabus* opposed to liberal ideas. Earlier, in October, Ricciardi decided to hold at Naples an anti-Catholic council[4] to sit at the same time as the papal one. William Michael Rossetti and Swinburne determined to send a joint letter of sympathy to the Italian radical. Their message was written by W. M. Rossetti, and modified and enlarged by Swinburne. Having been translated into Italian by W. M. Rossetti, it was sent off in November 1869. In their letter to Ricciardi, Swinburne said that "the Church or priests, and the Republic,* are natural and internecine enemies." The Anti-Council did meet in December 1869, but was suppressed, for it was too much like irreverent parody. Swinburne intended to have read before the Anti-Catholic Council his "Hymn of Man," of which he said:

> I have written a modern companion in arms and metre to my "Hymn to Proserpine" called "Hymn of Man" (during the Session in Rome of the Oecumenical Council), by the side of which "Queen Mab" is as it were an archdeacon's charge and my own previous blasphemies are models of Catholic devotion.

Indirectly thus, Ricciardi had inspired Swinburne to poetry.

§ 2. Giovanni Ruffini was perhaps the finest English stylist among a select group of at least bilingual Italian exiles. This judgment of his mastery of English is not merely relative, for he wrote in a manner so genuinely delightful that David Masson[5] and others accorded him very high praise.

He had been with his unfortunate brother, Dr. Iacopo, a chief of *Young Italy* in Genoa and had taken a part in the plots of 1833, which Charles Albert of Piedmont crushed with great severity.

* After the ideas of Mazzini.

Giovanni Ruffini came to London with another brother, Agostino, and shared with Mazzini the wretchedness of exile. All three became acquainted with Carlyle, who would alarm the Ruffinis, at least, with his tremendous tirades. Giovanni used to worry about a possible entanglement[6] between Mrs. Carlyle and Mazzini.

Gradually, the Ruffinis drew away from the programme of *Young Italy*, and were reconciled to seeing their country united under a monarchy, that of Piedmont. It was no doubt in recognition of these altered opinions that Charles Albert in 1848 made Giovanni Ruffini ambassador to France.

However, our chief interest in Giovanni is as a man of English letters of no mean order. Making his literary *début* in 1853, he published anonymously from Edinburgh an autobiographical novel* called *Lorenzo Benoni*. Like many other first works, it was a compilation of actual experiences, for it recapitulated events of the most poignant kind in the early history of *Young Italy*. The father of Lorenzo Benoni [Giovanni Ruffini] lived in Genoa; and one uncle, the Canon, resided in a small country town between Nice and Genoa, where he managed an estate belonging to Lorenzo's mother. The ecclesiastic would worry about olives and hope for the next year's crops. Lorenzo himself was the youngest of three brothers, who, as each attained the age of seven, were sent from Genoa to the Canon in order to learn Latin. Thence they would go on to the Royal College of Genoa. The Canon's housekeeper regarded Lorenzo as an intruder and illtreated him; consequently, he was glad at the age of nine to enter the Royal College in 1818. Here he was under a strict surveillance which did not differentiate between supervision and espionage. As he moved forward in school classes, he helped overthrow the rule of a cowardly bully named Anastasius, an ugly leader of a "gang" which took toll of their schoolmates' edibles. Lorenzo was a bright lad and in

* Several other Italians published autobiographies thinly disguised as fiction.

the competitions for school prizes won numerous scholastic honours. When he read a book on the *Index Librorum Prohibitorum*, a translation of Milton's *Paradise Lost*, he was punished by being confined in a cell at the Royal College. Eventually, he graduated with honours—*all* the prizes were his, but his father was not overcome with pleasure, for scholastic distinction was usual in the family. Lorenzo was intended for the law. On reading the life of a missionary martyr, however, he wanted to become a monk—an idea which he abandoned at the discoveries that he was not fond of flagellation and that he could not be comfortable while walking with gravel in his shoes. These considerations weighed more heavily than the joys of martyrdom; besides, his uncle John said that the Capuchins wore dirty clothes.

Next, Lorenzo entered the University of Genoa, which had just reopened after the failure of the revolution of 1821 in Piedmont. Here he soon became aware that independent thinking by students was deliberately discouraged and that only reactionary ideas were permissible. Hand in hand with a repressive government was a co-operative church, and between the two it was ordered that students observe strict religious requirements. Each university man had to have a certificate of good conduct from his parish priest to the effect that he had attended church regularly for six months, that he had confessed once a month, and that he had received the sacrament. At the University, Lorenzo met Fantasio [Mazzini], who early showed a capacity for social and political indignation and an extraordinary brilliancy. Also in attendance, but as a student of medicine, was Lorenzo's brother Caesar [Iacopo Ruffini].

Charged with an offence, of which he was not guilty, Lorenzo was suspended for a year. During this period of rustication, his father was unpleasant. Meanwhile, Fantasio read of the Greek Revolution and plotted for a free Italy. Even Piedmont in those days had no liberty of the press, for King Victor Emmanuel I had, in 1814, abandoned the Code of Napoleon for the repressive laws of 1770. (Indeed, the revived penal code was interpreted to include this provision: if a political prisoner obtained permission to shave, he might do so provided that behind him stood a soldier with a naked sabre. Naturally, Lorenzo's attempt to manifest his liberalism in the form of a moustache was effectively discouraged.)

The more ardent Fantasio busied himself with *Young Italy*, mingled in politics, and somehow found time to devote to romantic literature, including Byron. He had become disgusted with the mummery of the Carbonari, of which he himself, Lorenzo, and Caesar were members.

Lorenzo, now a doctor of laws, carried on an intrigue with a lady named Lilla, but neither the woman nor the details of their liaison are of any interest. In the meantime, Fantasio was arrested as a Carbonaro but was freed on a legal technicality—that there was only *one* witness against him. He proceeded to Marseilles, whence he directed *Young Italy*. Lorenzo and Caesar joined it and propagandized in its behalf. The organization spread rapidly, but unfortunately was disclosed through a quarrel of two drunken men. Military trials, imprisonments, and executions followed in a horrible sequence. Caesar Benoni died in prison, but we are not told how. Lorenzo escaped, reached Marseilles, and there saw Fantasio, haggard and careworn.

Lorenzo Banoni was indeed a fine account of Italian manners, of Piedmont in reaction about 1834 and before that time, of Mazzini and the beginnings of *Young Italy*. It was not a mere record, for its characterization is really notable. Uncle John, the brother of Lorenzo's mother, is a flesh-and-blood character, of a sardonic, yet tender humour; Fantasio is an extraordinary and sympathetic sketch of an important historical figure; and Caesar Benoni is affectionately drawn. These people move about in a *milieu* surprisingly modern. Students attend university lectures at the crowded homes of their professors because the government seeks to prevent large gatherings. Professors and students spy upon one another and are in turn under surveillance. An insolent soldiery, an alert censor, a strict priesthood, and a prison system based on torture bind a great people. *Lorenzo Benoni* is written in a style remarkably attractive. There is nothing unidiomatic. One could be unaware, except for the subject matter, that its author is not British, and one suspects from his manner that he has read Mrs. Gaskell and Jane Austen with a close devotion.

The Athenaeum did not like this novel, but *The Dublin University Magazine* (August, 1853) was very laudatory. *Tait's* called it the *Uncle Tom's Cabin* of the Italian question.[7] *Fraser's* was unstinted in its praise and commented that "the Italian nation, bound hand and foot, and abandoned to the stupidity and brutality of the stranger, [presented] a lamentable and revolting spectacle."[8] David Masson, in an unsigned review, was almost ecstatic, for he pronounced Ruffini's style "really beautiful—easy, sprightly, graceful . . . ."[9] However, though that conservative organ, *The Quarterly Review*,[10] acknowledged Ruffini's "uncommon mastery" of English, it used his novel as a text for a sermon against political conspiracy and dissidence. *Lorenzo Benoni* was hailed as a second *Gil Blas*, had an immense popularity, and ran through several English editions.[11]

Two years later, Giovanni Ruffini followed up the success of *Lorenzo Benoni* with a second anonymous novel, *Doctor Antonio*. In plot it was nothing distinguished, but again the limpid style of its author made it highly acceptable. The heroine, Lucy Davenne, travelling with her haughty father, the baronet Sir John of ancient lineage, by accident breaks her leg. They have been touring in a carriage during this year of 1840, and have come to an out-of-the-way place, on the Ligurian littoral, called Bordighera, a small hamlet in the Kingdom of Sardinia. A Doctor Antonio, political exile from Sicily because he had been the physician of a dying friend involved in conspiracy, attends to her. Lucy, in delicate health, is compelled to remain for some months in

Bordighera, and her father, the baronet, fumes uselessly. Sir John is an interesting character, with a supreme contempt for foreigners and a great deal of pride. It is related of him that while he was at Rome, he lived as if it were London—nothing strange to say about Victorian travellers. Doctor Antonio gradually softens Sir John, and by his infinite resource, refinement, delicacy, and charm helps restore Lucy's damaged health. The Italian's conversation is various—on a landscape, the history and wrongs of Sicily, the disunity of Italy and her cause, a botany lesson on the scent-organs of flowers—, for his object is to interest Lucy so that she may want to live. Doctor and patient fall in love, but never express it; and their idyll is broken up by the coming of the boisterous Captain Aubrey Davenne, who does not care for a foreign brother-in-law. So Lucy goes away to marry the rising politician, twenty-five years her senior, the Viscount Cleverton. Widowed at his death, she returns to Italy and eventually finds Doctor Antonio politically active (1848) in the Kingdom of Naples. He belongs to the moderates or constitutional monarchists, whose programme, mild as it was, was detestable to Ferdinand II. On May 15, 1848, riots break out in Naples. Doctor Antonio, who had tended the wounded, is arrested; and then follows the famous and protracted trial scene—the mockery of all justice by which Poerio and Settembrini and others, including our doctor, are condemned. Doctor Antonio is sent to the horrible prison of Ischia, from which Lucy tries to help him escape. Since he will not desert his comrades in misfortune, he refuses the aid of her yacht. Lucy dies, and Doctor Antonio is left in prison, the victim of a system which Gladstone called the negation of God.

Doctor Antonio had also an excellent sale both in England and in America, for the reviews were very good. *The Athenaeum* was favourable, and *Tait's*[12] enthusiastic. David Masson[13] spoke of its gentleness and purity of tone, sustained and unforced devotion of feeling, and its idiomatic language.

It is known[14] that this novel had a marked influence on English public opinion in favour of a united Italy. Some British travellers even made it a special point to visit places mentioned in *Lorenzo Benoni* and in *Doctor Antonio*.

There is in *Doctor Antonio* perhaps too much undiluted propaganda. It clearly reveals that Giovanni Ruffini had abandoned the views of *Young Italy*. His hero is no republican but rather a unitarian and constitutional monarchist. One portrait is of great interest, that of the Signora Eleanora, a widow, whose two sons are in exile. In reality, Ruffini was lovingly describing his own mother, the Marchesa Eleonora Curlo-Ruffini; and her sons are himself and his brother Agostino.

His third novel, *Lavinia*, 1860, has only brief, indirect, and retrospective views of the struggle for Italian nationalism—side lights on the atrocious Cardinal Antonelli, the defence of Rome, Garibaldi, the gallant Luciano Manara, and the noble Daniel Manin as an exile in Paris, giving Italian lessons. The hero, Paolo Mancini, a painter, fights with Manara's Lombards at Rome in 1848. Eventually, he meets Manin in Paris, who urges him to campaign with the Piedmontese contingent in the Crimea. Manin is shown as no doctrinaire republican, for he would be content if Italy were united under the House of Savoy. The plot itself is very simple and rather pleasant. Paolo and an English girl, Lavinia Holywell, fall in love; and after much trouble and long separation are united. The significant thing about this novel is that it stresses one point: the unity of Italy, be it republican or monarchical, was more important than the manner of its accomplishment. Also, Ruffini struck a democratic note in having the hero scorn his title of *marchese*.

Giovanni Ruffini's next novel, *Vincenzo*,* was readable, but less satisfactory than its predecessors, for its characters lacked definiteness and were selected only to establish a

* It ran in serial form in *Macmillan's Magazine* from May 1862 to November 1863.

thesis. The purpose of the story was to show the undercurrents of contemporary domestic life in Italy and to present the baneful effects of priestly influence on the women of the country and, through the women, on the noblest and most cultivated men and on the highest interests of the land. The heroine, Rose, is a pretty doll—well-shaped, comely, insipid, and characterless except for a blind piety and stubbornness. She marries her father's *protégé*, Vincenzo, and turns into a querulous, discontented, selfish, mischief-making wife, preferring the control of the bigoted priest, Don Pio, to the influence of her husband, whose political character she narrows and whose career in public life she compels him to abandon because the government of King Victor Emmanuel, which he serves, has passed anti-clerical legislation. Naturally, he becomes a despondent idler who lives on her wealth; yet he is determined to educate their daughter in the hope that she may not grow to be so narrow-minded as her mother.

The background of this novel is not without interest—the struggle of the Church against the State. Since the new United Italy had in its immediate past anti-clerical legislation, the priests tried to sabotage the constitutional government by their influence over the convent-trained women folk. This internal hostility, from 1848 to 1863, is clearly described. One learns that the clerics asserted it was a sign of God's wrath against the "atheist" government when Victor Emmanuel's mother, wife, and brother died in close succession;* that the last sacraments were refused to the Cabinet minister, Santa Rosa, who had abetted anti-papal legislation; and that in the village parishes the local priest habitually

* *Cf.* Henry Lushington's lines of consolation "To King Victor Emmanuel" (in *La Nation Boutiquière and Other Poems, Chiefly Political*, Cambridge, England, 1855, pp. 35–38):

"Win freely, ere thou die,
The calumnies that witness best to glory:
Be thine the foremost name in Savoy's story,—
And let the Jesuits lie."

used his influence against his flock's observing the anniversary of the granting of a constitution by King Charles Albert because the holiday was a *liberal* and not a *divine* festival.

Of course, *Vincenzo* was a novel of propaganda; and Ruffini's style, winning, soft, persuasive, could not atone for an unfortunate tendency merely to chronicle the contemporaneous and to create illustrative puppets in place of people. To demonstrate his fairness, Ruffini does have a *liberal* priest to offset his reactionary colleague, but one is absolutely sure that he considers the second type of cleric more usual. Priests, it is said, mumble "nonsense in Latin" and fatten "on other people's sweat."

It is interesting to catch a glimpse of Cavour in Turin, but recently elected as a deputy, practising oratory with a tremendous earnestness; of Gioberti addressing the Turinese in a weak voice and an eloquence without strength or audacity; of Cavour again, always the Anglophile, advising Vincenzo to study political economy, English, and the English blue books. Primarily, this is a story of an internal Italian tension which persists despite Mussolini's recent concordat with the Vatican.

Giovanni Ruffini also contributed pleasant sketches to *Macmillan's Magazine*,[15] wrote a few books of travel, and never lost his gift of an amiable style. As a writer of English fiction, he was not only the most successful among his fellow Italian exiles—he was the only one of genuine worth.

§ 3. Agostino Ruffini was a younger brother of Giovanni's, less memorable as a man of letters than as an attractive personality. He came to London, remained there only for a short while, and settled in Edinburgh in 1840. Here he was assisted by Mrs. Eliza Fletcher,[16] who thereby earned Mazzini's thanks. Agostino did not long adhere to that prophet's doctrines and has therefore been called[17] grossly ungrateful to his friend. However, a judgment as harsh as this might be thought somewhat partisan.

In Edinburgh, Agostino taught Italian and became the centre of a group of *Ruffinians*—that is, people who liked Ruffini, and they were very many. There was, for one, David Masson, who knew the man and loved him very much. It was he who described[18] Agostino as very British in his habits, being accustomed even to correct himself for the un-English mannerism of gesticulating by writing on the margins of the books he most often used: "Ruffini, don't gesticulate." He succeeded, said Masson, but not quite.

Agostino won Masson's sympathy for Italy, and the Scot learned to detest a despotism which expelled a man like this from his own land. The exile was very quiet in manner and seldom allowed the events of his past to emerge in conversation. Once, however, he told Masson an anecdote which illustrated the spirit of the Italian rebels in 1833:

> A bridge was to be taken somewhere. It was to be done by a band of insurgents. . . . After some preliminary explanations, their commander thus addressed them: "As you are marching towards the bridge, they will fire at you. Never mind; you march on. They will fire again. You are not hit; you still march on. They will again fire, and you are wounded. Never mind; you march on. Again they will fire, and you are killed this time. Never mind; march on still.[19]

On Masson, Agostino exerted a very deep intellectual influence, introducing the Britisher to Vico and defending Machiavelli from the usual accusation of diabolical malevolence. Agostino Ruffini has been thus described in the most sympathetic manner:

> What penetration he had; how he understood a case half-told; how gravely he would nod in silence for a time as he listened; and then how distinct the further questioning, and how exact the judgment! And no feigning or flattery![20]

No work of letters (except a good sonnet[21] in Italian on Carlyle, whose *Past and Present* he admired and in whom he discerned both Socrates and Diogenes) by Agostino Ruffini is known, though he often talked of the novel that he was going to write. Did it become part of his brother's *Doctor Antonio*? He appears in Mrs. Gaskell's *Round the Sofa*, 1859, as Mr. Sperano,[22] an Italian exile in Edinburgh, who had been banished even from France and now was teaching Italian with meek diligence; and David Masson wrote excellent biographical essays about him.

In person, he was of spare build and of middle height, fastidious in his habits, and of delicate health. He could not endure the British climate, which visited upon him the tortures of rheumatism and neuralgia. Masson admired his beautiful handwriting, was grateful for his opinions on Dante, Machiavelli, Vico, and Leopardi,[23] and loved the man's character. Said Masson:

> Nature never made a man in a nobler, finer mould. He was sent among us to show what manner of man an Italian might be. Wise, calm, fervid, honourable, proud; capable of being so stern, and withal so courteous! Ever open and considerate to the sorrows of others, ever secret and jealous of his own! To those who saw him but once, he was the type of a thoughtful and most gentle man; to those who saw him often, a fountain of the richest and the rarest pleasure.[24]

The younger Ruffini was known to Masson from 1840 to 1847.

In 1848, when Italy was struggling against despotism, Agostino returned to Genoa, and was elected in due course to the Sardinian Chamber of Deputies. He became paralysed and died on January 3, 1855.

Before one leaves Agostino Ruffini, one might perhaps consider this conjecture—that he was the prototype of Professor Pesca in Wilkie Collins's *The Woman in White*. One is told that Pesca was formerly of the University of Padua and that he left Italy for political reasons. An Italian tutor in London, he aspires to become a typical Britisher by carrying an umbrella, wearing gaiters and a white hat, and attempting to take up English sports. In person he is small.

A few more details are significant in identifying Pesca as Agostino Ruffini: his endeavour to be very English in speech, his habit of repeating certain colloquial expressions, and his likeable character.

§ 4. Antonio Gallenga (1812–95) was a very able man whose Italian patriotism underwent an alteration similar to that of many of his countrymen. He had begun as a Mazzinian of the most ardent zeal, joining *Young Italy* at Marseilles, and had become long before the end of his career a conservative so implacable in his views as to be distrusted in radical circles in London.

When Charles Albert of Piedmont crushed with terrible severity a liberal movement in Genoa, Gallenga went to Mazzini in 1833 and laid bare his resolution to assassinate the king and thus avenge the Genoese executions. Mazzini tried to discourage him, pointed out the perils of the enterprise and the undesirability of the procedure, but all was said in vain. Seeing that nothing could deter Gallenga, Mazzini gave him a dagger and money and sent him on to Turin. A sympathetic judgment of the whole matter is that Mazzini was making a symbolic gesture of defiance to despotism. Equally theoretical was Gallenga's resolution, for his courage failed him and Charles Albert lived for many more years.

In 1839, Gallenga, who had first gone to New York in 1836 and had later given Italian lessons and lectures on Italian literature near Harvard University, settled in London, ready to begin his notable career as a writer of books in English, usually under the pseudonym of Luigi Mariotti. He was not yet estranged from Mazzini when he published in 1841 the collected lectures which he had first delivered in Boston. His *Italy: General Views of Its History and Literature* was a rapid summary of her fortunes from the fall of the Roman Empire to his own day, and it had a definite purpose: to defend his countrymen from the aspersions of foreigners and to arouse them to efforts at national regeneration. Gallenga endeavoured to promote English sympathy for his fallen land, and demonstrated that her people, though of mixed descent, were culturally homogeneous and manifestly destined to be united. He called the Austrian rule over Italy a species of slavery, maintained in an atmosphere of terrified silence, and he told the Italians that they must emancipate themselves.

This work, notable for an excellent bird's-eye view of Italian history and literature, revealed in the author an astonishing command of English. It probably helped to rehabilitate the Italians in the eyes of English readers and to vindicate their national rights.

In 1846, Gallenga was one of the supporters[25] of Mazzini's Italian free school in Hatton Garden, London, where he sometimes delivered lectures. His *Blackgown Papers* of the same year included one story[26] propagandizing in behalf of the school, and also another tale (*Irene*) which described the fearful nature of the Carbonari and their oaths. The scene of the latter work was laid in Modena, about 1821, when its duke was Francis IV. The Carbonari, led by a Father Romualdo, vote for the death of one of their number, Vincenzo Besini, whose treachery has been rewarded by the office of director of police. Odoardo Besini also casts his ballot for the assassination of his brother. A young medical student carries out the orders of his "cousins" in conspiracy, escapes arrest, takes part in the central Italian disturbances of 1831, and eventually marries a kinswoman, Irene by name. One feels certain that this story is somewhat autobiographical. In any case, Gallenga's tales are further evidence of his mastery of English.

About 1847, Gallenga was teaching Italian at Eton College[27] and continuing to write various things. To *The New Monthly Magazine* he contributed in May an article on Dante, stressing the great poet's desire for Italian unity; and during the following July he also wrote a story of Tuscany, called *The Casino*, notable for its good local colour. More important was Gallenga's pamphlet, addressed to Lord Palmerston and entitled *Latest News from Italy*. He described (1847) the excitement throughout the peninsula, the stir of liberalism, the new journalistic freedom in Rome, Charles Albert's desire to possess Lombardy, the anti-Austrian feeling. The pamphleteer urged the Pope to expel the Austrians from Ferrara, which they had re-occupied, by way of warning lest Pius IX's liberalism go too far. All Italy, he declared, would go to the Pope's defence. Like many other Italians before 1848, Gallenga believed in the liberalism of this particular pope and considered him an Italian first. Indeed, he expressed the wish to see the Pope as the head of an Italian federation of states, for His Holiness seemed the champion of the Italian cause.

The next year, 1848, Gallenga published his *Italy, Past and Present*, a historical work with emphasis on Italian nationality, and another treatise called the *Present State and Prospects of Italy*. In the latter, he revealed how unhappy was the situation—a prying, arbitrary police, censorship, bad schools—and he gave a solution: the expulsion of the Austrians. There were chapters on Mazzini, Foscolo, Manzoni, Grossi, Pellico, and Giusti; accounts of Enrico Mayer, the Livornese educator, Gioberti and his neo-Guelph ideas, Massimo d'Azeglio; and other significant contemporaneous material. This was, of course, a survey of the Italian scene. Gallenga did not omit championing the worth of the Italians by his emphasis on the existence of capable and talented men of letters and thought. In other words, the Italians were worthy of separate nationality since they had produced writers of genius. Here was good pro-Italian propaganda, which marked, however, a change in Gallenga's allegiance: it is very clear to a careful reader that he had by this time begun to desert Mazzini and his programme. After 1848, neither had any use for the other, a state of affairs which Mazzini[28] ascribed to wounded vanity.

As one has seen, Gallenga wrote rather frequently on the problems of Italian unity. In 1851, he produced a well-documented and able history of the recent events in his native land. *Italy in 1848* was anti-Mazzinian in tone, for Gallenga had attached himself to those who believed that Italy could be unified only under the House of Savoy and that the leader of *Young Italy* was now a handicap. His hatred of Mazzini was not disguised, and yet it was tempered by a show of respect. One item in Gallenga's history is of interest particularly to Americans. He told how the Lombards read in Botta's *History of the American War of Independence* an account of the Boston tea party and imitated its technique by refusing to smoke in order to reduce Austrian revenues.

When Gallenga attempted the novel, he was not too successful, as is shown by his more or less autobiographical *Castellamonte* (1854), a tale of the insurrection of 1831. This book was dedicated to the patriot, Cesare Balbo, recently deceased. Gallenga's purpose was propaganda—in the guise of fiction, to arouse English indignation against the despots of Italy. But a passage of this sort was not calculated to make the British public respect the Italians:

> From the battle of Fornovo to that of Novara, during three and a half centuries, the Italians scarcely ever showed their faces on the battlefield except to be beaten,—and this especially when under the command of native leaders—especially when they took arms for the sacred cause of their country . . . and the less an Italian says about martial prowess, the better for himself and his country.[29]

However, the numerous incidents of tryannical cruelty included in *Castellamonte* probably did the Italian cause no harm. Thanks to a few grimly humorous anecdotes, the book is fairly readable. On one occasion, the hero escaped in a coffin, which was being carried through the town-gate. The custom-house officer asked: "Any contraband goods?" "Nothing but fresh pork, your honour," was the reply.

Gallenga had by 1855 become the spokesman in England

of the Piedmontese point of view. His *History of Piedmont* stressed the constitutional nature of her government, the toleration of freedom of inquiry, and the existence of a genuine freedom of the press. He described the Piedmontese as sober, discreet, manly, and above all things self-possessed —in other words, a nation capable of self-government since it reconciled liberty with order. That is to say, Gallenga was trying to prove that some Italians were after all so many Latin John Bulls. The ultimate aim of his history was to inform the English that only the constitutional monarchy of Piedmont was capable of uniting the Italian peninsula. As a friend of Mazzini's, David Masson belittled[30] Gallenga's *History of Piedmont*.

In 1858, Gallenga tried again to win the English over to the Piedmontese as the future saviours of Italy. *Country Life in Piedmont* was evidence that the people were generous, dignified, firm, certainly fit to rule themselves, and respectful of the institution of private property. It painted them as morally clean, kind-hearted, and of a winning frankness of speech. It also emphasized that English capitalists could profitably invest their money in various enterprises in Piedmont. Already, Gallenga said, English railway contractors had done well. Why shouldn't the English sell cheap coal to these Italians? There were good workmen and engineers available—

> could not companies be formed [in England] for the construction of bridges and dykes, the draining of marshes, and rescuing waste lands from the beds of overflowed rivers? Would it not be worth while for some of your speculators to help the Piedmontese in the war in which they must needs engage against Nature, and come in for a fair share of the spoils of victory?[31]

Yet England, he added, could profit even more generously from Italian investments provided that the Austrians, the Pope, and other reactionary forces were eliminated. Once more, Gallenga had tried to win English sympathy for

Italy, and this time through an appeal to mutual business interests.

During the Austro-French war of 1859, Gallenga served as correspondent for *The Times* of London. In 1860, he was expelled from Rome. When the American Civil War broke out, he reported the shifting fortunes of the North and the South. After the unity of Italy was an accomplished fact, he sympathetically presented[32] for English consumption the State's side of the case in 1879, when the Church of Rome and the Italian government were especially unfriendly. Gallenga died in England at the great age of eighty-three, an Italian whose English had been perfect and at the ready service of his fatherland. He had known Crabb Robinson, Henry Layard, Leigh Hunt, Thackeray, Dickens, Disraeli, Bulwer-Lytton, and Carlyle; and had served as a link beween English and Italian letters.

The evolution which his career shows, from Mazzinian to Moderate, was after all typical of the actual history of his countrymen. If their change of heart was not treachery, neither was his—and that is the fairest opinion of Gallenga's life.

CHAPTER XI

The Aftermath of the 'Forty-eight: Gavazzi, Lacaita, Saffi, Orsini

§ 1. For his part in the Italian risings of 1848, the apostate Father Alessandro Gavazzi was termed not only "a Savonarola gone madder"[1] but also a maniac. The truth is that these opinions are those of perhaps the most reactionary of Victorian publicists, Charles MacFarlane. Gavazzi was merely a seeker of the limelight with a genuine talent for florid eloquence and bombastic patriotism.

In Italy, Gavazzi had been a Barnabite monk. He became a master showman, going after 1849 on what has been described[2] as starring tours in the Anglo-Saxon world. During the campaign against "Papal Aggression" (the phrase used for the Pope's re-establishing of the ancient Roman Catholic bishoprics in England), Father Gavazzi fed the public on highly spiced tirades. He attained a dubious acclaim on long lecture trips and from the coign of vantage of an evangelical church, founded by him in London for a single purpose—to sully the Scarlet Woman of Rome and thus feed the prejudice of Protestant England. Probably his bigotry was more than patriotic—it was profitable.

From the very beginning of his English stay, Gavazzi was an attraction of great interest. It has been said that he was the original of Vittorio Santo, the verbose monk of Sydney Dobell's long dramatic poem, "The Roman" (1850). Santo is represented as delivering tirades in an endeavour to arouse the Italians to win their independence and union:

> You tell me you are Romans!
> Yet they were lords and you are slaves; the earth

Heard them and shook. It shakes, perchance, for you;
Shakes with the laugh of scorn that there are things
Who lick the dust that falls from Austrian feet,
And call the gods their fathers!

Italy, ruled by native tyrants and the foreigner, is described by Santo:

Every limb
Own'd by some separate savage—each charm lent
To some peculiar lust. The form that served
The world for signs of beauty, parcell'd out
A carcase on the shambles, where small kings,
Like unclean birds, hang round the expected carrion,
And chaffer for the corpse which shall not die!
Look on that mother and behold her sons!
Alas, she might be Rome if there were Romans!

Santo's fate resembles more the martyrdom of another monk, Ugo Bassi, than Gavazzi's career, for Dobell has him sentenced, by an Austrian military tribunal, to execution. His trial is portrayed in the manner of Browning's later poetry:

. . . the judgment-seat
Of Wollustling von Bauerhund von Bosen,
Baron of Herrschwuth and Scheinheiligkeit,
Count d'Omicidio, Marshal in the armies
Of that dread sovereign Apostolical
Our Liege and thine—the imperial Ferdinand,
Emperor of Austria—King. . . .

Ruskin in 1850 broke an engagement to hear Gavazzi lecture;[3] and Carlyle told his wife that the Italian was a blockhead, who was making a furore at Glasgow and elsewhere. What had annoyed Carlyle was that somebody in a Glasgow paper had praised Gavazzi as resembling "our grand hater of shams, T. Carlyle."[4] Out into industrial Northumberland, the great magnate, Joseph Cowen of Tyneside, brought Gavazzi and other exiles to propagandize for Italian unity; and in London, such notables as Palmerston and Earl Russell would sometimes hear lectures by the former monk.[5]

His fellow exiles toiled faithfully to enhance his influence. One of them, Campanella, wrote a *Life of Father Gavazzi*, which was all eulogy: Gavazzi had escaped to England only "that he might in this free land . . . proclaim the faithlessness of the Pope to those who have of late listened with too willing an ear to the seductions of Rome."[6] It might have reasonably been supposed that Gavazzi had wished to avoid a firing squad. In the same year, 1851, Giovanni Battista Nicolini* published another enthusiastic account of Gavazzi.

At this time, the former Barnabite hired the Princess's Theatre in London, where he would deliver "orations"[7] amid the cheers of his audiences, applauding alternately his denunciations of the Roman Catholic hierachy and his allusions to the wrongs of his country. However, it was not roses all the way, for Charles MacFarlane[8] castigated Gavazzi as a nonbeliever.

In 1853, Gavazzi made a very successful speaking tour in America. When he came back, he attacked Puseyism in the Church of England, the Jesuits, and Roman Catholics in general. His message was: "Englishmen, the foe is within you." At Brighton, he repeated his thesis in a speech delivered against the Tractarian movement; and in 1857 he replied to Cardinal Wiseman, who had praised the last four popes. What Wiseman had pronounced good, Gavazzi called bad. The impartial judge in this controversy will grant Gavazzi a superior style for lecturing and a real gift for satire. It is true that he picked up filth and threw it, but what indignation, what fire, and what highly seasoned bits of gossip on the tonsured folk, from whom he was an apostate!

> Good Pius IX is an old comedian, and Wiseman his London fiddler, and music among such companions is the most natural mode of communication. But as an Italian, I too will have my own music. And it shall be the music of a

* This Nicolini had been a deputy to the Tuscan Constituent Assembly and an officer of the General Staff of the Roman Army in the days of Mazzini's Republic.

> hundred guns at the bombardment of Rome [1849]; the music of that breach by which the new barbarians inundated the Eternal City; the music of palaces and monuments riddled to ruins for ever by the paternal blessings of a conquering Pope; the music of the hundreds of bleaching carcases left unburied by order of the priesthood to horrify the living; the music of chains and sighs; the music of weeping and despair; the music of the dungeons; the music of desolate exiles; the music of the scaffolds; the music of the martyrs expiating the crime of patriots to their country! And above all shall ring the music of execration and revenge, till Italy shall have destroyed the fatal institutions of the Pope, spared Wiseman future eloquence, and Italians the bonds of slavery![9]

In 1859, Gavazzi was chaplain of Garibaldi's men in the Alpine campaign. A short while previously, he had published in London his stirring oration, *Italy for the Italians*, a plea for her independence and her separate nationality. The Italians constituted a people, were of the same race, lived within a definite territory, spoke the same language—why ought they not to be free? Imagine, said Gavazzi to the English by way of analogy, that the Russians ruled Great Britain and sent her inhabitants to Siberia. Under the Hapsburg rule, Lombardo-Venetia, only a seventh part of the Austrian empire, paid one fourth of the imperial revenue. Under that same rule, the teaching of Italian was to be forbidden in Austrian Italy by 1860. Italy, declared Gavazzi, could be united if Scotland, Ireland, Wales, Cornwall, England, and Cumberland had been. He asked merely for English sympathy for Italy's cause. "When the day shall arrive for us to cross arms with the Austrians, all that we ask from England is to send to Russia, France, Prussia, this only word, 'do not interfere.' "* Then only could Italy be free—despite the Pope, despots, the Jesuits.

Gavazzi figures in several novels in English. J. R. D. Beste, who disliked him, used him as a character in *Modern*

* *Cf.* the international combat on Spanish soil, 1936–39.

Society in Rome, a story of the siege of 1849. He also appears in Miss Margaret Roberts's *Mademoiselle Mori*, 1860, where he is shown haranguing the Roman populace. The Roman Catholic priest, Antonio Bresciani, wrote that egregious story, *The Jew of Verona*, with no admiration whatsoever for the apostate Barnabite.

No one can deny to the colourful Gavazzi credit for having been very useful to the Italian cause in England; and few will contest the fact that he was a master of a vigorous and denunciatory style of speaking. None the less, fewer still will admire his lack of dignity, his unhesitating use of scandal, his evangelical vanity like that of a Los Angeles saver of souls.

§ 2. Sir James Lacaita, said the ninth Duke of Argyll,[10] was *persona gratissima* in English society. He was more than merely a gentleman of great charm, acceptable to great English political figures and to the panjandrums of polite London circles. He was a very important influence in the attainment of Italian unity, and twice by his intervention advanced the fortunes of his country.

Lacaita had been the legal adviser of the British Embassy at Naples. When Gladstone came to southern Italy in 1850, Lacaita told the Englishman a great deal about King Ferdinand's rule and showed him much more. It was not to be expected that Lacaita would go scot-free, and promptly the Neapolitan government arrested him on a political charge. Only the influence of Sir William Temple, the English minister, saved him from Poerio's fate. Lacaita had twice been warned of the Bourbon displeasure. As he was walking on the Toledo in Naples, a man whispered in his ear, "*Fuggite*"; a second person also repeated the admonition.[11] Such was authentic melodrama in southern Italy before Garibaldi came as a new Perseus.

Italy clearly not being a safe place for anybody suspected by *Bomba* of being a Mazzinian, Lacaita went into exile in

Edinburgh. There he married Maria Carmichael. Very soon after, he settled in London and taught Italian at Queen's College from 1853 to 1856. In the latter year, despite the offer of an annual salary of £200, he declined the chair of Italian letters at the University of Dublin. Since he was an authority on Dante, he assisted Lord Vernon in his great edition of the poet. In the spring of 1854, Lacaita gave a weekly course in Italian literature and history to a well-educated group of listeners. During April, he delivered four lectures in Italian, at the residence of the Duke of Sutherland, to an audience including Macaulay, Hallam, and Dean Milman.[12] Having already published an Italian anthology, Lacaita in 1855 revised Murray's *Handbook for Travellers in Southern Italy*. From 1857 to 1860 he wrote articles for the *Encyclopaedia Britannica*. Meanwhile, he had become friendly with Panizzi, and was concerned in the plot to rescue Settembrini and the other Neapolitan prisoners.[13] With Gladstone, Lacaita remained on terms of the greatest cordiality, acting as a secretary on a salary of £60 a month when the statesman in 1858 went on a mission to the Ionian Islands. From 1857 to 1863, Lacaita was secretary to Lord Lansdowne, and may have influenced what Matthew Arnold wrote in his pro-Italian pamphlet, *England and the Italian Question*, 1859.

Eventually, Lacaita, now not only a British subject (1854) but also Sir James thanks to Gladstone, was comfortably placed in London as a Civil Service Examiner. At this time (1860), Garibaldi was ready to cross over from Sicily to Naples and so complete the rescue of southern Italy from Bourbon misrule. Lord John Russell[14] was about to agree to a proposal of France to stop Garibaldi from crossing the Straits and entering Naples. The Italian cause was saved because Cavour, getting wind of this, spoke to the English minister at Turin, Hudson, who told him to send Sir James Lacaita, intimate friend of the Russell family, to explain the whole affair to Lord John. Lacaita was then very ill, but, at the request of Emmanuel d'Azeglio, Piedmontese minister to England, he called on Russell. Unfortunately, the statesman was closeted with the French minister, Persigny. Then Lacaita took out a card and addressed these words to Lady John Russell, who happened also to be ill: "For the love you bear the memory of your father [Gilbert Elliot, second Earl of Minto, friend of Italy and of Lacaita] see me this instant." A servant took up the card, and Lady John Russell saw him at her bedside. He persuaded her to send down to her husband a simple and peremptory message: "Come up at once." Lord John, who had been compelled to think that his wife had suddenly had a turn for the worse, left Persigny abruptly, rushed upstairs, and found himself with Lacaita. The Italian won Russell over, and the latter told Lacaita that he should go home and to bed—there was no need to worry. Sir James Lacaita went back to enjoy his illness, but Persigny must have experienced a sensation of baffled amazement at the about-face of the English minister. This episode is the basis of one scene in Mr. John Drinkwater's chronicle play on Garibaldi.

Ironically enough. King Francis II of Naples tried to enlist Lacaita's influence in England in order to stop Garibaldi's progress. Although the monarch offered to make Lacaita a Neapolitan marquis, to give him a large sum of money, and to appoint him as Neapolitan minister to England on a munificent salary, Lacaita was scarcely interested.[15]

In 1868, an English poetaster named Irby[16] dedicated a volume of pro-Italian verse to Lacaita. Though the poems were meretricious, this dedication to Lacaita was evidence that he had helped bring together Englishmen and Italians during the era of the making of Italy. In a more practical way, he had associated English capital and Italian business by his holdings in English companies interested commercially in Italy, especially in railways. One more detail is not without interest—his son once made the statement that Sir James had been the matchmaker of the famous marriage of Hannah Rothschild and Lord Rosebery,[17] a union of high finance and of high social position. Money and station had also united in Lacaita's career in England.

§ 3. Count Aurelio Saffi, man of letters and patriot, was, despite the accident of his title, a Mazzinian of the inner circle, and had served as one of the triumvirs of the Roman Republic. From 1851 he was, like his friend and chief, Mazzini, an exile in England. His way had been prepared for him, and without much difficulty he was able to obtain access to periodicals, whence he drew in part his livelihood.

At Mazzini's intercession, Mrs. Carlyle obtained tutorial employment for Saffi with the Sterlings and the Wedgwoods. Her husband took such a great liking to him that it aroused her gratified and astonished comment.[18] Mazzini also saw to it that his friend was admitted to radical coteries in London, and Saffi became known to George Jacob Holyoake, David Masson, and William Shaen. Everywhere, his gentle nature, dreamy and melancholy, made him welcome.

So far as one can tell, it was Saffi who took advantage of Gladstone's airing of the Poerio trial in order to translate, anonymously, in 1851, Poerio's speech in his own defence before the extraordinary grand court at Naples. Probably, Saffi wrote the article entitled "Religion in Italy" (*The Westminster Review*, October 1853), which was in tone Mazzinian and antipapal. Since he was an Italian nationalist, Saffi described the dignitaries of the Church as mere placemen, and said that the Pope's voice only swelled the chorus of European despots. Italy suffered, he declared, under the double tyranny of sword and crosier.

During 1856–57, Saffi and Miss Jessie White lectured[19] in the provinces on the Italian cause, speaking among other places at Manchester, Leeds, Newcastle, Edinburgh, and Glasgow. At Tyneside, the influential Joseph Cowen made them especially welcome. for their purpose was to raise money to finance one of Mazzini's revolutionary schemes. The Society of the Friends of Italy, in whose name they spoke, secured for Saffi in 1856* a post at the Taylorian Institute of Oxford, where he taught Italian. Swinburne had him for a teacher and was as a result confirmed in his Mazzinian sympathies. Frederic Harrison[20] studied Dante under Saffi, and became even more pro-Italian than he had heretofore been.

Saffi had appointed for himself a definite educational programme, which he explained in a letter from Oxford to Francesco Crispi:

> I am preparing some letters on Italian affairs to give English people a grasp of the situation, in which I want to set forth as well and as clearly as possible, the true conditions of the national problem, the features and tendencies of the Italian movement, and the responsibilities devolving upon the British nation, from the point of view of that international solidarity to which all civilized nations should aspire. In spite of a growing intercourse and sympathy with Italy, public opinion here is marked by a great deal of indecision and confusion concerning our capability to redeem and create a country of our own. . . .[21]

One wonders whether Swinburne's *Ode to Mazzini* is not a product of this deliberate statement of policy by his adored teacher, Aurelio Saffi.

When the attempt by Orsini on the life of Napoleon III was the subject of European discussion, and the French government tried to have the English Cabinet expel Italian refugees from London—"The School for Assassins," it was Saffi who wrote the pamphlet, *Carlo Poerio and the Neapolitan Police*, 1858, to show that tyrannical rule fostered conspiracy. He denounced any yielding on the part of the British government, for he believed that it ought never, at the bidding of despots, to organize a band of police to play into

* But Saffi, then living at 71, High Street, had taught Italian in Oxford as early as November 1853. See the *Edizione nazionale degli scritti di Giuseppe Mazzini*, L, 141.

the hands of Naples and Austria, to pay domiciliary visits to already unhappy aliens, or to violate the sanctuaries of their miserable homes and ransack their private papers. Saffi then gave an account of the horrible, arbitrary nature of Neapolitan justice, and said that the bastinado was allowed under the Bourbon code. Anywhere from ten to one hundred blows might be given to a political victim. Denying that Italian revolutionists were either terrorists or anarchists, he asserted that the Italians were fit for self-government, but what they had by way of rule was a system of repression not only illegal and despotic, but utterly immoral and criminal—all in the name of legitimacy and religion. It may be that this particular pamphlet by Saffi, written with a high-spirited and moving eloquence, was responsible in some slight degree for the fall of Palmerston's ministry, which had attempted to appease French demands for strict alien laws in England.

In 1859, Frederic Harrison and Professor Francis Newman* set about to form a band of writers to support the Italian cause in the press. Since Harrison hoped that some good would come from Napoleon III's interest in Italian affairs, Saffi and his friends never forgave him.[22] Like their leader, wholehearted Mazzinians in those days were unable to compromise reasonably on even a question of tactics.

Saffi married an English lady, a Miss Georgina Craufurd,[23] whose brother was a member of Parliament. Countess Saffi was a descendant of Sir Robert Walpole. It is interesting to observe how many of these Italian exiles married English girls, a fact which explains why such unions were fairly common themes in novels of the period.

In *Macmillan's Magazine*, July 1860, Saffi published an article on "Garibaldi and the Sicilian Revolution." Skilfully written, it explained the background of the Sicilian expedition: the perfidious behaviour of the Bourbon rulers towards the ancient Sicilian constitution, and the new feeling

* Brother of the Cardinal.

of *Italian* nationality. Saffi treated in detail Mazzini's single-hearted devotion to the Italian cause, described the preparatory work of Rosolino Pilo in Sicily, and asked for non-interference in Italy. England, he urged, should discountenance any foreign intervention. Only thus could Italian unity be achieved, and European peace be preserved. Two political articles by Saffi appeared in Holyoake's organ, *The Reasoner*, in March 1861; and one in *Macmillan's Magazine* for July 1863. The last expressed hope for backward southern Italy and the wish that Rome and Venice might be free. In December 1866, and April 1867, there appeared in *The Fortnightly Review* under Saffi's signature two able essays on "Italy and the Pope," in which he considered the question of Church and State and argued against the Church in general and against its temporal power in particular.

Saffi appears as a character in Miss Margaret Roberts's novel, *Mademoiselle Mori*; and is known to have influenced Dante Gabriel Rossetti's *Early Italian Poets*, the manuscript of which he had seen.[24] He was also on terms of close friendship with William Michael Rossetti, the more politically minded brother, who was a Mazzinian by whole-hearted conviction. Swinburne, of course, loved Saffi very much, and addressed several of his poetic efforts to the former Roman triumvir: "To Aurelio Saffi," written after Mazzini's death in 1872; and the dedication to the play, *Marino Faliero*, 1885. In the latter, Swinburne records his pride at having met Saffi at Oxford "where Isis whispers to the murmuring shade." Saffi, he said, had acted a sublime *rôle* at the time of the Roman Republic.

After Mazzini's death, Saffi became the leader of the Italian republican party. Whenever he was in England, he was in the habit of calling on Swinburne. The death of Saffi in 1890 evoked from Swinburne the fine, yet uneven verses, "In Memory of Aurelio Saffi." Swinburne praised the purity of Saffi's life and was certain of his immortality.

Six years later, he wrote another memorial poem and characteristically said about the same things as before: Saffi could stand with Dante and with Mazzini. On the other hand, Carlyle once vividly remarked that Saffi gave lectures at Oxford "in a moth-eaten voice."[25] One is made to forget by a gibe of this sort the great love which his students had felt for a distinguished exile.

§ 4. The most notorious of the Italian exiles in Great Britain was not Mazzini but a man whose single deed of violence made a universal stir—Felice Orsini. He first came to London in 1853 after the failure of Mazzini's *coup d'état* in Milan on February 6th, and reported to his principal. Malwida von Meysenbug,[26] who met him at Alexander Herzen's about this time, thought him handsome and very much like a *condottiere* of the Middle Ages.

The next news of Orsini was his arrest at Hermannstadt in 1854 on suspicion of being a revolutionary. He was shifted from prison to prison within the Austrian empire, and made a miraculous escape from the Mantuan fortress of S. Giorgio in 1856. The same year saw him again in London. Though his funds were very low, he was not discouraged but contemplated writing and teaching.

Orsini now made the acquaintance of influential people. At Bath, he was the guest of Walter Savage Landor[27] (a fellow believer in the virtue of tyrannicide); he went up to Tyneside and lectured for Italy under the auspices of Joseph Cowen of Newcastle; and he met Jessie Meriton White.

Orsini had ready in manuscript a narrative of his fifteen months' imprisonment and final escape from Mantua. This work Miss White ably translated as *The Austrian Dungeons in Italy* (1856), a vivid story of patriotism, suffering, daring, triumph. His object was to strengthen his countrymen against the Austrian and "to impress on the minds of the English and American friends of Italy, that deeds, not words, must make their sympathy . . . useful." In reality, he wanted

Italian exiles sent back from England fitly armed. Orsini's descriptions of his various cells form a frightful pattern—filth and vermin and bad smells, loathsome food and vile water, bastinadoing of prisoners fastened by means of vices, cross-examinations by jailers in order to trap their charges into making damaging admissions, an execution now and then to be carried out with a grotesque and dreadful pageantry. Apparently, Orsini had a long record as a political malcontent, for he acknowledged that he had been imprisoned at Bologna in 1844, at Florence in 1847, in Piedmont in 1853, in Switzerland in 1854, and—later in the same year—at Hermannstadt. His escape from Mantua compels one unreservedly to admire his courage and ingenuity, in both of which qualities he had been strengthened by a reading of Byron, especially by the tale of "Mazeppa."[28] After all, Mazeppa too had broken loose from torment.

Without the editorial assistance of Jessie White, Orsini published at Edinburgh in 1857 his *Memoirs and Adventures*. This second autobiography was occupied with his history from 1819 to about 1856, and excluded much of the material of his previous book. Sentenced in 1844 to the galleys for life, he was freed in 1846 by a papal amnesty. He took part in the defence of the Roman Republic under Mazzini and escaped by means of an English passport. One thing is noteworthy: *Memoirs and Adventures* clearly reveals that between 1856 and 1857 Orsini had broken off friendly relations with Mazzini. To this estrangement, Justin McCarthy, who heard Orsini lecture in Liverpool in 1857, has testified.

Now Orsini, freed from the control of Mazzini, whom he had contemptuously judged too timid, began making plans for his last and most desperate project. This was his plot to assassinate Napoleon III, whom he regarded as the enemy of Italian liberty. He spent a great deal of time in experimenting with various types of bombs, and even had George Jacob Holyoake[29] test them out. The English agitator observed that Orsini seemed upset about something and thought that he had fallen in love with a red-haired girl—in all probability, Jessie White.

It is possible that Orsini was in London in January 1858. At any rate, on the fourteenth of that month he was in Paris with an English passport made out in the name of Mr. Thomas Allsop of brewing fame. With Orsini were three accomplices: Pierri, De Rudio, and Gomez. When the desperate plotters hurled three pear-shaped grenades at their imperial quarry, Napoleon III was on his way to the opera. Later evidence indicates that Orsini and company had taken with them five bombs, which had been made by a Mr. Taylor of Birmingham. In addition, the conspirators were heavily armed with revolvers. Orsini was struck by a fragment of the hand grenade which he himself had thrown and was tracked by the traces of his own blood. De Rudio had hurled the other two bombs. One hundred and fifty-six men, women, and children, who had been watching the Emperor's progress, sustained a total of 511 wounds. Some of the wounded died of their injuries. Napoleon III, however, had not been harmed at all.

Pierri was executed. The death sentence of De Rudio was commuted to life imprisonment. Gomez was sent to jail at hard labour for life. Orsini was arrested and sentenced to death. At his trial, he displayed great dignity and spoke eloquently in the cause of Italian freedom. He was adulated by ladies of high social rank, some of whom were moved to tears at his execution.

The whole affair had international repercussions. The French, through Count Walewski, attempted to influence the English House of Commons to pass Lord Palmerston's Conspiracy Bill. Neither Lord Clarendon nor the Commons felt disposed to restrict the humane right of political refuge, and the measure not only failed but caused the fall of the ministry. The recent attempt at pressure by the French aroused a great deal of popular resentment in England, as was shown by leaders in *The Times* and by a London jury's acquitting Simon Bernard, an accomplice of Orsini. Though the facts were against Bernard, he was permitted to go free and was even vigorously applauded.

In literary circles, there was much commotion also. Mrs. Browning, conceding Orsini a death more noble than his life, thought Mazzini at the bottom of it all, and pleaded with Jessie White Mario* to make a public declaration of her hatred of political assassination, but the fiery Mme. Mario answered that in her opinion Napoleon III (who had achieved power through a bloody *coup d'état*) was a greater murderer than Orsini.[30] Swinburne bought a copy of Orsini's picture (a Regent Street shopkeeper demanded a shilling admission fee of those who wished to examine the original of Swinburne's ikon), and genuflected before it in his Oxford chambers. Landor found himself involved in a great deal of trouble. The old man was shocked that Orsini, once his guest, had actually endeavoured to carry out his own sentiments on tyrannicide. *The Times* (March 15, 1858) printed a long account of Orsini's execution and quoted the real Thomas Allsop as saying that Landor had offered a reward for the killing of Napoleon III. A letter to *The Times* two days later contained Landor's denial that he had ever countenanced assassination. One is amused by his hair-line distinction between assassination and tyrannicide—the former was base, the latter a sublime virtue, and that was that! Since, said Landor, Napoleon had been elected by the suffrage of his countrymen, he could be no tyrant but was a legitimate sovereign. Landor also wrote some verses, "Orsini's Last Thoughts,"[31] which described the Italian as considering himself condemned to death by a fellow Carbonaro of the past. According to Landor's poem, Orsini, certain of the eventual freedom of Rome, desired to say farewell to his wife and children. Another poet, Sydney Dobell, regarded the attempt on the Emperor not as

* She married Alberto Mario in 1857.

assassination but as an act of open war, always in progress between Louis Napoleon and the Italian refugees whom he had injured.[32]

The French government, very much disgruntled at the failure of the Conspiracy Bill, termed England a den of assassins. Landor, who had by now recovered from his fright, published in the London *Daily News* this "Reply from the 'Den' ":

> We encourage assassins! Sir! Have no fear,
> No hold has the murderer or sympathies here:
> England loathes an assassin, and loathes him no less
> Whether shameful by failure or great by success—
> Whether hiding from sight, or set high on a throne—
> Whether killer of thousands, or killer of one—
> Whether bribe or revenge, or the hope of a name,
> Or the dream of a "Destiny" "damn him to fame."
> Whatever the prompting, whatever the end,
> Has he slaughtered a people he swore to defend:
> Has he banded with ruffians, like him, to strike
> At a brother assassin—we loathe him alike!
>
> E'en where, Cain-like, by Providence guarded from ill,
> With a mark set upon him that no man may kill;
> Where prosperity seems all his projects to crown,
> We've no faith in his Favour—no fear of his Frown:
> Undismayed by his Fortunes—unawed by his Fate,
> We smile at his "Destiny"—WATCH him and WAIT.[33]

It is very evident that he was just a little sorry at Orsini's failure to kill the new "Man of Destiny." By December 1860, Landor had become entirely regretful that Orsini had blown up the wrong people. As he told Robert Browning, tyrannicide—meaning the assassination of Napoleon the Less—was glorious and beneficent![34]

Swinburne, unlike Landor, never felt abashed about the *affaire Orsini*. Indeed, he even wrote a sonnet, "For a Portrait* of Felice Orsini,"[35] in which he said that this was the face of a hero—steadfast, sad, and sweet. But he followed Landor's

* Probably the one which he kept in his Oxford chambers.

cue to some degree as these lines show: Orsini was one "who thought to vanquish wrong with wrong, Erring. . . ."

It was, however, the future Mrs. Hamilton King[36] who took most deeply to heart the execution of Felice Orsini. With her father, she entered the shop in Regent Street where the assassin's portrait was on exhibition, and gazed at it steadfastly and intently. Previously, she had followed with fascination the *Times* accounts of the entire matter. Very soon, she began work on what she considered her best poem, *The Execution of Felice Orsini*, and was occupied with it for a year and a half. It was finished early 1860. This long poem is characterized by an earnestness, a solemnity of tone, and an intensity of mood which are seldom found in the poetry of a girl scarcely out of her 'teens. At the beginning, she pictured Paris on the day of Orsini's execution, March 13, 1858: the crowds that waited all night or came very early to see; the Emperor in the Tuileries sleepless and ill at ease, for he had been a Carbonaro and had taken the same oath as Orsini; the soldiers on horseback pressing back the curious throngs; everything against a background of grayness and sorrow. She greeted the new day and described it sombrely:

> A day to be much remembered,
>   Sad and sublime;
> Written in letters of red
>   In the book of Time.
> Not a coronation morning,
>   With its light of purple and gold,
> And floods of mighty music
>   In hallelujahs rolled:
> Not a young bride led home
>   From royal halls afar,
> All pallid and pearl-glittering,
>   A sweet and tremulous Star:
> Not a conqueror's state entry,
>   With his armies marching back
> Under triumphal arches,
>   A glittering scarlet track,

When the wide streets glare in sunshine,
  And the bells ring out all day,
And the people shout together,
  Knowing not what they say:—
Only a winter's morning,
  Crowds standing silent by,
A prison and a scaffold,
  And a man brought out to die.

Then her attention wandered in horror to the guillotine:

Where the hideous frame
  Rises gaunt and tall,
Its cords wound up for working,
  Dull red painted all;
The hard block ready laid,
The overhanging blade,
  Horribly they loom
  Through the thinning gloom.

In the second part, called "The Prison," Mrs. King portrayed Orsini behind bars: his hair turned white in a week, his anguish, and his calm. She recalled his life, his joining a secret society, and his imprisonment in the Papal States. Then she rehearsed his part in 1849, first at the defence of Rome, "The third Rome in her bridal prime," and then in putting down disorder at Ancona, which had been kept in a state of terror by brigands and assassins. Next, she told of his career from 1849 to 1856—his exile:

All that story, yet half-told,*
Of danger strange and manifold,
Thirst and hunger, heat and cold,
Wanderings wild by field and flood,
Deeds of daring, wounds and blood,
    In peril and in pain.
  Often into prison cast,
  Yet no bonds could hold thee fast;
  From their hands escap'd and past,
    And forward once again.

* Later, she contemplated a biography of Orsini.

After this, Mrs. King related the story of his revolutionary mission in December 1854, through Hungary, Austria, and Transylvania; his intrepidity in the face of great peril; his escape from Mantua in March 1856; and finally, his life in England until December 1857, when he tried to induce the government and the people to act for Italy. This is her summary of his English life of exile:

> Bread of exile once more thine,
> Full of bitterness and brine;
> Damp, downward-pressing skies,
> Cold looks from stranger eyes;
> Passionate pleadings thrown away,
> Homesick pining day by day,
> Strong health fretted to decay. . . .

She concluded the second part of her poem by telling of Orsini's work at the dangerous task of making the bombs; his journey to France in the cause of tyrannicide; his trial, conducted with direful ceremony; and his great speech, on February 25, 1858, in his own defence.

In the third part of *The Execution of Felice Orsini*, the poet described the procession to the scaffold—slow and solemn, the lighted tapers flickering, and the hymn sad and subdued. She regarded him as a martyr and took delight in recording his final shout before his execution: "Vive la France! Viva l'Italia!" At the end, she imagined that the eclipse of the sun two days after was a sign of universal mourning.

Only an actual reading of her poem can reproduce its moving intensity. One feels that it was composed at a white heat. *The Execution of Felice Orsini* is a simple, almost stark poem—but not the worst of the Victorian age.

A year after Orsini's attempt on the life of Napoleon III, Swinburne had so far forgotten that he had in a very mild fashion expressed regret at the deed as to deliver a speech[37] at the Oxford Union on the duty of tyrannicide. This was about November 1859, probably when the Prince of Wales was visiting Oxford! But Swinburne had only in mind "Jonathan Wild the Less"—that is, Napoleon III.

When Napoleon III went to war against Austria in 1859, many Englishmen thought that he was fighting for Italy in order to silence the threats of those who wielded Italian daggers. In fact, it was held generally in Europe that the Emperor's desire to do something for Italian nationalism was motivated by his fear of another Orsini, and that he had once been a Carbonaro.

W B. Brooke's novel, *Out with Garibaldi* (1861), called Orsini "that noble-minded, but wrong-headed and cruelly belied patriot." Similarly in 1864, a Protestant clergyman, the Reverend Gavin Carlyle, deplored Orsini's fanaticism but defended "the character of this heroic man. . . . His method of action was mistaken; but his purpose was good. . . ."[38]

Orsini is mentioned in a few Victorian novels either directly or indirectly: in H. F. Chorley's *Roccabella*, 1859; in Charles Lever's *Tony Butler*, 1865; and elsewhere. There are also a few collections of very minor contemporary poetry which refer to his crime against Napoleon III. However, if one omits Mrs. King's long poems,[39] it is Swinburne* who most touchingly deals with the career of the executed assassin. In the "Song of Italy," Orsini is numbered among the Italian martyrs and is sorrowfully called the "foiled tyrannicide." It is of interest to note that when John Morley brought J. S. Mill† news of the declaration of war by France on Prussia (July 14, 1870), Mill violently struck his chair and exclaimed with passion, "What a pity the bombs

* The hitherto unknown and fragmentary play, the text of which E. H. W. Meyerstein reproduces in the *London Mercury and Bookman* article (No. 220, February 1938, pp. 415–23) entitled "Two Scenes from a Tragedy by Algernon Charles Swinburne," has a character named Orsini. It is conjectured that the drama was written after 1860.

† The long footnote (concerning the lawfulness of disseminating the doctrine of tyrannicide) at the beginning of the second chapter of his great essay, *On Liberty*, 1859, was inspired by the Orsini case.

of Orsini missed their mark, and left the crime-stained usurper alive!"[40]

In 1881, William Michael Rossetti wrote a sonnet on Orsini, which his brother, Dante Gabriel, praised.[41] The poem, appearing in the younger Rossetti's *Democratic Sonnets*,[42] asserted that Orsini had not died in vain, for

> be it fear or shame,
> Napoleon, arming, hushed the Lombard moan.

Of Felice Orsini, contemporary opinions were mixed, but none would deny that he had been the most desperate of all the Italian exiles of London.

CHAPTER XII

Gladstone and *Bomba's* Victims

The most celebrated political prisoners of the middle of the nineteenth century were the mild liberals: Baron Carlo Poerio, Luigi Settembrini, and Sigismondo Castromediano, Duke of Moriano. Probably the most detested ruler in the world was their jailer, Ferdinand II of Naples, better known as King *Bomba*, whose fortresses were said to hold some twenty thousand of his subjects on charges of treason, in many cases without any trial at all.

The former Cabinet minister Carlo Poerio came of a family of patriots, for his brother Alessandro and his father Giuseppe had also been politically active. In the 'thirties of the last century, Giuseppe Poerio had been a refugee in England, not exactly unheralded, since a novel (1825) by the Marquess of Normanby had praised his skill as a lawyer.[1] Luigi Settembrini, friend and fellow martyr with Carlo Poerio, had been arrested in 1839 on the charge of being a member of *Young Italy* and had then been released because proof of his guilt was lacking. Settembrini first attracted attention in England by his *Protesta del Popolo delle due Sicilie* of 1848 (which Swinburne read).[2] But what made these Italians known to the Anglo-Saxon world was the fact that in the winter of 1850–51 Gladstone heard their trial for treason.

Carlo Poerio was condemned to twenty-four years in irons, fined six hundred ducats, and bound to common malefactors by chains, which were never undone, night or day. After years of this existence, he came back into the world, ruined in health and with a permanent wound in his leg, where the iron had eaten into the flesh. Settembrini, having first been taken into preventive custody, was sentenced to death. Eventually, his punishment was commuted to imprisonment for the duration of life. Castromediano was sent to the galleys for thirty years.

The evolution of Gladstone's opinions on Italian unity is also the evolution of British popular sentiment on this subject. At the end of his career, he was an enthusiast on the subject of Italy's unity under the King of Piedmont. Before that, he had helped spread the reputation of Piedmont as an orderly, progressive state. Still earlier, he had laid bare the egregious nature of Bourbon misrule in southern Italy. But at the beginning he did not believe in "Italy a nation." From the point of view that Italian reform was necessary, both the British public and its guide progressed to accept also the notion that the union of Italy was equally and even previously essential. In a word, Gladstone had become one of the greatest of the friends of Italy. It is not for nothing that when the news of Gladstone's death in 1898 reached Italy, her premier expressed the feelings of the nation in the following words: "Italy has not forgotten, and will never forget, the interest and sympathy of Mr. Gladstone in the events that led to its independence." People who were there at the time said that the grief was real and universal, and resembled that displayed at the death of Garibaldi.[3]

For Italy, Gladstone's sympathy was cultural and political in origin. Like many another English statesman, he had been brought up to regard Rome as the heart of political civilization. At his public school where the classics were almost the whole curriculum, he had been taught the ancient models of eloquence and statecraft. It is not therefore incorrect to say that the ruins of the Forum were as sacred to Gladstone as to Mazzini himself. As a young man, Gladstone had spent six months in Italy and had become thereafter an assiduous reader of Dante. Besides knowing the Rome of the Caesars and her language, he had thus acquired an exact knowledge of Italian (which he spoke and wrote very well, said Panizzi)[4] and was even able nobly to render Manzoni's great ode on the death of Napoleon, *Il Cinque Maggio*, in English.[5] About 1843, Gladstone became acquainted with Panizzi, and from their friendship grew perceptibly his enthusiasm for Italy.[6] Yet it may be said with certainty that as late as 1848 Gladstone was hostile to the thesis that Italy ought to be united.[7]

But the next year marked the beginning of his alteration of sentiment: he was preparing an article on Leopardi for *The Quarterly Review*, and Panizzi was helping him with it. That is doubtless why the critique, which appeared in March 1850, contained a sympathetic reference to the misfortunes of Leopardi's fatherland and quoted almost the whole of the mournful and indignant *canzone*, *All' Italia*, with its picture of the walls and arches, columns and statues, and lone ancestral towers of Italy, all mute witnesses of her former greatness, and with its contrasting description of her present defenceless misery.

In the autumn of 1850, the Gladstones made a journey to southern Italy with the idea of benefiting the eyesight of one of their daughters. Gladstone, said Morley,[8] went to Naples with no purpose of political propaganda, and his prejudices were at that time rather strongly in favour of established governments—even that of the Neapolitan Bourbons. It may be that Gladstone had read Alexander Baillie Cochrane's *Young Italy*, which contained a sketch of a Neapolitan cell—prisoners in rags, many of them ignorant of what they were accused of, in an atmosphere as thick as a London fog permeated with a damp, fetid, noxious vapour. Cochrane had reported finding only about 614 political offenders in jail, all being held without trial, and had spoken, he said, frankly to King Ferdinand about them.[9] On November 16, 1850, Gladstone met James Lacaita, a friend of the English minister, Sir William Temple, and legal adviser to the British legation at Naples, with whom thereafter he discussed politics and literature, especially

Dante.[10] Though Charles Lacaita, his son, has denied it, it is probable that Lacaita induced Gladstone to inspect the Neapolitan prisons and to visit the law courts, and that he served as the Englishman's political mentor. From June 1850 until February 1851, the trial of Poerio, Settembrini, and about forty others went on. Gladstone watched the proceedings with a horrified interest, heard the witness, Jervolino, perjure away Poerio's liberty, and with a mounting anger learnt of Poerio's sentence. Next, he visited the Vicaria prison in Naples (reckoned the best in southern Italy), and then went to Nisida, where he found Poerio and other political prisoners chained to common felons. The prisoners told Gladstone not to consider the further punishments that they would suffer if he exposed the inhuman treatment—but to go ahead and publish his conclusions.

At the very time Gladstone was in Naples, Nassau Senior, the economist, was also there and was being informed by a high-placed Neapolitan, Carlo Troja, about prison conditions. Senior recorded in his journal[11] that even before trial, prisoners were chained together, two by two, in irons weighing between thirty and forty pounds, and never taken off for any purpose whatever. At the Vicaria, the cells, holding three persons, were about eight feet square, received light and air only from a hole in the top, far below the level of the ground, reeked with damp, and swarmed with vermin and loathsome reptiles. In Nisida, Senior learnt, there were rooms not twenty feet square in which seventeen or eighteen persons had been confined for months, and had been fed only with the blackest bread and with soup of which the smell was unbearable. And Nassau Senior observed that the foregoing was the treatment meted out to untried persons—persons whom the laws of almost every other country treated as innocent and detained only to insure their safe custody. The economist declared that even the medical men who undertook to visit the prisons, and were paid for doing so, were not required to enter the lower dungeons. The prisoners were brought up to them. Between Gladstone and Senior there is an extraordinary difference of behaviour—Senior, ever the proponent, evidently, of *laissez-faire*, merely made notes in his diary; Gladstone gave way to his humane feelings. However, in fairness to Senior, it must be admitted that had he made known what he had seen, he would have endangered many Neapolitans.

On December 20, 1850, Senior attended the trial of Poerio; and wrote, two days later, that almost to a man the Neapolitan moderate or constitutional party was in exile, or in irons, or had perished in the dungeons of the Vicaria or of Nisida.

> Every member of the many thousand families whose fortunes and happiness the King has destroyed, whose fathers and brothers he has driven from their homes, or slowly tortured to death in his prisons, and of the many thousand others who feel that the same fate is awaiting them, is one of a conspiracy against him, not the less real for being mutually uncommunicated.

And as if to prophesy the necessity of a Garibaldi, Senior added: "The lava is rapidly accumulating. You might as well expect Vesuvius to remain quiescent as Naples."[12] M. Manna, former Neapolitan Minister of Commerce, told Senior that those judges in Naples who were mild were dismissed. Hence, many were cruel in their sentences in order to retain their posts. At Christmas, he visited Lady Holland's (in Naples) and was cautioned to keep his mouth shut before a Count L.: ". . . he is one of the royal spies, and receives 100 ducats a month for his reports!" Finally, on the thirtieth of December, Nassau Senior met the Gladstones in Naples.[13] Probably Senior discussed with Gladstone what he had seen and what had been told him. Anyhow, on January 3, 1851, the English statesman himself went to hear Poerio's speech in his own defence.[14]

On that very day Lacaita was arrested; and Gladstone, notified of his friend's plight, remarked at dinner:

> If Lacaita, who is a man of moderate opinions, and who has assured me that he has never conspired or belonged to any secret society, has been so suddenly arrested, this means that at Naples there is no security for anyone, and I think that my party, the Tories, who have always supported the Bourbons, ought to know . . . what the conditions of this country are.[15]

Lacaita was freed on the twelfth, but that made no difference to Gladstone. He had sat for long hours during the trial of Poerio, visited the prisons, conversed with Poerio chained in double irons to a common felon, watched sick prisoners toil upstairs to see the doctors for whom the lower regions were too foul. He had been stirred by the corruption of the courts and their vindictive sentences. He had beheld uncondemned and untried men languishing in jail. He had seen especially the violation of all law and of the constitution to which *Bomba* had sworn fidelity.[16] And he had to speak out. That in him which years later made him denounce Turkish atrocities in Bulgaria asserted itself now and found expression in one of the finest and most eloquent of all the pamphlets of the last century, the *Two Letters to the Earl of Aberdeen, on the State Prosecutions of the Neapolitan Government.*

On February 26, 1851, Gladstone reached London and was met at the station by his friend, Sir Robert J. Phillimore, who found him bursting with denunciation of the Neapolitan horrors and unable to talk of anything else. On March 4th, he sought out Lord Aberdeen and urged him to intervene. Gladstone and Aberdeen agreed on the use of private remonstrance, but by April the former had ready his first letter. On May 2nd, Aberdeen wrote to Prince Schwarzenberg concerning what Gladstone had seen in Naples and asked the Austrian to use his influence so as to bring Gladstone's statements to the notice of the King of Naples. Although Schwarzenberg (as if to say, "*You* are not the ones to pose as merciful") alluded to a rising in the Ionian islands in 1849 which the English had put down with savage measures, he acted in accordance with the request of the British Foreign Office.[17] Incidentally, Palmerston in 1849 had called the attention of Vienna to the evils of the Neapolitan government. Time passed, nothing was being done, and Gladstone became impatient with roundabout diplomatic methods. What he said in private conversation aroused, he told Lacaita, tremendous interest. Yet he waited some time longer; and not until July 11th did he publish the first Letter to Lord Aberdeen. This was followed in two weeks by a second Letter.[18] He had based what he had written on information furnished by Abbot Luigi Tosti of Monte Cassino and a Mr. Brown, English correspondent at Naples for the London *Morning Post*;[19] and he had been urged to print his sensational disclosures not only by Lord Palmerston, the Foreign Secretary, but also by many others.

Now Gladstone's pamphlet is not an ephemeral political document—it is literature. In the first Letter, he said that he had been between three and four months in Naples, that he had not gone with any idea of looking for grievances or to propagate ideas. Yet such was the nature of the practices of the government of Naples, in reference to real or supposed political offenders, as to constitute "an outrage upon religion, upon civilization, upon humanity, and upon decency." He declared that he did not describe mere imperfection, corruption in low quarters, or occasional severity. He had beheld the incessant, systematic, deliberate violation of the law by the government. He had seen the wholesale persecution of virtue when united with intelligence, the violation of every moral law under the stimulants of fear and vengeance, the prostitution of the Neapolitan judicial system, the reduction of law to odium. In a word, the government and its policies constituted "the negation of God erected into a system" of governance. Then Gladstone estimated the number of political prisoners in the Kingdom of the Two Sicilies as lying between 15,000 and 30,000, and intimated that each prisoner meant also a ruined family and the confiscation of its property. He added that of the full complement of 164 members of the Neapolitan Chamber of Deputies, seventy-six were under arrest or in exile. Next, he revealed how arrests were made. The police, without warrants, would pay nocturnal visits to homes and ransack houses, seize papers, and tear up floors. A prisoner was first placed in custody and then evidence was "found" against him in his papers. Thereupon, he would be heard in secret without a legal adviser and would, frequently, be grossly insulted in order that he might lose his temper and commit an indiscretion. In a prisoner's correspondence, things were read in isolation and not in context. Thoughts were forged in order that they might be punished. Moreover, the courts refused to hear counter-evidence for a prisoner. The jails were the extremes of filth and horror, the food was unfit for human consumption, the cells housed swarms of human beings in long, low-vaulted rooms without any light to speak of.

Gladstone said that Baron Porcari was lodged on the island of Ischia in a dungeon without light and many feet below sea-level; that Settembrini was being kept in double irons for life and was being subjected to torture* with sharp instruments thrust under his finger-nails; and that Poerio, another innocent man, had been imprisoned through the use of forged papers.

The judges, Gladstone said, were poorly paid and were the slaves of the government: if a judge acquitted a political prisoner, he lost his place. Hence, the jails were crowded with the victims of despotism. Gladstone was convinced of Poerio's innocence, esteeming him as a cultivated and accomplished gentleman. Therefore, he concluded, it was time that the veil should be lifted from scenes fitter for hell than earth, that an end be made of the gross and flagrant illegality of Neapolitan justice.

* Settembrini denied that he had been tortured.

In his second Letter, Gladstone said that the police were called *sbirri* or *sgherri*—words expressing degradation and loathing. He added that the constitution of 1848 had never been officially withdrawn by the King of Naples, but merely violated systematically by the government, especially the article which guaranteed personal liberty and arrest by warrant on a specific charge. Children were taught in the catechism that the sovereign power was divine and unlimited and that the king might or might not adhere to the constitution which he had sworn to uphold. The people of Naples were misjudged by the English, for they were mild, simple, truthful, of warm affection, anxious to oblige, and free from gross vice.

The influence of Gladstone's Letters was immense. In Italy, they were received with grateful exultation; in England, the burning phrases seared themselves deep into the minds of all and prepared the way for the good will with which Garibaldi's great exploit of 1860 was received; generally in Europe, they sent a shudder of disgust almost everywhere. The effect of the Letters, which went through eleven* editions in 1851, was strengthened by the fact that Gladstone was then a Conservative and hence a noted adherent of the English party least inclined to the view advocated.[20] Naturally, The Society of the Friends of Italy invited Gladstone to become a member.[21] The English press joined the cry against *Bomba*. In July, George Lewes's organ, *The Leader*, urged Gladstone, as a further step, to attack absolutism itself.[22] But in France, Gladstone was denounced, and a cousin with the same surname was blackballed in a Paris club. Guizot wrote a long letter to Gladstone, regretting the publication of the latter's disclosures. Lord Aberdeen complained too, but Palmerston had copies of Gladstone's pamphlet sent to the British representatives in all the courts of Europe, with orders to give one copy to each government. Nevertheless, Poerio and Settembrini

* Fourteen editions by 1859.

received the impact of Bomba's fury,[23] Poerio being transferred to Ischia, where he was interred in an even worse dungeon—a kind of damp cave through which ran a sewer.

Many Italians addressed grateful letters to Gladstone or rushed into print to proclaim to the world their thankfulness for his disclosures. A former deputy of the Neapolitan Parliament, in exile in Turin, Giuseppe Massari, published in August an exultant pamphlet in which he declared that the letters to Aberdeen were not only "a good and noble and holy deed, but a grand stroke of politics."[24] Massimo d'Azeglio, a distinguished novelist and politician, expressed his gratification in a letter to Lord Minto.[25] A refugee, Giovanni Battista Nicolini, took the occasion of the publication of Gladstone's pamphlet to add that it might serve as a description of the judicial system in the Papal States.[26] In prison at Procida, Castromediano read a smuggled copy and thought it would aid the Italian cause. Indeed, the King of Naples, unable to ignore the effect of these Letters on foreign public opinion, had two Englishmen friendly to him visit Duke Sigismondo, who had by now been transferred to Monte Sarchio. Nothing of advantage to Ferdinand II came of the whole matter, because the Englishmen refused to lie in order to refute Gladstone's testimony.[27] Finally, a certain Laura Beatrice Mancini-Oliva published an Italian *canzone*, '*A Sir G. Gladstone: un' esule napolitana*." In brief, the poem aid that the noble Briton, filled with most holy wrath, had seen the Neapolitan horrors; possessing a truly magnanimous heart, he had defended a groaning people, now about to revive as a result of his indignation!

Among the notable English figures who took a great interest in Gladstone's Neapolitan revelations were Richard Monckton Milnes,[28] Ruskin, Tennyson, Charles Lever, and Landor. The last even wrote a heated letter to *The Examiner* (August 16, 1851) urging English intervention in Naples and at Rome. "Mr. Gladstone, calm and circumspect," said

Landor, "has laid open to the world the island-prison in which the most sanguinary and most cowardly of despots chains down the faithfullest and bravest of his people."[29] Richard Cobden perused a critique of Gladstone's Letters in *The Economist*, believed the truth of their charges, and nevertheless urged that there be no English intervention in Naples except a moral one:

> Everybody, after reading Gladstone's letter, must feel . . . anxious to do something to rescue the victims from their present fate. What can be done? In my opinion, Mr. Gladstone has rendered more service to humanity, by holding up to infamy the Government of Naples, than could have been effected by our Foreign Minister* if he had been ever so well disposed.[30]

King Ferdinand's *régime* was not allowed to go undefended against Gladstone's onslaught. Reactionaries, Italian, French, and British, sprang up to exculpate the Bourbon ruler and to vilify Poerio and others of his victims. Charles MacFarlane, a Scottish resident of Naples and recipient of royal favours,[31] was the first to offer a refutation. In August 1851, he published an urbane pamphlet entitled *The Neapolitan Government and Mr. Gladstone* in which he asserted that Gladstone had obtained only one-sided information; that there were only about 2,000 prisoners—not between 15,000 and 30,000; that the Neapolitan prisons had been greatly improved. Moreover, MacFarlane described the King of Naples as moderate and gentle—"too forgiving in *all* things," and denounced Carlo Poerio for his confirmed revolutionary record.[32] A Frenchman, Alphonse Balleydier, next entered the lists with a pamphlet, *La Vérité sur les Affaires de Naples; Réfutation des Lettres de M. Gladstone*; and like MacFarlane, maintained that Gladstone had heard things from biased witnesses. There were only 2,024 political prisoners. Balleydier added that Gladstone had violated the laws of hospitality, and desired to know why the English

* Palmerston.

(with a notorious record in Ireland) did not mind their own business. His conclusion is vigorous enough:

> *L'œuvre de M. Gladstone est un manteau d'arlequin cousu de pièces et de morceaux, friperies usées jusqu'à la corde et ramassées çà et là dans les bas-fonds de la démocratie italienne.**

In November, Jules Gondon, another Frenchman (and conservative Catholic), published an edition in English of his ill-tempered defence of the King of Naples, *A Letter to . . . W. E. Gladstone in answer to his two Letters . . . on the State Prosecutions of the Neapolitan Government*, in which appeared a series of statements calculated to cause people to believe that Gladstone had built his letters on a scaffolding of lies. There were, of course, refutations by Italian hands; for example, a pamphlet published at Genoa and entitled *Risposta di un Italiano a due lettere del signor Gladstone a Lord Aberdeen*. Its anonymous author declared that Gladstone had availed himself of hearsay evidence; that English prisons were no palaces either; that Poerio was guilty of republicanism; that England had its corrupt judges also (Sir Francis Bacon, for instance); and finally, that the Neapolitans, not the king, had violated their constitution. In general, the writer of this *apologia* used *tu quoque* arguments and of course cited English rule in Ireland. Eventually, the Neapolitan government itself published a translation of its official defence, written by a Signor Mandarini.[33] This *Review of the errors and fallacies published by Mr. Gladstone . . .* attempted sincerity but achieved only a specious effect of pseudo-plausibility. In form, it was a point-by-point rejoinder in vague, general language. For example, the apologist said that Gladstone should not have called the catechism "a complete systematised philosophy of perjury for monarchs," since it was a religious document. Elsewhere, without being specific, the writer maintained that

* "Mr. Gladstone's work is a Harlequin's cloak sewn together from patches and fragments—threadbare cast-off clothes picked up here and there among the dregs of the Italian democratic party."

Poerio deserved his sentence. Lord Palmerston called this official counterblast "a tissue of bare assertion and reckless denial, mixed up with coarse ribaldry and commonplace abuse of public men and political parties,"[34] and sent a copy[35] to Gladstone.

Naturally, the defenders of Ferdinand's treatment of Poerio and other political prisoners must be answered. Gladstone had many to rally to his side. By way of preliminary, Poerio's excellent speech, delivered at his trial in his own defence, was printed* in England in 1851. The accused denied having conspired against the King of Naples or being, as had been charged, an adherent of the sect called *Italian Unity*. Indeed, he affirmed that there was nothing hidden or underhand in his conduct, and that for this reason he had been held prisoner for five days without knowing his alleged crimes. The inference to be drawn was that the Neapolitan government needed time to trump up a case. Then, too, Panizzi, who visited the prisons of southern Italy in order to confirm Gladstone's charges, reviewed the Letters to Aberdeen in *The Edinburgh Review* (October 1851) and corroborated every detail. Henry Lushington,† the capable translator of Giusti's poetry and himself a poet, published anonymously an excellent pamphlet, *A Detailed Exposure of the Apology Put Forth by the Neapolitan Government.* Moreover, the Reverend John Aiton independently arrived at Gladstone's conclusions regarding the Neapolitan horrors and denounced them with telling vigour.[36] He incorporated his charges in an open letter[37] to Palmerston, which he had written (he said) before he knew of Gladstone's work,

* Reprinted in an enlarged form in Aurelio Saffi's pamphlet, *Carlo Poerio and the Neapolitan Police*, London, 1858.

† In 1855, Lushington published a poem, "To King Victor Emmanuel," by way of consolation to the monarch on three recent deaths in the royal family. The Jesuits said that these were retribution for anticlerical legislation. Lushington urged the king not to be afraid of their words, for they praised only the hands that held *Poerio's* cell keys. See *La Nation Boutiquière and Other Poems, Chiefly Political*, pp. 35–38.

and called on England, alone if necessary, to bombard Naples.

It remained for the poet laureate, Tennyson, to voice in 1852 the typical English attitude towards the imprisonment of Poerio and the other Italian martyrs:

> A health to Europe's honest men!
>   Heaven guard them from her tyrant's jails!
> From wronged Poerio's noisome den,
>   From iron limbs and tortured nails!
> We curse the crimes of Southern kings. . . .[38]

And the enlightened German traveller, August Ludwig von Rochau, expressed a fairly common European sentiment when he wrote:

> They call it mercy when they seize a man like Carlo Poerio in the night, bind him hand to hand, and foot to foot to a bandit, fling him into a subterranean dungeon, and leave him there while day after day, year after year, drags on its dreadful changeless anguish.[39]

Thus, Poerio and the others had become symbols of Neapolitan injustice, an opinion which Landor also held[40] in his satirical *Ten Letters Addressed to His Eminence the Cardinal Wiseman by a True Believer* (1853).

Gladstone himself spoke a final word on Ferdinand and his victims, publishing in 1852 a devastating reply[41] to the official Neapolitan statement. Gladstone's new pamphlet was a very judicious annihilation of *Bomba's* apologist, and was written in a tone in no wise indicative of any loss of temper—only a cold, restrained severity. As a pamphleteer, he had proved himself beyond a doubt a man of letters.

It was Gladstone's stand against tyranny in Naples which made Landor dedicate to him the jingoistic *Letters of an American, Mainly on Russia and Revolution* (1854), a shilling pamphlet in favour of the Crimean War. Landor regarded Russia as a great despotic power and esteemed Gladstone as the opponent of autocracy. The anonymous authoress of *Angelo: A Romance of Modern Rome* (1854)—in reality, a

Victorian terror novel—had also been influenced by a reading of Gladstone's Letters to Aberdeen.

Not content with pamphleteering, Gladstone in 1854 called Lord Clarendon's attention to the wretched fate of Poerio, Settembrini, and the other prisoners; and he also took a great deal of trouble to raise and invest a fund for the Settembrini family. Early in the next year, he told Lord John Russell that if the Vienna Conferences [Crimean War] should touch upon Italy, the English mission ought to "plead for the unhappy prisoners in the kingdom of the Two Sicilies detained for political offences real or pretended."[42] Moreover, he urged on Russell the necessity for drastic reforms in Naples if that state were to be admitted to a league of western nations,[43] for there was a rumour that Naples might join the Crimean War allies.[44]

In 1855, Frederick Chamier, an English naval officer, added his own testimony[45] to Gladstone's, and made clear that the latter had not exaggerated about the prisons of southern Italy or its government. Chamier demonstrated that it was better for an Italian to be a fool, a spy, or an idler than a clever man like Poerio. In Naples at that time, being intelligent was usually reckoned equivalent to being dangerous. He added that a foreigner who was the namesake of a radical would be barred from entering Naples. That is, if a man were named Thomas Paine, the authorities might and did treat him as though he were actually the eighteenth-century radical, Tom Paine. On one occasion, Chamier met an elegant gentleman in Naples who was thankful that he had not invited Gladstone to his house during the winter of 1850–51.

The great English conspiracy to free Settembrini and the other political martyrs on the island of San Stefano has already been described. That effort proved abortive when the rescue ship sank. The illness of the English minister at Naples, Sir William Temple, caused the abandonment in 1856 of a new plan, to be carried out by Rosolino Pilo and

Carlo Pisacane, for rescuing Settembrini and the others. Again, Panizzi and Gladstone were leading figures in the scheme. During this latter year, the plight of Poerio and his companions in misery almost brought on an international incident. Lord Palmerston intended to send a fleet to the Bay of Naples to overawe *Bomba.* Incidentally, he thought that the flotilla might rescue Poerio![46]

In 1857, George Dennis, then engaged in writing a guidebook to Sicily for John Murray, the publisher, penetrated into the prison at Palermo and verified Gladstone's accusations that political prisoners were tortured in order that confessions might be exacted.[47] *The Westminster Review* for July of the same year had an article[48] retelling Poerio's sufferings and stressing Gladstone's essential reliability about conditions in Naples. This magazine called on the English government to protest strongly against *Bomba*'s misgovernment.

As English public feeling expressed itself more unmistakably,* King Ferdinand felt more uncomfortable about his prisoners. In 1857, he offered to ship Poerio and Settembrini to Argentina in order that he might put an end to foreign indignation. However, Panizzi opposed their acceptance of the offer, since he wanted them to demand a pardon.[49] So notorious was the case of the Neapolitan prisoners that it even made its appearance in a contemporary novel, Mrs. Charles G. Hamilton's *The Exiles of Italy*, where there is an account of the trial of Poerio and Settembrini with much emphasis placed on the perjured testimony of the government witnesses.

At last the cumulative effect of British public sentiment

* Both France and Great Britain withdrew their ministers from Naples in October 1856, *ostensibly*, in the case of the English, as a *moral* protest against misgovernment. Perhaps Parliament could not countenance either the Neapolitan government's rejection of the railway schemes of certain British capitalists or its reluctance during the Crimean War to furnish mules for transport purposes. See William Roscoe Thayer, *The Life and Times of Cavour*, I, 432–33.

proved too much* for the King of Naples. Early in 1859, he released some sixty-six of the most notable of his political victims, including Poerio, Settembrini, Castromediano, and Spaventa. Ferdinand had intended an American exile for them. They were placed aboard a Neapolitan steamer, the *Stromboli*, and taken to Cadiz, there to join an old American sailing vessel bound for New York. Settembrini's son, Raffaele, who had been an officer with the Peninsular and North African Company, happened to be in Cadiz. By design, he shipped aboard the *David Stewart* as one Juan Rodriguez of Havana, scullion to the Negro cook. As soon as the Neapolitan frigate had left the American vessel (which she escorted to some two hundred miles beyond Cape St. Vincent), Juan the scullion dramatically appeared on deck as an officer in the English merchant marine and frightened Captain Prentiss, of Baltimore, into sailing for Queenstown. In England, the public raised £18,000 for the purpose of taking the sixty-six exiles (via Bristol) to London and there maintaining them.

Arrived in London, the exiles were treated with extraordinary courtesy. Important people like Lord Granville, the dukes of Sutherland and Argyll, the Marquess of Lansdowne, Palmerston, Gladstone, and Lord John Russell were very hospitable[50] to the more distinguished; and Italian became the fashion with ladies of high station. Men like Poerio laid the foundations of future cordiality between Englishmen and Italians. When Gladstone met Castromediano, he asked the Italian whether it were true that the authorities at Montefusco [one of the prisons where the Duke had been kept] killed a nightingale because the

* Richard Cobden maintained in February 1858, that nothing could be done in England to rectify the noisome government of Naples and that Gladstone's generous impulses had merely increased Poerio's misery. Events proved that Gladstone's tactics of publicity for the purpose of arousing mass pressure had constituted the correct political line. See Mrs. Salis Schwabe's *Reminiscences of Richard Cobden*, London, 1895, pp. 297–98.

prisoners listened to its singing; on hearing that it was true, the Englishman said, with a shudder, "Horrible, horrible! I could not have believed it!"[51]

As we have already seen, Dickens wanted the exiles' stories for the magazine *Household Words*. Another man of letters, the aged Leigh Hunt, wrote a sonnet (in *The Spectator*) entitled "To Poerio and His Fellow-Patriots," on the occasion of their arrival in London. The old man called the refugees noble souls and admired their courage, since, though chained to felons and confined in horrible prisons, they had not faltered. Hunt, himself at one time a famous prisoner, concluded by wishing them long life in free England.[52] In 1859, a certain A. G. published a prose drama in three acts called *Poerio and the Neapolitan Prisoners Transported*. This play was not very good, but it was an additional proof of the friendly English interest in the coming of the exiles. The episode of the seizure of the *David Stewart* was used in Stephen Watson Fullom's long narrative poem, *The Exile's Daughter*, 1860. A Latin epigram, *De Libertate*, by Walter Savage Landor, celebrated Poerio's release.

It should be noted that Gladstone's Letters to Aberdeen had been read by the woman novelist who wrote *Niccolo Marini; or, the Mystery Solved: a Tale of Naples Life* (1862)—pretty nearly the usual mixture of the Italian tyrant, half a dozen insurgents, four or five preachers of liberty and equality, twenty reactionaries, one good spy, and a couple of lovers whose families are at mortal enmity. These ingredients are stirred together with a series of sympathetic comments on the woes of Italy. And Gladstone's account of Poerio's trial is not the least of the materials utilized by the authoress, wisely anonymous.

Carlo Poerio died in 1867 and was remembered in James Lockhart's elegy, *The Patriot's Grave*. It is not much of a poem, but it does reveal how strong was the impression which the dead man had made on English hearts. In 1891, Gladstone maintained[53] that Poerio had revealed himself a greater man in the struggle for Italian unity than Mazzini himself—a judgment largely biased, yet showing the noble character of the Neapolitan martyr. Castromediano died at a very great age, having occupied himself in his last years with his archaeological collections. His was a slow and peaceful sunset after a life of hardship. Luigi Settembrini bore the marks of his chains to the day of his death.

G. A. Henty's story, *Out with Garibaldi*, reveals a knowledge on the author's part of Gladstone's exposures. Henty has one of his characters write to the London *Times* on the loathsomeness of the Neapolitan prisons. S. C. Grier's *One Crowded Hour* is partly based on the authoress's acquaintance with Gladstone's testimony regarding Poerio and the dungeons of Naples. Finally, Mr. John Drinkwater's last play, *Garibaldi*, alludes to the English statesman's revelations.

There were, of course, many more Italian patriots in England during the *Risorgimento*, men like Francesco Crispi, the future prime minister of Italy, and Federico Campanella, who belonged to *Young Italy* and collaborated with Mazzini in the publishing of *Pensiero ed Azione* from London. The brief sketches, in the foregoing chapters, of the more outstanding of the exiles can only suggest how deeply the cause of Italian unity was indebted to English magnanimity; how much it owed to a government which, despite diplomatic pressure of the most frantic type, maintained at home the right of asylum for political victims and reckoned among its statesmen leaders like Gladstone, capable of reproving victorious Wrong abroad.

PART III

Statesman and Warrior: Cavour and Garibaldi

CHAPTER XIII

" Milord Camillo "

IN English eyes Count Camillo Benso di Cavour was never an idol like Garibaldi or a saint slightly damaged like Mazzini. On the whole, the British public thought of him as an adept in Machiavellianism—or what Cavour himself, with an engaging frankness, would have termed diplomatic scoundrelism. And since he was successful, the Victorian age found him respectable even if he did not satisfy its longing for either the heroic or the apostolic. After all, these were epithets severally applicable to the other two leading figures of the *Risorgimento*, and a statesman might be content with respect devoid of worship.

Both Garibaldi and Mazzini had an exotic flavour to the Anglo-Saxon palate; Cavour, on the other hand, was in some respects more English than the English themselves. He flattered them by imitating their manners, he profited by the history of their foreign relations (than which scarcely anything Italian has been more Machiavellian), and he adopted as the principles of his domestic policy the doctrines of the Manchester School. It was perhaps because he recognized the essentially English nature of Cavour that John Morley, having written on Cobden and Gladstone, considered preparing next an estimate of the Italian. To Morley, the unification of Italy had been an example of the evolution of European liberalism in its widest and grandest sense; and Cavour, who had been at the helm, was exactly what every English politician since the days of Edmund Burke has imagined himself to be: "a high-minded political idealist, without a touch of the narrow-minded doctrinaire;

. . . no evangelist and no pedant; a successful practitioner of expediency, but no empiric."[1] No doubt agreeing with this judgment, Frederic Harrison could pronounce Cavour the greatest statesman of the nineteenth century,[2] and Lord Palmerston had for his Piedmontese colleague an undisguised admiration. Morley, Harrison, and Palmerston are recognizable English types. It is, however, significant that an atypical Englishman like Swinburne was unable to forgive Cavour, since he was responsible for the exile of the poet's idol, Joseph Mazzini.

The present writer does not wish to stress here Cavour the *Realpolitiker*, of whom Metternich said: "Diplomacy is passing away, there is now only one diplomatist in Europe, and unfortunately he is against us. . . ."[3] Rather would he emphasize those traits in Cavour which made his fellow Italians call him Lord Camillo in derisive recognition of his Anglophile leanings. The statesman's admiration for English ways was in him an affair of conscious cultivation: in debate, he liked to cite English history, with which he was very well acquainted;[4] unlike many of his class, the Piedmontese nobility, he had through his study of English culture been confirmed in liberal tendencies, such as a belief in constitutional monarchy and a dislike for absolutism and clericalism; like a good many of the English peerage, he was interested in steam navigation, railways, and factories; he took for his models in statesmanship Pitt, Canning, and Peel;[5] he had an extraordinary faith in free trade; he subscribed to *The Times*, *The Morning Post*, and *The Economist*;* he read assiduously Adam Smith, Ricardo, and Jeremy Bentham; and he was on terms of friendship with Nassau Senior.

As a younger son of the house of Benso (hence born into the Piedmontese feudal aristocracy), Cavour served in the royal army from 1826 to 1831. About 1828, he met William

* He was especially fond of this publication, which he read from its initial issue in 1843.

Brockedon, the painter, in the Alps, and from him heard much of British liberty. The two used to converse in English on the political and social institutions of Great Britain, for which Cavour acquired a high regard. The result of this influence, maintained in correspondence, on the young Italian was soon apparent: within a year, he was describing (in a letter to an English friend) his countrymen as not unworthy of freedom.[6] On December 2, 1830, he told Brockedon that England was to be congratulated on the new Whig ministry under Earl Grey, for he regarded Wellington and the Tories as the props of "the rotten edifice of the Holy Alliance."[7] It is therefore not surprising that the Austrian police should have begun to distrust Cavour. They had opened a letter of his in transit and had investigated its author, since they had disliked his liberal tone. The Austrian minister at Turin, Count Bombelles, described Cavour thus: "I consider him a very dangerous person, and all attempts made to redeem him have been fruitless. He requires most careful watching."[8] Anybody who could rejoice, as Cavour did in 1832, at the triumph of the first Reform Bill was naturally exposing himself to the most reactionary espionage. Indeed, he thought then that the patently liberal English public opinion might even help his fatherland to obtain a more enlightened rule.

Three years later, the young Cavour paid his first visit to England, where, characteristically, he observed economic conditions, factories, political methods, workhouses for paupers, prisons, hospitals, docks, and railways. He conversed with Nassau Senior, and dined at John Murray's—between the publisher's wife and daughter, neither of whom could speak French, and unfortunately the visitor's English ran out![9] And like Marshal Haynau and Garibaldi years later, he inspected Barclay's brewery in London, but was nowise humiliated or adulated by the workmen.[10] What chiefly impressed him were the railways and, no doubt, the hives of commerce and industry in Manchester and Liverpool.[11]

In 1836, Cavour had trouble with the Austrian authorities in Lombardy, who examined his mail. What he was doing was innocent enough—he had gone only on business to Buffalora, a frontier station between Piedmont and Hapsburg Italy.[12] Meanwhile, he read Nassau Senior's *Outline of the Science of Political Economy*,[13] a subversive work for those days.

The passing years strengthened in Cavour his fondness for things English. For example, he helped found at Turin in 1841 the *Société du Whist*, a club modelled on English and French prototypes, where he indulged his only vice, gaming, amid high conversation and higher play. In a sense, he had only duplicated in Piedmont fashionable St. James's Street with its London gamblers drawn from the peerage and patronizing Brooks' and Almack's and Crockford's.

Cavour's second visit to England was in 1843, when he came primarily to study agricultural methods. But he kept his eyes open and fixed on the situation in Ireland. The result was an essay the next year on the Irish question, which was quoted in the House of Commons and twice translated into English. His judgment favoured the union of Ireland and England on economic grounds.[14] And since he had a short while before called Nassau Senior "the most enlightened thinker in Great Britain,"[15] one is entirely certain of the bases of his arguments. In 1845, he published a second essay, championing the repeal in England of the Corn Laws. It is significant that Cobden, the Free Trader, visited him at Turin.

Later in the year, Cavour plunged ardently into politics—as a journalist first, the editor of a newly established daily organ prophetically called *Il Risorgimento*. The initial issue was that of December 15, 1847. Associated in the enterprise were Cesare Balbo, Gioberti, Massimo d'Azeglio, and others; and its programme was national independence, union between princes and people, progress along the path of constitutional reform, and confederation among the Italian rulers. At this time, scoffers made fun of Cavour's extraordinary partiality for England and her institutions by dubbing him "Milord Camillo" or "Milord *Risorgimento*."[16]

Nevertheless, through his journal he did obtain influence over public opinion. The revolutions of 1848 were about to inaugurate the mid-century with the struggle of European nationalism. On March 23rd, news came to Turin of the Milanese Five Days. Thereupon, Cavour published an appeal to the House of Savoy to strike for Italy. What he had written was a flaming outcry for war. It may have served as the impulse which led Charles Albert, on the 25th, to declare hostilities against Austria. In June, Cavour was more directly involved in politics as a member of the new Piedmontese parliament. He did not hold office for long, since he was accused of being an Anglophile, but he was re-elected in July 1849. By October of the following year, he was Minister of Agriculture, Industry, and Commerce.

Nassau Senior met Cavour in Italy in 1850[17] and probably influenced the latter to negotiate free trade treaties between Piedmont and France, Belgium, Holland, Switzerland, the German Customs Union, and England.* Cavour had previously championed the Siccardi laws, which abolished ecclesiastical jurisdiction in civil and criminal cases, required nominations to benefices to be submitted to the state, did away with the right of asylum in churches, limited the number of holy days that had to be observed, forbade ecclesiastical corporations to acquire property without royal permission, and favoured civil marriage.[18] This kind of legislation pleased Lord Palmerston, for the English were very angry because the papal brief of September 15, 1850, had "insolently" re-established the Roman hierarchy in Great Britain.[19]

During 1851, Cavour assumed, in addition to his other duties, the portfolio of finance, and instituted an important

* February 27, 1851.

change in policy. He told E. d'Azeglio, Piedmontese minister to London, that the English banking house of C. Hambro could serve them best[20] and thereafter less frequently went for state loans to Rothschild of Paris ("this Jew who strangles us").[21] The House of Hambro lent Piedmont £3,500,000 to balance its budget,[22] and so increased England's stake in Italian affairs. One suspects that it would not have been feasible for any English Cabinet to pursue for long a pro-Austrian and anti-Piedmontese policy. Indeed, Cavour's diplomacy and commercial treaties had already begun to annoy the Austrian Prime Minister, Prince Schwarzenberg. The latter wrote to the Duke of Modena (April 10, 1851):

> From now on, Piedmont will be the citadel from which the bordering states will be menaced not only by an inundation of English goods . . . but also by the far more dangerous contraband of English subversive tendencies, whose action has been already so bitterly experienced by Italy.[23]

The next year was marked by Cavour's temporary retirement from politics and his third visit to England. He met Palmerston, who sympathized with his views; Panizzi of the British Museum; and Lord Malmesbury. Both Palmerston and Malmesbury preached prudence to him. He spent a great deal of his time like a good bourgeois traveller—seeing docks, arsenals, factories, and the like.[24] Whigs and Tories received him cordially, for he had taken the House of Commons as a model for the Chamber of Deputies at Turin, and Piedmont was pleasing to the English on account of the Siccardi Laws. England was then particularly antipapal on account of its unfavourable reaction to the secession of a few prominent Anglicans to Rome. Cavour found Edinburgh charming—and said it was a good place if ever he went into exile![25] Instead, he returned to Italy and became premier on November 4th.

Late in January of the following year, Lord Shaftesbury,

who was in Turin, wrote a letter of thanks to Cavour for his good will towards the Protestant Vaudois:

> I cannot, as an Englishman, be indifferent to the progress of religious and constitutional Liberty in Italy; and I am sure that I speak the sentiments of my Country when I say that it watches with deep anxiety, all the movements that tend to impair the internal, or external security of the Kingdom of Sardinia.
>
> Nothing, I am certain, would more excite the sympathies of England, than any menace, from whatever quarter it might come, directed against a State of thing[s] she so heartily and conscientiously admires.[26]

A few weeks after Shaftesbury's note, Cavour wrote to E. d'Azeglio that he believed the moment opportune for acting on the English public, which was showing itself more and more favourable to their country and to their political line. At the same time, he told Shaftesbury in unmistakable tones not to have any illusions that Piedmont was about to become Protestant.[27] Nevertheless, he tried unsuccessfully to have a Civil Marriage Bill passed.[28]

Cavour had in many respects modelled his policies on English experience. In January 1854, he wanted to have the opinions of Nassau Senior and Gladstone on the feasibility of a legacy tax.[29] And he did swing Piedmont into the Crimean War on the side of England, where the alliance was popular because the government had been made angry by the King of Naples' prohibition of the sale of mules for transport purposes in the East.[30] Piedmont sent 15,000 men, who won a victory against the Russians at Tchernaya. The English financed their ally by a loan of one and one-half millions of pounds.[31] What was Cavour's purpose in fighting Russia? To get powerful friends in Europe, who might help him attain for Piedmont territories in Italy. He wrote (February 19, 1855) to E. d'Azeglio in London:

> Whisper a few words to Lord John Russell on the future of Italy. Without doubt, he is the English statesman who

takes the most interest in the problem—he won't find it astonishing that we're waiting for him to do something for our poor peninsula.[32]

In addition, Cavour urged laws to suppress monastic orders unconnected with education, preaching, or charity—surely, legislation pleasing to Protestant England. The result was that the Earl of Shaftesbury, a zealous Protestant, later told E. d'Azeglio that Piedmont could count on the vigorous aid of *The Record*, *The Morning Herald*, and *The Morning Advertiser*; and the noble lord also spoke strongly to Palmerston, who expressed his full awareness of England's sympathies for Sardinia and its antipathy to Austria.[33] In September 1855, the Catholic Sir George Bowyer,[34] M.P., refuted the English notion that a Protestant Reformation was going on in Piedmont or that its people were anything but staunchly Roman Catholic. But Bowyer grudgingly testified to Cavour's popularity in England. *The Greville Memoirs*,[35] for example, record Lord Clarendon's high opinion, in 1855, of the Italian statesman.

The Crimean War came to its futile end, and the Congress of Paris met as a sort of diplomatic coroner's inquest. Cavour had been trying to influence Clarendon (English Foreign Secretary), who delivered a vehement speech condemning the government of Ferdinand II as a scandal and terming that of the Pope the worst in the world. Clarendon also lamented the presence in Italy of Austrian and French armies of occupation.[36] This outburst by Clarendon gave Cavour his chance to plead the Italian cause, for in drafting the protocol of the Congress the Austrians had tried to expunge every reference to the Italian question but had been opposed on this point by Cavour and the English. That is to say, a European congress had witnessed the placing of a stigma on the conduct of the King of Naples and on clerical rule in the Papal States.[37] Cavour had so contrived it that Piedmont had been treated as a great power, Austria had been isolated, Napoleon III had been compromised in

Italian problems, and Italy had become an international question to be settled if Europe was to have peace. Nevertheless, when he made his fourth and last trip to England in 1856, Cavour discovered a plethora of English sympathy for Italy—but no soldiers.[38] However, Mazzinian Englishmen like Bayle St. John distrusted Cavour and certain other Piedmontese leaders on the ground that these thought more of enlarging Piedmont than of attaining Italian independence.[39] St. John had seen Cavour in action in the Turin Chamber of Deputies and held that he tried to ape Sir Robert Peel's mannerisms. Moreover, this English traveller said that Cavour was unpopular in Piedmont, and repeated scandal about the Italian—he was a speculator who made use of inside information.[40]

Assiduously, Cavour cultivated English public opinion. For example, one learns from a letter[41] of Thornton Hunt's (early in 1857) that Cavour tried to influence the English press in behalf of Piedmont, and one suspects the use of tactics like those of the government of the Czar before the World War in the case of the notoriously venal fourth estate of Paris. However, *The Westminster Review's* good opinion of Cavour and the Italian cause was without the shadow of a doubt entirely honest. In April, John Bright, on a visit to Turin, conversed at great length with Cavour. In his diary, the great Victorian orator recorded this observation on the Italian: "has the appearance of an intelligent English gentleman farmer rather than of a *fine* and subtle Italian."[42] Clearly, Bright had taken to Cavour. When the latter tried to get definite assurances of concrete sympathy from an even more powerful English political figure, Palmerston merely offered advice, nothing more—Italy should not be on bad terms with Austria![43]

The Orsini case of 1858 plunged four* European powers into the most intense excitement. Piedmont, at Napoleon III's insistence, had to pass a strict law forbidding con-

* France, England, Piedmont, and Austria.

spiracy against foreign sovereigns. This measure was defended by Cavour in a notable speech delivered in April to the Chamber of Deputies at Turin. He took the occasion to uphold his system of alliances and to explain why Piedmont entered the Crimean War on the side of the Allies, and he referred slyly and incidentally to those who called him an Anglomaniac. This address was reprinted as an English pamphlet, so anxious was Cavour's ministry to bring its point of view to the attention of the British.

In the spring of 1859, on his way home from his mission to the Ionian Islands, Gladstone[44] stopped off at Turin and met Cavour, who tried to gain the Englishman's friendship for Italy. Cavour also instructed the war correspondent of the London *Daily News*, Count Carlo Arrivabene, to do everything to win over the English people to the Italian cause; and he sent Massimo d'Azeglio and Commendatore Nigra, toward the end of April, to induce the English Cabinet to believe that Austria was making peace impossible.[45] When the war of 1859 did break out and was finally settled by the unsatisfactory peace of Villafranca, Cavour had so skilfully guided opinion in England that a member of Parliament published in the same month a pamphlet denying that the conflict had been premeditated by the Italian statesman and Louis Napoleon, and urging non-intervention in Italy on the part of foreign powers.[46] That was the actual policy pursued by the English Cabinet, though its members, Gladstone for one, were disgusted with the treaty of peace, arranged between Austria and France without Piedmont's presence. The English press said that Napoleon was only a half-hearted friend of Italy. In reality, Cavour was now letting England and France bid against each other for Italy's favour.[47] At the same time, he was acquainting himself with expressions of British opinion, in this connexion probably reading Matthew Arnold's excessively rare pamphlet, *England and the Italian Question*,[48] essentially a defence of the war of 1859 and a refutation of three arguments then current in England: the Italians, having never since the fall of the Roman Empire been independent of foreign rulers, could not now gain their freedom; the principle of nationality, in virtue of which the Italians claimed their independence, was chimerical; the result of the third Napoleon's intervention in Italy could only be a French war of conquest, and the substitution, for the Italians, of French in the place of Austrian domination. It is not for nothing that late in November Mrs. Browning, who admired Cavour, called him "acute."[49] On the whole then, the Italian statesman had by 1859 reached a position of esteem in Great Britain: an anonymous pamphleteer dedicated *The Italian Cause: Its History and Its Hopes . . .* to him; and a contemporary history, Miss Manning's *The Story of Italy*, praised him lavishly.

Curiously enough, if Cavour was able to influence English opinion through the press, on the other hand English newspapers had a most limited effect in Italy. As a writer[50] pointed out then, all the articles *The Times* ever published on Italian affairs did not produce half the result of Cavour's speeches. But English diplomacy in respect to Italy was another matter—especially during the crucial year of 1860. For Napoleon III, who had fought for Italian independence, was not anxious for Italian unity, and Cavour had to neutralize the policy of the Emperor. He did so through the aid of Lord John Russell. In January, the Englishman persuaded Napoleon to accept the principle of non-intervention in Italy. Russell's dispatch of February 28th condemned Napoleon's solution of the problem of central Italy as "subversive of Italian independence," and thus enabled Cavour to annex Tuscany without too much dread of French chagrin.[51] England, however, did not like Cavour's compensatory yielding of Savoy and Nice to France. As Robert Browning[52] put it, the Emperor had "taken eighteenpence for" his help in the war of 1859. Incidentally, Garibaldi, a Nizzard, in the Turin Parliament bitterly attacked Cavour for having surrendered his birthplace. For the same reason, a letter to the Newcastle *Journal*, June 23, 1860, called Cavour a knave.[53] Cavour's adroit diplomacy influenced Lord John Russell not to agree to a proposal of France to stop Garibaldi's Thousand from crossing the Strait of Messina and entering Naples. Later, Cavour was not afraid to send troops to invade Naples (despite the fact that the Austrians were massing on the Piedmont frontier) once Palmerston's attitude had been sounded out.[54] The final triumph of Cavour's policy came, of course, with Lord John Russell's famous dispatch of October 27th, which recognized Italian unity in the face of a scandalized Europe already met in threatening congress. Years later, Russell expressed his pleasure[55] at Cavour's approval of this historic message (which the Italian had taken care to publicize widely throughout Italy and among the European powers!). Naturally, a contemporary English poetaster[56] considered Italy fortunate to be under Cavour's guiding hand; and George Eliot,[57] who saw him in Turin, estimated him a man of thought.

But the fates were preparing to use their inexorable shears, and the last year of Cavour's life, 1861, had its due place in the temporal procession. Late in January, he wrote a letter thanking Frederic Harrison,[58] the Positivist and critic, for a sympathetic political article in the current issue of *The Westminster Review*. Harrison had called him a statesman of principles, not bound too much by theories, a far-seeing organizer (who had railroads built of both commercial and military value), and had said many other kind things. On the other hand, Joseph Mazzini's pamphlet, *The Italian Question and the Republicans*, described Cavour as being at Napoleon III's beck and call. The truth was that Cavour had used the grandiose Emperor of the French. History has given its verdict, and Frederic Harrison's opinion, rather than Mazzini's, has prevailed in regard to Count Cavour's career. From the pen of the most conservative English spokesman, the first Marquess of Normanby,[59] appeared also an attack on Cavour. Normanby quoted the Italian's statement, "I have been a conspirator for the last twelve years," to show that the Piedmontese government was without moral obligation and capable of using the tactics of falsehood. It is significant that only extreme opinions in England, from either end of the political gamut, were unfavourable to Cavour shortly before his death. A typical British subject like Dudley Costello,[60] the author of an illustrated work for tourists in Italy, had nothing but enthusiasm for the prime minister of the new Italy; and *The Times* could find recourse only to an epithet like *sagacious* to describe his bold policy in central Italy.[61] Even Cavour's manner in debate evoked the approval of a competent English observer, Edward Dicey, who had been in Turin toward the end of May and had heard the statesman's last speeches in the Chamber of Deputies. Dicey admired Cavour's sensible oratory and remarked on the rather un-Italian absence of florid magniloquence.[62]

On June 6, 1861, Cavour died—like Lincoln, fortunate not to have lived long enough for time to damage his reputation, then at its zenith. Elizabeth Barrett Browning, taking his death very much to heart, wrote in her last letter: "If tears or blood could have saved him to us, he should have had mine. I feel yet as if I could scarcely comprehend the greatness of the vacancy. A hundred Garibaldis for such a man. . . . May God save Italy!"[63] In the House of Lords, Clanricarde, Brougham, and Malmesbury paid tribute to the dead statesman, and only the Marquess of Bath played the devil's advocate by asserting that Cavour had "violated every law, human and divine."[64] In the Commons, the younger Sir Robert Peel was generous and fair, and so was Lord John Russell. But the Irish and Catholic the O'Donoghue saw, amid protesting cries, "God's justice in the death of Count Cavour." Monckton Milnes was very eulogistic,[65] and Palmerston equally so:

> The tale with which his memory will be associated is one of the most extraordinary—I may say the most romantic—recorded in the annals of the world. We have seen under his influence and guidance a people who were supposed to have become torpid . . . enervated . . . and to have had no knowledge or feeling on politics, except what may have been derived from the traditions of their history and the jealousies of rival States—we have seen that people, under his guidance and at his call, rising from the slumber of ages . . . breaking that spell by which they had so long been bound, and displaying on great occasions the courage of heroes, the sagacity of statesmen, the wisdom of philosophers, and obtaining for themselves that unity of political existence which for centuries had been denied them.[66]

In general, contemporary British periodicals and newspapers were disposed to be extremely kind to the dead statesman. The London *Times* had a long leader in tribute to Cavour and also printed an extended biographical sketch (June 7, 1861); *The Saturday Review*, June 8, 1861, also devoted a leading article to the Piedmontese. *The Athenaeum* (June 29, 1861) stressed Cavour's reverence for the English constitution and spoke of his "*eminently English* style of argument." Both *The Edinburgh Review* and *The Quarterly Review* for July eulogized him. Unexpectedly, the latter even described him as the most remarkable man of the generation and declared his influence would probably be felt longer and more widely than that of any living being. But in the Catholic *Rambler* for the same month, Lord Acton, the historian, with cold and dry words, attacked Cavour for having trampled on his Church and for having broken the faith of treaties. Yet Acton did acknowledge the dead man's skill as a statesman.[67]

Late in June 1861, and only two days before her death, Mrs. Browning heard with pleasure of Baron Ricasoli's purpose to continue Cavour's policies.[68] A far lesser poet, Mrs. Phillipson, wrote a requiem, "On the Death of Count Cavour"[69]—noisy verse urging the Italians to win Venice and Rome if they wished to be worthy of kneeling on Cavour's grave! Another example of English praise is Sir Edward Dicey's *Cavour. A Memoir*, 1861, an excellent account though scarcely devoid of partisanship. On the whole, that staunch Mazzinian, William Michael Rossetti, put it best (in his sonnet, "Cavour, 1861"[70]): the statesman's *rôle* in the Italian cause had been to "accommodate, retard, force onward, lure."

It is interesting to note the difference in attitude towards Cavour on the part of Catholic and Protestant English poets. On the one hand, Aubrey de Vere in 1862 called Cavour and Victor Emmanuel traitors to the cause of liberty because they had attacked the Church. One wonders what de Vere meant by liberty since he did believe the papacy was a bulwark against "modern anarchy and socialism" by virtue of its authoritarian principles.[71] On the other hand, Mrs. Browning's posthumous *Last Poems*[72] defended Cavour's character with great and sweet vehemence.

Giovanni Ruffini's novel, *Vincenzo*, presents Cavour in an attractive light and stresses his fondness for English ways. A year later, in 1864, two English histories[73] emphasized the greatness of the statesman's character and his part in the winning of Italian unity. In 1868, Matthew Arnold's report[74] on Continental education indirectly praised the Piedmontese for having realized how important an agency toward the regeneration of Italy was a good system of public instruction. The Countess Marie Montemerli declared in her novel, *The Florentines* (1870), that the dead Cavour had been the soul of Victor Emmanuel's popularity.[75] There is in existence an elegiac poem on Cavour (1873) by James Lockhart,[76] whose muse is doleful in more than one sense. M. Hartley's excellent novel, *Beyond Man's Strength*, 1909, affords a glimpse of "Milord" Cavour (in 1847) editing the *Risorgimento*; Sydney Carlyon Grier's *One Crowded Hour* has a good account of Cavour's devious *rôle* at the time of Garibaldi's mad dash at the head of the Thousand; finally,

John Drinkwater's chronicle play of Italian freedom, *Garibaldi*, dramatizes Cavour's secret yachting trip* to Garibaldi's island home, Caprera, in March 1859, when the warrior and the statesman, after some preliminary conversation, planned the historic expedition of the Thousand. Later in the play, Mr. Drinkwater has a scene in which Cavour reproves certain officers of the regular Piedmontese army for displaying a malignant jealousy towards Garibaldi and his irregulars, fresh from their miraculous conquest of southern Italy in 1860.

It is easy to see why Cavour left no such impress on English letters as Mazzini or Garibaldi. The man who pulls the strings is never discernibly spectacular, and there was nothing romantic about the short, stout, ill-dressed figure, except for the nose, very much like Mr. Punch. Indeed, in thought he had been *consciously* as close as possible to those members of England's ruling caste who take *Punch* for their guide in matters of humour and in temper of life. After all, he had really been a kind of "Milord Camillo."

* Probably an invented incident.

CHAPTER XIV

Garibaldi and the British: Until the London Ovation of 1864

As the years recede from the day of his death, the melodrama of Garibaldi's spectacular career fades into the sober hues of historical record. The twentieth century sees in the colourful military adventurer nothing more than a naïve and warm-hearted man with a genius for action. Garibaldi could be so easily manipulated and could so magnificently carry out the schemes of others that a recent critic[1] has described him as one having fists of iron and brains of cheese. Such a judgment is, in a limited sense, true—but it is also a little unkind, for it squeezes the drama out of the man's life and leaves it a pulp without juice. Perhaps he was not shrewd, but no one should ignore the splendour of his deeds, which made his life a kind of synthesis of heroic biography.*

English boys like Richard Garnett[2] sat at the feet of their elders and listened to tales of the great Giuseppe Garibaldi. One of them, in later years the ninth Duke of Argyll, declared[3] that the *condottiere's* romantic figure seemed the very ideal of all that boys longed for: coolness in the hell

* *Cf.* Mr. Aldous Huxley's *Eyeless in Gaza*, New York and London, 1936, p. 254:

> "When one's young, one thinks one can tailor one's time into all sorts of splendid and fantastic garments—shakos and chasubles and Ph.D. gowns; Nijinsky's tights and Rimbaud's slate-blue trousers and Garibaldi's red shirt. But by the time you've lived ten thousand days, you begin to realize that you'll be lucky if you succeed in cutting one decent workaday suit out of the time at your disposal."

of battle; a leonine confidence that communicated courage to all around him; the fixed resolve to venture life and all on the cast of fortune, at the right time; the crusade against despotism, bigotry, and bad government of all sorts.

Not everybody, of course, idolized Garibaldi. A Tory like Charles Lever[4] could consider him ignorant and childish; a Mazzinian like Bolton King could pronounce him overrated. But these were not the usual reactions in England: Swinburne's self-abasement at the thought of the hero, T. A. Trollope's good opinion, old Gabriele Rossetti's esteem, and *The Westminster Review's* friendly regard are far more indicative of the contemporary British admiration. As Gladstone once told John Morley,[5] the Italian was, in English eyes, a fine combination of profound and unalterable simplicity with self-possession. In a word, there was something English about this blue-eyed Latin!

Looking back on his own life, Garibaldi could not understand it. Had he been asked what had made him attempt to stir up a mutiny in the Piedmontese navy; what had driven him to go to South America; what had compelled him, now to skirmish round the Italian Lakes in the north of Italy, now in Sicily to seize Palermo, now to be taken prisoner as he marched on Rome: he could not have answered logically. It may be that he was simply a man of extraordinary physical and emotional vitality, who needed action and danger, who craved the applause of devoted followers. It may be that he was unable to rationalize his yearning for the stimulants of adventure. In any case, Garibaldi's life has no consistency of pattern in respect to ideas. Deeds follow in rapid succession, and they reveal, but do not explain, his alterations. Nevertheless, whatsoever he did had somehow as a goal the unity of Italy. To attain it, he had always been an opportunist, hardly ever a doctrinaire.

At the outset of his career, Garibaldi affiliated himself with *Young Italy*, and under the pseudonym of Joseph Borel was at the service of Mazzini, whom he had met in Marseilles. In obedience to orders, Garibaldi joined the Royal Piedmontese navy as a common sailor so as to win the men over to *Young Italy*. Mazzini's plan involved an expedition into Piedmont by way of Savoy, and Garibaldi's assignment was to seize (February 4, 1834) the frigate *Euridice* and then the arsenal at Genoa. The plot was discovered, and Garibaldi had to flee for his life. He rejoined Mazzini in Marseilles; meanwhile, the Piedmontese government sentenced him to be executed—*in absentia*. By 1836, he was in South America and engaged in revolutionary activities against the dictator of Brazil. Here he laid the foundations of his supreme mastery of guerrilla warfare, by which he eventually won the signal victories resulting in the freedom of Uruguay, 1846. During the next year, he received news of the progressiveness of the new pope, Pius IX, who had amnestied political offenders. Although Garibaldi had not been in Italy for a long time. Mazzini took pains to broadcast accounts of his South American exploits; that is why Gallenga[6] could tell the Pope in 1847 that if he moved against Austria, none other than the great Garibaldi would lend aid.

Now began the second stage of Garibaldi's career. On June 24, 1848, he was back in his native Nice and ready to offer his services to King Charles Albert. These were declined, for the ruler of Piedmont would have nothing to do with former rebels. Yet Garibaldi did take part in the events of 1848, though his conduct was unfairly disparaged by the correspondent[7] of the very biased London *Times*, which favoured the Hapsburgs.

But the event which really made Garibaldi known to the English-speaking world was his defence of Mazzini's short-lived Roman Republic. Most of the contemporary accounts of his conduct during the siege of Rome present him as a very gallant hero. In the House of Lords, Howden praised him, and one historian wrote: "When the trumpet sounded for battle, he was everywhere, giving orders, encouraging his men, and fighting."[8] Eventually, the beleaguered city fell, and Garibaldi, exasperated by Mazzini's blunders, made one of the most difficult and romantic retreats known to history. He was pursued by French, Austrian, Neapolitan, Tuscan, and Spanish troops; yet somehow he escaped after disbanding his followers in the neutral republic of San Marino. Venice under Manin had not yet succumbed, and thither he attempted to head in fishing boats. When, however, the Austrian fleet cut him off, he took again to the shore, where his Amazon* companion, Anita, died near Comacchio, against a background of epic grandeur. The story of his marvellous flight through central Italy is quite rightly a frequent theme of nineteenth-century English literature.

While fighting was going on around Rome, *The Illustrated London News*[9] was printing pictures and sympathetic comment in the text, and was thereby laying the first foundations of the Garibaldian cult in Great Britain, which in the course of time grew to enormous dimensions. But *The Times* of London was exceedingly hostile, as is shown by a leading article of July 10, 1849:

> As Garibaldi fortunately marched out of Rome to the South at the head of his six thousand partisans, who are hotly pursued by the First Division of the French, the worst enemies of the country will probably be annihilated.

Four days before this editorial, Arthur Hugh Clough expressed the other and more sympathetic point of view: "There is a Mrs. Garibaldi; she went out with him to the Abruzzi. I hope the French won't cut them to pieces, but *vice versa.*[10]

As a result of the siege of Rome, Garibaldi became one of Walter Savage Landor's heroes. Anita Garibaldi is the subject of a Latin epitaph[11] by Landor, which declares that she died, worthy of her husband, by deserted ways over which menacing swords were waved. At this time another

* There is in Rome a dashing equestrian statue which was erected to her memory.

enthusiast was Bulwer-Lytton, the novelist. Even that reactionary member of Parliament, Alexander Baillie Cochrane,[12] paid Garibaldi a grudging tribute though adding that the Italian, with his picturesque brigands, was a study for Salvator Rosa.

Again an exile, Garibaldi came to New York in 1850 and earned a living on Staten Island by the manufacture of candles. Felice Foresti, one-time prisoner of Spielberg, who had become professor of Italian at Columbia College, tried to help him in various ways. It is perhaps to Garibaldi's life in America that the title of Gerald Massey's poem, "Garibaldi in Exile,"[13] alludes. The Chartist poet presents the hero thinking of Rome, yet to be freed and hopeful of an Italy soon to be united. The lines, long and rapid, are fairly good.

Across the Atlantic, Garibaldi was being discussed in 1851 from different points of view. For one thing, Emilio Dandolo,[14] who had fought at the defence of Rome, judged him a good leader of guerrillas, but no general for mass actions. An important history[15] of the recent Italian revolts called Garibaldi "a leader of banditti." But Henry Lushington,* more discerning, regarded the Garibaldi who retreated from Rome as a great romantic figure, and said that his flight was a saga, characterized by great pathos—the tragic episode of Anita's death.[16] The last is the subject of these tender lines in Mrs. Browning's *Casa Guidi Windows*:

Forlorn
Of thanks be, therefore, no one of these graves!
  Not Hers,—who, at her husband's side, in scorn,
Outfaced the whistling shot and hissing waves,
  Until she felt her little babe unborn
Recoil, within her, from the violent staves
  And bloodhounds of the world,—at which, her life
Dropt inwards from her eyes and followed it
  Beyond the hunters. Garibaldi's wife
And child died so. And now, the seaweeds fit
  Her body, like a proper shroud. . . .

* 1812–55. To him Tennyson dedicated "The Princess."

In 1853, Landor wrote an imaginary conversation between Garibaldi and Mazzini. Another to concern himself at this time with Garibaldi was Charles Lever, who earned £50 by an appreciative article.[17]

The next year, there appeared a rather poor novel, *Angelo: A Romance of Modern Rome*, which dealt with Garibaldi's efforts in behalf of the Roman Republic. The anonymous author was probably a Welsh lady without very much knowledge of the contemporaneous events which she used as background. Her novel was very unfriendly to the Italian, who is thinly disguised as "the notorious Gariboni," the "irresponsible and profligate" leader of a gang of plunderers. Gariboni's character is "singularly adapted for the execution of the bloody work"—that is, of assassination! but he is brave and determined even if without pity or remorse. This is Gariboni's costume:

> a green blouse, turned up with red and slashed sleeves; red trousers buttoned up the sides; a low hat with a large plume of black feathers; the collar of his shirt turned down to show his neck; an embroidered pelisse thrown across his shoulders; a lance in his hand, a carbine hanging by his side; a belt with a brace of pistols, a sword, and another brace of pistols in his holsters.

The novelist imagines Garibaldi having the Sanfedists (counter-revolutionaries) executed by compelling them to drink poison containing human blood. Such is the fate of the wicked Jesuit, Basino, a close relative of Mrs. Radcliffe's terrific Schedoni. In this novel is all the apparatus of the tale of terror: the deep-dyed villain whose eyes flash and roll, trap doors, sliding-panels, dreadful dungeons, secret and slow poisonings, midnight enormities.

The real Garibaldi came back to Europe in 1854, and in March was at Newcastle (as the commander of the *Commonwealth*), where he received, among other things, a sword with this inscription: "To General Garibaldi, by the people of Tyneside, friends of European freedom."[18] Working men had made up a penny subscription and had purchased the sword and also a telescope. Garibaldi accepted the admiration of the citizens of Newcastle, which was in part conveyed by the young Joseph Cowen in a handsome address on parchment. As the head of the welcoming deputation, Cowen declared that Englishmen hoped for the day when Italy would drive out the Austrians and become a republic. And so, the captain of the *Commonwealth*, who had ostensibly come only for a cargo of coal, left with the knowledge that the liberal British element held him in great esteem. There were also others who idolized him in a more tender fashion. When Garibaldi returned to Italy and began to live on the island of Caprera, a wealthy English widow, who had become engaged to the very susceptible Italian, made a journey to Italy. This lady preserved decorum by taking as a companion Jessie Meriton White,[19] who first met Garibaldi at Nice in 1854.

Elsewhere, there has been told the story of Garibaldi's part in Panizzi's scheme to rescue the Neapolitan political prisoners on the island of San Stefano. When he came to England in order to advance this project, he was a guest (February 1856) of Jessie White's family.[20]

J. R. D. Beste's poor novel of the same year, *Modern Society in Rome*, has an interesting picture of Garibaldi at the time of the Roman Republic—green scarf around the waist, red tunic, brown cloak, pistols, and daggers; and gives a romantic account of the marriage of Anita and Garibaldi. Despite the withdrawal of Charles Albert from the struggle against Austria, Beste indicates how resolute Garibaldi was to fight on, and that he went to Rome for its defence. Anita Garibaldi is represented as a bold warrior at the side of her husband. To be sure, Beste does not omit the familiar story of Garibaldi's remarkable retreat, which followed the inevitable entrance of the French troops into Rome. On the whole, the novel was very complimentary to Garibaldi.

Up to this time, Garibaldi had believed in Mazzini's programme—a united republican Italy. In the summer of 1857, the Italian National Society was founded to win freedom under the leadership of Piedmont. The new organization had as its chief figures converted republicans like Garibaldi, Pallavicino, La Farina, and Manin, and was modelled on the English Anti-Corn-Law League.[21] Another item which may have helped slightly to keep Garibaldi's name before British eyes was the publication of Mrs. C. G. Hamilton's novel, *The Exiles of Italy*, which rehearses, in part, the siege of Rome, his flight, and Anita's death, for these themes were as yet not threadbare.

The cult of Garibaldi was visibly growing. Hero-worshipping females like the Baroness von Schwartz visited "the Cincinnatus of our times"[22] on the island of Caprera. Landor addressed (1858) a poetic epistle "To the Children of Garibaldi" and said their father was that man whom

> Earth from every coast with loud applause
> Hails a deliverer. . . .

The poet declared that the Italian's children had a great name to live up to—"virtues so pure and courage so humane" are their heritage. Let them but follow their father's steps and march ever onward.

The war of Piedmont and France against Austria having begun, during May 1859, Garibaldi led his Hunters of the Alps against General Urban, who was kept too busy to help the other Hapsburg generals. Even the pro-Austrian London *Times* admired Garibaldi for his campaign at Varese in Lombardy.[23] That is the background of Gerald Massey's spirited poem, "Garibaldi on the March,"[24] of which one line is a sufficient sample:

> On, on, Garibaldi, for Freedom and Right!

The sudden Treaty of Villafranca, giving only Lombardy to Piedmont, put an end to his exploits and disappointed the

Italians. The English press, agreeing that Napoleon was only a half-hearted friend of Italy, idolized Garibaldi as the enemy of the Emperor of the French and of Austria alike.[25] People called the Italian a great man of action, some tried to establish a connection between him and their own Anglo-Saxon pride by emphasizing the act that his name was of Germanic origin and meant *bold spear*,[26] and contemporary English histories* of Italy united in praising him. A pseudonymous Colonel Exalbion summed up the current British opinion: "Whatever be the opinion concerning the strife, one man at least entered it with patriotism wholly disinterested, a reputation entirely unalloyed. . . ." Exalbion added that Garibaldi was neither a Bobadill nor a canting patriot, but more like a "well-bred English military or naval officer."[27]

However, the Catholic *Dublin Review*[28] for September 1859 called Garibaldi's men a vile faction; *The Westminster Review*[29] replied with an admiring article on their exploits in the Alps. Not much later, the editor of *Punch*, the prolific Tom Taylor (later famous for his poem on the assassinated Lincoln), dramatized Garibaldi's career in a play shown at Astley's Theatre in London. The production, entitled *Garibaldi*, began its run late in October. Its first act, concerned with the hero's residence in Uruguay in 1846, introduces a treacherous captain in the Italian Legion,† a certain Mancini, who is described as nursing a guilty passion for his general's wife, Anita. This villain hates Garibaldi, and throughout the melodrama appears in various disguises. He carries off the daughter of the Garibaldis, but happily she is restored in the last act when her father kills the dastardly wretch. The second act is a retelling of the siege of Rome; the third deals with Garibaldi's famous flight from that city and with the death of Anita. The fourth (and final) act summarizes Garibaldi's deeds in

* Some were published in shilling parts and were richly illustrated.

† Garibaldi commanded an Italian Legion in South America.

the war of 1859. What with a musical score and horses on the stage and gaudy uniforms, this was a rather colourful play to the Victorian public. But Mazzini felt disgusted at the idea of Garibaldi on the stage![30]

Waxing ecstatic as usual about his hero and delirious against Napoleon III,[31] Walter Savage Landor said in the London *Times* (November 29, 1859): "The warmest heart is the tenderest, and that heart is Garibaldi's." In December, he wrote to Browning that he wished he could give his estates to the Italian and declared that £200 a year would be enough for his own needs. In a subsequent letter to his fellow poet, he confessed that politics no longer interested him now that Garibaldi was not in arms.[32]

But the fame of the immortal Thousand, who embarked from Genoa for the conquest of southern Italy in 1860, was soon ringing throughout the world.* Garibaldi was again in arms, and Landor could not but follow Italian politics with a fascinated attention. Before the expedition left for Sicily, its leader contracted a second marriage with a lady, who (so Landor[33] gossiped to Browning, and Mazzini[34] to an English lady) had been too kind to a lover and was with child. Garibaldi made no fuss, but promptly left his new wife. More important things were in the air. In Turin, Laurence Oliphant, an adventurous English journalist, met him and found him very angry about the projected cession of his native Nice to France. Nevertheless, Garibaldi could not for long nurse his wrath. The Thousand were being assembled.

At the very start, Mrs. Browning had not much faith in the Sicilian expedition, for she regarded Garibaldi as a man of not too much brains. Of course, she wished him and his men the best of luck.[35] On May 11, 1860, the Thousand landed at Marsala in sight of the British vessels, *Intrepid* and

* *E.g.*, Friedrich Engels reported (at second hand) the Sicilian expedition for the New York *Tribune*. See Gustav Mayer, *Friedrich Engels: a Biography*, London, 1936, p. 164.

Argus, the presence of which delayed an attack by two Neapolitan cruisers on Garibaldi's two troopships. At this time, Lord John Russell[36] was doubtful of Garibaldi's chances for success. When he moved on to attack Palermo, American and English tourists openly revealed their sympathies.[37] The taking of Palermo was an extraordinary military achievement, since it was a walled city of 180,000 people and had been defended by a fleet and by an army of about 20,000 men. European powers other than England, France in particular, wanted to force a truce on Garibaldi, but the British Cabinet refused to allow interference. Significantly, negotiations were carried on aboard the *Hannibal*, in the cabin of the *English* admiral, Mundy, who had been ready to rescue Garibaldi if things went wrong. At Palermo and elsewhere in Sicily, Garibaldi founded schools for boys and girls and decreed a free press. Whatever he did, were it only to show tenderness to his wounded, pleased English nationals everywhere, from Malta[38] to the British Isles.

The previously unhopeful Elizabeth Barrett Browning now wrote: "We are all talking and dreaming Garibaldi just now in great anxiety. Scarcely since the world was a world has there been such a feat of arms. All modern heroes grow pale before him."[39] In his official reports,[40] Admiral Mundy deemed Garibaldi's conduct at Palermo noble and generous. Landor wrote a poem on "Nice, the Birthplace of Garibaldi," in which he regretted that the city now was bound to the perfidious power, France, as a result of foul political trafficking. Yet Nice, said the poet, was great because it had produced a supreme hero.[41]

Explaining the background of the Sicilian expedition to the readers of *Macmillan's Magazine*, Aurelio Saffi pleaded for non-interference in Italy. It is significant to observe that this same (July) issue of the magazine printed an excellent translation of Giusti's famous poem, "The Boot." Did David Masson, the editor, wish to imply that Garibaldi was the man to wear the Italian boot—to unify the Italian peninsula? Richard Cobden,[42] fearful because Garibaldi was among the "degraded" Sicilians, compared him to Washington and emphasized the greatness of his moral qualities. John Forster,[43] the biographer of Dickens, considered the overthrow of the Bourbon hegemony in Sicily a miraculous feat. What would come next? Lord John Russell now supposed that Garibaldi would be completely successful.[44]

A contemporary* poem by Sydney Dobell, "The Youth of England to Garibaldi's Legion," expressed the admiration felt throughout the English-speaking world for the deeds of the Thousand:

> Do ye dream what ye have done?
> What ye are and shall be? Nay,
> Comets rushing to the sun,
> And dyeing the tremendous way
> With glory, look not back, nor know
> How they blind the earth below.

Dobell declared that Garibaldi's men had surpassed Thermopylae; that they

> Untitle the proud Past and crown
> The heroic ages in our own!

In a similar vein, Gerald Massey wrote a poem[45] for the memory of a boy who had died heroically while fighting for Garibaldi. The mystical Harriet Eleanor Baillie Hamilton addressed "Two Sonnets to Garibaldi. August 1860."[46] The first affirmed that the hero had been sent to bring Christ's kingdom back to the world; the second praised him for his gentleness to his wounded men. Together, they completed a portrait of a warrior with grandeur of soul.

Also numbered among those who hailed anew the conquest of Sicily was Walter Savage Landor. His "Resurrection

* First published in *Macmillan's Magazine*, August 1860.

of Sicania,"* which appeared in *The Examiner*, August 4, 1860, has the finish of classic sculpture:

Again her brow Sicania rears
Above the tomb; two thousand years
Have sorely swept her beauteous breast,
And War forbidden her to rest.
Yet War at last becomes her friend;
And cries aloud, Thy grief should end:
Sicania, hear me, rise again—
A houseless† hero breaks thy chain.

Exactly a week later, the poet, in a letter "To Garibaldi" in the pages of *The London Review*, urged the hero to make himself king of Sicily: "only a crown can consolidate the ruinous state of Sicily" and "only one man has proved that he is worthy of wearing it." Landor seemed to believe that England and America would support the independence of Sicily. At the same time, he wrote an open letter "To Kossuth," in which he affirmed that the glory of Garibaldi and of the Hungarian would be eternal.[47] These two letters were succeeded by the publication of an imaginary conversation between "Garibaldi and Bosco":[48] Bosco had come to Sicily in order to assassinate Garibaldi but was turned aside by the hero's magnanimity. In September, Landor made Garibaldi one of the speakers in another of his imaginary conversations, "Garibaldi and the President of the Sicilian Senate."[49] The President of the Senate, in a very florid manner, expressed his thanks to Garibaldi for having freed Sicily from Bourbon rule. To these brief words the hero, now ready to depart across the Strait of Messina for Naples, replied with a long discourse, couched in dignified language. The words which Landor placed in Garibaldi's mouth are of some interest. The commander of the Thousand

* Landor sent a slightly different version of the poem to George Jacob Holyoake, August 20, 1860. See the latter's *Bygones Worth Remembering*, I, 235. Holyoake reprinted this poem in his organ, *The Reasoner*, XXV, 294 (September 9, 1860).

† Garibaldi's native city of Nice had been yielded to France.

urged the Sicilians to sweep away the crouching Bourbon, reminded them that they were the descendants of the great Normans, and recalled the ancient glories of Sicily—the greatness of Syracuse and Agrigentum and Messina. Significantly, Garibaldi is now made to say that the Sicilians should nominate a constitutional king from their own number.

On September 7th, Garibaldi entered Naples. Disraeli, eagerly following what was taking place, wrote, a few days later, a note to a friend which included this comment:

> What an immense event is the Italian Revolution! Since 1792 we have not had such affairs. This is real history—and what an imbroglio! A race between the red flag of Mazzini wafted on by the passions of centuries, and the cold diplomatic standard of mere Sardinian ambition. . . . Look out for great events.[50]

Typical of Disraeli in its theatricality, this diagnosis was, none the less, the true one. The conquest of southern Italy, largely prepared by Mazzinians,* was turned in the end to the advantage of the Kingdom of Sardinia. But even as late as October 16th, Disraeli was puzzled about Garibaldi's intentions. Was he for Cavour, or did he wish to set up a republic in Naples?

Some of Garibaldi's victories on the mainland were celebrated in contemporary English verse. For example, Mary Cowden Clark wrote a spirited poem on "The Battle of Melazzo."[51] King Victor Emmanuel's entrance into Naples (November 7, 1860) at the side of Garibaldi is the subject of Henry C. Barlow's "Ode to Garibaldi,"[52] written after the manner of Dryden's "Alexander's Feast." Incidentally,

* In December 1859, Mazzini told Emilie Ashurst Hawkes that he did not personally like Garibaldi but intended to use him for some good (that is, *Mazzinian*) scheme. The fact is that as early as March Mazzini had been plotting with Francesco Crispi, then in London, and it was Crispi who helped make the way in Sicily easier for Garibaldi's men. See the *Edizione nazionale degli scritti di Giuseppe Mazzini*, LXIII, 204, and LXV, 335.

Punch showed Garibaldi helping Victor Emmanuel to get his right leg into the boot (Italy).[53]

It is hard nowadays to realize how many English hearts throbbed with delight at the contemporary exploits of the Thousand and their red shirt leader. One must remember that it was Gladstone's letters to Aberdeen on Neapolitan misgovernment which had prepared the kind of public opinion ready, at a later date, to applaud Garibaldi's final attack on the Kingdom of the Two Sicilies. Another fortunate thing for Italy was the coming into power of a new Liberal ministry in 1859. Men like Palmerston, Russell, and Gladstone were pro-Italian; the preceding Conservative Cabinet had been pro-Austrian; so were Queen Victoria and the Royal Court.[54] Equally helpful to Garibaldi's Sicilian expedition had been the kind of propaganda for Italy which Poerio, Settembrini, and the other Neapolitan political victims promoted by their actual presence in London during 1859. Indeed, it is correct to say that in Europe only England applauded Garibaldi in southern Italy. However, English good will would have counted for nothing if he had not had in Sicily great courage and extraordinary luck. That lively Victorian diarist, Sir William Hardman, merely expressed a general Anglo-Saxon sentiment when he praised Garibaldi as "the embodiment of honour, fidelity, patriotism, truth, single-hearted simplicity, and loyalty."[55]

As we have seen, among those who exulted greatly during 1860 was Walter Savage Landor. Typical of his sentiments are these lines in a poem called "Syracuse," on Garibaldi in Sicily:

> Syracuse, raise again thy head,
> Long hast thou slept, but art not dead.
> A late avenger now is come
> Whose voice alone can split the tomb.
> Hearest thou not the world throughout
> Cry Garibaldi? One loud shout
> Arises, and there needs but one
> To shatter a polluted throne.[56]

Landor also adapted* some famous verses by the Roman poet, Ennius, on Quintus Fabius Maximus Cunctator and applied them to Garibaldi:

Unus homo Romae cunctando restituit Rem,
At non cunctando restituet melior:
Vive, vale, Garibalde! parat tibi certa triumphos,
Jam gladio fracto perfidus hostis abit.[57]

In effect, the poet said that one man by delay had restored the Roman state; by not lingering, Garibaldi would do better. And so Landor saluted the hero, for whom a triumph was certain. When Garibaldi was in Calabria, Landor was rather anxious lest something untoward happen. However, like Mrs. Browning,[58] he also was cheered by the success of the Thousand. In December 1860 he wrote in a letter to Browning that the profits (imaginary!) from the Italian version of a conversation between Savonarola and the Prior of San Marco were to go to Garibaldi's wounded.[59] Possibly during 1860, Landor composed the lines, "To America, on Italy,"[60] in which he expressed the opinion that Garibaldi equalled even Washington.

Others who admired the deeds of the Thousand at the time of their occurrence were the travellers, J. R. D. Beste[61] and W. G. Clark.[62] One should not omit English working-class sympathy for Garibaldi as a champion of European democracy. It was this class which read the adulatory *Illustrated Life and Career of Garibaldi*, 1860, a shilling pamphlet, embellished on the cover with a picture of a brigand in red with two pistols, and in the text with numerous and egregious illustrations.

British aid to Garibaldi's men did not merely take the form of words—it was financial, diplomatic, naval, and military. As Charles Lever then put it, what was, after all, the importance of the *moral* support of England in an era of

* Mr. H. C. Minchin prints a slightly different version of this Latin epigram by Landor, in his edition of *Walter Savage Landor. Last Days, Letters, and Conversations*, London, 1934, p. 47.

steel-plated frigates and Armstrong guns?[63] It is true that Admiral Mundy[64] testified to Lord John Russell's having ordered a strict observance of neutrality and non-interference. But the facts attest to the partisan stand taken by England in behalf of Garibaldi. In the first place, the Thousand obtained, when it was seen that they would be successful, excellent English rifles. Moreover, The Friends of Italy sent Bertani, who was in Genoa under Garibaldi's written directions, 100,000 lire through W. H. Ashurst, the hero's London financial agent. This sum was meant to promote the enlistment of volunteers and the purchase of arms and uniforms, and to finance an attack on the Papal States and Naples.[65] Then, too, W. J. Linton broadcast an appeal for English subscriptions to Garibaldi's venture in Sicily and said that each gift of £15 meant another armed member for the expedition.[66] Another who tried to raise money was George Jacob Holyoake, whose organ, *The Reasoner*, September 23, 1860, printed a picture of Garibaldi, and with it an urgent request for donations. Joseph Cowen, Mazzinian partisan, carried the fullest accounts in his newspaper, the Newcastle *Daily Chronicle*, of what was happening in southern Italy, and actively propagandized for Garibaldi. On October 2, 1860, a concert (and lecture) was given in order to raise funds for the Garibaldians.[67] One contemporary opinion[68] was that about £30,000 was raised in England by the "Pro Italia" Committees to be found in very nearly all the towns of the United Kingdom. Lady Byron, who died on May 16, 1860, left in her will £40 for Garibaldi, then in Sicily.[69]

Many Englishmen sailed for Italy to join the Garibaldian forces, and it was for this Anglo-Saxon contingent that the then Miss Harriet Hamilton wrote a spirited battle hymn on the victory at Volturno.[70] One of Garibaldi's most trusted lieutenants was the dashing Colonel Peard, of whom the war correspondent, Count Carlo Arrivabene, wrote: "He is a simple, unpretending man, who, like all true Englishmen, hates despotism and servitude."[71] Colonel Dunne, another and valuable English officer with Garibaldi, is known to have sabred cowards in his regiment of Picciotti, *i.e.*, Sicilian riffraff. Incidentally, the English officers formed an Albion Club for the consumption of wine and food in the British manner![72]

George Jacob Holyoake[73] was acting secretary of the group which enlisted the British Legion for Garibaldi. Men were enrolled at No. 8, Salisbury Street, Strand, London. The secretly sympathetic Lord John Russell did nothing to stop the British contingent from sailing on the *Melazzo*, although these men were going to attack a friendly power. Holyoake recruited 810 men, all well equipped, and Garibaldi is said to have paid most of the cost, £30,000. Very airily, Lord Palmerston commented that he had no right to prevent "excursionists" from seeing Mount Etna. Since Naples was unsettled, naturally tourists needed arms![74] However, there were vain protests* in England about the following advertisement in the London papers:

> *Excursion to Sicily and Naples.* All persons (particularly Members of Volunteer Rifle Corps) desirous of visiting Southern Italy and of *aiding* by their presence and influence the *Cause of Garibaldi* and *Italy*, may learn how to proceed by applying to the Garibaldi Committee. . . .

Some of those attracted thus to the Italian cause were toughs from Glasgow and London—not averse to a little plunder and a great deal of drink. As indulgent Italians put it, these men were not accustomed to a country where wine was cheap.[75] At any rate, they got a bad name for disorderliness and pilfering, and nearly shot King Victor Emmanuel by accident.[76] Five of them were condemned to be executed for various misdeeds, but their sentences were commuted to prison terms.[77] Included in the ranks of the

* See the pamphlet published at Manchester in 1860 for the Manchester Foreign Affairs Association: *English Aid to Garibaldi, on His Invasion of the Sicilies. Is it Lawful and Just?*

Redshirts were some sailors who had deserted from H.M.S. *Agamemnon* and had been made the crew of a battery. Other sailors, on leave from H.M.S. *Hannibal*, wanted to join and asked Jessie White Mario, the Florence Nightingale of the Thousand, to get muskets for them.[78]

All things considered, it was the attitude of the British Foreign Office which helped Garibaldi most—more than men, rifles, or money. Lord John Russell told the Queen it was no moral wrong, rather a merit, to overthrow a tyrannical government like that of Naples.[79] It has already been seen how thanks to Lacaita's intervention Lord John refused to oppose Garibaldi's passage across the Strait of Messina to the Italian mainland. When the Emperors of Russia and Austria and the King of Prussia met in Austria to consider undoing the dramatic work of the Garibaldian and the Piedmontese forces towards the unification of Italy, Russell issued his famous dispatch (October 27, 1860) in which he said some unkind things regarding the character of the papal and Neapolitan governments, and declared that the Italians were the best judges of their own interests:

> . . . her Majesty's Government can see no sufficient grounds for the severe censure with which Austria, France, Prussia, and Russia have visited the acts of the King of Sardinia. Her Majesty's Government will turn their eyes rather to the gratifying prospect of a people building up the edifice of their liberties, and consolidating the work of their independence, amid the sympathies and good wishes of Europe.[80]

There was joy in Italy when this statement was made public early in November, and one Italian said the message was worth an army of 100,000 men. Indeed, Admiral Mundy[81] was told by King Victor Emmanuel in Naples that Lord John Russell and Sir James Hudson had been the truest friends any country could have. Yet it should not be forgotten that what *The Westminster Review*[82] said then was significant: a free Italy meant valuable commerce for England.

Naturally, Garibaldi liked the English. They had given him arms and men and diplomatic protection. They had sold him two frigates for the transportation of his followers. Even the London *Times* correspondent, Eber, had assisted by furnishing valuable information to the Thousand. Lord John Russell had called Garibaldi in the Commons a man of most remarkable character. Admiral Sir George Rodney Mundy had been a friend in deed. In England, people sang Mercantini's "Garibaldi's Hymn," and were pleased when the hero gave land at Naples to the English for a Protestant church. This gift was confirmed in 1861 by the minister Ricasoli, a Protestant.[83]

His work done, Garibaldi left for his island home, Caprera, with a bag of seeds, another of vegetables, and a roll of salt codfish. He had been compelled to borrow 1,500 lire. Such was the return to private life of the new Cincinnatus, and the simplicity of his exit made a profound impression on the British. To illustrate, *Macmillan's Magazine*[84] printed a good sonnet on "Garibaldi's Retirement" in which the anonymous poet emphasized that even the manner of his withdrawal had been prophesied by his past career. In the same issue, an Englishwoman, who had been in Naples when Garibaldi entered the city, described him as being "too guileless and pure-minded for this world."[85] In justice to Victor Emmanuel, it should be recorded that the King in vain offered Garibaldi great honours—a palace, the title of general, a steamship, provision for his sons, a dowry for his daughter, a dukedom, and the Order of the Annunziata.[86]

As a result of the Sicilian expedition, some writers during 1860 utilized as material Garibaldi's exploits at an earlier period of his career; people wanted to know everything about the Redshirt. Therefore, Giovanni Ruffini's novel, *Lavinia*, gave some details about Garibaldi and the revolution of 1848–49; Miss Margaret Roberts's story, *Mademoiselle Mori*, dealt with the siege of Rome; and another, *Angelo San-*

martino, was concerned to some degree with Garibaldi and his Hunters of the Alps during the war of 1859. Stephen Watson Fullom's poem, *The Exile's Daughter*, has also some description of Garibaldi in the war against Austria. In addition, a certain H. L. wrote a long poetic tale, *Italy: Past—Present—and Future* (1860), which called Garibaldi a plain, straightforward soldier—in lines generally of such a lack of merit that one supposes each second verse to have been written for the purpose of rhyming with its predecessor.

The most amusing contemporary literary work on Garibaldi is Rosalind Davis's drawing-room operetta in two acts, *Garibaldi, or The Rival Patriots* (1860). The music was by H. Frederick Cowen, a boy of eight; the words by the seventeen-year-old Miss Davis; and the operetta itself was performed once, by the family and young friends of little Cowen (who was probably a scion of the very pro-Italian Tyneside family). In the first act Pietro, Garibaldi's aide-de-camp, bursts into this song:

> Oh! who shall say a soldier's life
> Consists of nought but war and strife?
> We have many pleasures too,
> And our duties are but few.
>
> If we are called up to fight,
> We obey with all our might,
> And if in battle we should fall,
> A man can die but once, that's all.
>
> Though we must leave the girls we love,
> Why, that their constancy does prove;
> And if too long from them we roam,
> They love us better when we come home.

The story of the operetta is pleasantly inane: Theresa, an Austrian by birth, feels that the Italians have been grossly wronged and have justice on their side. She is betrothed to Leopold, the Austrian commander, but is also loved by Garibaldi. When the latter, who under the pseudonym of

Ernesto has been playing the lovesick swain, learns that she loves another, he sings:

> And must I go, and bid farewell
> To all my dreams of thee,
> Must thy fair form within this heart
> No longer cherished be?

Theresa replies: Yes, he must go! To which Garibaldi gallantly sings:

> No, I will ne'er another wed,
> Since thee I've loved in vain;
> Then farewell, lady, never more
> On earth we'll meet again.

Eventually, the Austrians and the Italians join battle, and Leopold is captured by Garibaldi. Theresa enters the Italian camp to plead for her lover, and Garibaldi, revealing himself as the rejected Ernesto, magnanimously releases the Austrian leader. An evening like this at the Cowens' reveals the extent of the cult of Garibaldi in England.

By November 1860, *The Drapeau Rouge*, a volume of Mazzinian verse, had been written in greeting to Garibaldi and his companions in arms. The theme of this collection of uninspired English poetry is democracy, the champions of which are Garibaldi and Mazzini, against whom are ranged Napoleon III, the Neapolitan Bourbon, the Pope, and their cohorts. Allusion is made to the recent meeting of the autocrats of Europe for the purpose of preventing the union of Italy after Garibaldi's conquest of Sicily.

During 1861, English admiration for Garibaldi assumed the proportions of ecstasy. The aged Landor[87] was ready to devote his pen and his heart to the Redshirt, and the young Swinburne thought him the greatest man since Adam. Moreover, one writer in *The Westminster Review*[88] called Garibaldi a figure out of Plutarch; and similarly, Dudley Costello[89] said that he deserved to be ranked with the noblest heroes of antiquity. People dedicated novels[90] to

Garibaldi, or monotonously retold the story of the Thousand: the same skirmishes, the same joined battles. Of this latter type of literature, we have Reginald Charles Oldknow's atrocious *Garibaldi in Sicily, or the Adventures of Johnson; and Other Poems*; the dull novel by W. B. Brooke called *Out with Garibaldi*; and Miss Mary Elizabeth Braddon's* book, *Garibaldi and Other Poems*—endless and dull Spenserian stanzas on the conquest of Sicily. A certain Reverend William MacIlwaine perched himself on a mountain-top (figuratively), beheld *A Vision of Italy* in very blank verse, and then launched into a eulogy of Garibaldi as the freer of the oppressed. A typical example of MacIlwaine's afflatus is the following:

> "Lowing kine
> Signalled the milk pail."

It was, however, Mrs. Caroline Giffard Phillipson[91] who during 1861 maltreated the Muses most frightfully. On April 9th, she visited Garibaldi at Turin and obtained his permission to dedicate her verse to him. A month later, calling him in a poem the greatest hero of modern times and the purest known to fame, she visualized him as a wearer of the "golden crown" of "Christ's holy warriors." Mrs. Phillipson also perpetrated some lines "In Memoriam of a Visit to General Garibaldi." Apparently, the General had been ill, and she saw him on his sick-bed. In his eyes she beheld

> a radiance holy,
> Such as angel orbs might show,
> Gazing on us with their soft light,
> Moisten'd by the tender feelings in the heart that throbb'd below!

In other poems she urged the Italians to call on Garibaldi again that he might lead them to the conquest of Rome and Venice. Interestingly enough, she was anticipating the fiasco of Aspromonte.

* She was the author of *Lady Audley's Secret* and many other novels.

A Manchester reporter, one John B. Marsh, wrote *The Life and Adventures of Garibaldi, the Apostle of Liberty*, an admiring biography, but in its treatment reminding one of a modern tabloid newspaper concerned with the lurid career of an American public enemy. Marsh's account is full of apocryphal yarns and sounds like a sixpenny novel. Of the siege of Rome, we are told:

> Where the fire was hottest, the conflict fiercest, the danger greatest, there was Garibaldi; his hair floating in the wind, his face lighted with enthusiasm, like some good guardian angel, or some old Roman warrior risen from the grave—animating, fighting, conquering, and invincible.

Marsh quoted to advantage Garibaldi's famous speech* when he fled from Rome: "Soldiers! in recompense for the love you may show your country, I offer you hunger, thirst, cold, war, and death! Who accepts the terms let him follow me." At the end, our biographer reassuringly declared that Garibaldi merely rested now from his wearying labour; but only for a time, for the hero would never swerve from his sublime resolve to give liberty to the downtrodden and freedom to the oppressed.

About this time, Garibaldi was by some being compared with Cavour, and not to his own advantage. It is true that Frederic Harrison[92] wrote that Garibaldi, "the noblest soldier of our day," was a link between the two parties advocating the unification of Italy, the monarchist Moderates and the republican Mazzinians. But Sir Edward Dicey's memoir of Cavour depreciated Garibaldi in comparison with the dead statesman. As Sir James Hudson said to the Duke of Argyll, Garibaldi was a very brave man—"Honest and patriotic, but has no head."[93]

English politics were more concerned in 1861 with the American Civil War than with Garibaldi. However, *The Quarterly Review* pointed out that the English had rejoiced

* Used in Drinkwater's *Garibaldi* also.

at the success of the events in Italy and had not questioned the methods employed. They had been won by the romantic exploits of Garibaldi without realizing that he had violated the Foreign Enlistment Act by recruiting volunteers in England.[94] In the House of Commons, Lord John Russell, in reply to the taunts of Disraeli, said that the King of Naples had had about 100,000 soldiers, about 40,000 to 50,000 men in reserve, a fleet; yet Garibaldi and 1,800 men took the land. "Well," said Russell, "the inference to which I came, and that every man made for himself, was that the King of Naples was not very strong in the affections of his subjects."[95] It should not be supposed that British sympathizers were content with Garibaldi's deeds in southern Italy. In 1861, George Jacob Holyoake collected money for some thrust* by the hero at Venice or Rome; and there was in existence, to cite merely an example, a "Glasgow Garibaldi Fund Committee."[96]

Mrs. Browning's posthumous volume of *Last Poems*, 1862, included a poem on Garibaldi. Her verses described his grief at the cession of Nice, his birthplace, to France, and then retold the story of the Sicilian expedition, the successful conclusion of which was marked by the memorable telegram to Turin that Palermo had surrendered. "They have made me a foreigner," Mrs. Browning had Garibaldi say. But she emphasized that nothing had been able to alter the hero's devotion to Italy. The same collection by Mrs. Browning contained a poem called "The King's Gift": on the present of a diamond necklace to Teresita, Garibaldi's daughter, as a tribute from King Victor Emmanuel, since for himself, the conqueror of southern Italy had refused many great rewards.

But the foregoing was in the nature of an echo of the Italian events of 1860. In the offing was Garibaldi's mad

* For that matter, Ferdinand Lassalle visited Garibaldi, on the island of Caprera (1861), to discuss a fantastic Hungarian revolt. See Franz Mehring, *Karl Marx*, p. 334.

raid on Rome, which ended in the defeat of Aspromonte. During April, Mrs. Phillipson expressed the hopes of many English people when she wished, in verse,[97] to see Rome and Venice free, and hinted that Garibaldi was the man to carry out the task. In another poem called " 'Rome or Death,' " from the slogan of the men who were shortly to be dispersed before Rome, she urged Italian mothers and wives to let their men follow Garibaldi and win great praise. A certain Francis Alexander Mackay[98] even wrote a war chant for the new adventure, which was stirring and trite—the usual slogans: "Let us conquer or die!" "On to victory!" "Down with the tyrants!"

Meanwhile, money was being raised in England by a "Garibaldi Italian Unity Committee" composed of the following gentlemen: P. A. Taylor, M.P., chairman; W. H. Ashurst, treasurer; J. Sale Barker; W. J. Linton; W. T. Malleson; William Shaen; R. E. Wainewright; and J. M. Moir, secretary.[99] One observes that most of these were on very close terms with Mazzini. And it was Emilie Ashurst Venturi[100] who carried the money, collected in Great Britain through Mazzini, to Garibaldi. Garibaldi himself, as perpetual honorary president of the "United Associations of Working Men in Naples," wrote the president of the General Working Men's Association in London a letter calculated to win sympathy for his projected enterprise. He told these English workers that up to the present time there had been no freedom in schools, no liberty of speech, nor any free press in Italy; neither had the Italians had any right of association. Now they enjoyed more liberty than ever before. Nevertheless, Garibaldi pointed to those sections of Italy that were overrun by foreigners and by brigands. These elements laid waste the country, burned cities and villages, and slaughtered unoffending citizens. All this, he said, was the work of the Bourbons and of the priests. The Pope was in power in Rome, thanks only to the bayonets of French troops. In the midst of their difficulties, the Italians, declared

Garibaldi, had turned their thoughts to their fellow workmen in England. In the name of the love they bore to their own native land, in the name of the brotherhood of labour, of national rights, and of that universal freedom opposed so much by the Pope, he asked the British labouring classes to lend their sympathy and their influence towards making good the Italian cry, "Rome is the capital of Italy." About this time, Jessie White Mario returned to England in order to give lectures on the state of Italy, and no doubt to prepare public opinion when Garibaldi should march on Rome.[101]

Mrs. Gaskell, the novelist, wrote an introduction for Colonel Vecchi's biographical sketch of *Garibaldi at Caprera*, 1862, which appealed to the anti-Catholic sentiments of certain sections of the English people. Vecchi described Garibaldi as *perfect* in his private and public life and said that Caprera was "the den of the Italian Lion." He gave details about a phrenologist who visited Garibaldi and marvelled at his cranium, and related that the hero received many letters (mostly from Anglo-Saxon ladies) asking for his autograph and a lock of hair. The biographer even told a story of an English peer who came in his yacht to make Garibaldi's acquaintance. This nobleman asked Garibaldi for a souvenir—a pair of strong nailed shoes; and Garibaldi told him it was the only pair he had! Anyhow, Garibaldi gave the Englishman a red shirt and a stone from Caprera! Additional anecdotes to tickle the English antipapal fancy included this story—that Garibaldi had named his donkeys "Pio Nono," "Immaculate Conception," and "Lamoricière" (Lamoricière was the Frenchman who commanded the papal troops). Vecchi said that some people in Melbourne, Australia, had sent Garibaldi a sword which had cost three hundred pounds.

In addition to all this propaganda, Landor, who apparently had heard rumours, wrote a poem[102] exulting in the coming expedition against Rome:

Rejoice all ye
Who once were free,
And what ye were again shall be;
Freedom hastes home
To ruin'd Rome,
And Venice rises from the sea.

An admirer of Landor, Swinburne, published, on the very day before Garibaldi's men set out with their tremendous cheer of "Rome or Death!", "A Song in Time of Revolution, 1860." In this poem, the young poet, thinking of the Thousand in southern Italy and of the other Italian events of 1860 (such as the successful plebiscites in central Italy), said that

> The heart of the rulers is sick, and the high priest covers his head.

No doubt he wished again to see

> The priests . . . scattered like chaff, and the rulers broken like reeds;

and therefore one may suppose that although the poet was recalling events of the immediate past, he was really looking forward to Garibaldi's new adventure.

While English hearts rejoiced, the Garibaldians went towards Rome. Late in August 1862, the Piedmontese government sent a force of Bersaglieri to stop the march on Rome and so prevent international complications. Garibaldi ordered his men to desist from firing, but the royal troops began hostilities anyway and wounded the hero during the sanguinary conflict of Aspromonte. Although he wished to depart from Italy on an English ship, he was placed under arrest and imprisoned for a short time at Varignano. Miss Hamilton immediately began the verses, "Garibaldi at Varignano,"* attacking the haste of the Italian government to disown its benefactor: "This is royal recompense for

* Later renamed "Aspromonte" in the volume (1869) entitled *Aspromonte and Other Poems.*

service ever true." What was this Italian love which wounded the object of its affections? she asked. Her conclusion is that he had been no fool even though he

> might have been cross'd and starr'd
> With diamonds, and set among princes,
> And had gold for his reward.

Very acidly, Sir William Hardman pronounced Garibaldi idiotic and declared that with his sword he was a Bayard, but with his pen a Bombastes.[103] With an equal bitterness, Mrs. Carlyle observed[104] to her husband: "So Garibaldi . . is wounded and captured already—luck, I should say, to the poor fellows he was leading to destruction." Richard Monckton Milnes thought the Italians had only acted with common sense about Garibaldi. Lady Palmerston said that they were all sorry, but Garibaldi lacked sense and judgment.[105] However, Lord Palmerston sent him an invalid's bed; and the people of England, donating their pennies, raised more than £1,000, to be spent on medical treatment for the wounded man.[106] Indeed, English admirers, distrusting Italian physicians, even engaged Doctor Parker, a noted surgeon of the time, to look after Garibaldi at Varignano. Moreover, James Stansfeld[107] visited the wounded man for The Society of the Friends of Italy. Meanwhile, riots broke out in Hyde Park and at Birkenhead where the Catholic Irish and the English sympathizers with Garibaldi clashed *à la Donnybrook*. At Dundee, Scotland, the Victorian literary critic, George Gilfillan, made a speech declaring himself an enthusiast for Garibaldi and Italy's unity.[108]

Persons like Mrs. Phillipson were very angry at the King of Piedmont, and called him a traitor. This poetess said that Garibaldi in a jail was far worthier than the false Victor Emmanuel in his palace; and she also versified her wrath at the conduct of the Piedmontese ministry, whom she termed a "shallow-hearted crew.." When the king pardoned Garibaldi and amnestied his followers, Mrs. Phillipson modified her opinion of Victor Emmanuel. He was no longer a traitor, merely a coward. Yet she hoped that the king and Garibaldi would once more be friends and strive together for the union of all Italy.[109] Another to treat the contemporaneous subject of the wounded and incarcerated Garibaldi was a certain James Henry Powell, whose penny pamphlet, entitled *Garibaldi, the Prisoner of Spezzia. A Poem*, repeated the whole story of the Aspromonte fiasco. This poetaster declared that the right would triumph despite usurpers [Napoleon III] and Popes. More competently worded, Gerald Massey's poem, "Garibaldi at Aspromonte,"[110] expressed high praise for the Redshirt.

There are also in existence several anonymous poems on the events at Aspromonte, probably written within a few days of the disaster suffered by Garibaldi's men. For example, one provincial English newspaper printed these atrocious lines:

> Alas the day! 'twas fortune's frown!
>   Alas for Royal gratitude!
> The King to whom he gave a crown
>   Hath basely spilt the patriot's blood.
>   Wounded and low,
>   A prisoner now,
>   Yet glorious as he's great and good.
>
> But not in vain doth this befal;
>   From evil good will yet come out;
> Ghosts of Italian martyrs call—
>   To arms, Italian youth! they shout;
>   For Rome or death
>   The sword unsheath!
> That Rome is yours 'tis crime to doubt.[111]

As the *Daily Telegraph* wrote, Garibaldi had conspired only to increase the power and territory of his king.[112] Not regarded as a traitor, he lost no prestige in Great Britain. An English committee even sent a Mrs. Chambers[113] to his home on the island of Caprera with instructions to induce him to come to England. There, indeed, he had already become part and parcel of everyday commercial and social life. Stylish English women wore loose blouses called "Garibaldis"; and their children were fond of eating large square cakes with layers of currants, known as "Garibaldi biscuits," or relished a species of hard, round, boiled candies popularly sold under the name of "Garibaldi balls."[114]

During 1863, Garibaldi was by no means forgotten despite the fact that his Redshirts were no longer in action. A friend of Landor's, Mrs. Frederick West,[115] composed "Garibaldi's March," the musical qualities of which are somewhat dubious; and Landor himself published in his *Heroic Idyls* (1863) several Latin epigrams and some English verses eulogizing his idol. In one of his English poems, "The Later Day," the old poet fancied Garibaldi rising to pierce the cloud that hovered over the Italians, and then advised the new Italy in this pedestrian manner:

> Alone in Garibaldi place thy trust,
> There shalt thou find a guardian brave and just.

Some of the more considerable Victorian novelists were now thinking of writing stories with a Garibaldian flavour. There was, for example, Charles Lever, who had in mind a novel about an Irish member of the Thousand. This became his *Tony Butler*, which eventually appeared in *Blackwood's Edinburgh Magazine*.[116] Then, too, George Meredith, visiting Italy in 1863 with his friend, Lionel Robinson, made tours in Piedmont and saw the scene of Garibaldi's guerrilla fighting in 1848.[117] This trip influenced the composition of Meredith's vivid novel, *Vittoria*.

A certain Thomas Swann, whose Muse was vapid and garrulous, wrote *Modern Italy: A Poem* (1863), inspired apparently by the preparations for that first march on Rome which was ended by the defeat of Aspromonte. Swann indulges in much facile and nebulous praise of Garibaldi. In the same year, Rear Admiral Sir George Rodney Mundy published an interesting account[118] of his own conduct at Palermo and Naples during the stirring events of 1859–61. Though Mundy said he had tried to be neutral, his narrative is proof to the contrary and shows how much he had helped Garibaldi. The Admiral's sketch of the *condottiere* is valuable. Garibaldi was a man in his middle years, five feet seven inches in height, strongly built, with a lofty brow, reddish hair, a benevolent and intelligent face, a clear, silvery voice, and a simple and even tender manner. Other contemporary accounts agree with this description of the hero at the time of the Sicilian expedition. The Bishop of Lincoln, Christopher Wordsworth, recorded in his travel journal (1863) an interesting Italian comment on Garibaldi:

> You know that among heathen nations there are some objects which the Priests *taboo*, and no one dares touch them; the People of Italy idolize Garibaldi, they have *tabooed* him, and no one ventures to touch him.[119]

Well, when Garibaldi did go to England in the spring of 1864, it was soon evident that the people there had also "tabooed" him. No comparable popular welcome has perhaps ever been known with the exception of that which New York gave Charles Lindbergh, back from his flight to Paris.

CHAPTER XV

Garibaldi and the British: From the London Ovation until the Present

WHY did Garibaldi pay his famous visit to England? He himself gave as a pretext the necessity for consulting celebrated English surgeons about the wound which he had suffered at Aspromonte. But his real motive was to use English sympathy for him in such a way as to put pressure on Her Majesty's Government and to induce it to give him money and other support for a war against Austria, the rewards of which were to be Venice and the surrounding territory.[1] It was therefore neither his health nor the pleasures of adulation which took him to the British Isles, but rather the cause of Italian unity.

On March 24th, *The Times* of London printed a long leader on the approaching visit of Garibaldi, and rehearsed his career in terms of the most cordial praise. Elsewhere in the same issue was an account of the plans of the trade and friendly societies of London workmen for a grand welcome. Five days later, the "Thunderer" reported Garibaldi's arrival at Malta on the mail steamship *Ripon*. With him was a Colonel Chambers of the Liverpool Rifle Volunteers. In an interview, the great man said he was coming to London for medical advice. Some of the Bourbon adherents, who had left Naples and had obtained refuge in Malta, hissed him; but most people cheered. Meanwhile, the municipality of Southampton was making official plans for a reception. *The Times* of April 1st recorded Garibaldi's touching at Gibraltar.

On the 3rd, the hero landed at Southampton in the midst of tumultuous rejoicing, for, as one contemporary journalist[2] in the provinces wrote, he had excited the sympathy of all because he was the champion of the rights of all, without distinction of colour or race, and a man who throughout his public career had exhibited the unselfish patriotism of a Washington and the military genius of a Gustavus Adolphus. The *Morning Star* of Southampton grew lyrical in its editorial greeting to the visitor. Southampton was decked out like a bride, British and Italian flags waved from almost every house, a military band played "Garibaldi's Hymn" by Luigi Mercantini, and there was wild cheering. In London, *The Times* (April 5, 1864) devoted much space to what was going on at Southampton, including the effusive speech of G. Brinton, the provincial mayor, and announced that the Lord Provost of Edinburgh had invited Garibaldi to visit the Scottish capital. Already, Edinburgh working men were making plans for his welcome.

A little later, a London deputation called on Garibaldi and obtained his promise to visit the metropolis on Monday, April 11th, not on the preceding Saturday. A Birmingham group also issued a most cordial invitation to the hero to see their city too. The Garibaldian ecstasy was growing every moment. In London, the Lord Mayor was engrossed in preparations; and the London and South Western Railway Company was getting ready a special train of ten carriages for Garibaldi.

The Times of April 9th eulogized Garibaldi's character, and printed by way of news the fact that sums were being collected for a Testimonial Fund. Prominent among those making arrangements was P. A. Taylor, M.P., and friend of Mazzini. On the same day, the current issue of *Punch* had a fine cartoon of Garibaldi with this caption: "THIS IS THE NOBLEST ROMAN OF THEM ALL!" The humorous magazine ridiculed those who objected to the patriot hero's fraternizing with workers and who desired to render his stay as politically harmless as possible. A Mayfair and rather effeminate dandy thus expresses himself:

> If he dines with us, I should say, let all political subjects be most cahfully avoided, and let the convasation be weswtwicted as closely as possible to gastwonomy, hauces, and the faiaw sex![3]

At first, Garibaldi was entertained at the home of the wealthy Mr. Seely. Here William Allingham paid him a visit and was favourably impressed, especially when the hero, understanding Allingham to be a poet, called him *mio caro* and shook hands heartily.[4] On the 11th, *The Times* printed a tremendous editorial on Garibaldi, stressing the affection which the English had for him and the entertainments being planned by the highest society. Already he had obtained the freedom of the City of London. On the streets, newsboys were beginning to sell adoring broadsides* in verse, lurid pamphlets on the hero's exploits, and pictures of a Salvator Rosa brigand labelled

GENERAL GIUSEPPE GARIBALDI.

Monday, April 11th, witnessed the extraordinary reception given by London to its hero. More than half a million people lined some three miles of streets along which Garibaldi's carriage made hardly any progress. So dense was the crowd that it took more than four hours to cover the route from Nine Elms station to Stafford House, the town residence of the Duke of Sutherland. There were brass bands playing the inevitable "Garibaldi's Hymn," there were the trade societies massed to greet their champion, there were banners flying everywhere, and above all a steady roar of hurrahs. Like an American presidential candidate, Garibaldi kissed a baby with curls, and all were gratified! In the immense procession that saluted Garibaldi was a remarkable mixture of Odd Fellows, Freemasons, temperance societies, and

* *E.g.*, Miss M. B. Smedley's *Garibaldi. Why We Welcome Him*, London, 1864.

especially the working men, who in their address of welcome coupled his name with Mazzini's. From the balconies of government buildings dignitaries cheered and cheered. The Duchess of Argyll,[5] who was among those waiting for Garibaldi to pass in parade, thought his face sublime. But Alexander Herzen[6] confessed that he had been unable to see Garibaldi because of the sea of people flooding the streets and the squares. Wherever there was a coping, a balcony, or a window, people were perched, some having waited for as long as six hours. With shouts of "Hurrah!" men and women and children clung to the carriage of their hero, and all who could get close to him shook hands, kissed the edge of his cloak, and shouted "Welcome!" The carriage of the Duke of Sutherland, in which Garibaldi finally reached Stafford House, near St. James's Palace, literally fell to pieces in the stable, such had been the strength of the thousands of eager arms that had snatched at and held to its sides, for London was mad with joy.[7]

It was the working men who took Garibaldi most closely to heart, deserted their factories, and cheered him. It was they who carried the banners with inscriptions like these: "Welcome Garibaldi," "Welcome the Hero of Italy," "The Man of the People," "The Pure Patriot," "The Bravest of the Brave," "Garibaldi the Great and Good," "The Liberator of Italy," and other admiring epithets.[8] In a word, they had given way, without reserve, to one of the greatest outbursts of delirious enthusiasm which England was ever to know. Theirs was a poetic recognition of Garibaldi's heroic achievements, and in him they saw a fighter for democracy and for their own interests.*

However, the upper classes also felt a genuine admiration for the picturesque Redshirt. When the Duchess of Suther-

* Important British trade-union leaders like Allan of the engineers, Applegarth of the carpenters, Lucraft of the joiners, Cremer of the builders, Odger of the shoemakers, were prominent in organizing Garibaldi's triumphal reception. See Mehring, *Karl Marx*, p. 347.

land drove Garibaldi to Eton, both the boys and the masters cheered him.[9] On April 13th, the hero went through a strenuous round of social engagements. During the day, he called on Mr. Seely, and had luncheon with Lord and Lady Russell at Pembroke Lodge. In her diary, Lady Russell entered this record of her visitor: "Simple dignity in every word he utters."[10] At night, the Duke of Sutherland gave a magnificent banquet at Stafford House in Garibaldi's honour; and among those present were the Dukes of Sutherland and Argyll, Earl Russell, the Earls of Clarendon, Derby, Malmesbury, and Shaftesbury, Earl Grosvenor, Lord Palmerston, Mr. Gladstone, Henry Adams, the future American historian, and Panizzi of the British Museum. When Garibaldi was introduced to Gladstone, he shook hands and said "Précurseur!"—meaning that the statesman had paved the way for the Thousand by influencing public opinion in Italy and in England against the Bourbon misgovernment.[11] After the banquet followed an "assembly," at which many people were presented to the hero—dukes, marquesses, earls, lord mayors, foreign nobility, diplomats, Messrs. Stansfeld, Bright, and Cobden, Admiral Mundy, and of course the ladies.* As Herzen wrote:

> The men shook his hand with the vigour with which a man shakes his own when he has put his finger in boiling water; some said something as they did so, the majority grunted, remained dumb and bowed as they turned away. The ladies too were mute, but they gazed so long and so passionately at Garibaldi that there will certainly be a crop of children born this year in London with his features; and as the children even now are going about in red shirts like his, there will be nothing left to imitate but his cloak.[12]

Garibaldi enjoyed the ducal hospitality of Stafford House while he remained in London and was on several occasions *fêted* by the Dowager Duchess and the Duchess of Sutherland.

* Henry Adams recorded (*The Education of Henry Adams*, Boston and New York, 1918, p. 198) that he had seen "three duchesses literally" worshipping at Garibaldi's feet.

Meanwhile, his leg was being looked after by an eminent surgeon named William Fergusson. On April 14th, he received a Manchester deputation and also one of more than fifty officers from the London Fire Brigade. He visited Aubrey House, the residence of P. A. Taylor, and was surrounded by exiles like Mazzini, Venturi, Louis Blanc, and Ledru-Rollin; and at night he went in state to the Italian Opera in Covent Garden and heard *Norma* and *Masaniello*. People noticed his close attention to that portion of the second opera dealing with liberty and love of country; and they cheered the lines beginning "*O santo ardor di patrio amor.*" Ladies in the box above his dropped flowers upon him; and others, more advantageously seated, gazed with adoration. In between his social engagements of the morning and the evening, he somehow managed to sandwich in a visit to a girls' school conducted by Giuseppe M. Campanella, and was cheered by an immense crowd. More than two hundred English girls were presented to the great man.

The next day, he went to Bedford to see a steam plough in action. Workmen were very cordial to him when he visited a large factory, and indeed the whole city came out to greet him. At night, he dined in London with Panizzi and was again in the midst of nobility and great commoners like Gladstone. On the following day, he inspected Barclay's brewery in Southwark, principally, one supposes, because the workmen had mobbed and hustled the Austrian Marshal Haynau (known as Marshal Hyena or as the butcher of Brescia) when the latter paid them an ill-starred visit in September 1850. Later in the day, he went to the Crystal Palace (alas! since gone up in flames), was cheered again and again, listened to music by Handel, made a speech very complimentary to the English, heard once more the Garibaldi hymn, and received a sword from the Italian residents of London.

On April 18th, George Eliot[13] went to see Garibaldi, who had gone for a second time to the Crystal Palace. Again the working men made a tremendous demonstration for him, especially when some British members of the famous Thousand saluted their old leader. And again there was the inevitable business of hearing Mercantini's hymn sung by those present. Earlier in the day, he had called on a few of the revolutionary exiles of London like Karl Blind, Ledru-Rollin, and Louis Blanc. But at night he was in more conventional company—dining with the Marquess and Marchioness of Clanricarde and meeting swarms of peers and their ladies. Gladstone was there too, and also a member of the Rothschild family.

The next day, Garibaldi was entertained at William Ashurst's home, and later received some thousand people, mostly middle-class in addition to many of the peerage, at Mr. Seely's house. John Bright, who was there, discerned in him kindness and gentleness and simplicity. At night, he went again to the opera and heard *Lucrezia Borgia*. But all was not harmony. There was a report that the hero was leaving England on account of pressure by the Cabinet, and so the "Garibaldi Reception and Testimonial Fund" committee held a long and very stormy meeting.

The Times, April 20, 1864, had a long editorial on Garibaldi's return to Caprera, which was scheduled for the 22nd. The reason for his quitting England, said the "Thunderer," was simply that he had overtaxed his strength by

> calls, receptions, deputations, levées, concerts, entertainments, dinners, Operas, triumphal progresses, visits to arsenals and model farms, with never-ending noise, shaking of hands, and bowing; and every now and then a speech to be made. . . .

Yet this leader did hint at the displeasure of Napoleon III because of the warmth of England's greeting to Garibaldi, for Garibaldi was a friend of Mazzini* and in his own right an enemy of the Emperor of the French. Elsewhere in *The*

* Mazzini had but recently been falsely accused of being associated with one Greco in a plot to assassinate Louis Napoleon.

Times was printed a letter from Fergusson, Garibaldi's surgeon, indicating that the hero had been advised to return to Caprera on account of his health; and on the same page appeared a comforting item to the effect that £1,972 4s. had been raised for Garibaldi. Tennyson's name was down for a subscription of a guinea.

During the 20th, Garibaldi visited the City of London, where very many waited to see him. At the Guildhall, he signed the Roll of Honorary Citizenship and was officially lauded. Somehow, he managed to find time to visit Foscolo's grave. In the evening, Gladstone entertained him at a dinner attended by dukes, an archbishop, Panizzi, and others. Afterwards came a reception where he was again presented to throngs of diplomats, to English dignitaries like Monckton Milnes and Stansfeld, and of course to the House of Lords not in official session!

Why was Garibaldi leaving England at what many people believed was Gladstone's insistence, though the statesman had manifestly honoured him and was known to admire him sincerely, despite a disturbing lack of religious faith? Later, Gladstone told the Commons that Garibaldi had gone back to Caprera because of his health, that he had advised the hero not to kill himself by accepting too many invitations for receptions in provincial towns (Garibaldi had received more than thirty such invitations). But Garibaldi himself believed that his stay was embarrassing the English government.[14] For example, Disraeli, who regarded Garibaldi as the foe of constituted authority in Church and State, refused to meet him even when London went wild with enthusiasm. To Disraeli, he was merely a pirate.[15] Similarly, a certain R. Jermyn Cooper, addressing *Three Letters to the Conservatives of England . . . on the Subject of Garibaldi and Revolution* (1864), denounced the hero as the great fomenter of disturbances throughout Europe. Cooper said that whereas others had pointed their daggers to strike a secret and deadly blow, Garibaldi's proclaimed object had been to subvert kingdoms, overthrow thrones, and spread "the fatal Upas shade of democracy" over all the Continent. The acclaim given to Garibaldi "stinks in the nostrils!"

In any case, Palmerston had tried to render Garibaldi's stay in England as harmless as possible by turning him over to hosts like the Duke of Sutherland and Charles Seely to keep him busy. Philip Guedalla[16] repeats a delightfully appropriate anecdote which reveals the pugnacious statesman's breezy attitude. Palmerston *loquitur* on Garibaldi's visit: "Oh, let's marry him to the rich Miss ——." But, said some one, he has a wife. "Oh, then, we'll get —— to explain her away." As he said the last, did he look towards Gladstone? Probably! What Palmerston feared was that English and foreign republicans would make capital of Garibaldi's visit. He had seen a great deal of Louis Blanc, Mazzini (to whom, on April 17th, he paid an extraordinary public tribute), Ledru-Rollin, Karl Blind, and other exiles. These may have used Garibaldi; but as it was wittily observed,[17] only the servants at Stafford House profited materially. The housemaids made small fortunes by selling little bottles of soapsuds *said* to have come out of Garibaldi's basin! Sir William Hardman recorded in his extraordinary diary[18] a similar story: Garibaldi had sent a slipper to a surgical bandage maker's in order to have something made to fit his wounded foot. While this slipper was in the bandage maker's shop, more than two hundred women are said to have kissed the sainted relic!

Frederic Harrison[19] said that Garibaldi had to leave because of Gladstone's insistence and that the pretence of health was merely diplomatic gloss. On the other hand, George Jacob Holyoake was of the opinion that Garibaldi departed without any direct hint but merely because he sensed how embarrassing his presence was to the government.[20] None the less, Mazzini informed Holyoake that there was actual official pressure.[21] For not only had Napoleon III been angered, but Victor Emmanuel of

Piedmont was furious at England's reception to Garibaldi,[22] the rebel of Aspromonte. Foreign displeasure might have hurt certain British interests with heavy capital investments abroad and therefore might have indirectly given difficulty even to Gladstone's skill at budget-making.

Yet Garibaldi could not be allowed to depart abruptly. Hence, on the twenty-first, the members of the Reform Club gave a luncheon in honour of the hero, and in due course sang "Garibaldi's Hymn." When Garibaldi visited the Houses of Parliament, Earl Russell was most cordial. In the evening, the Italian went to Fishmongers' Hall, where the worshipful Company had a banquet ready. Among those present were the Duchess of Sutherland and the Dowager Duchess, the Duke and Duchess of Argyll, the Earl and Countess of Shaftesbury, and many other notables, who heard the innumerable toasts to their guest and beheld him getting the Honorary Freedom of the Company of Fishmongers. The present writer has seen a copy of the menu[23] and can merely say that it was amazing even for a Victorian function. The working people of London were so angry about their idol's leaving that *The Times* reprinted an article from *The Lancet*, the British medical journal, which said that Garibaldi's promised departure was due only to his health.

On the following day, April 22nd, *The Times* had an enormous leading article joining Garibaldi and Shakespeare's birthday in a rough amalgam of the Castor and Pollux species; and also printed a second editorial reproving the "Working Men's Reception Committee" for having said that the Government, especially Gladstone, were anxious to get rid of the visitor. Of the first *Times* leader, Sir William Hardman remarked that to associate Shakespeare with Garibaldi was to join a dead lion to a living ass.[24] On this very day when Garibaldi was to have left London (on the Duke of Sutherland's yacht) for Caprera, the Prince of Wales went to Stafford House and chatted with him for more than an hour.

Previously, Robert Browning[25] had shaken the hero's hand

and was very glad to have said a few words to him in Italian. The poet laureate and Mrs. Tennyson also called on Garibaldi in London,[26] and in return the Italian visited Farringford. After the visit, Tennyson[27] wrote to the Duke of Argyll:

> What a noble human being! I expected to see a hero and was not disappointed. One can not exactly say of him what Chaucer says of the ideal Knight, "as meke he was of port as is a made"; he is more majestic than meek, and his manners have a certain divine simplicity in them, such as I have never witnessed in a native of these islands, among men at least, and they are gentler than those of most young maidens whom I know.

Garibaldi had planted a tree (*Wellingtonia Gigantea*, said *Punch*) in Tennyson's garden, had quoted from Foscolo's *I Sepolcri*, had admired the primroses, and had kissed the children. On his part, Tennyson recited Manzoni's "*Il Cinque Maggio*," advised Garibaldi not to talk politics in England, for the Italian was very bitter against Napoleon III, and was charmed by his simplicity (but thought that in worldly matters he had the "divine stupidity of a hero"). Of their visitor, Mrs. Tennyson recorded her impressions in her diary, April 1864:

> a most striking figure in his picturesque white poncho lined with red, his embroidered red shirt and coloured tie over it. His face very noble, powerful, and sweet, his forehead high and square. Altogether he looked one of the great men of our Elizabethan age. His manner was simple and kind.

The Illustrated London News printed a full-page picture of Garibaldi's visit to Tennyson,[28] which is remembered in these lines of the laureate's:

> Or watch the waving pine which here
>   The warrior of Caprera set,
>   A name that earth will not forget
> Till earth has roll'd her latest year. . . .[29]

Unfortunately, some vandal broke off two branches from the tree which Garibaldi had planted, and by his misdeed earned the just wrath of *Punch* (April 23, 1864), versified in the poem, "On a Snob."

On the 23rd, Garibaldi inspected the Royal model farm at Windsor, where some farmers of the vicinity wanted to give him a steam plough. He refused their gift because his own farm on Caprera, consisting of only twenty-five acres, was too small for the economical use of the machine. The City of Manchester now sent him its regrets at his not being able to come. The great man of action, hitherto led like a show lion through drawing-rooms by a string of roses, was getting ready to leave for home. But first he addressed a letter of thanks* to the generally cordial London press. Naturally, *Punch*[30] printed a fine cartoon of Britannia shaking hands with the departing hero—"FAREWELL TO GARIBALDI." In the preceding issue of *Punch* had appeared a serious and dignified poem on the welcome by London to one who was a

> King; crowned by deeds and consecrate by fame.

Garibaldi did not leave unrebuked: for example, Captain Mayne Reid, the author of numerous adventure stories, took exception[31] to Garibaldi's statement, in a newspaper, that England had individual freedom, freedom of conscience, of domicile, of press, of speech, and of association. Reid, a man highly sympathetic towards the English working classes, whom he considered underprivileged, was using a quotation from Garibaldi as a springboard to launch his own radical ideas. Among other things, Reid said that freedom of speech was a matter of caprice in England because "whenever [it] becomes dangerous to important hereditary privileges, it will be quickly stifled. . . ."

* In reality, composed for Garibaldi by James Stansfeld. See J. L. and Barbara Hammond on *James Stansfeld* . . ., p. 84. Stansfeld was Garibaldi's most trusted adviser during his 1864 visit to England. Afterwards, Garibaldi called him the "type of English courage, loyalty, and consistency, the friend of Italy in her evil days, the champion of the weak and of the oppressed abroad" (*Dictionary of National Biography*, 1st supplement, III, 352–54).

On May 9th, Garibaldi returned to Caprera. Cardinal Manning on the following day published an open letter[32] on the subject of the hero's visit. His Eminence expressed an extreme dislike for the manner in which those in high place had thrown open their houses to honour Garibaldi; and denounced the furore over the "pirate," whose movements had been chronicled as by a Court newsman and for whom the red cloth had been spread to honour his entry. The Cardinal avowed his belief in the ultimate failure of Italian unity, for it was in "direct conflict with the providential order by which Christendom has been sustained for these thousand years."

On the other hand, the month of May saw: Charles Lever[33] publishing a very laudatory article in *Blackwood's* on the recent visit and the character of Garibaldi; George Meredith[34] working on an ode to the hero and thinking of a trip to Italy in order to get local colour for a novel [*i.e. Vittoria**]; and *Fraser's Magazine*[35] printing a facile poem, "To Garibaldi," by Sir John Kingston James,† who insisted on reviving the great deeds of the Redshirts in southern Italy under the "second Washington."

There were some English voices during 1864 raised to advance more accurate opinions on Garibaldi. The feminist and philanthropist, Miss Frances Power Cobbe,[36] an acute observer, said that he was only a military hero in "King Cambyses vein"—and not at all fit for times of peace. But a hero-worshipper like Lieutenant-Colonel Chambers, to whose military mind peace had no victories "no less renowned than war," exhausted even the empyrean reaches of blind adulation in his book on *Garibaldi and Italian Unity*, 1864—full of prating verbosity on "chivalry," "intrepidity," "honour," "virtue," and the rest of the abstractions of claptrap. Equally bad is an anonymous biography of Garibaldi

* Meredith first thought of calling this novel *Emilia in Italy*.

† He was also one of the innumerable English translators of Filicaia's great sonnet, "*All' Italia*." See *Macmillan's Magazine*, VII, 240 (January 1863).

(which had apparently been printed to take immediate advantage of the universal British madness over his visit), called descriptively *The life of Garibaldi, including his career in South America, Rome, Piedmont, and Lombardy; with full particulars of the Landing at Marsala and the Sicilian Campaign; his triumphal Entry into Naples; his Residence at Caprera; and the Disaster at Aspromonte. . . .* The author compared Garibaldi to Raleigh, Frobisher, and Drake, banally called him a "*chevalier sans peur et sans reproche*," and then said that both Scotland and Ireland claimed Garibaldi's ancestry—the Scots asserting that his name was derived from "Bartholomew or Baldy Garrow," the Irish maintaining that it was a corruption of "Garret Baldwin," and our biographer giving as his verdict the Scottish "Not proven"! Even worse was a certain Scott Hamilton's inane *Garibaldi; or, the Hero of Italy: a Grand Dramatic Ovation to "The Hero of the Age."*

The unfortunate chronicler who has had to read the fulsome praise for Garibaldi served up in the foregoing books almost sympathizes with those Greeks who tired of hearing Aristides called the Just. Nevertheless, the present writer cannot applaud a bitter attack on Garibaldi in a Catholic organ, *The Dublin Review* for July 1864, where it was said that he was nothing but a pirate and an associate of Mazzini, "the sheik of the assassins."

The furore aroused by Garibaldi's visit died away. Yet one rather minor English poet, George Walter Thornbury, when he heard in Venice, before 1866, the roll of drums preceding the determined march of Austrian soldiers with fixed bayonets, exclaimed:

> Hark! now the brutal German drum
>   Leads on the bayonets. See
> Insolent soldiers pacing round
>   A city once so free.
> Rise, hero of yon lovely isle,*
>   And give them liberty.[37]

* Garibaldi on Caprera.

Then there was Eleanor Darby, who dedicated her poems, *Ruggiero Vivaldi, and other lays of Italy . . .*, 1865, to Garibaldi and rhapsodized about his merits. "Ruggiero Vivaldi" has a hero of the same name who fights with Garibaldi in the war of 1859 and accompanies the Redshirt to Sicily the next year. Unfortunately, the poem is merely trite, if fluent verse: its story is exceedingly stupid, there is no talent for characterization, and the imagery is at best conventional, at worst asinine.

A far happier effort is Charles Lever's rollicking novel, *Tony Butler*, with its complement of Bobadills and its plethora of burlesque. The story is exceedingly slight: the adventures of a not very intelligent youth of good family who can ride and hunt and be a bit impudent, and who knows his own lack of brains. Tony Butler fights with Garibaldi in Calabria, inherits a convenient fortune of £36,000 a year from uncle Sir Omerod, and marries the *ingénue* heroine. As part of the background is a Bourbon scheme to enlist an Irish legion* of five or six thousand men for service in the Neapolitan army—"the *Cacciatori* of St. Patrick"—who are to maintain "the cause of order *versus* anarchy—the right to rule of the good, the virtuous, and the enlightened against the tyranny of the unlettered, the degraded, and the base." Some of these Hunters of St. Patrick go over to Garibaldi; many turn brigand and infest the Calabrian hills. One significant detail in this novel about the Thousand is the reaction of the ferocious Major Miles M'Caskey, *miles gloriosus*, to the meagre packs of the *Garibaldini*: "Why, the fellows have not even risen to the dignity of pillage!" *Tony Butler* is acceptable only because of its gaiety and brag. More to one's fancy is the excellent account (published in 1865) by Jessie White's husband, Alberto Mario, of episodes in his own career and in Garibaldi's during the dramatic days of the conquest of southern Italy. His odyssey, *The Red Shirt*, was very favourably reviewed by Anthony Trollope[38]—probably on account

* *Cf.* the Irish volunteers who fought with the Spanish rebels (1937).

of its brisk cheerfulness and its differentiation between what was heroic and what was comic opera in the progress of the Thousand.

Miss Amelia Blandford Edwards* published serially a novel entitled *Half a Million of Money*, which ran in Charles Dickens's magazine, *All the Year Round*, from April 22 to December 23, 1865. The fabulously wealthy hero, Saxon Trefalden, infatuated with a beautiful Italian girl of Mazzinian leanings, Olimpia Colonna, is represented as financing the Redshirts. The scene of much of the story is laid in southern Italy. Not only is the victory of Melazzo recounted, but there are glimpses of some English officers with the Thousand and also references to the siege of Gaeta, where the Bourbons made their last stand. Eventually, Olimpia Colonna, alienated from republicanism by the fiasco of Aspromonte, is convinced that only the Moderates (or Piedmontese monarchical party) can unite Italy. The foregoing outline scarcely suggests the tinsel, sensational plot of Miss Edwards's novel. For Signorina Colonna carries on numerous and simultaneous flirtations to make converts for the "Cause," and one is left with the vague impression that the overthrow of Bourbon Italy in 1860 was due to the machinations of an old gentleman (drawn from an already legendary Mazzini) and his handsome daughter, in the octagon tower of an English country-house. Yet the story has movement, and the present writer confesses to having enjoyed it. Anyhow, it boasts a perfectly gorgeous villain of the deepest dye and a set of English nobility of the most inane kind—like Mr. P. G. Wodehouse's characters.

After Aspromonte was to come the *débâcle* of Mentana, for Garibaldi always thought that he could repeat elsewhere his extraordinary success in Bourbon Italy. There was a section of British opinion which encouraged him in attempts aimed at freeing either Rome or Venice; and this English

* She was also an explorer and Egyptologist.

attitude was expressed by W. J. Linton in a poem, "Three Wishes," one of which was

> to be king of Italy at Garibaldi's side
> To tread Vienna's crowded streets, Napoleon's help denied,
> And there proclaim Venetia free, our Adriatic bride![39]

Garibaldi was almost the only prominent Italian military figure to do well during the war* of Italy and Prussia against Austria (1866), a fact which kept his name high in English esteem. When he began to lay plans for another dash on Rome, he probably included in his calculations English good will, English guns, and English money. About February 1867, he dined at Spezzia with Charles Lever, who explained to him that if he expressed sympathy for the Fenians, he would alienate English sentiments.[40] Indeed, Robert Browning thought him a good deal of a fool: "Garibaldi is just what I always took him for, once out of a mountain pass!"[41] But it was English money, raised mostly by the Mazzinians, that took Garibaldi again out of a mountain pass[42] and to another disaster. "Rome or Death!" was the shout of his men, and the outcome was not Rome.

Garibaldi's intentions were soon widely known. The Italian ministry did not wish any incident to mar its convention (1864) with the government of Napoleon III. According to the terms of the agreement, French troops were gradually to be withdrawn from the papal territory. In the meantime, a force was to be recruited to protect the Pope. At the end of 1866, the evacuation of Rome was complete, and the city was entirely denuded of French soldiery. The Italian government had agreed to respect the papal possessions and even to oppose by force any attack upon them from the outside. Prime Minister Rattazzi had Garibaldi arrested at Sinalunga on September 24, 1867 and shipped off to Caprera. On October 21st, the brothers Cairoli and

* George Meredith served as correspondent for *The Morning Post* of London.

about seventy-five other patriots were killed in an attempt to take Rome. The next day, Rattazzi resigned; and on the twenty-third, Garibaldi escaped from Caprera, got to Florence, and then started out for Rome with a motley host of men and boys, many armed with old-fashioned English muskets. Before his escape, Swinburne had written the poem called "In the Twilight," which questioned whether Garibaldi would submit to Victor Emmanuel's *no* or go on to Rome.[43] Well, he did go on to Rome; and while his men marched, *The Athenaeum* printed a "Translation of the *Inno Romano* [Roman Hymn], Written by Garibaldi for the Emancipators of Rome." The translator, "B.", conveyed in an adequate fashion the hackneyed frenzy of Garibaldi's verses—the "expel the tyrants! eject the priests!" variety of patriotic exuberance.[44]

Unfortunately for Garibaldi, Napoleon III sent an expeditionary force from Toulon. The Garibaldians, who had previously routed the papal troops, served to test a new type of French rifle. The experiment was a tremendous success, since Garibaldi's men were mowed down, at the beginning of November, in the bloody fiasco of Mentana.

In England, Swinburne, whose long "Song of Italy" had recently referred to the

> splendour of the sudden sword
> That drove the crews abhorred
> From Naples

and to "the Bitter Hill" of Aspromonte, now had as a subject the defeat of Mentana. The result was the poem known as "The Halt Before Rome," in the November *Fortnightly Review*. The poet could not yet believe that the Italian cause might sustain a check, for in Garibaldi's men was a flame to urge them on and at their head were great chiefs to lead. Next, he jibed at England, with "hands overflowing with gold," since she had not intervened for Italy, "mother of men." To Swinburne, the rout was only a halt—

Rome would yet be Italian. But now the city was curbed by one "swathed in the shroud of his creeds," by him

> who hath claws as a vulture,
> Plumage and beak as a dove.

It was he, the unspeakable Pope, whose words were "a savour of death unto death"; who fed his sheep with "ashes" and "grass from the graves of the dead"; who clasped Rome like an adder, for his lips, smoother and sweeter than oil, were full of poison. Under his sway, "life dies down in all lands"; and his blessings were curses. Mrs. Browning, said Swinburne, "song-bird beautiful-souled," erred when she praised Victor Emmanuel. "The Halt Before Rome" has been called the finest political rhapsody in our language, a possible judgment,[45] though not the present writer's.

An unfinished poem by Sydney Dobell, "Mentana,"[46] deals with a wife's grief for her husband, a slain Garibaldian. The poet prophesies a great and united Italy—"undivided by division," with "everlasting beauty, whole and one." Likewise, Francis Turner Palgrave wrote some lines in mourning for the dead who fell before Rome and declared that these had planted the seed of future victory. Palgrave's "Mentana"[47] does not pity the slain but rather asserts that with them and not with the French would lie the ultimate triumph. In tone, the poem is both martial and elegiac; though it is not great as verse, it does not lack spirit.

In *Blackwood's*[48] for November 1867, Charles Lever, who was in the English consular service in Italy, wrote an account of the inside politics behind the defeat of Mentana. He was of the opinion that the Italian government, headed by Rattazzi, had abetted Garibaldi in the march on Rome. But, said Lever, the man who had succeeded with the Thousand had tried only to repeat his own exploits. It is known that Lever was fond of Garibaldi. On the other hand, Browning, at the Athenaeum Club, liked nobody engaged in the

Mentana rout—neither the King of Italy nor Napoleon III nor Garibaldi: "well, it seems ordained that if you believe in heroes you will be sorry for it sooner or later."[49] Sir William Hardman was glad that the Garibaldians had been beaten.[50]

Garibaldi escaped from Mentana, was arrested, and released. Huge demonstrations in the streets of Milan and of other Italian cities had gained his freedom.

A very determined English lady, Miss Emma Pearson, travelled to Rome and was there when the French *chassepot* rifles made horrible work among the Garibaldians at Mentana. Her lively account of her experiences, *From Rome to Mentana* (1868), contains a defence of Garibaldi's men against the charge that they were *en masse* brigands and robbers. In contrast to her essentially Protestant sympathy with Garibaldi is the fact that a number of ardent English Catholics fought in 1867 with the Pontifical Zouaves.[51]

Years later, William Michael Rossetti, considering Garibaldi's career as a patriot from 1860 to 1867, composed a bitter and vigorous sonnet called "The Red Shirt." When the younger Rossetti, an ardent Mazzinian, thought of the honest King of Italy [*Il Re Galantuomo*, Victor Emmanuel], his gorge rose and found expression in a second sonnet, "Victor Emmanuel, 1867":

> Man of his word, and king. Scarce credible
> The combination.

Savoy and Nice, Aspromonte, and Mentana, all declared: "Put not thy trust in princes, Italy."[52]

F. W. Irby's[53] spirited song, "The Red Shirt" (1868), deals with the Thousand on their way to conquer the Kingdom of the Two Sicilies. In the same year, Sir Edwin Arnold, the author of "The Light of Asia," translated two *Political Poems by Victor Hugo and Garibaldi*. The first was the exile of Guernsey; the second, of Caprera. The foregoing volume has a preface by George Jacob Holyoake. Hugo's contribution was a bitter poem on Mentana; the poet mourned the slain six hundred, denounced the Pope for having blessed weapons capable of killing "a dozen men a minute" [the *chassepots*], and repeated his hatred for Napoleon III, the emperor who had the French fight in the proportions of ten to one! To Hugo, the Pope was the "sinister old man," who could meekly pray; and Garibaldi had been served like John Brown at Harper's Ferry. Furthermore, Victor Emmanuel was no "honest man" [*galantuomo*] but rather a turnkey for Sicily and Naples; and the Pope, like a jackal, fed on Italian flesh. Yet the chief criminal responsible for Mentana was neither the Pope nor the Italian king but rather the French Judas, Napoleon the Little! And Hugo concludes his energetic lines by calling on France, a sottish giant, to rise! Garibaldi's poem asked whether the France which once drove the tyrants far and wide could be enslaved to that false Napoleon, that "Ape of Caesar, this Sham Jove." Tactfully, Garibaldi paid tribute to England for having forbidden any interference when he wished in 1860 to cross the Strait of Messina from Sicily to Naples. It is interesting to observe how well both writers can beat the drum of rhetoric, but Hugo is more concrete in his imagery than Garibaldi. George Meredith[54] asked Swinburne to lend him a copy of Hugo's poem and also expressed an interest in Garibaldi's verses.

When the first anniversary of Mentana came round in the autumn of 1868, Swinburne recalled in a vague poem[55] the dead Garibaldians, whom he saw hopefully as the seed of liberty. And the poet called on the living Italians to march ever forward to their goal, a land entirely united and including Rome. Swinburne celebrated the second anniversary of Mentana in two sonnets, devoted mostly to Napoleon III. The Emperor of the French was named a "dog," born of "a whorish womb"; and our sonneteer frenziedly prayed:[56]

> Cancel his bond of life, dear God, I pray,
> That I may live to say, The dog is dead!

Significantly, Swinburne barely mentioned Garibaldi, since the latter had recently quarrelled with the poet's idol, Mazzini.[57] However, Mrs. Hamilton King's second poem on Orsini, "To the Memory of Felice Orsini,"[58] does not neglect Garibaldi and his deeds. On the third anniversary of Mentana, Swinburne responded to the stimulus of the theme with his usual reaction of rabid verse against Napoleon III. The Emperor's throne had been overturned by the Prussian armies; and Swinburne positively gloated, by means of two sonnets,[59] at the downfall of the "Accursed," whom he visualized as feeding the worms and then entering hell as naked bones! Garibaldi is scarcely even noticed by our poet, so preoccupied is he with a furious rage against the fallen ruler.

In 1870, Disraeli published his tremendously successful novel, *Lothair*, in part dealing with the Mentana affair of three years before. One character, Mrs. Putney Giles, is described as having "thrown herself in ecstatic idolatry at the feet of the hero of Caprera." The historical background is rapidly sketched in—the French troops have left Rome; and the Italian revolutionary party, though in need of money, is stirring. But Monsignor Berwick placidly observes: "The Aspromonte expedition drained their private resources; and as for further aid, that is out of the question; the galantuomo [Victor Emmanuel] is bankrupt." Disraeli indicates that Garibaldi has refused to stir against Rome without the sanction of the King of Italy, and Mirandola [Mazzini] says with savage exasperation: " 'He wants to get wounded in his other foot. Will he never weary of being betrayed?' " [Garibaldi was wounded at Aspromonte.] Eventually, Garibaldi is persuaded to lead the march on Rome, but is arrested at Rattazzi's orders. However, he escapes from Caprera, moves towards Rome, and is overwhelmed at Mentana, where Lothair, the hero of the novel, is wounded. The reader is told that Lothair, heir to immense wealth, has helped finance the expedition. Disraeli has an interesting picture of high-born English Roman Catholics assisting in the hospital department during the defence of Rome against the Garibaldians. Captain Bruges in *Lothair*—described as a man without imagination or sentiment, but nowise lacking in sympathy and honesty, and in conduct disinterested and in speech very simple—is really Disraeli's notion of Garibaldi's character. Yet Disraeli had refused to meet Garibaldi in 1864, for the politician Disraeli was a different person from the novelist of the identical name.

Still another English novel published during 1870 deals with Mentana—the Countess Marie Montemerli's story, *The Florentines*. Its real theme is the conflict between Church and State in Italy, and the expression of that hostility is the Mentana campaign. The authoress, who favours the side of the state, tells how the central government tried to prevent the departure of Italian volunteers for Garibaldi's raid on Rome. Then follows a picture of the great *condottiere*, escaped from Caprera where four vessels had watched the island, haranguing the people of Florence. With him are his stalwart sons, Menotti and Ricciotti, and General Nicotera. There are rumours that Victor Emmanuel is financing the *Putsch*. When disaster overtakes the Garibaldians, the women of Italy, accustomed to reverence the Pope, become more attached to the cause of the state. Countess Montemerli makes clear how ill-equipped and comparatively few in numbers were the forces that were slaughtered by the new French *chassepot* rifles.

Garibaldi himself, his resources very low, had turned novelist. In 1870 appeared an English translation of his atrocious story, *The Rule of the Monk*. These are his theses: that priests in Rome seduced girls and practiced infanticide of their offspring, that the clergy by improper influence induced the wealthy to cut off their heirs and leave their property to the Church, that the priesthood did not hesitate to use poison for its own ends, that cardinals had servants to act as procurers, that torture was employed in the jails of

Rome, that there was an unholy alliance between the papal government and the brigands, and that the priests with the assistance of the nuns and their female parishioners were responsible for the large number of illegitimate births in Rome. Quite rightly, the novel was placed on the *Index Librorum Prohibitorum.* In an *obiter dictum*, Garibaldi again acknowledged his debt to the English for having proclaimed non-intervention in 1860, when he wished to cross the Strait of Messina.

The Rule of the Monk is absolutely without organization, its plot is of no importance, its style is even vapid, its characterization is non-existent. What is significant is that it indicates the bitterness of the enmity between the clergy and many Italian nationalists. As a contemporary reviewer[60] pointed out, no such Rome as the city of its pages existed outside the bounds of a disordered imagination. It was scarcely credible that almost all priests were monsters of licentiousness and cruelty, daily perpetrating atrocious crimes for the gratification of carnal lusts; and it was equally unbelievable that anybody could write such a jejune mixture of feeble love story, patriotic reflections and rhapsodies, and arrant nonsense.

As a novelist, it may be added that Garibaldi revealed himself to be an egregious egotist. One would rather remember him in these lines from Eleanor Darby's contemporary poem, "The Giant of the Andes":

> that more wondrous warrior, whose bright fame,
> That shot its morning rays o'er Monte Video,
> Beams, like the sun, from the Old World to the New.[61]

The rest of Garibaldi's life mostly belongs not to the world of action but to that of recollection, for there are, with a single exception, no more deeds of guerrilla warfare, no more perilous escapes, no more futile marches on Rome. The war of 1870 between France and Prussia simultaneously marked the unification of two nations—Germany and Italy;

and the Pope became the prisoner of the Vatican, to remain in indignant seclusion until the days of Mussolini. When a new French republic was proclaimed, Garibaldi fought against the Germans and for France. He had risen above any petty spleen and had forgotten the Gallic bullets which had expelled him from Rome in 1849 and had slaughtered his men at Mentana. Besides, this was no longer the France of the Second Empire. The Garibaldi who opposed von Moltke's soldiers is the subject of Gerald Massey's poem, "France and Garibaldi," which pays a fine tribute to the old campaigner.[62] It was Massey's fancy that Garibaldi stood

> peerless, towering o'er the time,
> With *none beside him.*

In another poem, "Garibaldi's Prophecy,"[63] Massey and Garibaldi reached a conclusion on which both would have agreed, for the Italian is made to predict the fall of the Roman Catholic Church, and thus becomes the spokesman of Massey's Protestant zeal.

Garibaldi as a theme for writers in English never lost its popularity. A British journalist[64] remarked, twelve long years after Garibaldi handed over Naples to Victor Emmanuel in person, that true stories like this still had the power to stir him as if they were part of only yesterday. Indeed, a minor poet, Charles Edward Mudie[65] (of circulating library fame), did refer vividly in 1872 to Garibaldi and the Thousand in Naples.

During 1873, Mrs. Hamilton King was at work on the remarkable Mazzinian poems of the *Risorgimento* which compose *The Disciples.* Early in the year, she wrote to Garibaldi for more information on the martyr, Ugo Bassi, and received an amiable, but not helpful, answer.[66] The episode of Ugo Bassi deals superbly with the story of the monk's services as chaplain to Garibaldi's legion at the defence of Rome; the taking of the city by the French; Garibaldi's flight in order to maintain the struggle, though he promised his followers only the certainty of death—but not even a grave; and the pursuit of the fugitives into the wild Apennines by the armies of many nations. With those who fled, said Mrs. King, went hunger, thirst, and death as companions while the vultures wheeled overhead in dreadful flight. Her narrative describes the fortunes of the fugitives. Rejected by the tiny republic of San Marino on account of Austrian threats, nine hundred surrendered to General Gorzhowski and suffered treachery. The rest fled on with Garibaldi, who made for Venice, but his boats were forced to return to the shore. Then Mrs. King repeats the tragic story of Anita Garibaldi's death near Ravenna and Garibaldi's sad departure to America.

Linda White's insipid novel, *Courtship and a Campaign*, 1873, is concerned to some extent with Garibaldi's part in the war of 1866. The authoress, a Mazzinian in her convictions, was very bitter against the Italian government, accusing it of having given Garibaldi's irregulars the refuse of the royal arsenals—old muskets and shoddy clothing. Furthermore, she charged that the generals of the Italian Regular Army treated Garibaldi with discourtesy although he was the only leader to do well against the Austrians (that is, in his campaign in the Tyrol).

Alfred Austin's* long poem in ottava rima, *Rome or Death!*, 1873, has for its subject the Mentana campaign of 1867. The poet invokes the bellicose muse in this epic parody:

I

O Thou, the worthiest of the tuneful quire,
Muse of the pricking spear and tented field,
So long unwooed by any mortal lyre,
Wake! and to my presumptuous summons yield.
Oh! make my rhymes resound with that quick fire
Which, instant, flashes from thy stricken shield!
My verse like bounding war-horse scour the plain;
And blow thy shrilly trumpets through the strain!

* Poet Laureate after Tennyson.

II

For I who first with low satiric flight,
Skimming the mortal earth, attempted wing,
Then, bolder grown, of Love's short-lived delight,
And cruel Faith's resolves, did loftier sing,
Now must ascend to empyrean height,
Where lightnings speak and deafening thunders ring,
And to the heaven of heavens of song must soar:—
Muse! help me weak—who helped the strong of yore!

III

And thou too, lovely land! where long a guest
I happy dwelt, and whom I loved so well,
When only fair,—now not more fair than blest,—
Who breathed thy genius into Tasso's shell,
And with thy fire warmed Ariosto's breast,
Aid me! 'tis of thy hope deferred* I tell.
Smile upon me, that erst upon them smiled,—
Their all too feeble but still faithful child.

In lines of anaemic sentimentality, Austin describes Capri, where dwell Godfrid and Miriam, brother and sister. She, we are told, is loved by Gilbert. Truly, these are Italian names! When the summons from Garibaldi, "Rome or Death!" comes, our Capriotes row to the mainland while Miriam chants a bombastic prophecy that Italy shall be free:

Awake, ye deaf! Arise, ye thralls!
Country cries, Freedom calls;
And by all the Gods, maugre all the Gauls,
O Italy, my Italy,
Thou shalt be one and free!

Confident that France will not defend the Pontiff and that the Italian king will abet this expedition against Rome by not intervening, the Italians gather. Garibaldi, who had been arrested, soon comes to lead the Redshirts. With tinsel glitter, Austin describes the petty success of Monte Rotondo; and makes Garibaldi deliver speeches in which rant and

* Garibaldi's defeat at Mentana.

classical heroes and associations contend for control, and sense is never attained. Then comes the disaster of Mentana when the *chassepots* of the French crush the Garibaldians. Godfrid and Gilbert are both killed, but first our poet must unite in marriage the dying Gilbert to Miriam. In the midst of the strife, she chants a battle piece to encourage the men—who presumably take time out, from fighting for their lives, to listen. And when the rout is on, she sings a prophetic song of the defeat of the French, the rape of their women, the payment of tribute to the victors, and internal strife [the Commune, which Austin witnessed]. In spite of almost interminable epic similes, the poem ends with the return of the victorious French and the conquered Italians to Rome, where the Pope marches in thankful procession and with awesome ceremony.

Ernest Myers[67] retold in rhyming couplets of long, swinging lines the story of the patriot at *The Defence of Rome* in the days of Mazzini's republic when the revolutionary leaders,

> with the faithful who followed, their hearts unshaken of fear,
> Stood forth against odds overwhelming and fell in the front with a cheer,
> These, with the hundreds more who should live in their country's praise
> By the lips of men and of maidens, the camp's and the hearth-stone's lays.
> Nay, let not the glory sleep or the high deeds suffer wrong
> That should march to the music of time and the tide of sonorous song.
> By these from her ancient abasement was Italy lifted on high,
> From these come the breath of her life, for they proved that her sons could die.*

A year before Garibaldi's death in 1882, W. M. Rossetti wrote a sonnet on the hero's career through 1871 and sum-

* General Oudinot had said that the Italians could not fight.

marized with precision the chief events of his life: South America, the defence of Rome, the campaign in the Tyrol in 1859, the Thousand, Mentana, the fighting with France against Germany. "Garibaldi, 1871,"[68] is not a great sonnet but it quite deserves the praise which Dante Gabriel Rossetti[69] gave to it.

If a poet was already at hand to sum up a great life within the narrow compass of a sonnet, then a greater Maker was prepared to write its conclusion. On June 2, 1882, Garibaldi's death plunged Italy into grief and made a universal sensation, for he had been, to use W. M. Rossetti's words, "The Hero of the World." On the first anniversary of his passing, Gladstone[70] at Stafford House uttered a generous tribute to the simple nobility of his demeanour, manners, and actions. Above all, Gladstone praised the union in Garibaldi of the most profound and tender humanity with a fiery valour, praised it even more than "his splendid integrity, and his wide and universal sympathies," or his "seductive simplicity of manner," or "that inborn and native grace which seemed to attend all his actions."

Garibaldi makes an appearance in Tighe Hopkins's *For Freedom*; Henty's *Out with Garibaldi*; Herbert Hayens's juvenile yarn, *One of the Red Shirts*, 1901; Miss S. C. Grier's *One Crowded Hour*: all on the Thousand in Sicily and Calabria. Warwick Deeping's *The Lame Englishman* is concerned with Garibaldi's defence of the Roman Republic in 1849. The foregoing novels are on the whole adequate but not much more than that.

When the one hundredth anniversary of Garibaldi's birth was at hand, George Meredith wrote for the London *Times* that excellent memorial poem, "The Centenary of Garibaldi."[71] He had been one of three great men, said Meredith, who had made Italy live anew. It was not for him to possess the fervour of Mazzini or the calculating brain of Cavour. Rather was his "a single blade against a circling horde." Though in character he was as simple as a child, yet in battle he was "leopard dashed with fox." Therefore, Meredith concluded,

> Proudly Italia names his place of birth!
> The bosom of Humanity his grave.

One must also rank very high, not merely as history but also as *belles lettres*, those three studies which George Macaulay Trevelyan has devoted, with manifest respect, to the greatest of all the Italian *condottieri*. In addition, there is Drinkwater's disappointing play on Garibaldi—disappointing because episodic, wrong in details (for history is unsuccessfully distorted so as to be more dramatic), occasionally silly, wooden in characterization, and lacking in vitality. Indeed, the *dramatis personae* seem to act as if they knew what posterity says and expects of them. Yet it is refreshing to chance upon an occasional speech or upon an epigrammatic remark worthy of praise: *e.g.*, "The trouble with Mazzini [1859] is that he's always known the right thing to do, and never the right time to do it." Mr. Drinkwater's thesis was that Garibaldi always wanted to see the unity of Italy achieved and did not care how it was done, whether by republicans or by monarchists. Such an idea is too simple, for the truth is that Garibaldi accepted the notion of a *monarchical* unitarian Italy with considerable reluctance and sometimes with peevish grace.

Of Joseph Garibaldi, not much more is to be said here save that he leaves with the serious reader an impression of astonishing modernity. After all, he was the first of the "shirts," who plague us during these difficult times; he revived the Italian habit of marching on Rome; and he did believe in dictatorships—though solely of a temporary kind. Nevertheless, in memory of his aid to the third French Republic, there was a "Garibaldi" brigade fighting with the international anti-Fascistic forces against the Spanish rebels (1937–38). The name assumed by the foregoing military contingent, composed of Italians in exile, is appropriate, for the man thus commemorated had, about 1871, welcomed the First International as the "rising sun of the future."[72]

Conclusion

PRIMARILY, *Italian Nationalism and English Letters* has been a literary study, but in part it has described the heritage of good will which the fourth Rome of Mussolini acquired through Anglo-Saxon admiration for Mazzini's lifelong prophecy of the refulgent third Rome of the People, Garibaldi's magnificent career, and Cavour's constitutional monarchy. From its pages can be seen how powerful an influence nationalism has been. Rightly, the most sagacious minds of the last century were reluctant to sneer at the forces centripetally acting on European peoples of similar speech and customs and dwelling in contiguous territories. If nineteenth-century history was turned into a political seismogram, it is nevertheless true that a seismogram is a chart of periods of equilibrium as well as of shock. Unfortunately, the twentieth century witnesses the spectacle of nationality elevated to godhead. With the utmost detachment, scientists like Julian Huxley to-day repeat, if only by way of comment on this new apotheosis of blood and soil, a mocking but sorrowful epigram: a nation is a society joined by a common error as to its origin and by a common aversion to its neighbours.

Whatever may be the implications of contemporary nationalism, the unification of Italy was, as Byron said, the very poetry of politics. To recall that this theme not only inspired some of the finest work of Shelley, Landor, Clough, Elizabeth and Robert Browning, Meredith, and Swinburne, but also appeared in the writings of many others, is to realize its importance in the history of English literature.

Notes

Introduction

1. George Macaulay Trevelyan, *Garibaldi and the Thousand*, London, 1909, pp. 22–24.
2. Walter Savage Landor, "Mr. More O'Ferrall," letter to *The Examiner*, September 22, 1849, p. 597.
3. *The Reasoner*, ed. George Jacob Holyoake, London, 1846–61, VII, 347.
4. *British Parliamentary Papers* (Blue Books), 1852, LIV, 76.
5. *Ibid.*, 1852, LIV, 88.
6. *Ibid.*, 1852, LIV, 96.
7. George Jacob Holyoake, *Sixty Years of an Agitator's Life*, 4th edition, London, 1900, II, 40–41.

CHAPTER I

Doctrine and Personality

1. Richard Garnett, *A History of Italian Literature*, New York and London, 1928, p. 374.
2. Ernesto Masi, *Il Risorgimento italiano*, Florence, 1917, I, 535.
3. *Ibid.*, I, 532.
4. G. L. Bickersteth, "*Giuseppe Mazzini*," *Carducci: A Selection of his Poems, with Verse Translations, Notes, and Three Introductory Essays*, London, 1913, pp. 112–13.
5. William Roscoe Thayer, *The Life and Times of Cavour*, Boston and New York, 1911, I, 588.
6. Arthur James Beresford Whyte, *The Early Life and Letters of Cavour*, 1810–1848, London, 1925, p. xvi.
7. Cecil Scott Forester, *Victor Emmanuel II and the Union of Italy*, London, 1927, p. 123.
8. Gaetano Salvemini, *Mazzini*, Florence, 1925, pp. 1–3 and 7.
9. Gaetano Salvemini, "Mazzini," *Encyclopaedia of the Social Sciences*, ed. Edwin R. A. Seligman and Alvin Johnson, New York, 1933, X, 240–41.
10. René Galland, *George Meredith, les cinquante premières années* (1828–1878), Paris, 1923, pp. 255–56.
11. Salvemini, *Mazzini*, p. 35.
12. *Ibid.*, p. 43.
13. *Ibid.*, p. 53.
14. Masi, *op. cit.*, I, 533.

15. M. Mansfield, "England and Italy," *The Dublin Review*, CXCVIII, 22 (January 1936).
16. Joseph Mazzini, *Essays*, tr. Thomas Okey, ed. Bolton King, London, 1894, pp. x–xi.
17. George Macaulay Trevelyan, *Garibaldi and the Thousand*, London, pp. 22–24.
18. William Watkin Davies, *Gladstone and the Unification of Italy*, Oxford, 1918, p. 9.
19. *Mazzini's Letters*, tr. Alice de Rosen Jervis, ed. Bolton King, London, 1930, p. x.
20. Niccolò Machiavelli, *The Prince*, tr. Luigi Ricci, revised by E. R. P. Vincent, London, 1935, p. 75.
21. John Morley, *Recollections*, London, 1917, I, 246.
22. *Ibid.*, I, 75–76.
23. *Ibid.*, I, 76–77.
24. *Ibid.*, I, 78–79.
25. William Roscoe Thayer, *Italica: Studies in Italian Life and Letters*, Boston, 1908, pp. 67–68.
26. *Ibid.*, p. 70.
27. Frederic Harrison, *Autobiographic Memoirs*, London, 1911, I, 97–99.
28. Hallam (2nd Baron) Tennyson, *Alfred Lord Tennyson: a Memoir*, London, 1897, II, 2–3.
29. David Masson, *Memories of London in the 'Forties*, Edinburgh and London, 1908, pp. 194–96.
30. *Ibid.*, p. 209.
31. Moncure Daniel Conway, *Autobiography: Memories and Experiences*, Boston and New York, 1904, II, 58.
32. George Jacob Holyoake, *Bygones Worth Remembering*, London, 1905, I, 204.
33. George Macaulay Trevelyan, *English Songs of Italian Freedom*, London, 1911, p. xxi.
34. *Ibid.*, pp. xix–xx.

CHAPTER II

Mazzini's Early Career, 1805–36

1. Emilie Ashurst Venturi, *Joseph Mazzini: a Memoir*, London, 1875, p. 7.
2. *Edizione nazionale degli scritti di Giuseppe Mazzini*, Imola, 1906–37, XIV, 384.
3. Venturi, *op. cit.*, pp. 7–8.
4. *Ibid.*, p. 14.
5. Joseph Mazzini, *Life and Writings*, London, 1864–70, I, 2.
6. *Ibid.*, I, 4.
7. Jessie White Mario, *The Birth of Modern Italy*, ed. the Duke Litta-Visconti-Arese, London, 1909, p. 4.

8. Stringfellow Barr, *Mazzini: Portrait of an Exile*, New York, 1935, p. 295.
9. Janet Penrose Trevelyan, *A Short History of the Italian People*, 3rd edition, London, 1929, p. 477.
10. Gwilym Oswald Griffith, *Mazzini: Prophet of Modern Europe*, London, 1932, p. 57.
11. Bolton King, *Mazzini*, London, 1902, p. 18.
12. *Ibid.*, p. 21.
13. Margaret Josephine Shaen, *William Shaen: a Brief Sketch*, London, 1912, p. 19.
14. White Mario, *op. cit.*, p. 10.
15. Thomas Frost, *The Secret Societies of the European Revolution*, 1776–1876, London, 1876, II, 141.
16. *Ibid.*, I, 213.
17. *Ibid.*, I, 219.
18. *Ibid.*, I, 226.
19. *Ibid.*, I, 229.
20. *Ibid.*, I, 233.
21. *Ibid.*, I, 249.
22. *Ibid.*, I, 251.
23. *Ibid.*, II, 146–47.
24. *Ibid.*, II, 147–49.
25. *Ibid.*, II, 151.
26. *Ibid.*, II, 154.
27. *Mazzini's Letters*, tr. Alice de Rosen Jervis, ed. Bolton King, London, 1930, p. 5.
28. Samuel C. Chew, *Swinburne*, Boston, 1929, pp. 106–07.
29. Mazzini, *Life and Writings*, I, 225–26.
30. *Mazzini's Letters to an English Family, 1844–72*, ed. E. F. Richards, London, 1920–22, III, 214–15.
31. *Edizione nazionale degli scritti di Giuseppe Mazzini*, I, 354–61.
32. Edward George Earle Lytton Bulwer-Lytton, *The Last Days of Pompeii*, The New Household Edition, Boston, 1891, Vol. V, Book II, Chapter IV, p. 112. First published in 1834.
33. Mazzini, *Life and Writings*, I, 227.
34. William James Linton, *European Republicans; Recollections of Mazzini and His Friends*, London, 1893, p. 30.
35. White Mario, *op. cit.*, p. 14.
36. *Ibid.*, p. 16.
37. *Edizione nazionale degli scritti di Giuseppe Mazzini*, I, 377–81.
38. *Memoirs of Prince Metternich*, tr. Mrs. Alexander Napier, London, 1880–82, V, 411–12.
39. Arthur James Beresford Whyte, *The Early Life and Letters of Cavour, 1810–1848*, London, 1925, p. 260.
40. Joseph Mazzini, *Essays*, tr. Thomas Okey, ed. Bolton King, London, 1894, pp. 34–35.

CHAPTER III

First Years in London

1. *Edizione nazionale degli scritti di Giuseppe Mazzini*, Imola, 1906–37, XIV, 23.
2. *Ibid.*, XVIII, 251–52.
3. David Alec Wilson, *Carlyle to "The French Revolution" (1826–1837)*, London, 1924, p. 400.
4. Mrs. Eliza Fletcher, *Autobiography*, Edinburgh, 1875, pp. 229–33.
5. Stringfellow Barr, *Mazzini: Portrait of an Exile*, New York, 1935, p. 122.
6. Gwilym Oswald Griffith, *Mazzini: Prophet of Modern Europe*, London, 1932, p. 147.
7. *Edizione nazionale degli scritti di Giuseppe Mazzini*, XIV, 261.
8. Griffith, *op. cit.*, pp. 357–58.
9. *Mazzini's Letters to an English Family, 1844–72*, ed. E. F. Richards, London, 1920–22, I, 266.
10. Barr, *op. cit.*, p. 123.
11. Ross Douglas Waller, *The Rossetti Family, 1824–1854*, Manchester, 1932, p. 59.
12. Count Carlo Pepoli, *On the Language and Literature of Italy. An Inaugural Lecture, delivered in University College, London, on 6th November, 1838*, London, 1838, pp. 25–26.
13. Mrs. Fletcher, *op. cit.*, p. 244.
14. *Edizione nazionale degli scritti di Giuseppe Mazzini*, XVIII, 251–52.
15. *Ibid.*, XVIII, 291 and 295.
16. *Ibid.*, XVIII, 298–99.
17. *Ibid.*, XVIII, 335.
18. *a.* Griffith, *op. cit.*, p. 135.
    b. Edizione nazionale degli scritti di Giuseppe Mazzini, XXXII, 7.
19. David Alec Wilson, *Carlyle on Cromwell and Others (1837–48)*, London, 1925, pp. 58–59.
20. Joseph Mazzini, *Life and Writings*, London, 1864–70, VI.
21. *Edizione nazionale degli scritti di Giuseppe Mazzini*, XVIII, 366.
22. *Ibid.*, XIX, 32 and 57.
23. *Ibid.*, XIX, 104.
24. *Ibid.*, XIX, 239–41.
25. Wilson, *Carlyle on Cromwell . . .*, p. 127.
26. Griffith, *op. cit.*, p. 149.
27. Jessie White Mario, *The Birth of Modern Italy*, ed. the Duke Litta-Visconti-Arese, London, 1909, p. 34.
28. *Ibid.*, p. 35.
29. *Ibid.*, p. 41.
30. *Ibid.*, pp. 36–37.
31. *Ibid.*, pp. 50–51.

32. *Mazzini's Letters*, tr. Alice de Rosen Jervis, ed. Bolton King, London, 1930, p. 77.
33. William Michael Rossetti, *Gabriele Rossetti. A Versified Autobiography*, London, 1901, p. 160.
34. Barr, *op. cit.*, p. 161.
35. White Mario, *op. cit.*, pp. 52–53.
36. *Edizione nazionale degli scritti di Giuseppe Mazzini*, XXIII, 63 and 79–80.
37. *Ibid.*, XXIII, 127.
38. Jane Welsh Carlyle, *Letters to her Family, 1839–1863*, ed. Leonard Huxley, London, 1924, p. 30.
39. *Ibid.*, p. 34.
40. *Ibid.*, pp. 39–40.
41. *Ibid.*, p. 48.
42. *Ibid.*, pp. 51–52.
43. *New Letters of Thomas Carlyle*, ed. Alexander Carlyle, London and New York, 1904, I, 264.
44. *Edizione nazionale degli scritti di Giuseppe Mazzini*, XXIV, 154–55.
45. *Ibid.*, XXIV, 4.
46. White Mario, *op. cit.*, pp. 63–64.
47. Mazzini, *Life and Writings*, IV.
48. Jane Welsh Carlyle, *op. cit.*, p. 129.
49. *Ibid.*, pp. 138–41.
50. *Letters and Memorials of Jane Welsh Carlyle*, ed. James Anthony Froude, London, 1883, I, 248.
51. *Ibid.*, I, 251.
52. *Edizione nazionale degli scritti di Giuseppe Mazzini*, XXVI, 121–22.

CHAPTER IV

Lord Aberdeen Spies on Mazzini's Letters

1. Gwilym Oswald Griffith, *Mazzini: Prophet of Modern Europe*, London, 1932, pp. 163–64.
2. Carrington C. Tutwiler, jun., *Reflections of the Early Risorgimento in Contemporary Victorian Literature*, unpublished Princeton University dissertation, 1934, II, 282.
3. Griffith, *op. cit.*, p. 165.
4. Frederick W. Hoeing, "Letters of Mazzini to W. J. Linton," *The Journal of Modern History*, V, 56 (March 1933).
5. Jessie White Mario, *The Birth of Modern Italy*, ed. the Duke Litta-Visconti-Arese, London, 1909, pp. 85–87.
6. *Mazzini's Letters to an English Family, 1844–72*, ed. E. F. Richards, London, 1920–22, I, 20–23.
7. Francis W. Hirst, *Early Life and Letters of John Morley*, London, 1927, II, 140–41.

8. Mrs. Edyth Hinkley, *Mazzini, The story of a great Italian*, London, 1924, p. 77.
9. *New Letters and Memorials of Jane Welsh Carlyle*, ed. Alexander Carlyle, with an introduction by Sir James Crichton-Browne, London and New York, 1903, I, 151.
10. James Anthony Froude, *Thomas Carlyle: a History of his Life in London, 1834–81*, London, 1884, I, 343–44.
11. David Alec Wilson, *Carlyle on Cromwell and Others (1837–48)*, London, 1925, p. 265.
12. Bolton King, *A History of Italian Unity. Being a Political History of Italy from 1814 to 1871*, London, 1899, II, 388.
13. William Nassau Molesworth, *The History of England from the Year 1830–1874*, London 1874, II, 133–35.
14. [Antonio Panizzi], "Post-Office Espionage," *The North British Review*, November 1844, pp. 265–69.
15. *Ibid.*, pp. 271–72.
16. *Ibid.*, pp. 258–59.
17. White Mario, *op. cit.*, p. 81.
18. Robert Esmonde Sencourt, *The Life of George Meredith*, London, 1929, p. 139.
19. T. Wemyss Reid, *The Life, Letters, and Friendships of Richard Monckton Milnes, First Lord Houghton*, London, 1890, I, 330.
20. *Dickens to his Oldest Friend. The Letters of a Lifetime from Charles Dickens to Thomas Beard*, ed. Walter Dexter, London and New York, 1932, p. 88.
21. John Forster, *The Life of Charles Dickens*, Memorial edition, London, 1911, I, 345–46.
22. [Giovanni Domenico Ruffini], *Doctor Antonio*, Edinburgh, 1855, p. 316.
23. William Flavelle Monypenny and George Earle Buckle, *The Life of Benjamin Disraeli, Earl of Beaconsfield*, London, 1910–20, II, 311–13.
24. Joseph Mazzini, *Life and Writings*, London, 1864–70, I, 232.
25. George Macaulay Trevelyan, *English Songs of Italian Freedom*, London, 1911, p. 50.
26. Mrs. Sutherland Orr, *A Handbook to the Works of Robert Browning*, London, 1902, p. 306.
27. Griffith, *op. cit.*, p. 167.
28. *Mazzini's Letters*, tr. Alice de Rosen Jervis, ed. Bolton King, London, 1930, p. 98.
29. White Mario, *op. cit.*, pp. 97–101.
30. J. L. and Barbara Hammond, *James Stansfield: a Victorian Champion of Sex Equality*, London, 1932, p. 18.
31. *Mazzini's Letters to an English Family, 1844–72*, I, 37.
32. *Ibid.*, I, 45.
33. Jane Welsh Carlyle, *Letters to her Family, 1839–1863*, ed. Leonard Huxley, London, 1924, pp. 261 and 270.
34. Froude, *op. cit.*, I, 381–82.

35. Froude, *op. cit.*, I, 384–85.
36. *Edizione nazionale degli scritti di Giuseppe Mazzini*, Imola, 1906–37, XXX, 373.
37. Froude, *op. cit.*, I, 402.
38. Mrs. Edyth Hinkley, *op. cit.*, p. 89.
39. *The Life of Thomas Cooper: Written by Himself*, London, 1872, p. 299.
40. *Edizione nazionale degli scritti di Giuseppe Mazzini*, XXXIII, 75–76.
41. White Mario, *op. cit.*, pp. 107–08.
42. John Frederick Stanford, *The Patriots of Italy: An Appeal in their Behalf*, London, August 1847, pp. 8–9.
43. Edmund Downey, *Charles Lever: His Life in His Letters*, London, 1906, I, 265–66.
44. *Edizione nazionale degli scritti di Giuseppe Mazzini*, XXXII, 72–73.
45. *Ibid.*, XXXII, 263.

CHAPTER V

The Sunset of the 'Forty-eight

1. Mrs. Eliza Fletcher, *Autobiography*, Edinburgh, 1875, p. 267.
2. Thomas Adolphus Trollope, *Tuscany in 1849 and 1859*, London, 1859, p. 128.
3. Antonio Carlo Napoleone Gallenga (also known as Luigi Mariotti), *Present State and Prospects of Italy*, London, 1848, pp. 18–20.
4. Charles MacFarlane, *A Glance at Revolutionized Italy . . . in the Summer of 1848*, London, 1849, I, vii.
5. *Ibid.*, II, 8.
6. *Ibid.*, II, 66–67.
7. Emilio Dandolo, *The Italian Volunteers and Lombard Rifle Brigade . . .*, London, 1851, p. 257.
8. *Autobiography of G. Garibaldi*, authorized translation by A. Werner, with a supplement by Jessie White Mario, London, 1889, II, 9 and 12.
9. Mrs. Fletcher, *op. cit.*, pp. 273–74.
10. *Punch*, XVII, 35 (July to December 1849).
11. Gwilym Oswald Griffith, *Mazzini: Prophet of Modern Europe*, London, 1932, p. 225.
12. Elizabeth Barrett Browning, *Letters to her Sister, 1846–1859*, ed. Leonard Huxley, London, 1929, pp. 100–01.
13. *Ibid.*, pp. 105–06.
14. Jane Welsh Carlyle, *Letters to her Family, 1839–1863*, ed. Leonard Huxley, London, 1924, p. 325.
15. *Ibid.*, p. 334.
16. James Anthony Froude, *Thomas Carlyle: a History of His Life in London, 1834–81*, London, 1884, I, 454.
17. Arthur Hugh Clough, *Letters and Remains*, London, 1865, p. 121.

18. Griffith, *op. cit.*, p. 214.
19. Clough, *op. cit.*, pp. 123–25.
20. *Ibid.*, p. 128.
21. *Ibid.*, pp. 144–45.
22. Arthur Hugh Clough, *Poems*, 6th edition, ed. Charles Whibley, London, 1913, p. 288.
23. Margaret Josephine Shaen, *Memorials of Two Sisters, Susanna and Catherine Winkworth*, London, 1908, p. 38.
24. George Macaulay Trevelyan, *Garibaldi's Defence of the Roman Republic*, London, 1907, pp. 109–10.
25. Wilfrid Ward, *The Life of John Henry Cardinal Newman*, New York and London, 1912, I, 195–96.
26. [Hamilton Geale], *Ernesto di Ripalto: a Tale of the Italian Revolution*, London, 1849, I, 239.
27. *Memoirs of Margaret Fuller Ossoli*, London, 1852, III, 217.
28. *Mazzini's Letters*, tr. Alice de Rosen Jervis, ed. Bolton King, London, 1930, p. 139.
29. *Mazzini's Letters to an English Family, 1844–72*, ed. E. F. Richards, London, 1920–22, I, 195.
30. *Ibid.*, I, 126–27.
31. Sidney Colvin, *Landor*, London, 1881, p. 196.
32. William James Linton, *Claribel and Other Poems*, London, 1865, pp. 254–55.
33. Henry Lushington, *The Italian War, 1848–9, and the Last Italian Poet*, London, 1859, p. 188.
34. Victor Alexander George Robert Lytton, Second Earl of Lytton, *The Life of Edward Bulwer, First Lord Lytton*, London, 1913, II, 127.
35. *Mazzini's Letters to an English Family, 1844–72*, I, 132.
36. Alexander Herzen, *My Past and Thoughts. The Memoirs of Alexander Herzen . . .*, tr. Constance Garnett, London, 1924–27, III, 68.
37. Jessie White Mario, *The Birth of Modern Italy*, ed. the Duke Litta-Visconti-Arese, London, 1909, pp. 219–20.
38. David Alec Wilson, *Carlyle at His Zenith (1848–53)*, London, 1927, p. 208.
39. *Edizione nazionale degli scritti di Giuseppe Mazzini*, Imola, 1906–37, XLII, 314.
40. Jane Welsh Carlyle, *op. cit.*, pp. 344–45.
41. *Letters of Mrs. Gaskell and Charles Eliot Norton, 1855–1865*, ed. Jane Whitehill, London, 1932, p. ix.
42. Georges Lafourcade, *La Jeunesse de Swinburne (1837–1867)*, Paris, 1928, I, 121.
43. M. J. Shaen, *op. cit.*, pp. 59–60.
44. Ross Douglas Waller, *The Rossetti Family, 1824–1854*, Manchester, 1932, p. 70.
45. *Military Events in Italy, 1848–1849*, tr. from the German by the Earl of Ellesmere, London, 1851, p. 313.
46. Gallenga, *Italy in 1848*, London, 1851, p. 389.

47. Nassau William Senior, *Journals Kept in France and Italy from 1848 to 1852*, London, 1871, II, 233.
48. Luigi Carlo Farini, *The Roman State, from 1815 to 1850*. Of the four volumes, the first three were translated by William Ewart Gladstone, and the last by a lady under his direction. London, 1851–54, IV, 115.
49. Gustav Mayer, *Friedrich Engels: A Biography*, London, 1936, p. 128.
50. *The Quarterly Review*, CCLXVIII, 176 (January 1937).
51. *Edizione nazionale degli scritti di Giuseppe Mazzini*, XLIV, 41.
52. *Ibid.*, XLVII, 83–84.

CHAPTER VI

The Ebbing of the Mazzinian Tide

1. *The Charge of Terrorism in Rome, during the Government of the Republic, Refuted by Facts and Documents. The Documents Furnished by Mr. Mazzini*, Tract 2 of The Society of the Friends of Italy, London, 1851, pp. 27–28.
2. *Letters of Thomas Carlyle to John Stuart Mill, John Sterling, and Robert Browning*, ed. Alexander Carlyle, London, 1923, p. 287.
3. Bolton King, *Mazzini*, London, 1902, pp. 85–87.
4. *The Correspondence of Thomas Carlyle and Ralph Waldo Emerson, 1834–1872*, ed. Charles Eliot Norton, London, 1883, II, 199.
5. Elizabeth Barrett Browning, *Poetical Works*, ed. Frederic G. Kenyon, London, 1897, pp. 346–48.
6. Howard R. Marraro, *American Opinion on the Unification of Italy, 1846–1861*, New York, 1932, p. 207.
7. *Edizione nazionale degli scritti di Giuseppe Mazzini*, Imola, 1906–37, XLV, 119.
8. *New Letters and Memorials of Jane Welsh Carlyle*, ed. Alexander Carlyle, with an introduction by Sir James Crichton-Browne, London and New York, 1903, II, 39.
9. Elizabeth Barrett Browning, *Letters*, ed. Frederic G. Kenyon, London, 1897, II, 78.
10. *Letters and Memorials of Jane Welsh Carlyle*, ed. James Anthony Froude, London, 1883, II, 178.
11. Margaret Josephine Shaen, *Memorials of Two Sisters, Susanna and Catherine Winkworth*, London, 1908, p. 87.
12. *Ibid.*, pp. 91–92.
13. *Letter from Signor Mazzini to Mr. G. J. Holyoake*, London, June 1852.
14. George Jacob Holyoake, *Sixty Years of an Agitator's Life*, 4th edition, London, 1900, I, 266.
15. Holyoake, *Bygones Worth Remembering*, London, 1905, I, 216.
16. *Ibid.*, I, 209.
17. *Ibid.*, I, 203.

18. Anna Theresa Kitchel, *George Lewes and George Eliot, A Review of Records*, New York, 1933, pp. 64–70.
19. John Walter Cross, *George Eliot's Life as Related in Her Letters and Journals*, London, 1885, I, 269.
20. *Ibid.*, I, 275.
21. Frederick W. Hoeing, "Letters of Mazzini to W. J. Linton," *The Journal of Modern History*, V, 60 (March 1933).
22. Miles Thomas Stapleton, Eighth Baron Beaumont, *France and Austria in Central Italy*, London, 1852, p. 36.
23. Dr. Julius Casto, *Italy and the Italian Question*, London, 1852.
24. F. W. Newman, *The Place and Duty of England in Europe*, Tract 5 of The Society of the Friends of Italy, London, 1852, p. 20.
25. Count Carl Ludwig von Ficquelmont, *Lord Palmerston, L'Angleterre et le Continent*, Paris, 1852, I, 112.
26. August Ludwig von Rochau, *Wanderings through the Cities of Italy in 1850 and 1851*, tr. Mrs. Percy Sinnett, London, 1853, I, 219.
27. Pietro Orsi, *Cavour and the Making of Modern Italy, 1810–1861*, London and New York, 1926, pp. 188–90.
28. Emily Jolly, *The Life and Letters of Sydney Dobell*, London, 1878, I, 280–85.
29. *The Diaries of John Bright*, ed. R. A. J. Walling, London, 1930, p. 136.
30. Gwilym Oswald Griffith, *Mazzini: Prophet of Modern Europe*, London, 1932, p. 267.
31. *New Letters of Thomas Carlyle*, ed. Alexander Carlyle, London and New York, 1904, II, 144.
32. *Ibid.*, II, 150.
33. *Edizione nazionale degli scritti di Giuseppe Mazzini*, XLIX, 349.
34. William Roscoe Thayer, *The Life and Times of Cavour*, Boston and New York, 1911, I, 274.
35. James Howard Harris, Third Earl of Malmesbury, *Memoirs of an Ex-Minister: An Autobiography*, London, 1884, I, 385.
36. Felice Orsini, *Memoirs and Adventures*, tr. [H.] George Carbonel, Edinburgh, 1857, p. 111.
37. Elizabeth Barrett Browning, *Letters*, II, 109.
38. *New Letters and Memorials of Jane Welsh Carlyle*, II, 68–69.
39. *Edizione nazionale degli scritti di Giuseppe Mazzini*, XLVII, 369–73.
40. Griffith, *op. cit.*, p. 252.
41. Walter Savage Landor, *Complete Works*, ed. T. Earle Welby and Stephen Wheeler, London, 1927–36, III, 293–95.
42. Walter Savage Landor, *Works*, ed. C. G. Crump, London, 1891–93, VIII, 227.
43. [Giovanni Domenico Ruffini], *Lorenzo Benoni*, Edinburgh, 1853, pp. 189–90.
44. *Ibid.*, p. 192.
45. *a.* Gaby Vinant, *Un Esprit Cosmopolite au XIXe Siècle, Malwida de Meysenbug (1816–1903): Sa Vie et Ses Amis*, Paris, 1932, p. 137.
    b. Sir Charles Gavan Duffy, *Conversations with Carlyle*, New York, 1892, pp. 109–10.

46. Gerald Massey, *My Lyrical Life: Poems Old and New*, 2nd series, London, 1889, pp. 329–30.
47. *Edizione nazionale degli scritti di Giuseppe Mazzini*, LII, 8–9.
48. *Ibid.*, LIII, 20.
49. Harriet Martineau, *Autobiography with Memorials*, 3rd edition, London, 1877, I, 378–80.
50. Richard Heber Wrightson, *A History of Modern Italy, from the First French Revolution to the Year 1850*, London, 1855, pp. v, xii–xiii, 21, and 315.
51. William Flavelle Monypenny and George Earle Buckle, *The Life of Benjamin Disraeli, Earl of Beaconsfield*, London, 1910–20, IV, 247.
52. *Edizione nazionale degli scritti di Giuseppe Mazzini*, LIV, 69 and 143.
53. Gaby Vinant, *op. cit.*, p. 141.
54. *Edizione nazionale degli scritti di Giuseppe Mazzini*, LIV, 173–76.
55. *Ibid.*, LIV, 216.
56. Bolton King, *op. cit.*, p. 165.
57. Bayle St. John, *The Subalpine Kingdom; or, Experiences and Studies in Savoy, Piedmont, and Genoa*, London, 1856, II, 68.
58. *Ibid.*, II, 222.
59. *Cavour e l'Inghilterra*, Bologna, 1933, II, 34, letter 589.
60. *Sketches on Italy: Its Last Revolution, Its Actual Condition, Its Tendencies and Hopes*, London, 1856, p. 40.
61. John Richard Digby Beste, *Modern Society in Rome. A Novel*, London. 1856, I, 6.
62. *Ibid.*, I, 138.
63. Orsini, *The Austrian Dungeons in Italy*, tr. Jessie Meriton White, London, July, 1856, p. 93.
64. Jessie White Mario, *The Birth of Modern Italy*, ed. the Duke Litta-Visconti-Arese, London, 1909, p. 260.
65. King, *op. cit.*, p. 153.
66. Orsini, *Memoirs and Adventures*, p. 77.
67. *Edizione nazionale degli scritti di Giuseppe Mazzini*, LVIII, 31–33.
68. *Ibid.*, LVIII, 43–44.
69. Griffith, *op. cit.*, pp. 274–76.
70. William Michael Rossetti, *Some Reminiscences*, London, 1906, I, 244.
71. Stringfellow Barr, *Mazzini: Portrait of an Exile*, New York, 1935, p. 273.
72. Marchesa Bice Pareto Magliano, "Some First-Hand Recollections of Mazzini," *The Contemporary Review*, November 1917, pp. 568–70.
73. Mrs. Edyth Hinkley, *Mazzini. The Story of a Great Italian*, London, 1924, p. 177.
74. Arthur James Beresford Whyte, *The Political Life and Letters of Cavour, 1848–1861*, London, 1930, pp. 383–84.
75. Algernon Charles Swinburne, *Ode to Mazzini*, preface by Edmund Gosse, twenty copies printed for T. Watts-Dunton, London, 1909, pp. 5–8.

76. Georges Lafourcade, *La Jeunesse de Swinburne (1837–1867)*, Paris, 1928, I, 121–22.
77. *Ibid.*, II, 19.
78. Sir Edmund Gosse, *The Life of Algernon Charles Swinburne, The Complete Works of Algernon Charles Swinburne*, the Bonchurch edition, ed. Sir Edmund Gosse and Thomas James Wise, London, 1925–27, XIX, 40.
79. Lafourcade, *op. cit.*, II, 22–28.
80. Griffith, *op. cit.*, p. 283.
81. Whyte, *op. cit.*, pp. 383–84.
82. Francesco Crispi, *Memoirs*, tr. Mary Prichard-Agnetti, London, 1912, I, 95–96.
83. *Autobiography of G. Garibaldi*, authorized translation by A. Werner, with a supplement by Jessie White Mario, London, 1889, III, 147.
84. *Edizione nazionale degli scritti di Giuseppe Mazzini*, LXI, 3–4
85. *Ibid.*, LXI, 332–33.
86. *Ibid.*, LXI, 188–89.
87. Amelia L. V. Gretton, *The Vicissitudes of Italy, Since the Congress of Vienna*, London, 1859, p. 11.
88. [Anne Manning], *The Story of Italy*, London, 1859, p. 308.
89. Elizabeth Barrett Browning, *Letters to Her Sister, 1846–1859*, ed. Leonard Huxley, London, 1929, pp. 314–16.
90. Elizabeth Barrett Browning, *Letters*, II, 329.
91. Gosse, *op. cit.*, XIX, 56.
92. [Henry Fothergill Chorley], "Paul Bell," *Roccabella: a Tale of a Woman's Life*, London, [1859], I, 296.
93. *Ibid.*, II, 83–84.
94. Margaret Josephine Shaen, *op. cit.*, p. 195.
95. *Memoir of Joseph Mazzini*, reprinted from *The London Review*, November 17, 1860, London, 1861, pp. 5–6.

CHAPTER VII

Mazzini's Last Years

1. Rev. George Tooker Hoare, *Notes on North Italy, and the Seat of War in 1859*, London, 1860, p. 61.
2. *The Letters of Charles Dickens*, ed. Georgina Hogarth and Mamie Dickens, London, 1880[79]–1882[81], III, 191–92.
3. Kate Crichton, *Before the Dawn. A Tale of Italy*, London, 1860, II, 142.
4. Harriet Martineau, "Political Agitators," *Once a Week*, V, 698 (December 14, 1861).
5. Elizabeth Barrett Browning, *Letters*, ed. Frederic G. Kenyon, London, 1897, II, 442.
6. Gwilym Oswald Griffith, *Mazzini: Prophet of Modern Europe*, London, 1932, p. 318.

7. Sir Edward Dicey, *Cavour. A Memoir*, Cambridge, England, 1861, p. 240.
8. Fredrika Bremer, *Two Years in Switzerland and Italy*, tr. Mary Howitt, London, 1861, I, 216.
9. *The Reasoner*, XXVI, 99.
10. William B. Brooke, *Out with Garibaldi; or, From Melazzo to Capua*, London, 1861, p. 198.
11. [Frederic Harrison], "Cavour and Garibaldi," *The Westminster Review*, new series, XIX, 177 (January 1861).
12. Mrs. Harriet Eleanor Baillie Hamilton King, *Letters and Recollections of Mazzini*, ed. G. M. Trevelyan, London, 1912, pp. 10–17.
13. Count Charles Arrivabene, *Italy under Victor Emmanuel*, London, 1862, II, 211.
14. David Masson, "The Poems of Arthur Hugh Clough," *Macmillan's Magazine*, VI, 329–30 (August 1862).
15. Frederick W. Hoeing, "Letters of Mazzini to W. J. Linton," *The Journal of Modern History*, V, 62 (March 1933).
16. Mrs. Hamilton King, *op. cit.*, pp. 18–28.
17. *Ibid.*, pp. 31–32.
18. Justin McCarthy, *Portraits of the Sixties*, London, 1903, pp. 310–16.
19. William Flavelle Monypenny and George Earle Buckle, *The Life of Benjamin Disraeli, Earl of Beaconsfield*, London, 1910–20, I, 241.
20. Edmund Downey, *Charles Lever: His Life in His Letters*, London, 1906, II, 25.
21. Paul Frischauer, *Garibaldi—The Man and the Nation*, London, 1935, p. 345.
22. John Sale Barker, *Two Lectures on Italian Unity and the National Movement in Europe*, London, 1864.
23. Camillo Mapei, *Italy, Illustrated and Described* . . ., with a supplementary essay by the Rev. Gavin Carlyle, 2nd edition, Glasgow and London, 1864, p. cx.
24. Edward Henry Nolan, *The Liberators of Italy* . . ., [London, 1864].
25. *The Letters of George Meredith*, ed. William Maxse Meredith, London, 1912, I, 141.
26. Mrs. Hamilton King, *op. cit.*, p. 47.
27. *Ibid.*, pp. 41–42.
28. *Letters of Robert Browning to Miss Isa Blagden*, ed. A. J. Armstrong, Waco, Texas, 1923, p. 114.
29. John Walter Cross, *George Eliot's Life as Related in Her Letters and Journals*, London, 1885, II, 406–08.
30. William James Linton, *Prose and Verse . . . 1836–1886*, twenty volumes assembled by Linton and presented by him to the British Museum in 1895, XVI, 140–41.
31. Stewart Marsh Ellis, *George Meredith: His Life and Friends in Relation to His Work*, London, 1919, pp. 221–23.
32. George Meredith, *Vittoria*, the Memorial Edition, London, 1909–11, I, 9–10.

33. George Meredith, *Vittoria*, the Memorial Edition, London, 1909–11, I, 115–16.
34. *Ibid.*, I, 252.
35. *Ibid.*, I, 200–01.
36. Georges Lafourcade, *La Jeunesse de Swinburne* (*1837–1867*), Paris, 1928, I, 251–52.
37. *Ibid.*, II, 301–18.
38. *Mazzini's Letters to an English Family, 1844–72*, ed. E. F. Richards, London, 1920–22, III, 154.
39. W. Brooks Drayton Henderson, *Swinburne and Landor*, London, 1918, p. 178.
40. Sir Edmund Gosse, *The Life of Algernon Charles Swinburne*, *The Complete Works of Algernon Charles Swinburne*, the Bonchurch edition, ed. Sir Edmund Gosse and Thomas James Wise, London, 1925–27, XIX, 153.
41. *Ibid.*, 153–54.
42. Evelyn Abbot and Lewis Campbell, *The Life and Letters of Benjamin Jowett*, London, 1897, II, 10–12.
43. Lafourcade, *op. cit.*, I, 253–54.
44. William Michael Rossetti, *Rossetti Papers 1862 to 1870*, London, 1903, p. 226.
45. *Mazzini's Letters to an English Family, 1844–72*, III, 156.
46. Lafourcade, *op. cit.*, I, 254–56.
47. Gosse, *op. cit.*, XIX, 154.
48. Mrs. Disney Leith, *The Boyhood of Algernon Charles Swinburne. Personal Recollections . . . With Extracts from Some of his Private Letters*, London, 1917, pp. 91–94.
49. *The Complete Works of Algernon Charles Swinburne*, the Bonchurch edition, ed. Sir Edmund Gosse and Thomas James Wise, London, 1925–27, II, 315–16.
50. Gosse, *op. cit.*, XIX, 160.
51. Mrs. Disney Leith, *op. cit.*, pp. 80–81.
52. *Mazzini's Letters to an English Family, 1844–72*, III, 164.
53. William Michael Rossetti, *op. cit.*, p. 231.
54. Mrs. Disney Leith, *op. cit.*, pp. 94–95.
55. Georges Lafourcade, *Swinburne: A Literary Biography*, London, 1932, p. 168.
56. Gosse, *op. cit.*, XIX, 161–62.
57. William Michael Rossetti, *op. cit.*, p. 245.
58. *Mazzini's Letters to an English Family, 1844–72*, III, 195–96.
59. Lafourcade, *Swinburne: A Literary Biography*, p. 170.
60. *Mazzini's Letters to an English Family, 1844–72*, III, 199.
61. Gosse, *op. cit.*, XIX, 164–66.
62. F. W. Irby, *Italy: Original Poems and Translations*, London, 1868, p. 44.
63. William Michael Rossetti, *op. cit.*, p. 407.
64. Lafourcade, *La Jeunesse de Swinburne* (*1837–1867*), I, 187.
65. "A Counsel," *The Complete Works of Algernon Charles Swinburne*, II, 356.

66. Lafourcade, *Swinburne: A Literary Biography*, p. 170.
67. *Mazzini's Letters to an English Family, 1844–72*, III, 214–15.
68. Bolton King, *Mazzini*, London, 1902, p. 217.
69. Benjamin Disraeli, Earl of Beaconsfield, *Lothair*, Hughenden edition, London, 1881, X, 164–68.
70. *Mazzini's Letters to an English Family, 1844–72*, III, 248.
71. William Michael Rossetti, *Democratic Sonnets*, London, 1907, II, 17.
72. *Mazzini's Letters to an English Family, 1844–72*, III, 232–39.
73. Lafourcade, *Swinburne: A Literary Biography*, pp. 171–72.
74. *Ibid.*, p. 177.
75. Mrs. Disney Leith, *op. cit.*, p. 96.
76. John Morley, *Recollections*, London, 1917, I, 72–73.
77. *a.* Joseph Mazzini, "A Letter to the Members of the Oecumenical Council. *From the Council to God*," *The Fortnightly Review*, XIII, 725–51 (June 1, 1870).
    b. Richard Garnett, *A History of Italian Literature*, New York and London, 1928, p. 373.
78. Joseph Mazzini, "Italy and the Republic," *The Fortnightly Review*, March 1, 1871, pp. 289–309.
79. *Mazzini's Letters to an English Family, 1844–72*, III, 263.
80. Thomas Carlyle, *Reminiscences*, ed. C. E. Norton, London and New York, 1932, p. 75.
81. Abbot and Campbell, *op. cit.*, II, 10–12.
82. *Mazzini's Letters to an English Family, 1844–72*, III, 280.
83. Mrs. Hamilton King, *op. cit.*, p. 97.
84. Lafourcade, *Swinburne: A Literary Biography*, p. 160.
85. *The Complete Works of Algernon Charles Swinburne*, XVIII, 83–84.
86. Gosse, *op. cit.*, XIX, 174–78.
87. Harold Nicolson, *Swinburne*, London, 1926, pp. 131–32.
88. *Mazzini's Letters to an English Family, 1844–72*, III, 299.
89. Bolton King, *op. cit.*, p. 221.

CHAPTER VIII

Epilogue

1. Mrs. Harriet Eleanor Baillie Hamilton King, *Letters and Recollections of Mazzini*, ed. G. M. Trevelyan, London, 1912, p. 103.
2. Moncure Daniel Conway, *Autobiography: Memories and Experiences*, Boston and New York, 1904, II, 66–67.
3. *William Allingham. A Diary*, ed. H. Allingham and D. Radford, London, 1907, p. 208.
4. Mrs. Disney Leith, *The Boyhood of Algernon Charles Swinburne. Personal Recollections . . . With Extracts from Some of his Private Letters*, London, 1917, pp. 98–99.
5. John Walter Cross, *George Eliot's Life as Related in Her Letters and Journals*, London, 1885, III, 156.

6. David Masson, *Memories of London in the 'Forties*, Edinburgh and London, 1908.
7. [Charles Edward Mudie], *Stray Leaves*, 2nd edition, [London?], 1872, pp. 48–50.
8. William Lloyd Garrison, *Joseph Mazzini: His Life, Writings, and Political Principles*, New York, 1872.
9. Mrs. Hamilton King, *op. cit.*, p. 107.
10. *Ibid.*, p. 139.
11. Mrs. Hamilton King, *The Disciples*, London, 1873, p. 1.
12. *Ibid.*, pp. 7–8.
13. Isabella Blagden, *Poems*, Edinburgh and London, 1873, pp. 77–82.
14. David Alec Wilson and David Wilson MacArthur, *Carlyle in Old Age (1865–1881)*, London, 1934, p. 352.
15. Thomas Hake and Arthur Compton-Rickett, *Letters of Algernon Charles Swinburne. With Some Personal Recollections*, London, 1918, pp. 151–52.
16. *The Complete Works of Algernon Charles Swinburne*, the Bonchurch edition, ed. Sir Edmund Gosse and Thomas James Wise, London, 1925–27, XVIII, 275 and 280.
17. Thomas Adolphus Trollope, *The Story of the Life of Pius the Ninth*, London, 1877, I, 144.
18. William James Linton, *Prose and Verse . . . 1836–1886*, twenty volumes assembled by Linton and presented by him to the British Museum in 1895, XX, 5–11.
19. Arnold Toynbee, *Lectures on the Industrial Revolution in England. . .*, with a memoir by Benjamin Jowett, London, 1884, p. 200.
20. Thomas Carlyle, *Reminiscences*, ed. James Anthony Froude, London, 1881, II, 182.
21. "Lines on the Monument of Giuseppe Mazzini," *The Complete Works of Algernon Charles Swinburne*, V, 335–36.
22. Oscar Fingall O'Flahertie Wilde, *Poems*, ed. Robert Ross, London, 1909, pp. 187–208.
23. *Ibid.*, pp. 198–201.
24. Margaret Josephine Shaen, *William Shaen: A Brief Sketch*, London, 1912, pp. 14–20.
25. Alice Galimberti, *L'Aedo d'Italia: Algernon Charles Swinburne*, Palermo, 1925, p. 45.
26. John Purves, letter to *The* [London] *Times Literary Supplement*, September 24, 1931, pp. 729–30.
27. *The Complete Works of Algernon Charles Swinburne*, X, 119.
28. *Ibid.*, X, 3–5.
29. *The Works of John Ruskin*, ed. E. T. Cook and Alexander Wedderburn, London, 1903–12, XXXV, 44.
30. *Letters of Lord Acton to Mary Gladstone*, ed. Herbert Paul, London, 1913, p. 167.
31. *The Collected Works of William Morris*, ed. May Morris, London and New York, 1910–15, XXIV, 382–83

32. *The Complete Works of Algernon Charles Swinburne*, XIII, 57.
33. Georges Lafourcade, *Swinburne: A Literary Biography*, London, 1932, pp. 288–89.
34. *The Complete Works of Algernon Charles Swinburne*, VI, 171–74.
35. John Morley, *The Life of William Ewart Gladstone*, London, 1903, III, 478.
36. Mrs. Disney Leith, *op. cit.*, p. 90.
37. Algernon Charles Swinburne, *Collected Poetical Works*, London, 1927, I, viii–ix.
38. William Hale White, *Clara Hopgood*, London, 1896, p. 269.
39. Gaetano Salvemini, "Mazzini," *Encyclopaedia of the Social Sciences*, ed. Edwin R. A. Seligman and Alvin Johnson, New York, 1933, X, 240–41.

CHAPTER IX

The First Generation of Italian Exiles in Great Britain: Foscolo, Rossetti, Panizzi

1. Edmund Garratt Gardner, *Italian Literature*, London, 1927, p. 59.
2. Gaudence Megaro, *Vittorio Alfieri: Forerunner of Italian Nationalism*, New York, 1930, p. 144.
3. "*Buonaparte Liberatore, Oda del liber' uomo Niccolò Ugo Foscolo 1797, prima del 12 maggio.*"
4. *Catalogo dei Manoscritti Foscoliani*, Rome, 1885, p. 47.
5. Sir Spencer Walpole, *The Life of Lord John Russell*, London, 1889, I, 109.
6. Constance Brooks, *Antonio Panizzi, Scholar and Patriot*, Manchester, 1931, p. 21.
7. John Cam Hobhouse, First Baron Broughton, *Italy: Remarks made in Several Visits from the Year 1816 to 1854*, London, 1859–61, II, 291–379.
8. Francesco Viglione, *Ugo Foscolo in Inghilterra*, Catania, 1910, pp. 319–21.
9. "Narrative and Romantic Poems of the Italians," *The Quarterly Review*, XXI, 486–556 (April 1819).
10. *North American Review*, XCI, 245 (July 1860).
11. Ugo Foscolo, *Opere edite e postume*, Florence, 1850–99, VIII, 9.
12. Guglielmo Pepe, *Memoirs. Comprising the Principal Military and Political Events of Modern Italy*, London, 1846, III, 231.
13. "Italian Tragedy," *The Quarterly Review*, XXIV, 90–97 and 101 (October 1820).
14. "To Ugo Foscolo," *The New Monthly Magazine*, II, 453 (1821).
15. Antonio Carlo Napoleone Gallenga (also known as Luigi Mariotti), *Present State and Prospects of Italy*, London, 1848, p. 38.

16. Cyrus Redding, *Fifty Years' Recollections, Literary and Personal, with Observations of Men and Things*, London, 1858, II, 197. Redding's translation.
17. *The Journal of Sir Walter Scott*, Edinburgh, 1890, I, 14–15.
18. Redding, *op. cit.*, II, 187–93.
19. John Purves, "Macready and Ugo Foscolo," letter to *The* [London] *Times Literary Supplement*, August 17, 1933, p. 549.
20. Angelo Ottolini, *Bibliografia Foscoliana*, Florence, 1921, p. 51.
21. "Memoir of Ugo Foscolo," *The London Magazine*, October 1827, pp. 238–44.
22. *The Foreign Review, and Continental Miscellany*, II, 177 (1828).
23. *Ibid.*, II, 410–31 (1828).
24. "Modern Poets and Poetry of Italy," *The Westminster Review*, October 1859, pp. 427–56.
25. *The Oxford Book of Italian Verse*, ed. St. John Lucas, Oxford, 1910, p. 562.
26. E. R. Vincent, *Gabriele Rossetti in England*, Oxford and London, 1936, p. xi.
27. W. M. Rossetti, *Gabriele Rossetti. A Versified Autobiography*, London, 1901, p. 75.
28. Vincent, *op. cit.*, pp. 3–5.
29. *Ibid.*, pp. 72–76.
30. *Ibid.*, p. 14.
31. *Ibid.*, pp. 17–19.
32. *Ibid.*, p. 39.
33. *Ibid.*, pp. 22–25.
34. *The Athenaeum*, May 19, 1832, pp. 318–19.
35. Vincent, *op. cit.*, p. 85.
36. Gabriele Rossetti, *Disquisitions on the Anti-Papal Spirit Which Produced the Reformation; Its Secret Influence, etc.*, tr. Miss Caroline Ward, London, 1834, II, 205.
37. *The Athenaeum*, August 17, 1833, pp. 553–54. Review of Gabriele Rossetti's *Iddio e L'Uomo: Salterio.*
38. Arthur Henry Hallam, *Remains in Verse and Prose*, London, 1863, pp. 211–93.
39. A. W. Schlegel, "*Dante, Pétrarque et Boccace, A Propos De L'Ouvrage De M. Rossetti,*" *Revue des Deux Mondes*, August 1836, pp. 400–18.
40. Vincent, *op. cit.*, pp. 56,.58, and 109.
41. W. Holman Hunt, *Pre-Raphaelitism and the Pre-Raphaelite Brotherhood*, London, 1905, I, 154–55.
42. James Whiteside, *Italy in the Nineteenth Century, Contrasied with Its Past Condition*, 1st edition, London, 1848, III, 174–78.
43. William Michael Rossetti, *Democratic Sonnets*, London, 1907, II, 9.
44. Brooks, *op. cit.*, p. 11.
45. Countess Evelyn Martinengo-Cesaresco, *The Liberation of Italy, 1815–1870*, London, 1902, p. 52.

46. Antonio Panizzi, *Extracts from Italian Prose Writers for the Use of Students in the London University*, London, 1828.
47. *The Athenaeum*, October 1, 1828, p. 772.
48. David Alec Wilson, *Carlyle to "The French Revolution" (1826–1837)*, London, 1924, pp. 362–63.
49. Vincent, *op. cit.*, p. 26.
50. Louis Fagan, *The Life and Correspondence of Sir Anthony Panizzi*, Boston and New York, 1881, I, 146–47.
51. *Edizione nazionale degli scritti di Giuseppe Mazzini*, Imola, 1906–37, XVIII, 141.
52. Fagan, *op. cit.*, I, 186.
53. *Ibid.*, I, 186.
54. *Ibid.*, I, 191.
55. David Alec Wilson, *Carlyle to Threescore-and-Ten (1853–1865)*, London, 1931, p. 176.
56. Brooks, *op. cit.*, p. 88.
57. William Ewart Gladstone, "Giacomo Leopardi," reprinted from *The Quarterly Review*, March 1850, in *Gleanings of Past Years, 1845–76*, London, 1879, II, 65–129. See II, 65, for this reference.
58. Fagan, *op. cit.*, I, 287–89.
59. *Ibid.*, II, 105–13.
60. *Ibid.*, II, 103.
61. Jessie White Mario, *The Birth of Modern Italy*, ed. the Duke Litta-Visconti-Arese, London, 1909, p. 256.
62. Fagan, *op. cit.*, II, 15–16.
63. William Flavelle Monypenny and George Earle Buckle, *The Life of Benjamin Disraeli, Earl of Beaconsfield*, London, 1910–20, IV, 400–01.
64. David Masson, *Memories of London in the 'Forties*, Edinburgh and London, 1908, p. 133.
65. *The Letters of Charles Dickens*, ed. Georgina Hogarth and Mamie Dickens, London, 1880[79]–1882[81], II, 89–90.
66. John Morley, *The Life of William Ewart Gladstone*, London, 1903, II, 151–52.
67. *Ibid.*, II, 196–97.

CHAPTER X

Some Italian Exiles of the 1830's: Ricciardi, the Brothers Ruffini, Gallenga

1. Count Giuseppe Napoleone Ricciardi, *The Autobiography of an Italian Rebel*, London, 1860, p. 63.
2. Ross Douglas Waller, *The Rossetti Family, 1824–1854*, Manchester, 1932, p. 69.
3. Ricciardi, *op. cit.*

4. Georges Lafourcade, *Swinburne: A Literary Biography*, London, 1932, pp. 172–74.
5. David Masson, *Memories of Two Cities, Edinburgh and Aberdeen*, Edinburgh and London, 1911, p. 121.
6. Jessie White Mario, *The Birth of Modern Italy*, ed. the Duke Litta-Visconti-Arese, London, 1909, p. 44.
7. *Tait's Edinburgh Magazine*, XXII, 683 (1855).
8. *Fraser's Magazine*, XLVIII, 88 (July 1853).
9. *The North British Review*, XIX, 186 (May 1853).
10. *The Quarterly Review*, XCIII, 117–28 (July 1853).
11. Gwilym Oswald Griffith, *Mazzini: Prophet of Modern Europe*, London, 1932, pp. 357–58.
12. *Tait's Edinburgh Magazine*, XXII, 683–90 (1855).
13. *The North British Review*, XXIV, 538–48 (February 1856).
14. G. S. Godkin, *Life of Victor Emmanuel II, First King of Italy*, London, 1879, II, 43.
15. *Macmillan's Magazine:* "A Contemporary Hobby," III, 467–73 (April 1861); "A Quiet Nook," V, 277–94, 371–78, 496–504 (February, March, April 1862); "Sanremo Revisited," XI, 374–87 (March 1865).
16. Mrs. Eliza Fletcher, *Autobiography*, Edinburgh, 1875, pp. 233–34.
17. Bolton King, *Mazzini*, London, 1902, p. 7.
18. Masson, *op. cit.*, p. 124.
19. *Ibid.*, p. 127.
20. *Ibid.*, p. 136.
21. Felice Momigliano, "*Mazzini e Carlyle*," *Rassegna Italo-Britannica*, August 1918, p. 56.
22. Joseph Mazzini, *Essays*, tr. Thomas Okey, ed. Bolton King, London, 1894, p. 229.
23. David Masson, "Dead Men Whom I Have Known; or, Recollections of Three Cities," *Macmillan's Magazine*, XI, 324–25 (February 1865).
24. *The North British Review*, XIX, 207 (May 1853).
25. *The People's Journal*, II, 147–48 (1846).
26. Antonio Carlo Napoleone Gallenga (also known as Luigi Mariotti), "Morello, or the Organ-Boy's Progress," *The Blackgown Papers*, London, 1846, II, 1–100.
27. Hon. William Warren Vernon, *Recollections of Seventy-two Years*, London, 1917, p. 71.
28. *Edizione nazionale degli scritti di Giuseppe Mazzini*, Imola, 1906–37, XLII, 58–59.
29. Gallenga, *Castellamonte . . .*, London, 1854, II, 44.
30. *The North British Review*, XXIV, 548–68 (February 1856).
31. Gallenga, *Country Life in Piedmont*, London, 1858, p. 126.
32. Gallenga, *The Pope and the King; the War between Church and State in Italy*, London, 1879.

CHAPTER XI

The Aftermath of the 'Forty-eight: Gavazzi, Lacaita, Saffi, Orsini

1. Charles MacFarlane, *A Glance at Revolutionized Italy . . . in the Summer of 1848*, London, 1849, II, 12.
2. George Macaulay Trevelyan, *Garibaldi's Defence of the Roman Republic*, London, 1907, p. 76.
3. John Ruskin, *Letters upon Subjects of General Interest . . . to Various Correspondents*, London, 1892, p. 13.
4. James Anthony Froude, *Thomas Carlyle: A History of his Life in London, 1834–81*, London, 1884, II, 83.
5. Giuseppe Maria Campanella, *Life in the Cloister, in the Papal Court and in Exile*, London, 1877, p. 135.
6. Campanella, *The Life of Father Gavazzi*, London, 1851, p. 54.
7. Father Gavazzi, *Orations*, London, 1851.
8. MacFarlane, *The Neapolitan Government and Mr. Gladstone, etc.*, London, August 1851, p. 23.
9. Alessandro Gavazzi, *The Four Last Popes. A Lecture Delivered . . . in Reply to "Recollections" by Dr. Wiseman on the Same Subject*, London, 1857, p. 64.
10. John George Edward Henry Douglas Sutherland Campbell, Ninth Duke of Argyll, *Passages from the Past*, London, 1907, pp. 109–10.
11. Hon. William Warren Vernon, *Recollections of Seventy-two Years*, London, 1917, p. 199.
12. Charles Lacaita, *An Italian Englishman: Sir James Lacaita, 1813–1895*, London, 1933, pp. 63–65.
13. Louis Fagan, *The Life and Correspondence of Sir Anthony Panizzi*, Boston and New York, 1881, II, 131.
14. Trevelyan, *Garibaldi and the Making of Italy*, London, 1911, pp. 105–08.
15. Fagan, *op. cit.*, II, 208.
16. F. W. Irby, *Italy: Original Poems and Treanslations*, London, 1868.
17. Lacaita, *op. cit.*, p. 241.
18. Jane Welsh Carlyle, *New Letters and Memorials*, ed. Alexander Carlyle, with an introduction by Sir James Crichton-Browne, London and New York, 1903, II, 33.
19. Jessie White Mario, *The Birth of Modern Italy*, ed. the Duke Litta-Visconti-Arese, London, 1909, p. xxii.
20. Frederic Harrison, *Autobiographic Memoirs*, London, 1911, I, 95.
21. Francesco Crispi, *Memoirs*, tr. Mary Prichard-Agnetti, London, 1912, I, 87–88.
22. Harrison, *op. cit.*, I, 189.
23. George Jacob Holyoake, *Sixty Years of an Agitator's Life*, 4th edition, London, 1900, I, 284.

24. Dante Gabriel Rossetti, *Letters . . . to William Allingham, 1854–1870*, ed. G. B. Hill, London, 1897, p. 54.
25. David Alec Wilson and David Wilson MacArthur, *Carlyle in Old Age (1865–1881)*, London, 1934, p. 352.
26. Malwida von Meysenbug, *Gesammelte Werke*, ed. Berta Schleicher, Leipzig, 1922, I, 402–03.
27. John Forster, *The Works and Life of Walter Savage Landor*, London, 1876, I, 456.
28. Felice Orsini, *The Austrian Dungeons in Italy*, tr. Jessie Meriton White, later Mme. Mario, London, July, 1856, p. 105.
29. Holyoake, *op. cit.*, II, 23–25.
30. *The Evening Post*, New York, February 7, 1859.
31. Walter Savage Landor, *Letters and Other Unpublished Writings*, ed. Stephen Wheeler, London, 1897, pp. 209–11.
32. Emily Jolly, *The Life and Letters of Sydney Dobell*, London, 1878, II, 130.
33. Holyoake, *op. cit.*, II, 56–57.
34. H. C. Minchin, *Walter Savage Landor. Last Days, Letters and Conversations*, London, 1934, pp. 107–08.
35. *The Complete Works of Algernon Charles Swinburne*, the Bonchurch edition, ed. Sir Edmund Gosse and Thomas James Wise, London, 1925–27, IV, 301.
36. Mrs. Harriet Eleanor Baillie Hamilton King, *Letters and Recollections of Mazzini*, ed. G. M. Trevelyan, London, 1912, pp. 4–8.
37. Georges Lafourcade, *La Jeunesse de Swinburne (1837–1867)*, Paris, 1928, I, 149–50.
38. Camillo Mapei, *Italy, Illustrated and Described . . . with a Supplementary Essay by the Rev. Gavin Carlyle*, 2nd edition, Glasgow and London, 1864, p. cxx.
39. Mrs. Hamilton King:
    a. *The Execution of Felice Orsini, March 13th, 1858* [London? 1860?]. Reprinted in *Aspromonte and Other Poems*, London, 1869.
    b. "Ugo Bassi" in *The Disciples*, London, 1873.
40. John Morley, *Recollections*, London, 1917, I, 55.
41. William Michael Rossetti, *Dante Gabriel Rossetti: His Family Letters . . .*, London, 1895, II, 378.
42. W. M. Rossetti, *Democratic Sonnets*, London, 1907, II, 10.

CHAPTER XII

Gladstone and *Bomba's* Victims

1. [Constantine Henry Phipps, First Marquess of Normanby], *The English in Italy*, London, 1825, III, 280–81.
2. Georges Lafourcade, *La Jeunesse de Swinburne (1837–1867)*, Paris, 1928, II, 18.

3. William Waktin Davies, *Gladstone and the Unification of Italy*, Oxford, 1918, p. 12.
4. Louis Fagan, *The Life and Correspondence of Sir Anthony Panizzi*, Boston and New York, 1881, II, 86.
5. John Morley, *The Life of William Ewart Gladstone*, London, 1903, III, 549–50.
6. Constance Brooks, *Antonio Panizzi, Scholar and Patriot*, Manchester, 1931, p. 69.
7. George Macaulay Trevelyan, *Englishmen and Italians: Some Aspects of their Relations Past and Present*, annual Italian lecture of the British Academy, London, 1919, p. 16.
8. Morley, *op. cit.*, I, 388.
9. Alexander Baillie Cochrane, *Young Italy*, London, 1850, pp. 270–75.
10. Charles Lacaita, *An Italian Englishman: Sir James Lacaita, 1813–1895*, London, 1933, pp. 25–26.
11. Nassau William Senior, *Journals Kept in France and Italy from 1848 to 1852*, London, 1871, II, 5.
12. *Ibid.*, II, 16–21.
13. *Ibid.*, II, 22–29.
14. *Ibid.*, II, 32–33.
15. Lacaita, *op. cit.*, pp. 27–29.
16. Morley, *op. cit.*, I, 390–92.
17. *Ibid.*, I, 603.
18. *Ibid.*, I, 393–96.
19. Lacaita, *op. cit.*, p. 33.
20. Trevelyan, *Garibaldi and the Thousand*, London, 1909, p. 53.
21. Morley, *op. cit.*, I, 396.
22. Anna Theresa Kitchel, *George Lewes and George Eliot. A Review of Records*, New York, 1933, p. 70.
23. Morley, *op. cit.*, I, 398–401.
24. Giuseppe Massari, *Al Sig. Guglielmo Gladstone Parole di Gratitudine*, Turin, 1851, p. 4.
25. Massimo Taparelli d'Azeglio, *Scritti Postumi*, Florence, 1872, pp. 189–94.
26. Giovanni Battista Nicolini, *The History of the Pontificate of Pius the Ninth*, Edinburgh, 1851, pp. 160–63.
27. Countess Evelyn Martinengo-Cesaresco, *Italian Characters in the Epoch of Unification*, London, 1901, pp. 7–10.
28. T. Wemyss Reid, *The Life, Letters, and Friendships of Richard Monckton Milnes, First Lord Houghton*, London, 1890, I, 451.
29. *Letters of Walter Savage Landor Private and Public*, ed. Stephen Wheeler, London, 1899, pp. 335–36.
30. Mrs. Salis Schwabe, *Reminiscences of Richard Cobden*, London, 1895, pp. 151–55.
31. William Roscoe Thayer, *The Life and Times of Cavour*, Boston and New York, 1911, I, 200.

32. Charles MacFarlane, *The Neapolitan Government and Mr. Gladstonc, etc.*, London, August 1851, p. 18.
33. Lacaita, *op. cit.*, p. 34.
34. Philip Guedalla, *Gladstone and Palmerston*, London, 1928, p. 40.
35. *Ibid.*, p. 84.
36. John Aiton, *The Lands of the Messiah, Mahomet, and the Pope; as Visited in 1851*, 2nd ed., London, 1852, pp. 490–505.
37. Aiton, *Letter to the Right Hon. Lord Palmerston . . . on the Political Imprisonments and Present Condition of Naples*, Edinburgh, 1851.
38. "Hands All Round," *The Poetic and Dramatic Works of Alfred Lord Tennyson*, Cambridge edition, ed. W. J. Rolfe, Boston and New York, 1898, p. 868.
39. August Ludwig von Rochau, *Wanderings through the Cities of Italy in 1850 and 1851*, tr. Mrs. Percy Sinnett, London, 1853, I, 292.
40. Walter Savage Landor, *Complete Works*, ed. T. Earle Welby and Stephen Wheeler, London, 1927–36, XII, 127.
41. William Ewart Gladstone, *An Examination of the Official Reply of the Neapolitan Government*, London, 1852.
42. *The Later Correspondence of Lord John Russell, 1840–1878*, ed. G. P. Gooch, London, 1925, II, 190.
43. Davies, *op. cit.*, pp. 16–17.
44. Morley, *op. cit.*, II, 11–12.
45. Frederick Chamier, *My Travels; or an unsentimental journey through France, Switzerland, and Italy*, London, 1855, *passim.*
46. *The Later Correspondence of Lord John Russell, 1840–1878*, II, 219.
47. Tina Scalia Whitaker, *Sicily and England: Political and Social Reminiscences, 1848–1870*, London, 1907, pp. 266–67.
48. "Naples and Diplomatic Intervention," *The Westminster Review*, July 1857, pp. 186–213.
49. Fagan, *op. cit.*, II, 147–50.
50. *Ibid.*, II, 173–74.
51. Martinengo-Cesaresco, *op. cit.*, pp. 10–11.
52. *The Poetical Works of Leigh Hunt*, ed. H. S. Milford, London, [1922], p. 253.
53. Morley, *op. cit.*, III, 478.

CHAPTER XIII

"Milord Camillo"

1. John Morley, *Recollections*, London, 1917, II, 135–36.
2. Frederic Harrison, *Autobiographic Memoirs*, London, 1911, I, 295.
3. John Webb Probyn, *Italy: from the Fall of Napoleon I, in 1815, to the Death of Victor Emmanuel, in 1878*, London, 1884, p. 237.
4. Count Carlo Arrivabene, *Italy under Victor Emmanuel*, London, 1862, II, 10.

5. Arthur James Beresford Whyte, *The Early Life and Letters of Cavour, 1810–1848*, London, 1925, p. xvii.
6. Edward Cadogan, *The Life of Cavour*, London, 1907, p. 14.
7. William Roscoe Thayer, *The Life and Times of Cavour*, Boston and New York, 1911, I, 20.
8. Whyte, *op. cit.*, pp. 64–65.
9. Thayer, *op. cit.*, I, 51–53.
10. Whyte, *op. cit.*, p. 124.
11. *Ibid.*, pp. 128 and 132.
12. *Ibid.*, pp. 65 and 67.
13. *Ibid.*, p. 159.
14. *Ibid.*, pp. 291–92.
15. *Count Cavour and Madame de Circourt*, tr. Arthur J. Butler, ed. Count Nigra, London, 1894, p. 46.
16. Countess Evelyn Martinengo-Cesaresco, *Cavour*, London, 1898, p. 44.
17. Nassau William Senior, *Journals Kept in France and Italy from 1848 to 1852*, London, 1871, I, 293.
18. Thayer, *op. cit.*, I, 288.
19. *Ibid.*, I, 291 and 304.
20. *Cavour e l'Inghilterra*, Bologna, 1933, I, 6.
21. Thayer, *op. cit.*, I, 135.
22. Arthur James Beresford Whyte, *The Political Life and Letters of Cavour, 1848–1861*, London, 1930, p. 7.
23. Thayer, *op. cit.*, I, 204–05.
24. Whyte, *The Political Life and Letters of Cavour, 1848–1861*, p. 93.
25. Thayer, *op. cit.*, I, 140 and 147–48.
26. *Cavour e l'Inghilterra*, I, 13.
27. *Ibid.*, I, 15.
28. Thayer, *op. cit.*, I, 214–16.
29. *Cavour e l'Inghilterra*, I, 21.
30. Martinengo-Cesaresco, *op. cit.*, p. 87.
31. *Cavour e l'Inghilterra*, I, 358–59.
32. *Ibid.*, I, 42.
33. *Ibid.*, I, 131.
34. Sir George Bowyer, *Rome and Sardinia*, London, 1856. Reprinted from *The Dublin Review*, XXXIX, 164–99 (September 1855).
35. Charles Cavendish Fulke Greville, *The Greville Memoirs*, ed. Henry Reeve, London, 1888, VII, 307.
36. Mary Clive Bayley, *The Making of Modern Italy*, London, 1919, pp. 162–63.
37. Thayer, *op. cit.*, I, 384–86.
38. Whyte, *The Political Life and Letters of Cavour, 1848–1861*, p. 221.
39. Bayle St. John, *The Subalpine Kingdom; or, Experiences and Studies in Savoy, Piedmont, and Genoa*, London, 1856, I, xii–xiii.
40. *Ibid.*, II, 153–66.
41. *Cavour e l'Inghilterra*, II, 112.
42. *The Diaries of John Bright*, ed. R. A. J. Walling, London, 1930, p. 226.

43. Cadogan, *op. cit.*, p. 181.
44. John Morley, *The Life of William Ewart Gladstone*, London, 1903, II, 5.
45. Arrivabene, *op. cit.*, I, 12.
46. *Observations on the Negotiations Respecting the Affairs of Italy*, by an M.P., London, July 1859.
47. George Macaulay Trevelyan, *Englishmen and Italians: Some Aspects of their Relations Past and Present*, annual Italian lecture of the British Academy, London, 1919, p. 15.
48. *Letters of Matthew Arnold, 1848–1888*, ed. George W. E. Russell, London, 1901, I, 124.
49. Elizabeth Barrett Browning, *Letters*, ed. Frederic G. Kenyon, London, 1897, II, 352.
50. Sir Edward Dicey, *Rome in 1860*, Cambridge, England, 1861, p. 237.
51. Whyte, *The Political Life and Letters of Cavour, 1848–1861*, p. xii.
52. Elizabeth Barrett Browning, *op. cit.*, II, 385.
53. Manchester Foreign Affairs Association, *English Aid to Garibaldi, on his invasion of the Sicilies. Is it lawful and just?*, Manchester, 1860, p. 4.
54. Thayer, *op. cit.*, II, 404.
55. John Earl Russell, *Recollections and Suggestions, 1813–1873*, London, 1875, p. 285.
56. H. L., *Italy: Past—Present—and Future*, London, 1860, p. 24.
57. John Walter Cross, *George Eliot's Life as Related in Her Letters and Journals*, London, 1885, II, 167.
58. Harrison, *op. cit.*, I, 202.
59. Constantine Henry Phipps, First Marquess of Normanby, *A Vindication of the Duke of Modena from the charges of Mr. Gladstone*, 1st edition, London, 1861.
60. Dudley Costello, *Piedmont and Italy from the Alps to the Tiber, Illustrated in a Series of Views Taken on the Spot*, London, 1861, I, 58.
61. Matthew Arnold, *Friendship's Garland*, London, 1871, pp. 150–53.
62. Sir Edward Dicey, "Recollections of Cavour's Last Debate," *Macmillan's Magazine*, IV, 249–56 (July 1861).
63. Elizabeth Barrett Browning, *op. cit.*, II, 449.
64. *Hansard's Parliamentary Debates*, 3rd series, CLXIII, 623–25.
65. *Ibid.*, 3rd series, CLXIII, 772–78.
66. Herbert Clifford F. Bell, *Lord Palmerston*, London, 1936, II, 279.
67. John Emerich Edward Dalberg Acton, Baron Acton, *Historical Essays and Studies*, ed. J. N. Figgis and R. V. Laurence, London, 1907, pp. 174–203.
68. W. Hall Griffin and Harry Christopher Minchin, *The Life of Robert Browning*, London, 1910, p. 222.
69. Mrs. Caroline Giffard Phillipson, *Songs of Italy; and Other Poems*, London, 1862, pp. 109–11.
70. William Michael Rossetti, *Democratic Sonnets*, London, 1907, II, 13.
71. Wilfrid Ward, *Aubrey de Vere: a Memoir Based on His Unpublished Diaries and Correspondence*, London, 1904, pp. 291 and 364–65.

72. Elizabeth Barrett Browning, "Summing Up In Italy. (Inscribed to Intelligent Publics Out Of It)," *Poetical Works*, ed. Frederic G. Kenyon, London, 1897, pp. 540–41.
73. *a.* Camillo Mapei, *Italy, Illustrated and Described* . . ., with a supplementary essay by the Rev. Gavin Carlyle, 2nd edition, Glasgow and London, 1864.
    b. Edward Henry Nolan, *The Liberators of Italy* . . ., [London, 1864].
74. Matthew Arnold, *Schools and Universities on the Continent*, London, 1868, p. 118.
75. Countess Marie Montemerli, *The Florentines. A Story of Home-Life in Italy*, London, 1870, II, 97.
76. James Lockhart, *Cavour. Patria e Gloria. Poem Dedicated to the Sons of Italy*, Florence, 1873.

CHAPTER XIV

Garibaldi and the British: Until the London Ovation of 1864

1. Arthur Livingston, review of *Mazzini: Portrait of an Exile* by Stringfellow Barr, *New York Herald Tribune Books*, October 20, 1935, section VII, 8.
2. *The Memoirs of Garibaldi*, ed. Alexander Dumas, tr. R. S. Garnett, London, 1931, p. v.
3. John George Edward Henry Douglas Sutherland Campbell, Ninth Duke of Argyll, *Passages from the Past*, London, 1907, I, 114.
4. William John Fitzpatrick, *The Life of Charles Lever*, new and revised edition, London, 1884, p. 321.
5. John Morley, *The Life of Wiliam Ewart Gladstone*, London, 1903, II, 109–10.
6. Antonio Carlo Napoleone Gallenga (also known as Luigi Mariotti), *Latest News from Italy*, London, 1847, p. 14.
7. Michael Burke Honan, *The Personal Adventures of "Our Own Correspondent" in Italy*, London, 1852, I, 265.
8. Luigi Carlo Farini, *The Roman State, from 1815 to 1850*, London, 1851–54, IV, 86.
9. George Macaulay Trevelyan, *Garibaldi's Defence of the Roman Republic*, London, 1907, p. 110.
10. *Ibid.*, p. 237.
11. Walter Savage Landor, *Heroic Idyls, with Additional Poems*, London, 1863, p. 314.
12. Alexander Baillie Cochrane, *Young Italy*, London, 1850, pp. 112–14.
13. Gerald Massey, *My Lyrical Life: Poems Old and New*, 2nd series, London, 1889, pp. 115–17.
14. Emilio Dandolo, *The Italian Volunteers and Lombard Rifle Brigade* . . ., London, 1851, p. 235.
15. *Military Events in Italy, 1848–1849*, tr. from the German by the Earl of Ellesmere, London, 1851, p. 328.

16. Henry Lushington, *The Italian War, 1848–9, and the Last Italian Poet*, London, 1859, p. 197.
17. Edmund Downey, *Charles Lever: His Life in His Letters*, London, 1906, I, 332.
18. *Autobiography of G. Garibaldi*, authorized translation by A. Werner, with a supplement by Jessie White Mario, London, 1889, III, 123
19. Jessie White Mario, *The Birth of Modern Italy*, ed. the Duke Litta-Visconti-Arese, London, 1909, pp. xxi and 249.
20. *Edizione nazionale degli scritti di Giuseppe Mazzini*, Imola, 1906–37, LVII, 100.
21. George Macaulay Trevelyan, *Garibaldi and the Thousand*, London, 1909, p. 65.
22. [Baroness M. E. von Schwartz], *Recollections of General Garibaldi . . . etc.*, tr. E. Field, London, 1861, p. 174.
23. William Roscoe Thayer, *The Life and Times of Cavour*, Boston and New York, 1911, II, 21.
24. Massey, *op. cit.*, pp. 117–20.
25. George Macaulay Trevelyan, *Englishmen and Italians: Some Aspects of their Relations Past and Present*, annual Italian lecture of the British Academy, London, 1919, p. 15.
26. *The Reasoner*, ed. George Jacob Holyoake, London, 1846–61, XXIV, 275 (August 28, 1859).
27. Colonel Exalbion, *Garibaldi: His Life, Exploits, and the Italian Campaigns*, London, [1859], pp. 5–6 and 306.
28. "The Massacre of Perugia," *The Dublin Review*, XLVII, 260 (September 1859).
29. "Garibaldi and the Italian Volunteers," *The Westminster Review*, October 1859, pp. 478–503.
30. *Edizione nazionale degli scritti di Giuseppe Mazzini*, LXVII, 111.
31. Walter Savage Landor, "To Garibaldi," *To Elizabeth Barrett Browning and other Verses*, one of thirty copies printed, for private circulation, for Thomas J. Wise, London, 1917, p. 17.
32. H. C. Minchin, *Walter Savage Landor. Last Days, Letters and Conversations*, London, 1934, pp. 37 and 40.
33. *Ibid.*, p. 84 (February 11, 1860).
34. *Edizione nazionale degli scritti di Giuseppe Mazzini*, LXVII, 86–87.
35. Elizabeth Barrett Browning, *Letters*, ed. Frederic G. Kenyon, London, 1897, II, 386.
36. *The Later Correspondence of Lord John Russell, 1840–1878*, ed. G. P. Gooch, London, 1925, II, 260.
37. *Autobiography of G. Garibaldi*, II, 179.
38. *The Memoirs of Francesco Crispi*, tr. Mary Prichard-Agnetti, London, 1912, I, 201.
39. Elizabeth Barrett Browning, *op. cit.*, II, 398.
40. *British Parliamentary Papers* (Blue Books), 1860, LXVIII, 371 (June 3, 1860).

41. Walter Savage Landor, *Letters and Other Unpublished Writings*, ed. Stephen Wheeler, London, 1897, pp. 211–13.
42. Mrs. Salis Schwabe, *Reminiscences of Richard Cobden*, London, 1895, pp. 314–15.
43. Victor Alexander George Robert Lytton, Second Earl of Lytton, *The Life of Edward Bulwer, First Lord Lytton*, London, 1913, II, 332.
44. *The Later Correspondence of Lord John Russell, 1840–1878*, II, 266.
45. Massey, "One of Garibaldi's Men," *op. cit.*, pp. 121–23.
46. Mrs. Harriet Eleanor Baillie Hamilton King, *Aspromonte and Other Poems*, London, 1869, pp. 69–70.
47. Walter Savage Landor, letters to *The London Review*, August 11, 1860, pp. 124–25.
48. *The Athenaeum*, August 18, 1860, pp. 313–14.
49. *The Athenaeum*, September 1, 1860, pp. 289–90.
50. William Flavelle Monypenny and George Earle Buckle, *The Life of Benjamin Disraeli, Earl of Beaconsfield*, London, 1910–20, IV, 321.
51. *The Athenaeum*, September 22, 1860, p. 384.
52. Henry C. Barlow, *Rome from Monte Mario, with Other Way-Side Sketches*, London, 1860, pp. 33–35.
53. George Macaulay Trevelyan, *Garibaldi and the Making of Italy*, London, 1911, pp. 266–67.
54. Trevelyan, *Garibaldi and the Thousand*, p. 117.
55. S. M. Ellis, *A Mid-Victorian Pepys: The Letters and Memoirs of Sir William Hardman*, London, 1923, pp. 11–12.
56. John Forster, *The Works of Walter Savage Landor*, London, 1876, VIII, 314.
57. Walter Savage Landor, *Heroic Idyls, with Additional Poems*, p. 308.
58. W. Hall Griffin and Harry Christopher Minchin, *The Life of Robert Browning*, London, 1910, p. 221.
59. H. C. Minchin, *Walter Savage Landor. Last Days, Letters and Conversations*, p. 109.
60. Walter Savage Landor, *Letters and Other Unpublished Writings*, pp. 208–09.
61. John Richard Digby Beste, *Nowadays: or, Courts, Courtiers, Churchmen, Garibaldians, Lawyers and Brigands, at Home and Abroad*, London, 1870, II.
62. W. G. Clark, "Naples and Garibaldi," *Vacation Tourists and Notes of Travel in 1860*, ed. Sir Francis Galton, London, 1861, p. 1.
63. Downey, *op. cit.*, I, 362.
64. Rear Admiral Sir George Rodney Mundy, *H.M.S. "Hannibal" at Palermo and Naples, during the Italian Revolution, 1859–61*, London, 1863, p. 8.
65. Thayer, *op. cit.*, II, 341–42.
66. William James Linton, *Prose and Verse . . . 1836–1886*, twenty volumes assembled by Linton and presented by him to the British Museum in 1895, XVI, 62.
67. *The Reasoner*, XXV, 296–319.

68. Sir Charles Stuart Forbes, *The Campaign of Garibaldi in the Two Sicilies: a Personal Narrative*, London and Edinburgh, 1861, p. 309.
69. *Edizione nazionale degli scritti di Giuseppe Mazzini*, LXVIII, 18.
70. Mrs. Hamilton King, "Battle Hymn for Garibaldi's British Legion. Volturno, 1860," *op. cit.*, pp. 63–68.
71. Count Carlo Arrivabene, *Italy under Victor Emmanuel*, London, 1862, I, 124.
72. *Ibid.*, II, 71–72 and 77.
73. George Jacob Holyoake, *Bygones Worth Remembering*, London, 1905, I, 243–49.
74. Joseph McCabe, *George Jacob Holyoake*, London, 1922, pp. 54–55.
75. Trevelyan, *Garibaldi and the Making of Italy*; pp. 259–60.
76. Bolton King, *A History of Italian Unity. Being a Political History of Italy from 1814 to 1871*, London, 1899, II, 177.
77. Trevelyan, *Garibaldi and the Making of Italy*, p. 151.
78. *Ibid.*, pp. 235 and 251.
79. Thayer, *op. cit.*, II, 312.
80. Sir Spencer Walpole, *The Life of Lord John Russell*, London, 1889, II, 326–27.
81. Mundy, *op. cit.*, p. 292.
82. *The Westminster Review*, October 1860, p. 410.
83. *Autobiography of G. Garibaldi*, III, 156 and 275.
84. *Macmillan's Magazine*, III, 160 (December 1860).
85. *Ibid.*, III, 157 (December 1860).
86. Thayer, *op. cit.*, II, 421–23.
87. Maltus Questell Holyoake, "The Last Writings of Landor," *The Gentleman's Magazine*, CCLXXXVI, 13 (January 1899).
88. *The Westminster Review*, January 1861, p. 130.
89. Dudley Costello, *Piedmont and Italy from the Alps to the Tiber, Illustrated in a Series of Views Taken on the Spot*, London, 1861, I, 142.
90. *E.g.*, *Alfio Balzani; or, Extracts from the Diary of a Proscribed Sicilian*, New York and London, 1861.
91. Mrs. Caroline Giffard Phillipson, *Songs on Italy; and Other Poems*, London, 1862.
92. [Frederic Harrison], "Cavour and Garibaldi," *The Westminster Review*, new series, XIX, 172–201 (January 1861).
93. John G. E. H. D. Sutherland Campbell, Ninth Duke of Argyll, *op. cit.*, I, 291.
94. "Italy," *The Quarterly Review*, CIX, 133–77 (January 1861).
95. *Italy. Corrected report of the Speeches of . . . Lord John Russell delivered in the House of Commons . . . February 5, and . . . 6, 1861*, pp. 8–9.
96. Lieutenant-Colonel O. W. S. Chambers, *Garibaldi and Italian Unity*, London, 1864, p. 150.
97. Mrs. Phillipson, "One Year Ago," *op. cit.*, pp. 10–12.
98. Francis Alexander Mackay, "Hurra! For Garibaldi! A War Chant," *Lays and Poems on Italy*, London, 1862, pp. 112–14.

99. James Stansfeld, *The Italian Movement and Italian Parties*, London, [March 1862].
100. *Mazzini's Letters to an English Family, 1844–72*, ed. E. F. Richards, London, 1920–22, III, 32.
101. Chambers, *op. cit.*, pp. 170–74.
102. Forster, *op. cit.*, VIII, 338.
103. Ellis, *op. cit.*, p. 191.
104. *Letters and Memorials of Jane Welsh Carlyle*, ed. James Anthony Froude, London, 1883, III, 114.
105. T. Wemyss Reid, *The Life, Letters, and Friendships of Richard Monckton Milnes, First Lord Houghton*, London, 1890, II, 83–84.
106. Bolton King, *op. cit.*, II, 247.
107. J. L. and Barbara Hammond, *James Stansfeld: a Victorian Champion of Sex Equality*, London, 1932, p. 48.
108. Robert A. and Elizabeth S. Watson, *George Gilfillan: Letters and Journals, with Memoir*, London, 1892, pp. 422–25.
109. Mrs. Phillipson, *op. cit.*, pp. 1–6 and 156–59.
110. Massey, *op. cit.*, pp. 124–27.
111. *Garibaldi: his career and exploits. Reprinted with additions from the "Morning Star" of April 2, 1864; with a descriptive narrative of the hero's reception at Southampton. . .*, London, 1864, p. 2.
112. Chambers, *op. cit.*, p. 259.
113. David Larg, *Giuseppe Garibaldi: a Biography*, London, 1934, p. 310.
114. *Notes and Queries*, 12th series, XI, 217 and 238.
115. *Letters of Walter Savage Landor Private and Public*, ed. Stephen Wheeler, London, 1899, p. 228.
116. Downey, *op. cit.*, I, 369.
117. Mrs. Amy Foster Watson, *Meredith and Italy*, London, 1919, p. 6.
118. Mundy, *op. cit.*
119. Christopher Wordsworth, Bishop of Lincoln, *Journal of a Tour in Italy, with Reflections on the Present Condition and Prospects of Religion in that Country*, London, 1863, I, 79.

CHAPTER XV

Garibaldi and the British: From the London Ovation Until the Present

1. Pietro Orsi, *Cavour and the Making of Modern Italy, 1810–1861*, London and New York, 1926, p. 357.
2. *Garibaldi: His Career and Exploits*, London, 1864, pp. 3, 12, and 15.
3. *Punch*, April 9, 1864, pp. 146 and 149.
4. *William Allingham, A Diary*, ed. H. Allingham and D. Radford, London, 1907, p. 99.
5. John G. E. H. D. Sutherland Campbell, Ninth Duke of Argyll, *Passages from the Past*, London, 1907, I, 121.

6. Alexander Herzen, *My Past and Thoughts. The Memoirs of Alexander Herzen*, tr. Constance Garnett, London, 1924–27, V, 51–52.
7. George Macaulay Trevelyan, *Garibaldi and the Making of Italy*, London, 1911, p. 289.
8. Edward Henry Nolan, *The Liberators of Italy . . .*, [London, 1864], p. 230.
9. Trevelyan, *op. cit.*, p. 290.
10. Desmond McCarthy and Lady Mary Agatha Russell, *Lady John Russell. A Memoir . . .*, London, 1910, p. 189.
11. John G. E. H. D. Sutherland Campbell, Ninth Duke of Argyll, *op. cit.*, I, 118.
12. Herzen, *op. cit.*, V, 78.
13. John Walter Cross, *George Eliot's Life as Related in Her Letters and Journals*, London, 1885, II, 382.
14. John Morley, *The Life of William Ewart Gladstone*, London, 1903, II, 112–13.
15. William Flavelle Monypenny and George Earle Buckle, *The Life of Benjamin Disraeli, Earl of Beaconsfield*, London, 1910–20, IV, 327–28.
16. Philip Guedalla, *Palmerston*, London, 1926, p. 452.
17. William Warren Vernon, *Recollections of Seventy-two Years*, London, 1917, p. 240.
18. *The Letters and Memoirs of Sir William Hardman, Second Series: 1863–1865*, ed. S. M. Ellis, New York, 1926, p. 171.
19. Frederic Harrison, *Autobiographic Memoirs*, London, 1911, I, 357.
20. George Jacob Holyoake, *Bygones Worth Remembering*, London, 1905, I, 241.
21. Pia Onnis, "*Battaglie democratiche e Risorgimento in un carteggio inedito di Giuseppe Mazzini e George Jacob Holyoake*," *Rassegna Storica del Risorgimento*, Rome, December 1935, p. 926.
22. T. Wemyss Reid, *The Life, Letters, and Friendships of Richard Monckton Milnes, First Lord Houghton*, London, 1890, II, 124.
23. James Weston, *General Garibaldi at Fishmongers' Hall*, London, May 1864, p. 8.
24. *The Letters and Memoirs of Sir William Hardman . . .*, p. 170.
25. *Letters of Robert Browning Collected by Thomas J. Wise*, ed. Thurman L. Hood, London, 1933, p. 79.
26. Herzen, *op. cit.*, V, 43.
27. Hallam Tennyson, Second Baron Tennyson, *Alfred Lord Tennyson: a Memoir*, London, 1897, II, 1–4.
28. Harold G. Nicolson, *Tennyson: Aspects of His Life, Character, and Poetry*, London, 1923, p. 182.
29. "To Ulysses," *The Poetic and Dramatic Works of Alfred Lord Tennyson*, Cambridge edition, ed. W. J. Rolfe, Boston and New York, 1898, p. 546.
30. *Punch*, April 30, 1864, p. 181.
31. Captain Mayne Reid, *Garibaldi Rebuked by One of His Best Friends, etc.*, London, 1864.

32. Henry Edward Cardinal Manning, *The Visit of Garibaldi to England. A Letter to the Right Hon. E. Cardwell, etc.*, London, 1864.
33. Charles Lever, "Cornelius O'Dowd upon Men and Women, and Other Things in General," *Blackwood's Edinburgh Magazine*, May 1864, pp. 614–18.
34. *The Letters of George Meredith*, ed. William Maxse Meredith, London, 1912, I, 141–42.
35. Sir John Kingston James, "To Garibaldi," *Fraser's Magazine*, May 1864, pp. 625–26.
36. Miss Frances Power Cobbe, *Italics. Brief Notes on Politics, People, and Places in Italy, in 1864*, London, 1864, pp. 183 and 435.
37. George Walter Thornbury, "In my Gondola," *Historical and Legendary Ballads and Songs*, illustrated by Whistler, Tenniel, etc., London, 1876[1875], pp. 124–26.
38. *The Fortnightly Review*, III, 775–77 (February 1, 1866).
39. William James Linton, *Prose and Verse . . . 1836–1886*, twenty volumes assembled by Linton and presented by him to the British Museum in 1895, XVI, 147.
40. Edmund Downey, *Charles Lever: His Life in His Letters*, London, 1906, II, 29.
41. *Letters of Robert Browning Collected by Thomas J. Wise*, p. 113.
42. Cecil Scott Forester, *Victor Emmanuel II and the Union of Italy*, London, 1927, p. 172.
43. Thomas Earle Welby, *A Study of Swinburne*, London, 1926, p. 100.
44. *The Athenaeum*, October 26, 1867, p. 537.
45. George Macaulay Trevelyan, *English Songs of Italian Freedom*, London, 1911, p. 221.
46. *The Poetical Works of Sydney Dobell*, with a memoir by John Nichol, London, 1875, II, 419–23.
47. Francis Turner Palgrave, *Lyrical Poems*, London, 1871, pp. 141–43.
48. Charles Lever, "Garibaldi's Last," *Blackwood's Edinburgh Magazine*, November 1867, pp. 609–12. Lever wrote under the name of Cornelius O'Dowd.
49. *Letters of Robert Browning to Miss Isa Blagden*, ed. A. J. Armstrong, Waco, Texas, 1923, p. 150.
50. *The Hardman Papers*, a further selection, 1865–68, from the letters and memoirs of Sir William Hardman, ed. S. M. Ellis, London, 1930, p. 286.
51. Joseph Powell, *Two Years in the Pontifical Zouaves, a Narrative of Travel, Residence, and Experience in the Roman States*, London, 1871.
52. William Michael Rossetti, *Democratic Sonnets*, London, 1907, II, 12 and 15.
53. F. W. Irby, *Italy: Original Poems and Translations*, London, 1868, p. 51.
54. *The Letters of George Meredith*, I, 190.
55. *The Complete Works of Algernon Charles Swinburne*, the Bonchurch edition, ed. Sir Edmund Gosse and Thomas James Wise, London, 1925–27, II, 119–22.

56. *The Complete Works of Algernon Charles Swinburne*, the Bonchurch edition, ed. Sir Edmund Gosse and Thomas James Wise, London, 1925–27, II, 361.
57. Georges Lafourcade, *La Jeunesse de Swinburne (1837–1867)*, Paris, 1928, I, 187.
58. Mrs. Harriet Eleanor Baillie Hamilton King, *Aspromonte and Other Poems*, London, 1869, pp. 71–74.
59. *The Complete Works of Algernon Charles Swinburne*, II, 362.
60. *The Athenaeum*, March 5, 1870, pp. 319–20.
61. Mrs. Eleanor Darby, *Legends of Many Lands; Sonnets, Songs, and Other Poems*, London, 1870, p. 149.
62. Gerald Massey, *My Lyrical Life: Poems Old and New*, 2nd series, London, 1889, pp. 127–28.
63. *Ibid.*, p. 128.
64. Alexander Mackie, *Italy and France. An Editor's Holiday*, London, 1874, p. 65.
65. [Charles Edward Mudie], "The Tricolor in Naples. May 1859," *Stray Leaves*, 2nd edition, [London?], 1872, pp. 39–47.
66. Mrs. Hamilton King, *Letters and Recollections of Mazzini*, ed. G. M. Trevelyan, London 1912, p. 105.
67. Ernest Myers, *The Defence of Rome and Other Poems*, London and Oxford, 1880.
68. W. M. Rossetti, *op. cit.*, II, 18.
69. William Michael Rossetti, *Dante Gabriel Rossetti: His Family-Letters . . .*, London, 1895, II, 369.
70. Morley, *op. cit.*, II, 109.
71. George Meredith, *The Poetical Works*, ed. G. M. Trevelyan, London, 1912, pp. 562–64.
72. Franz Mehring, *Karl Marx: The Story of His Life*, tr. Edward Fitzgerald, London, 1935, p. 495.

Bibliography

I

General and Miscellaneous

Abba, Giuseppe Cesare, *Meditazioni sul Risorgimento*, Turin, 1913.

Letters of Lord Acton to Mary Gladstone, ed. Herbert Paul, London, 1913.

dell'Agostino, Erminia, *Cenni sulla poesia patriottica, popolare e popolareggiante nel Lombardo-veneto, 1847–1866*, Sondrio, Italy, 1921.

Ambrosini, Luigi, *Cronache del Risorgimento e scritti letterari con una introduzione biografica*, Milan, 1931.

Campbell, John George Edward Henry Douglas Sutherland, Ninth Duke of Argyll, *Passages from the Past*, London, 1907, 2 vols.

d'Azeglio, Massimo Taparelli, *Scritti postumi*, Florence, 1872.

Balbo, Cesare, *Le Speranze d'Italia*, Turin, 1920.

Barbiera, Raffaello, "*Un inglese fautore del Risorgimento italiano: John Webb Probyn*," *Rassegna Italo-Britannica*, May 1918, pp. 60–64.

Bayley, Mary Clive, *The Making of Modern Italy*, London, 1919.

Berkeley, George Fitz-Hardinge, *The Irish Battalion in the Papal Army of 1860*, Dublin, 1929.

Berkeley, George Fitz-Hardinge, *Italy in the Making, 1815 to 1846*, Cambridge, England, 1932.

Berkeley, George Fitz-Hardinge and J., *Italy in the Making, June 1846 to 1 January 1848*, London and Cambridge, England, 1936.

Berkeley, George Fitz-Hardinge, "The Mental Development of Italian Nationality, 1815–1848," *The Nineteenth Century and After*, CXXI, 91–102 (January 1937).

Bini, Arturo and Fatini, Giuseppe, *I Canti della patria: la lirica patriottica nella letteratura italiana*, Milan, 1916, 2 vols.

The Diaries of John Bright, ed. R. A. J. Walling, London, 1930.

Brinton, Crane, *English Political Thought in the Nineteenth Century*, London, 1933.

Brinton, Crane, *The Political Ideas of the English Romanticists*, London, 1926.

British Parliamentary Papers (Blue Books), London, 1848–71.

Browning, Oscar, "Italy in the 'Sixties," *Anglo-Italian Review*, II, 253–56, 357–60; III, 78–81, 171–74, 272–74 (1918–19).

The Cambridge History of English Literature, ed. A. W. Ward and A. R. Waller, New York, 1933, 15 vols.

The Cambridge Modern History, ed. A. W. Ward, G. W. Prothero, Stanley Leathes, Cambridge, England, 1902–11, 13 vols.

Carnovale, Luigi, *The Most Tragic Struggle of the Centuries: the Italian Risorgimento*, Chicago, 1929.

Carpi, Leone, *Il Risorgimento italiano: Biografie storico-politiche d'illustri Italiani contemporanei*, Milan, 1884.

Carr, Edward Hallett, *The Romantic Exiles*, London, 1933.

Carter, John and Pollard, Graham, *An Enquiry into the Nature of Certain Nineteenth Century Pamphlets*, London and New York, 1934.

Casella, Maria Elena, "*Il Risorgimento Italiano nella poesia inglese*," *La Rassegna Nazionale*, CXC, 35–53 (Florence, March 1913).

Cazamian, Louis, *Le Roman Social En Angleterre (1830–1850): Dickens—Disraeli—Mrs. Gaskell—Kingsley*, Paris, 1904.

Colombo, Adolfo, *L'Inghilterra nel Risorgimento italiano*, Milan, [1917].

De Sanctis, Francesco, *History of Italian Literature*, ed. Benedetto Croce, tr. Joan Redfern, London, 1932, 2 vols.

De Sanctis, Francesco, *La Letteratura italiana nel secolo XIX*, Naples, 1898.

The Dictionary of National Biography, ed. Sir Leslie Stephen and Sir Sidney Lee, London, 1885–1901, 66 vols.

The Dictionary of National Biography, Second Supplement, ed. Sir Sidney Lee, New York, 1912, 3 vols.

Dizionario del Risorgimento nazionale, ed. Michele Rosi, Milan, 1930–33, 3 vols.

Ehrsam, Theodore G., Deily, Robert H., and Smith, Robert M., *Bibliographies of Twelve Victorian Authors*, New York, 1936.

Enciclopedia Italiana, Milan and Rome, 1929–37, 35 vols.

The Encyclopaedia Britannica, 11th edition, ed. Hugh Chisholm, Cambridge, England, and New York, 1910–11, 29 vols.; 14th edition, ed. J. L. Garvin, London and New York, 1936, 24 vols.

Filippi, Sir Filippo de, *The Relations of the House of Savoy with the Court of England*, London, 1920.

Flamini, Francesco, *A History of Italian Literature* (1265–1907), tr. Evangeline M. O'Connor, with an introduction by W. M. Rossetti, 1907.

Foresti, Eleuterio Felice, *The Fate of the Carbonari: Memoirs of Felice Foresti*, tr. Howard R. Marraro, New York, 1932.

Frost, Thomas, *The Secret Societies of the European Revolution, 1776–1876*, London, 1876, 2 vols.

Gardner, Edmund Garratt, *The National Idea in Italian Literature*, Manchester, 1921.

Gardner, Edmund Garratt, *Italian Literature*, London, 1927.

Garnett, Richard, *A History of Italian Literature*, New York and London, 1928.

Graham, Walter James, *Tory Criticism in the Quarterly Review, 1809–1853*, New York, 1921.

Greenfield, Kent Roberts, "The Historiography of the Risorgimento since 1920," *The Journal of Modern History*, VII, 49–67 (March 1935).

Greville, Charles Cavendish Fulke, *The Greville Memoirs*, ed. Henry Reeve, London, 1888, 8 vols.

Hancock, William Keith, *Ricasoli and the Risorgimento in Tuscany*, London, 1926.

Hanley, Constance, *The Risorgimento in the Works of Landor, Swinburne, Mrs. Browning, and Meredith*, unpublished Columbia University M.A. Thesis, 1927.

Ellis, S. M., *A Mid-Victorian Pepys: The Letters and Memoirs of Sir William Hardman*, London, 1923.

Ellis, S. M., *The Letters and Memoirs of Sir William Hardman, Second Series: 1863–1865*, New York, 1926.

Ellis, S. M., *The Hardman Papers*, a further selection (1865–68) from the Letters and Memoirs of Sir William Hardman, London, 1930.

Holland, Rupert Sargent, *Builders of United Italy*, New York, 1908.

Howells, William Dean, *Modern Italian Poets; Essays and Versions*, New York, 1887.

Johnson, Rossiter, *An Anthology of Italian Authors . . . (1270–1907)*, [New York], 1907.

Johnston, Robert Matteson, *The Napoleonic Empire in Southern Italy and the Rise of the Secret Societies*, London, 1904, 2 vols.

Johnston, Robert Matteson, *The Roman Theocracy and the Republic, 1846–1849*, London, 1901.

Jones, Dora M., "English Writers and the Making of Italy," *The London Quarterly Review*, July 1912, pp. 84–98.

King, Bolton, *A History of Italian Unity. Being a Political History of Italy from 1814 to 1871*, London, 1899, 2 vols.

Longfellow, Henry Wadsworth (editor), *Italy* in *Poems of Places*, Boston, 1876–79, 3 vols.

de Luca, Pasquale, *I Liberatori. Glorie e figure del Risorgimento (1821–1870)*, Bergamo, 1909.

The Oxford Book of Italian Verse, ed. St. John Lucas, Oxford, 1910.

de'Lucchi, Lorna, *An Anthology of Italian Poems, 13th-19th Century*, London, 1922.

Luzio, Alessandro, *Carlo Alberto e Giuseppe Mazzini. Studi e ricerche di storia del Risorgimento*, Turin, 1923.

Luzio, Alessandro, *Garibaldi, Cavour, Verdi. Nuova serie di studi e ricerche sulla storia del Risorgimento*, Turin, 1924.

Maccoby, Simon, *English Radicalism, 1832–1852*, London, 1935.

Machiavelli, Niccolò, *Il Principe*, ed. L. Arthur Burd, with an introduction by Lord Acton, Oxford, 1891.

Machiavelli, Niccolò, *The Prince*, tr. Luigi Ricci, revised by E. R. P. Vincent, London, 1935.

Harris, James Howard, Third Earl of Malmesbury, *Memoirs of an Ex-Minister: An Autobiography*, London, 1884, 2 vols.

Marraro, Howard R., *American Opinion on the Unification of Italy, 1846–1861*, New York, 1932.

Marshall, Roderick, *Italy in English Literature, 1755–1815: Origins of the Romantic Interest in Italy*, New York, 1934.

Martin, Sir Theodore, *The Life of His Royal Highness the Prince Consort*, London, 1875–80, 5 vols.

Martinengo-Cesaresco, Countess Evelyn, *Italian Characters in the Epoch of Unification*, London, 1901.

Martinengo-Cesaresco, Countess Evelyn, *The Liberation of Italy, 1815–1870*, London, 1902.

Masi, Ernesto, *Il Risorgimento italiano*, Florence, 1917, 2 vols.

Masi, Ernesto, *La Storia del Risorgimento nei Libri*, Bologna, 1911.

Mayer, Gustav, *Friedrich Engels: A Biography*, London, 1936.

McClellan, George Brinton, *Modern Italy: A Short History*, Princeton, New Jersey, 1933.

Mead, William Edward, "Italy in English Poetry," *Publication of the Modern Language Association*, XXIII, 421–70 (1908).

Mehring, Franz, *Karl Marx: The Story of His Life*, tr. Edward Fitzgerald, New York, 1935.

von Metternich-Winneburg, Clemens Wenzeslaus Nepomuk Lothar, *Memoirs of Prince Metternich*, tr. Mrs. Alexander Napier, London, 1880–82, 5 vols.

Miles, Alfred H. (editor), *The Poets and the Poetry of the Century*, London, [1891], 10 vols.

Molesworth, William Nassau, *The History of England from the Year 1830–1874*, London, 1874, 3 vols.

Early Life and Letters of John Morley, ed. Francis W. Hirst, London, 1927, 2 vols.

Morley, John, *Recollections*, London, 1917, 2 vols.

Pasolini, Pietro Desiderio dall'Onda, *Memoir of Count Giuseppe Pasolini*, tr. and abridged by the Dowager Countess of Dalhousie, London, 1885.

Pons, Amilda A., *The Holocaust: Italy's Struggle with the Hapsburg*, London, 1919.

Prezzolini, Giuseppe, *Repertorio bibliografico della Storia e della Critica della Letteratura italiana dal 1902 al 1932*, Rome, 1936, Vol. I (A–L).

Probyn, John Webb, *Italy: From the Fall of Napoleon I, in 1815, to the Death of Victor Emmanuel, in 1878*, London, 1884.

Vincent, Charles W., *Catalogue of the Library of the Reform Club, etc.*, London, 1894.

Reform Club, *Catalogue of Panizzi Pamphlets*, London, 1920.

Rodd, Sir Rennell, "English Poets on the Italian Risorgimento," *Rassegna Italo-Britannica*, May 1918, pp. 5–8.

Salis Schwabe, Mrs., *Reminiscences of Richard Cobden*, London, 1895.

Schauffler, Robert Haven, *Through Italy with the Poets*, New York, 1908.

Schuyler, Eugene, *Italian Influences*, New York, 1901.

Scott, Sir Walter, *Life of Napoleon*, in *Miscellaneous Works*, Edinburgh, 1870–82, 30 vols. (Vols. 8–16).

Shields, Nancy Catchings, *Italian Translations in America*, New York, 1931.

Spellanzon, Cesare, *Storia del Risorgimento e dell'Unità d'Italia*, Milan, 1933–34, 2 vols.

Stillman, W. J., *The Union of Italy, 1815–1895*, new edition, revised, with an epilogue by G. M. Trevelyan, London, 1909.

von Stockmar, Baron E., *Memoirs* (of Baron Christian Friedrich von Stockmar), ed. F. Max Müller, London, 1872, 2 vols.

Taylor, A. J. P., *The Italian Problem in European Diplomacy, 1847–1849*, Manchester, 1934.

Thayer, William Roscoe, *The Dawn of Italian Independence: Italy from the Congress of Vienna, 1814, to the Fall of Venice, 1849*, Boston, 1893, 2 vols.

Thayer, William Roscoe, *Italica: Studies in Italian Life and Letters*, Boston, 1908.

Tivaroni, Carlo, *Storia critica del Risorgimento italiano, 1735–1870*, Turin and Rome, 1888–97, 9 vols.

Trail, Florence, *An Italian Anthology*, Boston, 1926.

Trevelyan, George Macaulay, *English Songs of Italian Freedom*, London, 1911.

Trevelyan, George Macaulay, *Manin and the Venetian Revolution of 1848*, London, 1923.

Trevelyan, Janet Penrose, *A Short History of the Italian People*, 3rd edition, revised and enlarged, London, 1929.

Tutwiler, jun., Carrington C., *Reflections of the Early Risorgimento in Contemporary Victorian Literature*, unpublished Ph.D. dissertation, Princeton, 1934.

Van Horne, John, *Il Risorgimento*, Chicago, 1922.

Vernon, William Warren, *Recollections of Seventy-two Years*, London, 1917.

Forester, Cecil Scott, *Victor Fmmanuel II and the Union of Italy*, London, 1927.

Godkin, G. S., *Life of Victor Emmanuel II, First King of Italy*, London, 1879, 2 vols.

Visconti di Modrone, Guido Carlo, *England and Italy. An Historical Survey of a Great Friendship*, [London], 1932.

Visconti Venosta, Giovanni, *Memoirs of Youth: Things Seen and Known, 1847–1860*, London, 1914.

Wellesley, Arthur, First Duke of Wellington, *Supplementary Despatches, Correspondence, and Memoranda*, London, 1862–65, Vols. IX–XII.

Whitaker, Tina Scalia, *Sicily and England: Political and Social Reminiscences, 1848–1870*, London, 1907.

Wicks, Margaret C. W., *The Italian Exiles in London, 1816–1848*, Manchester, 1937.

Wollaston, George Hyde, *The Englishman in Italy: Being a Collection of Verses Written by Some of Those Who Have Loved Italy*, Oxford, 1909.

Young, George Malcolm (editor), *Early Victorian England, 1830–1865*, London, 1934, 2 vols.

II

Contemporary Biography, History, Pamphleteering, and Periodical Writing: A Chronological Record

Fox, Henry Richard Vassall, Third Baron Holland, *Letter to a Neapolitan from an Englishman*, London, 1818. Reprinted as *Sketch of a Constitution for the Kingdom of Naples, Suggested in 1815 to the Duca di Gallo*, London 1848.

Hobhouse, John Cam, First Baron Broughton, "Essay on the Present Literature of Italy," *Historical Illustrations of the Fourth Canto of "Childe Harold,"* 2nd edition, London, 1818.

"General Reflections Suggested by Italy, Seen in the Years 1818 and 1819," *The London Magazine*, January 1820, pp. 3–7.

[Eastlake, Sir Charles], *Memoirs of the Secret Societies of the South of Italy, Particularly the Carbonari*, London, 1821.

Morgan, Lady (Sydney Owenson), *The Life and Times of Salvator Rosa*, London, 1824, 2 vols.

[Benefit concert for Spanish and Italian refugees], *The Athenaeum*, April 8, 1829, pp. 220–21.

d'Azeglio, Massimo Taparelli, *The Present Movement in Italy*, tr. F[ortunato] P[randi], London, 1847.

Stanford, John Frederick, *The Patriots of Italy: An Appeal in their Behalf*, London, August 1847.

d'Azeglio, Massimo Taparelli, *Austrian Assassinations in Lombardy*, tr. Fortunato Prandi, London, 1848.

de Boni, Filippo, *Lo Straniero in Lombardia*, Losanna, 1848.

Bowyer, Sir George, *Lombardy, the Pope, and Austria*, London, 1848.

[*Letter to Lord Palmerston. Dated London, 25 April, 1848.*]

Granville, A. B., *The Italian Question. A second Letter to Lord Palmerston . . . with a refutation of certain misrepresentations by Lord Brougham, Mr. D'Israeli, and the "Quarterly Review," respecting the rights of Austria and the Lombardo-Venetians*, London, October 1848.

The Italian Question. A Very Humble Remonstrance to the Right Honourable Lord Brougham. By a Sardinian, London, 1848.

[*Miscellanee Politiche Genovesi*], Genoese political poetry, etc., Genoa, 1848 (British Museum, 804. k. 13).

[*A number of broadsides relating principally to political events in Naples and in Sicily*], 1848 (British Museum, 1851. c. 26).

Whiteside, James, *Italy in the Nineteenth Century, Contrasted with Its Past Condition*, 1st edition, London, 1848, 3 vols.

Stapleton, Miles Thomas, Eighth Baron Beaumont, *Austria and Central Italy*, London, 1849.

Brougham, Henry, Baron Brougham and Vaux, *Lord Brougham's Speech on Foreign Affairs, in the House of Lords, July 20, 1849*, London, 1849.

Foster, M. E., *A Hand-Book of Modern European Literature, for the use of schools and private families*, London, 1849.

MacFarlane, Charles, *A Glance at Revolutionized Italy . . . in the Summer of 1848*, London, 1849, 2 vols.

Sicily and England. A Sketch of events in Sicily in 1812 and 1848, illustrated by vouchers and state papers, London, 1849.

Cochrane, Alexander Baillie, *Young Italy*, London, 1850.

Fox, Henry Richard Vassall, Third Baron Holland, *Foreign Reminiscences*, London, 1850.

Pasqualino, the Marchesa, *Letters from Sicily: containing some account of the political events in that island, during the spring of 1849*, ed. W. H. [Charlton], London, July 1850.

Rome in 1848–49, [London, 1850].

Aiton, John, *Letter to the Right Hon. Lord Palmerston . . . on the political imprisonments and present condition of Naples*, Edinburgh, 1851.

Dandolo, Emilio, *The Italian Volunteers and Lombard Rifle Brigade . . .*, tr. R. M., London, 1851.

Military Events in Italy, 1848–1849, tr. from the German by the Earl of Ellesmere, London, 1851.

Nicolini, Giovanni Battista (of Rome, deputy to the Tuscan Constituent Assembly), *The History of the Pontificate of Pius the Ninth*, Edinburgh, 1851.

Venice, a brief history, London, 1851.

Casto, Dr. Julius, *Italy and the Italian Question*, London, 1852.

["Piedmont"], *The Edinburgh Review*, XCVI, 36–54 (July 1852).

Honan, Michael Burke, *The Personal Adventures of "Our Own Correspondent" in Italy*, London, 1852, 2 vols.

Stapleton, Miles Thomas, Eighth Baron Beaumont, *France and Austria in Central Italy*, London, 1852.

Vane, Charles William Stewart, Viscount Castlereagh, Third Marquess of Londonderry, *Correspondence, Despatches, and Other Papers*, London, 1853, 4 vols.

Constitutionalist, A, *Southern Italy, As It Now Is*, London, 1853.

Foster, Margaret E., *Italian Literature*, Edinburgh, 1853.

Wrightson, Richard Heber, *A History of Modern Italy, from the First French Revolution to the Year 1850*, London, 1855.

Bowyer, Sir George, *Rome and Sardinia*, London, 1856. Reprinted from the *Dublin Review*, XXXIX, 164–99 (September 1855).

Litton, Letablère John, *A Voice from History; or, an inquiry as to the Justice, Expediency, and Utility of our Intervention at Naples*, Dublin, October 1856.

Sketches on Italy: Its Last Revolution, Its Actual Condition, Its Tendencies and Hopes, London, 1856.

"State of Parties in Italy since 1848," *The Westminster Review*, January 1857, pp. 98–133.

"Naples and Diplomatic Intervention," *The Westminster Review*, July 1857, pp. 186–213.
Colletta, Pietro, *History of the Kingdom of Naples*, tr. and supplemented by Susan Horner, Edinburgh, 1858, 2 vols.
Dawbarn, Miss Elizabeth, *Naples and King Ferdinand*, London, 1858.
Wiseman, Nicholas Patrick Stephen, Cardinal, *Recollections of the Last Four Popes and of Rome in their Times*, London, 1858.
English Liberal, An, *Italy: Its Condition. Great Britain: Its Policy. A Series of Letters Addressed to Lord John Russell, M.P.*, London, February 1859.
"The Italian Question," *The Westminster Review*, April 1859, pp. 444–86.
Harris, James Howard, Third Earl of Malmesbury, *Official Correspondence on the Italian Question*, January–May 1859, London, 1859.
"The Roman Question," *The Westminster Review*, July 1859, pp. 186–214.
"Austrian Interventions," *The Westminster Review*, July 1859, pp. 215–42.
M.P., An, *Observations on the Negotiations Respecting the Affairs of Italy*, London, July 1859.
"The Massacre of Perugia," *Dublin Review*, September 1859, pp. 168–264.
"Modern Poets and Poetry of Italy," *The Westminster Review*, October 1859, pp. 427–56.
"Bonapartism in Italy," *The Westminster Review*, October 1859, pp. 526–66.
Tuscany Da Sé. An Ower True Tale, London, October 1859.
Lushington, Franklin, "The Crisis of Italian Freedom," *Macmillan's Magazine*, I, 55–63 (November 1859).
About, Edmond François Valentin, *The Roman Question*, tr. H. C. Coape, London, 1859.
d'Azeglio, Roberto, *The Court of Rome and the Gospel*, tr., with a preface, by A. H. Layard, London, 1859.
English Liberal, An, *Napoleon III in Italy*, London, [1859].
A Few Words About the Italian Question, London, 1859.
Fyers, William Augustus, *The Italian Crisis. A Letter Addressed to . . . Parliament and to the British Nation*, London, 1859.
Germany and Italy, 2nd enlarged edition, translated from the German, London, 1859.
Gibson, Edward, *The Future of Italy*, Dublin, 1859.
Gretton, Amelia L. V., *The Vicissitudes of Italy, since the Congress of Vienna*, London, 1859.
The Italian Cause: its History and its Hopes. Italy's Appeal to a Free Nation, London, 1859.
[Lance, Adolphus], *The History of the Italian Peninsula, commencing with the fall of Venice*, London and Leipzig, [1859–62], 2 vols. Printed in 36 shilling parts, with illustrations.
Man in Manchester, A, *Napoleon III and Italy. What Will Be Done and Why*, London, 1859.
[Manning, Miss Anne], *The Story of Italy*, London, 1859.
Mapei, Camillo, *Italy, Classical, Historical, and Picturesque*, 1st edition, tr. David Dundas Scott, Glasgow, 1859.

Nolan, Edward Henry, *The War in Italy, etc.*, London, [1859]. Unfinished. Planned to appear in monthly parts. Only Part I.

Phipps, Constantine Henry, First Marquess of Normanby, *Speech . . . in the House of Lords . . . June 7th, 1859 . . . with an Appendix on Italian Affairs*, London, 1859.

Strafforello, Gustavo, *L'Italia nei canti dei poeti stranieri contemperanei*, Turin, 1859.

Urquhart, David, *Mr. Urquhart on the Italian War . . .*, London, 1859.

The War in Italy. From Drawings by Carlo Bossoli with a Descriptive Narrative by the Author of "The Times" Letters from the Allied Camp, London, 1859.

Ward, H. M., *The Past and Future of the Present Crisis*, London, 1859.

"Italy: the Designs of Louis Napoleon," *The Westminster Review*, January 1860, pp. 218–66.

"Sicily as it Was and Is," *The Westminster Review*, January 1860, pp. 121–67.

Ludlow, J. M., "The 'Idea' of Nationality: Savoy," *Macmillan's Magazine*, I, 354–63 (March 1860).

Hughes, Thomas, "Italy Resurgent and Britain Looking On," *Macmillan's Magazine*, 494–96 (April 1860).

"Manin, and Venice in 1848–9," *The Westminster Review*, April 1860, pp. 363–400.

"The Organization of Italy," *The Westminster Review*, October 1860, pp. 386–410.

Barker, John Sale, "Italian Unity and the National Movement in Europe," *Macmillan's Magazine*, III, 71–80 (November 1860).

Burgess, Rev. Richard, *A City for the Pope: or the Solution of the Roman Question*, London, 1860.

Butt, Isaac, *The History of Italy, from the abdication of Napoleon I, with introductory references to that of earlier times*, London, 1860, 2 vols.

Central Italy and Diplomatic Interference, London, 1860.

England and Napoleon III. The Truth on the Italian Question, London, 1860.

Hoare, Rev. George Tooker, *Notes on North Italy, and the Seat of War in 1850*, London, 1860.

Horner, Susan, *A Century of Despotism in Naples and Sicily*, Edinburgh, 1860.

Italy, the Past and Present, London, 1860.

Salvagnoli, Vincenzo, *The Independence of Italy*, London, 1860.

Whiteside, James, *Italy in the Nineteenth Century*, 2nd edition, revised and abridged, London, 1860.

Wiseman, Nicholas Patrick Stephen, Cardinal, *Pastoral Letter . . . Enjoining a Collection . . . for . . . the Pope*, London, 1860.

"Italy," *The Quarterly Review*, CIX, 133–77 (January 1861).

Macdonnell, R., "Venetia and the Peace of Europe," *Macmillan's Magazine*, III, 235–46 (January 1861).

"The Neapolitan and Roman Questions," *The Westminster Review*, new series, XIX, 114–52 (January 1861).

Waring, George, "Victor Amadeus, the First King of Sardinia," *Macmillan's Magazine*, III, 337–48 (March 1861).

"The Sicilian Revolution," *The Westminster Review*, April 1861, pp. 337–63.

Dicey, Edward, "The Naples Question," *Macmillan's Magazine*, IV, 499–504 (October 1861).

Dicey, Edward, "The Passaglia Phase of the Papal Question," *Macmillan's Magazine*, V, 168–76 (December 1861).

Dicey, Edward, *Rome in 1860*, dedicated to Mr. and Mrs. Robert Browning, Cambridge, England, 1861.

Phipps, Constantine Henry, First Marquess of Normanby, *A Vindication of the Duke of Modena from the Charges of Mr. Gladstone*, London, 1861. A second edition of this pamphlet appeared in 1861, and a French translation was published in Paris in 1862.

Dall'Ongaro, Francesco, *Baron Ricasoli, Prime Minister of Italy*, London, 1861.

Trollope, Theodosia Garrow, *Social Aspects of the Italian Revolution, in a series of letters from Florence, reprinted from the Athenaeum; with a sketch of subsequent events up to the present time*, London, 1861.

Arrivabene, Carlo, *Italy under Victor Emmanuel*, London, 1862, 2 vols.

Martin, Henri, *Daniel Manin and Venice in 1848–49*, tr. Charles Martel, with an introduction by Isaac Butt, London, 1862.

Cartan, Lieutenant-Colonel William, *Eight Letters on the Italian Reformation*, London, [1863].

La Question de Naples et le Parlement Anglais, report of the Commons debate of May 8, 1863, Paris, 1863.

Barker, John Sale, *Two Lectures on Italian Unity and the National Movement in Europe*, London, 1864.

Mapei, Camillo, *Italy, Illustrated and Described . . .*, 2nd edition, with an additional introductory essay by Gavin Carlyle, Glasgow and London, 1864.

The State of Sicily. From the official reports of the debates in the Parliament of Turin, London, 1864.

Mario Alberto, *The Red Shirt*, London, 1865. Reviewed by Anthony Trollope in *The Fortnightly Review*, III, 775–77 (February 1, 1866).

Dicey, Edward, "The Campaign in Italy," *Macmillan's Magazine*, XIV, 241–51 (August 1866).

Wylie, Rev. James Aitken, *The Awakening of Italy and the Crisis of Rome*, London, [1866].

[Conder, Frances Roubiliac], *The Trinity of Italy: or the Pope, the Bourbon, and the Victor*, London, 1867.

du Camp, Maxime, *Orient et Italie; souvenirs de voyage et de lectures*, Paris, 1868.

Probyn, John Webb, *Essays on Italy, Ireland, and the United States of America*, London, 1868.

Maguire, John Francis, *Pontificate of Pius the Ninth*, 3rd edition, London, 1870.

Powell, Joseph, *Two Years in the Pontifical Zouaves, a narrative of Travel, Residence, and Experience in the Roman States*, London, 1871.

Arthur, William, *The Pope, the Kings and the Peoples*, London, 1877, 2 vols.

III

Travels and Guidebooks

The Journal of John Mayne during a tour on the Continent upon its reopening after the fall of Napoleon, 1814, ed. John Mayne Colles, London, 1909.

Frye, William Edward, *After Waterloo: reminiscences of European travel, 1815–1819*, ed. Salomon Reinach, London, 1908.

Beyle, Marie Henri, *Rome, Naples, and Florence, in 1817*, London, 1818.

Sass, Henry, *A Journey to Rome and Naples . . . in 1817*, London, 1818.

Hoare, Sir Richard Colt, *A Classical Tour through Italy and Sicily*, 2nd edition, London, 1819, 2 vols.

Lullin de Chateauvieux, Jacob Frédéric, *Italy, its Agriculture, etc.*, tr. Edward Rigby, Norwich, England, 1819.

Rose, William Stewart, *Letters from the North of Italy. Addressed to Henry Hallam, Esq.*, London, 1819, 2 vols.

Cadell, William Archibald, *A Journey in Carniola, Italy, and France, in the Years 1817, 1818*, Edinburgh, 1820, 2 vols.

Galiffe, Jacques Augustin, *Italy and its Inhabitants; an account of a tour in that country in 1816 and 1817*, London, 1820, 2 vols.

Matthews, Henry, *The Diary of an Invalid; being the Journal of a Tour . . . in Portugal, Italy, Switzerland, and France in the years 1817, 1818, and 1819*, London, 1820.

Monson, William John, Baron Monson, *Extracts from a Journal*, London, 1820.

Starke, Mariana, *Travels on the Continent: written for the use and particular information of travellers*, London, 1820.

Williams, Hugh William, *Travels in Italy, etc.*, Edinburgh, 1820, 2 vols.

Craven, Richard Keppel, *A Tour through the Southern Provinces of the Kingdom of Naples . . . To Which Is Subjoined A Sketch Of The Immediate Circumstances Attending The Late Revolution*, London, 1821.

Morgan, Lady (Sydney Owenson), *Italy*, London, 1821, 3 vols.

Tarchiani, Nello, "Lady Morgan," *Le Vie d'Italia*, Milan, April 1926, pp. 367–78.

Foreign Officer in the British Service, A, [André Vieusseux], *Italy and the Italians in the Nineteenth Century*, London, 1821.

Galignani's Traveller's Guide through Italy . . . compiled from the works of Coxe, Eustace, Forsyth, Reichard, etc., 6th edition, Paris, 1822.

Sherer, Joseph Moyle, *Scenes and Impressions in Egypt and in Italy*, London, 1824.

Stanley, Arthur Penrhyn, *The Life and Correspondence of Thomas Arnold*, 10th edition, London, 1877, 2 vols. Thomas Arnold had travelled in Italy at various times from 1825 to 1840.

[Beste, John Richard Digby], *Transalpine Memoirs; or, Anecdotes and Observations, Shewing the Actual State of Italy and the Italians*, Bath, England, 1826, 2 vols.

Hazlitt, William, *Notes of a Journey through France and Italy*, London, 1826. *The Complete Works of William Hazlitt*, Centenary Edition, ed. P. P. Howe, London, 1930–34, 21 vols.

Jameson, Anna Brownell, *Diary of an Ennuyée*, London, 1826.

Erskine, Mrs. Steuart, *Anna Jameson: Letters and Friendships* (1812–1860), London, 1915.

Beste, Henry Digby, *Italy As It Is; or, Narrative of an English Family's Residence for Three Years in That Country*, London, 1828.

Simond, Louis, *A Tour in Italy and Sicily*, London, 1828.

Duppa, Richard, *Travels in Italy, Sicily, and the Lipari Islands*, 1st edition, London, 1828.

Duppa, Richard, *Travels on the Continent, Sicily, and the Lipari Islands*, 2nd edition, London, 1829.

Robinson, Henry Crabb, *Diary, Reminiscences, and Correspondence*, ed. Thomas Sadler, Boston, 1869, 2 vols. Robinson had travelled in Italy from 1829 to 1831, and with Wordsworth in 1837.

Morley, Edith J., *The Correspondence of Henry Crabb Robinson with the Wordsworth Circle*, Oxford, 1927, 2 vols.

Sinclair, J. D., *An Autumn in Italy, being a personal narrative of a tour in the Austrian, Tuscan, Roman and Sardinian States, in* 1827, Edinburgh, 1829.

Cobbett, James Paul, *Journal of a Tour in Italy, and also in part of France and Switzerland; . . . from October, 1828, to September, 1829*, London, 1830.

Conder, Josiah, *Italy*, London, 1831, 3 vols.

Johnson, James, *Change of Air, or the Diary of a Philosopher in pursuit of health and recreation*, London, 1831.

Linton, William, *Sketches in Italy . . .*, London, 1832.

Roscoe, Thomas, *The Tourist in Italy*, [London?], 1832–33, 2 vols.

Tobin, J. J., *Journal of a Tour . . . in . . . 1828–29, through Syria, Carniola, and Italy, whilst accompanying the late Sir Humphry Davy*, London, 1832.

[Carne, John], *Letters from Switzerland and Italy, during a late Tour*, 1st edition, London, 1834.

Carne, John, *The Journal of a Tour through Switzerland and Italy*, 2nd edition, London, 1840.

Brockedon, William, *Road-Book, from London to Naples*, London, 1835.

Herbert, Charles, *Italy and Italian Literature*, London, 1835.

Thomson, William, *Two Journeys through Italy and Switzerland*, London, 1835.

Craven, Richard Keppel, *Excursions in the Abruzzi and Northern Provinces of Naples*, London, 1838, 2 vols.

Taylor, Sir Herbert, "Notes," *The Taylor Papers*, London, 1913. Travels in 1838.

Gardiner, Marguerite P. F., Countess of Blessington, *The Idler in Italy*, London, 1839–40, 3 vols.

von Raumer, Friedrich Ludwig Georg, *Italy and the Italians*, London, 1840, 2 vols.

White, Thomas Henry, *Fragments of Italy and the Rhineland*, London, 1841.

Laing, Samuel, *Notes of a Traveller on the social and political state of France, Prussia, Switzerland, Italy, and other parts of Europe, during the present century*, London, 1842, 2 vols.

Trollope, Mrs. Frances M., *A Visit to Italy*, London, 1842, 2 vols.

Shelley, Mrs. Mary W. Godwin, *Rambles in Germany and Italy in 1840, 1842, and 1843*, London, 1844, 2 vols.

Yates, Mrs. F. M. L., *A Winter In Italy; in a series of letters to a friend*, London, 1844, 2 vols.

Griffith, Lucinda Darby, *A Journey across the Desert . . . comprising sketches of Aden . . . Malta, Sicily and Italy*, London, 1845, 2 vols.

Stisted, Clotilda Elizabeth, *Letters from the Bye-ways of Italy*, London, 1845.

Costello, Louisa Stuart, *A Tour to and from Venice by the Vaudois and the Tyrol*, London, 1846.

Francis, J. G., *Notes from a Journal Kept in Italy and Sicily . . . 1844–46*, London, 1847.

Gardiner, William, *Sights in Italy, with some account of the present state of music and the sister arts in that country*, Leicester, England, 1847.

Butler, Mrs. Frances Anne Kemble, *A Year of Consolation*, London, 1847, 2 vols.

Kemble, Frances Anne, *Record of a Girlhood*, London, 1878–79, 3 vols.

Savonarola, Don Jeremy [Francis Sylvester Mahony], *Facts and Figures from Italy . . . addressed . . . to Charles Dickens, Esq., being an appendix to his "Pictures,"* London, 1847.

Buckingham, James Silk, *France, Piedmont, Italy, Lombardy, the Tyrol, and Bavaria: an Autumnal Tour*, London, 1848, 2 vols.

Geale, Hamilton, *Notes of a Two Years' Residence in Italy*, Dublin, 1848.

Townsend, George, *Journal of a Tour in Italy, in 1850, with an account of an interview with the Pope at the Vatican*, London, 1850.

Beldam, Joseph, *Recollections of Scenes and Institutions in Italy and the East*, London, 1851, 2 vols.

Aiton, John, *The Lands of the Messiah, Mahomet, and the Pope; as Visited in 1851*, 2nd edition, London, 1852.

Baxter, William Edward, *The Tagus and the Tiber; or, Notes of Travel in Portugal, Spain, and Italy, in 1850–1*, London, 1852, 2 vols.

Gregorovius, Ferdinand, *The Roman Journals . . . 1852–1874*, tr. Mrs. Gustavus W. Hamilton, London, 1907.

Letters from Italy and Vienna, Cambridge, England, 1852.

Hillard, George Stillman, *Six Months in Italy*, London, 1853, 2 vols.

von Rochau, August Ludwig, *Wanderings through the Cities of Italy in 1850 and 1851*, tr. Mrs. Percy Sinnett, London, 1853, 2 vols.

Chamier, Frederick, *My Travels; or an unsentimental journey through France, Switzerland, and Italy*, London, 1855, 3 vols.

Street, George Edmund, *Brick and Marble in the Middle Ages: notes of a tour in the north of Italy*, London, 1855.

Wylie, Rev. James Aitken, *Pilgrimage from the Alps to the Tiber, or the Influence of Romanism on Trade, Justice, and Knowledge*, Edinburgh, 1855.

St. John, Bayle, *The Subalpine Kingdom; or, Experiences and Studies in Savoy, Piedmont, and Genoa*, London, 1856, 2 vols.

Forester, Thomas, *Rambles in the islands of Corsica and Sardinia, etc.*, 1st edition, London, 1858.

Kavanagh, Julia, *A Summer and Winter in the two Sicilies*, London, 1858, 2 vols.

Hobhouse, John Cam, First Baron Broughton, *Italy: Remarks made in several visits from the year 1816 to 1854*, London, 1859–61, 2 vols.

"Extracts from the Journal of an Englishwoman at Naples," *Macmillan's Magazine*, III, 152–60 (December 1860).

Gretton, Mrs. G., *The Englishwoman in Italy: impressions of life in the Roman States and Sardinia, during a ten years' residence*, London, 1860, 2 vols.

Bremer, Fredrika, *Two Years in Switzerland and Italy*, tr. Mary Howitt, London, 1861, 2 vols.

Catlow, Agnes; and Catlow, Maria E., *Sketching Rambles; or, Nature in the Alps and the Apennines*, London, 1861, 2 vols.

Costello, Dudley, *Piedmont and Italy from the Alps to the Tiber, Illustrated in a Series of Views Taken on the Spot*, London, 1861, 2 vols.

Crichton, Kate, *Six Years in Italy*, London, 1861, 2 vols.

Forester, Thomas, *The Island of Sardinia: with remarks on its resources, and its relations to British interests in the Mediterranean. Being the preface to the second edition of "Rambles in the islands of Corsica and Sardinia, etc.,"* London, 1861.

Arthur, William, *Italy in Transition: Public Scenes and Private Opinion in the Spring of 1860*, 6th edition, London, 1862.

Grenville, Richard, Duke of Buckingham and Chandos, *Private Diary*, London, 1862, 4 vols.

Chambers, William, *Something of Italy*, London and Edinburgh, 1862.

Mendelssohn-Bartholdy, Felix, *Letters from Italy and Switzerland*, tr. Lady Wallace, London, 1862.

Wordsworth, Christopher, Bishop of Lincoln, *Journal of a Tour in Italy, with Reflections on the Present Condition and Prospects of Religion in that Country*, London, 1863, 2 vols.

Cobbe, Miss Frances Power, *Italics. Brief Notes on politics, people, and places in Italy, in 1864*, London, 1864.

Moens, William J. C., *English Travellers and Italian Brigands. A Narrative of Capture and Captivity*, London, 1866, 2 vols.

[Tuckett, Miss Elizabeth], *Beaten Tracks: or, Pen and Pencil Sketches in Italy*, London, 1866.

[Pearson, Miss Emma], *From Rome to Mentana*, London, 1868.

Ramage, Craufurd Tait, *The Nooks and By-Ways of Italy*, Liverpool, 1868.

Browning, S., *A Holiday Tour; being a Few Weeks Passed Among the Swiss and Italian Lakes*, 2nd edition, London, 1869.

Hawthorne, Mrs. Sophia A. P., *Notes in England and Italy*, New York, 1869.

Maclaren, Charles, *Select Writings . . . of The Late Charles Maclaren*, Edinburgh, 1869, 2 vols.

Sala, George Augustus, *Rome and Venice, with other Wanderings in Italy, in 1866–7*, London, 1869.

Beste, John Richard Digby, *Nowadays: or, Courts, Courtiers, Churchmen, Garibaldians, Lawyers and Brigands, at Home and Abroad*, London, 1870, 2 vols.

Evill, William, *A Winter Journey to Rome and Back, with an account of the opening of the Oecumenical Council, etc.*, London, 1870.

Elliot, Frances Minto, *Diary of an Idle Woman in Italy*, London, 1871.

Senior, Nassau William, *Journals Kept in France and Italy from 1848 to 1852*, London, 1871, 2 vols.

Castelar y Ripoll, Emilio, *Old Rome and New Italy*, tr. Mrs. Arthur Arnold, London, 1873.

Mackie, Alexander, *Italy and France. An Editor's Holiday*, London, 1874.

IV

Italian Patriots and the British

CAMPANELLA, GIUSEPPE MARIA

My Life and what I learnt in it, London, 1874.

Life in the Cloister, in the Papal Court and in exile, London, 1877.

CAVOUR

Cavour e l'Inghilterra, Bologna, 1933, 3 vols.

Count Cavour and Madame de Circourt, ed. Count Nigra, tr. Arthur J. Butler, London, 1894.

Count Cavour's Inedited Letters, and British Diplomacy in 1856, London, 1862.

The Speech of Count Camillo Cavour . . . at the sitting of the 16th April, 1858, on the Proposed Law Relative to Conspiracy Against Foreign Sovereigns . . ., London, 1858.

Acton, John Emerich Edward Dalberg, Baron Acton, *Historical Essays and Studies*, ed. J. N. Figgis and R. V. Laurence, London, 1907.

The Athenaeum, June 29, 1861, pp. 851–55.

Cadogan, Edward, *The Life of Cavour*, London, 1907.

Dicey, Sir Edward, *Cavour. A Memoir*, Cambridge, England, 1861.

Dicey, Sir Edward, "Recollections of Cavour's Last Debate," *Macmillan's Magazine*, IV, 249–56 (July 1861).

The Edinburgh Review, July, 1861, pp. 267–77.

Hansard's Parliamentary Debates, 3rd series, CLXIII, 623–25, 772–78 (June 6–7, 1861).

Lockhart, James, *Cavour. Patria e Gloria. Poem Dedicated to the Sons of Italy*, Florence, 1873.

Martinengo-Cesaresco, Countess Evelyn, *Cavour*, London, 1898.

Orsi, Pietro, *Cavour and the Making of Modern Italy, 1810–1861*, London and New York, 1926.

The Quarterly Review, CX, 208 (July 1861).

Ruffini, Francesco, *L'Insegnamento di Cavour*, Milan, 1916.

The Saturday Review, June 8, 1861, pp. 569–70.

Thayer, William Roscoe, *The Life and Times of Cavour*, Boston and New York, 1911, 2 vols.

The [London] *Times*, June 7, 1861, pp. 8–9; June 10, 1861, p. 9.

Whyte, Arthur James Beresford, *The Early Life and Letters of Cavour*, 1810–1848, London, 1925.

Whyte, Arthur James Beresford, *The Political Life and Letters of Cavour, 1848–1861*, London, 1930.

CRISPI, FRANCESCO

The Memoirs of Francesco Crispi, tr. Mary Prichard-Agnetti, London, 1912, 3 vols.

FOSCOLO, NICCOLÒ UGO

Foscolo, N. U., *Essays on Petrarch*, London, 1823.
——, *Opere edite e postume*, Florence, 1850–99, 12 vols.
Edinburgh Review Articles by Foscolo:
"Dante," XXIX, 453–74 (February 1818).
"Dante," XXX, 317–51 (September 1818).
"Life of Pius VI," XXXI, 271–95 (March 1819).
"Parga," XXXII, 263–93 (October 1819).
"History of the Democratical Constitution of Venice," XLVI, 75–106 (June 1827).
London Magazine Articles by Foscolo:
"Ancient Encaustic Painting of Cleopatra, with an Engraving," May 1826, pp. 65–71.
"Boccaccio," June 1826, pp. 145–57.
"Angeloni on Political Force," (?), June 1826, pp. 231–42.
"The Women of Italy," October 1826, pp. 204–19.
New Monthly Magazine Articles by Foscolo:
"Michel Angelo," IV, 339–47 (1822).
"Frederick the Second, and Pietro delle Vigne," IV, 455–62 (1822).
"Guido Cavalcanti," V, 1–9 (1822).
"The Lyric Poetry of Tasso," V, 373–80 (1822).
Quarterly Review Articles by Foscolo:
"Narrative and Romantic Poems of the Italians," XXI, 486–556 (April 1819).
"State of Female Society in Greece," (?), XXII, 163–203 (July 1819).
"Modern Greece," (?), XXIII, 325–59 (July 1820).
"Pétrarque et Laure," XXIV, 529–66 (January 1821).
"History of the Aeolic Digamma," XXVII, 39–70 (April 1822).
Retrospective Review Article by Foscolo:
"On the Antiquarians and Critics of Italian History," XIV, 136–53 (1826).
Westminster Review Articles by Foscolo:
"Wiffen's *Tasso*," October 1826, pp. 404–45.
"Memoirs of Casanova," April 1827, pp. 400–16.
Foscolo, N. U., *Letters of Ortis*, tr. F. B., 2nd edition, London, 1818.
Ricciarda by Foscolo, reviewed in *Blackwood's Edinburgh Magazine*, XXII, 571–84 (November 1827); in *The Quarterly Review*, XXIV, 90–97 (October 1820).
Foscolo, N. U., "Dei Sepolcri," tr. C., *Tait's Edinburgh Magazine*, XXII, 595–97 (1855).
——, *The Sepulchres*, tr. S. C., [London, 1860?].

The Works of Ugo Foscolo, reviewed in *The Foreign Review, and Continental Miscellany*, II, 410–31 (1828).

Anglomane, "Foscolo and English Hospitality," *Fraser's Magazine*, XXXI, 401–14 (April 1845).

Caraccio, Armand, "*Ugo Foscolo 'comparatiste,'*" *Revue de Littérature Comparée*, Paris, April 1937, pp. 261–98.

Caraccio, Armand, *Ugo Foscolo: L'Homme et le Poète (1778–1827)*, Paris, 1934.

Catalogo dei Monoscritti Foscoliani, Rome, 1885.

Cippico, Antonio, *The Poetry of Ugo Foscolo*, London, 1924.

Copinger, W. A., *On the Authorship of the First Hundred Numbers of the "Edinburgh Review,"* Manchester, 1895.

"Life and Writings of Ugo Foscolo," *The Westminster Review*, April 1851, pp. 237–45.

"Memoir of Ugo Foscolo," *The London Magazine*, October 1827, pp. 238–44.

Noad, A. S., "Ugo Foscolo and Some Englishmen," *University of Toronto Quarterly*, I, 105–22 (October 1931).

Ottolini, Angelo, *Bibliografia Foscoliana*, Florence, 1921.

Ugo Foscolo nel centenario del suo insegnamento all'Università di Pavia, 1809–1909, Pavia, 1910.

Pecchio, Giuseppe, *Vita di Ugo Foscolo*, Lugano, 1830. Reviewed in *The New Monthly Magazine*, XXXIV, 153–68 (1832).

Picciotto, James, "Ugo Foscolo and His Age," *Dublin University Magazine*, LXXVIII, 87–98 (July 1871).

Purves, John, "Macready and Ugo Foscolo," letter to *The* [London] *Times Literary Supplement*, August 17, 1933, p. 549.

The Quarterly Review, XXIV, 101 (January 1822).

Redding, Cyrus, *Fifty Years' Recollections, Literary and Personal, with Observations of Men and Things*, London, 1858, 3 vols.

The Journal of Sir Walter Scott, Edinburgh, 1890, 2 vols.

"To Ugo Foscolo," a poem, *The New Monthly Magazine*, II, 453 (1821),

"Ugo Foscolo," *North American Review*, XCI, 213–58 (July 1860).

Viglione, Francesco, *Ugo Foscolo in Inghilterra*, Catania, 1910.

Vincent, E. R., "An Attack on Foscolo," *The Modern Language Review* XXXII, 441–45 (London, July 1937).

GALLENGA, ANTONIO CARLO NAPOLEONE (ALSO KNOWN AS LUIGI MARIOTTI)

Gallenga, A. C. N., *Italy: General Views of Its History and Literature*, London, 1841, 2 vols.

——, *The Blackgown Papers*, London, 1846, 2 vols.

——, "The Spirit of Dante," *The New Monthly Magazine*, LXXX, 1–19 (May 1847).

——, "The Casino," *The New Monthly Magazine*, LXXX, 253–68 (July 1847).

Gallenga, A. C. N., *Latest News from Italy*, London, 1847.
——, *Italy, Past and Present*, London, 1848, 2 vols.
——, *Present State and Prospects of Italy*, London, 1848.
——, *Scenes from Italian Life*, London, 1850.
——, *Italy in* 1848, London, 1851.
——, *Castellamonte; an autobiographical sketch illustrative of Italian life during the insurrection of 1831*, 1st edition, London, 1854, 2 vols. A second edition appeared in 1856.
——, *History of Piedmont*, London, 1855, 3 vols.
——, *Country Life in Piedmont*, London, 1858.
——, *The Pope and the King; the War between Church and State in Italy*, London, 1879, 2 vols.

GARIBALDI, GIUSEPPE

Garibaldi, G., *Autobiography*, authorized translation by A. Werner, with a supplement by Jessie White Mario, London, 1889, 3 vols.
——, *Memoirs*, ed. Alexander Dumas, tr. R. S. Garnett, London, 1931.
——, *The Rule of the Monk; or, Rome in the Nineteenth Century*, London, [1870], 2 vols. Reviewed in *The Athenaeum*, March 5, 1870, pp. 319–20.
——, "Translation of the *Inno Romano*, Written by Garibaldi for the Emancipators of Rome," *The Athenaeum*, October 26, 1867, p. 537.
Hugo, Victor; and Garibaldi, Giuseppe, *Political Poems by Victor Hugo and Garibaldi. Done into English by an Oxford Graduate* [Sir Edwin Arnold], London, 1868. George Jacob Holyoake wrote the preface.
Adams, Henry, *The Education of Henry Adams*, Boston and New York, 1918.
The Athenaeum, April 16, 1864, p. 535; July 30, 1864, p. 147. On Garibaldi's visit to England.
Bicknell, Algernon Sidney, *In the Track of the Garibaldians through Italy and Sicily*, London, 1861.
Braddon, Miss Mary Elizabeth, *Garibaldi and Other Poems*, London, 1861.
Chambers, O. W. S., *Garibaldi and Italian Unity*, London, 1864.
Chesterton, G. K., *Letters to an Old Garibaldian*, London, 1915.
Clark, Mary Cowden, "The Battle of Melazzo," a poem, *The Athenaeum* September 22, 1860, p. 384.
Clark, W. G., "Naples and Garibaldi," pp. 1–75 of *Vacation tourists and Notes of Travel in 1860*, ed. Sir Francis Galton, London, 1861.
Cooper, R. Jermyn, *Three letters to the Conservatives of England . . . on the subject of Garibaldi and revolution*, London, 1864.
[Davis], Rosalind, *Garibaldi, or The Rival Patriots, a Drawing Room Operetta, in Two Acts*, with music by H. Frederick Cowen, London, 1860.
Dobell, Sydney, "The Youth of England to Garibaldi's Legion," a poem, *Macmillan's Magazine*, II, 324–28 (August 1860).
The Drapeau Rouge. Chants from Britain in greeting to Giuseppe Garibaldi and his companions in arms, dedicated to Mazzini, London, 1861.

Drinkwater, John, *Garibaldi: A Chronicle Play of Italian Freedom in Ten Scenes*, London, 1936.

The Dublin Review, July 1864, pp. 132–55. On Garibaldi's visit to England.

Exalbion, Colonel, *Garibaldi: his Life, Exploits, and the Italian Campaigns* London, [1859].

Forbes, Sir Charles Stuart, Third Baronet, *The Campaign of Garibaldi in the Two Sicilies; A Personal Narrative*, London and Edinburgh, 1861.

Frischauer, Paul, *Garibaldi—The Man and the Nation*, London, 1935.

"Garibaldi and the Italian Volunteers," *The Westminster Review*, October 1859, pp. 478–503.

Garibaldi: his career and exploits. Reprinted with additions from the "Morning Star" of April 2, 1864; with a descriptive narrative of the hero's reception at Southampton . . ., London, 1864.

"Garibaldi's Retirement," a sonnet, *Macmillan's Magazine*, III, 160 (December 1860).

Guerzoni, Giuseppe, *Garibaldi*, Florence, 1882, 2 vols.

Hamilton, Scott, *Garibaldi; or, the Hero of Italy: a Grand Dramatic Ovation to "The Hero of the Age,"* a prose play, Belfast, [1864?].

Huch, Ricarda, *Garibaldi and the New Italy*, New York, 1928–29, 2 vols.

The illustrated life and career of Garibaldi: containing full details of his conduct . . ., London, [1860].

James, J. Kingston, "To Garibaldi," a poem, *Fraser's Magazine*, May 1864, pp. 625–26.

Larg, David, *Giuseppe Garibaldi: a Biography*, London, 1934.

The Life of Garibaldi, including his career in South America, Rome, Piedmont and Lombardy; with full particulars of the Landing at Marsala and the Sicilian Campaign; his triumphant Entry into Naples; his Residence at Caprera; and the Disaster at Aspromonte . . ., London, 1864.

Manchester Foreign Affairs Association, *English Aid to Garibaldi, on his invasion of the Sicilies. Is it lawful and just?*, Manchester, 1860.

Manning, Henry Edward, Cardinal, *The Visit of Garibaldi to England. A letter to the Right Hon. E. Cardwell, etc.*, London, 1864.

Marsh, John B., *The Life and Adventures of Garibaldi, the Apostle of Liberty*, Manchester, [1861].

Mundy, Rear-Admiral Sir George Rodney, *H.M.S. "Hannibal" at Palermo and Naples, during the Italian Revolution, 1859–1861*, London, 1863.

Nolan, Edward Henry, *The Liberators of Italy* . . ., London, [1864].

Notes and Queries, 12th series, XI, 217 (September 9, 1922); 12th series, XI, 238 (September 16, 1922).

Oldknow, Reginald Charles, *Garibaldi in Sicily, or the Adventures of Johnson; and Other Poems*, London, 1861.

Oliphant, Laurence, *Episodes in a Life of Adventure; or, Moss from a Rolling Stone*, Edinburgh and London, 1887.

Powell, James Henry, *Garibaldi, the Prisoner of Spezzia. A Poem*, London, [1862].

Punch on Garibaldi's visit to England:
April 9, 1864, pp. 146 and 149.
"Rome: Naples: London. The Welcomes of Garibaldi," a poem, April 23, 1864, pp. 168–69.
"On a Snob," a poem, April 23, 1864, p. 174.
April 30, 1864, p. 181.

Reid, Mayne (Captain), *Garibaldi rebuked by one of his best friends, etc.*, London, 1864.

Saffi, Aurelio, "Garibaldi and the Sicilian Revolution," *Macmillan's Magazine*, II, 235–44 (July 1860).

[von Schwartz, Baroness M. E.], *Recollections of General Garibaldi . . . etc.*, tr. E. Field, London, 1861.

S[medley], Miss M. [B.], *Garibaldi. Why we welcome him*, verse, London, 1864.

Stiavelli, G., *Garibaldi nella letteratura italiana*, Rome, 1901.

Taylor, Tom, review in *The Athenaeum*, October 29, 1859, p. 571, of Taylor's dramatization of Garibaldi's life.

The [London] *Times* on Garibaldi's visit to England in 1864:
March 24th, pp. 8 and 9.
March 29th, p. 4.
April 1st, p. 9.
April 5th, p. 11.
April 7th, p. 14.
April 8th, p. 12.
April 9th, p. 14.
April 11th, pp. 8 and 12.
April 12th, pp. 9 and 12.
April 14th, p. 14.
April 15th, p. 9.
April 16th, p. 11.
April 18th, p. 9.
April 19th, p. 11.
April 20th, pp. 9 and 12.
April 21st, p. 14.
April 22nd, pp. 7, 11, 10–11.
April 23rd, p. 11.
April 25th, p. 11.
April 28th, p. 7.

Trevelyan, George Macaulay, *Garibaldi's Defence of the Roman Republic*, London, 1907.

Trevelyan, George Macaulay, *Garibaldi and the Thousand*, London, 1909.

Trevelyan, George Macaulay, *Garibaldi and the Making of Italy*, London, 1911.

Vecchi, C. Augusto, *Garibaldi at Caprera*, with a preface by Mrs. Gaskell, London, 1862.

Weston, James, *General Garibaldi at Fishmongers' Hall*, [London], May 1864.

GAVAZZI, ALESSANDRO

Gavazzi, A., *Orations by Father Gavazzi*, London, 1851.

——, *Father Gavazzi's Oration, delivered April 5th, 1854, at the Assembly Rooms, Kennington Park, London*, London, [1854].

——, *Gavazzi's Orations: delivered at the Town Hall, Brighton*, Brighton, England, [1855].

——, *The Four Last Popes. A lecture, delivered . . . in reply to "Recollections" by Dr. Wiseman on the same subject*, London, 1857.

——, *Italy for the Italians. An Oration*, London, [1859].

——, *A Scheme for Church and Union in Italy, and its opponents*, London, 1865.

Campanella, Giuseppe Maria, *The Life of Father Gavazzi*, London, 1851.

LACAITA, SIR JAMES

Lacaita, Charles, *An Italian Englishman: Sir James Lacaita, 1813–1895*, London, 1933.

MAZZINI AND THE CARLYLES

William Allingham, A Diary, ed. H. Allingham and D. Radford, London, 1907.

Letters to William Allingham, ed. H. Allingham and E. Baumer Williams, London, 1911.

Carlyle, Jane Welsh, *Letters and Memorials*, ed. James Anthony Froude, London, 1883, 3 vols.

Carlyle, Jane Welsh, *Letters to her Family, 1839–1863*, ed. Leonard Huxley, London, 1924.

Carlyle, Jane Welsh, *New Letters and Memorials*, ed. Alexander Carlyle, with an introduction by Sir James Crichton-Browne, London and New York, 1903, 2 vols.

The Correspondence of Thomas Carlyle and Ralph Waldo Emerson, 1834–1872, ed. Charles Eliot Norton, London, 1883, 2 vols.

Letters of Thomas Carlyle to John Stuart Mill, John Sterling and Robert Browning, ed. Alexander Carlyle, London, 1923.

Carlyle, Thomas, letter to *The* [London] *Times*, June 19, 1844.

Carlyle, Thomas, *New Letters*, ed. Alexander Carlyle, London and New York, 1904, 2 vols.

Carlyle, Thomas, *Reminiscences*, ed. James Anthony Froude, London, 1881, 2 vols.

Carlyle, Thomas, *Reminiscences*, ed. C. E. Norton, London and New York, 1932.

Conway, Moncure Daniel, *Autobiography: Memories and Experiences*, Boston and New York, 1904, 2 vols.

Duffy, Sir Charles Gavan, *Conversations with Carlyle*, New York, 1892.

Froude, James Anthony, *Thomas Carlyle: a history of his life in London, 1834–81*, London, 1884, 2 vols.

Gray, W. Forbes, "Carlyle and John Forster: An Unpublished Correspondence," *The Quarterly Review*, CCLXVIII, 271–87 (April 1937).

Momigliano, Felice, "*Mazzini e Carlyle*," *Rassegna Italo-Britannica*, I, 52–62 (Milan, August 1918).

Nichol, John, *Thomas Carlyle*, London, 1904. "English Men of Letters" series.

Ralli, Augustus, *Guide to Carlyle*, London, 1920, 2 vols.

Wilson, David Alec:

Carlyle Till Marriage (1795–1826), London, 1923.

Carlyle to "The French Revolution" (1826–1837), London, 1924.

Carlyle on Cromwell and Others (1837–48), London, 1925.

Carlyle at His Zenith (1848–53), London, 1927.

Carlyle to Threescore-and-Ten (1853–1865), London, 1931.

Wilson, David Alec; and MacArthur, David Wilson, *Carlyle in Old Age (1865–1881)*, London, 1934.

MAZZINI, JOSEPH

[Mazzini, Joseph], "Mazzini and the Ethics of Politicians," *The Westminster Review*; XLII, 225–51 (September 1844).

Mazzini, J., *Italy, Austria, and the Pope. A Letter to Sir James Graham, Bart.*, London, May 1845.

——, *The People's Journal* (1846): "Attilio and Emilio Bandiera," I, 121–23; "Jacopo Ruffini (1833)," I, 293–94.

——, *Royalty and Republicanism in Italy; or, Notes and Documents relating to the Lombard Insurrection and to the Royal War of 1848*, London, 1850. Reviewed in *The Edinburgh Review*, January 1851, pp. 33–71.

——, "Europe: its Condition and Prospects," *The Westminster Review*, April 1852, pp. 442–67.

——, *Letter from Signor Mazzini to Mr. G. J. Holyoake*, [London, June 1852].

——, *Two Letters to the People of England on the* [Crimean] *war*, London, 1855.

——, *Mazzini's letters to D. Manin . . . on the Theory of the Dagger . . . the Piedmontese Question . . . the Case of Italy . . .*, London, 1856.

——, *To Louis Napoleon*, 2nd edition, London, 1858.

——, *The Late Genoese Insurrection Defended*, London, 1858.

——, *The Italian Question and the Republicans*, London, March 1861.

——, *The Duties of Man*, tr. Mme. E. A. Venturi, London, 1862.

——, "On Caesarism," *Macmillan's Magazine*, XII, 259–66 (July 1865).

——, "A Letter to the Members of the Oecumenical Council. *From the Council to God*," *The Fortnightly Review*, XIII, 725–51 (June 1, 1870).

——, "Italy and the Republic," *The Fortnightly Review*, March 1, 1871, pp. 289–309.

——, *The War and the Commune*, London, 1871.

Mazzini, J., "Mazzini on the Eastern Question," *The Fortnightly Review*, XXVII, 559–79 (April 1, 1877). Two articles translated by Mme. E. A. Venturi, with a foreword by James Stansfeld.

——, *Edizione nazionale degli scritti di Giuseppe Mazzini*, Imola, 1906–37, 75 vols.

——, *Life and Writings*, London, 1864–70, 6 vols. First 3 volumes reviewed by C. E. Maurice, *Macmillan's Magazine*, XVI, 54–61 (May 1867).

——, *Essays*, tr. Thomas Okey, ed. Bolton King, London, 1894.

——, *Mazzini's Letters*, tr. Alice de Rosen Jervis, ed. Bolton King, London, 1930.

—— *Mazzini's Letters to an English Family* [the Ashursts], 1844–72, ed. E. F. Richards, London, 1920–22, 3 vols.

Abbott, Evelyn; and Campbell, Lewis, *The Life and Letters of Benjamin Jowett*, London, 1897, 2 vols.

Arias, Gino, "*Les idées économiques et sociales de Giuseppe Mazzini*," *Revue d'Économie Politique*, May 1919, pp. 261–77.

Barr, Stringfellow, *Mazzini: Portrait of an Exile*, New York, 1935. Reviewed by Arthur Livingston in *New York Herald Tribune Books*, October 20, 1935, VII, 8.

Bryce, James, *Modern Democracies*, New York and London, 1921, 2 vols.

Conway, Moncure Daniel, *Mazzini*, [London?, 1872?]. A memorial discourse delivered on March 17, 1872.

Cooper, Thomas, *The Life of Thomas Cooper: written by himself*, London, 1872.

Fletcher, Mrs. Eliza, *Autobiography*, Edinburgh, 1875.

Galimberti, Alice, *Giuseppe Mazzini nel pensiero inglese*, Rome, 1919.

Garrison, William Lloyd, *Joseph Mazzini: His Life, Writings, and Political Principles*, New York, 1872.

Gay, H. Nelson, "*Mazzini e Antonio Gallenga: Apostoli dell'Indipendenza Italiana in Inghilterra*," *Nuova Antologia*, CCLX, 206–22 (Rome, July 16, 1928).

Griffith, Gwilym Oswald, *Mazzini: Prophet of Modern Europe*, London, 1932.

Herzen, Alexander, *My Past and Thoughts. The Memoirs of Alexander Herzen* . . ., tr. Constance Garnett, London, 1924–27, 6 vols.

Hinkley, Mrs. Edyth, *Mazzini. The Story of a great Italian*, London, 1924.

Hoeing, Frederick, W., "Letters of Mazzini to W. J. Linton," *The Journal of Modern History*, V, 55–68 (March 1933).

Howe, Susanne, *Geraldine Jewsbury: Her Life and Errors*, London, 1935.

King, Bolton, *Mazzini*, London, 1902.

King, Mrs. Harriet Eleanor Baillie Hamilton, *Letters and Recollections of Mazzini*, ed. G. M. Trevelyan, London, 1912.

King, Mrs. Harriet Eleanor Baillie Hamilton, "The Religion of Mazzini," *The Dublin Review*, CLII, 41–67 (January 1913).

Lightbody, W. M., "Mazzini: A Study in Political Idealism," *The Westminster Review*, CLXX, 176–85 (August 1908).

Linton, William James, "The Italian Gratuitous School," *The People's Journal*, II, 147–48 (1846).

Linton, William James, *European Republicans; Recollections of Mazzini and His Friends*, London, 1893.

Lloyd, Henry Demarest, *Mazzini and Other Essays*, New York, 1910.

Luzio, Alessandro, "Mazzini's Metamorphoses," *The Living Age*, October 1, 1921, pp. 44–48.

MacCunn, John, *Six Radical Thinkers*, London, 1907.

Magliano, Marchesa Bice Pareto, "Some First-Hand Recollections of Mazzini," *The Contemporary Review*, November 1917, pp. 565–72.

Mansfield, M., "England and Italy," *The Dublin Review*, CXCVIII, 17–28 (January 1936).

Mario, Jessie White, *The Birth of Modern Italy*, ed. the Duke Litta-Visconti-Arese, London, 1909. Reviewed in *The Athenaeum*, September 25, 1909, pp. 356–57.

Marraro, Howard R., "Two Unpublished Letters of Giuseppe Mazzini," *The Journal of Modern History*, VIII, 194–99 (June 1936).

Martineau, Harriet, *Autobiography with Memorials* [by Maria Weston], 3rd edition, London, 1877, 3 vols.

Martineau, Harriet, "Political Agitators," *Once a Week*, V, 698 (December 14, 1861).

Memoir of Joseph Mazzini, London, 1861. From the *London Review*, November 17, 1860.

von Meysenbug, Malwida, *Gesammelte Werke*, ed. Berta Schleicher, Leipzig, 1922, 5 vols.

Märchenfrau und Malerdichter: Malwida von Meysenbug und Ludwig Sigismund Ruhl, letters edited by Berta Schleicher, Munich, 1929.

Rebel in Bombazine: Memoirs of Malwida von Meysenbug, tr. Elsa von Meysenbug Lyons, ed. Mildred Adams, New York, 1936.

Vinant, Gaby, *Un Esprit Cosmopolite au XIXe Siècle, Malwida de Meysenbug (1816–1903) : Sa Vie et Ses Amis*, Paris, 1932.

Morris, William, "The Pilgrims of Hope," XXIV, 382–83, in *Collected Works*, ed. Miss May Morris, London and New York, 1910–15, 24 vols.

Myers, Frederic W. H., "Giuseppe Mazzini," *The Fortnightly Review*, April 1, 1878, pp. 513–28; May 1, 1878, pp. 710–28.

Newman, John Henry, Cardinal, *Historical Sketches*, London, 1903–08, 3 vols.

Ward, Wilfrid, *The Life of John Henry Cardinal Newman*, New York and London, 1912, 2 vols.

Onnis, Pia, "*Battaglie Democratiche e Risorgimento in un Carteggio Inedito di Giuseppe Mazzini e George Jacob Holyoake*," *Rassegna Storica del Risorgimento*, Rome, December 1935, pp. 885–927.

Ossoli, Margaret Fuller, *Memoirs*, London, 1852, 3 vols.

[Panizzi, Antonio], "Post-Office Espionage," *The North British Review*, Edinburgh, November 1844, pp. 257–95

Punch on the letter-opening case of 1844, VII, 2–3, 7, 10, 15, 118 (1844).

Punch on Mazzini and the Roman Republic, XVI, 215; XVII, 21 and 35 (1849).

The Quarterly Review, CCLXVIII, 176 (January 1937).

Ravenna, Leona, "*I giornali di Giuseppe Mazzini*," *Archivio Storico Italiano*, No. 363, Vol. II, pp. 78–88 (Florence, 1937).

Report from the Secret Committee [of the House of Lords] *relative to the Post Office*, London, 1844.

Rosselli, Nello, *Mazzini e Bakounine*, Turin, 1927.

Rudman, Arthur, *Mazzini: Patriot and Prophet*, London, 1922.

Saager, Adolf, *Giuseppe Mazzini. Die Tragödie eines Idealisten*, Zürich, 1935.

Salucci, Arturo, *Amori Mazziniani*, Florence, 1928.

Salvemini, Gaetano, *Mazzini*, Florence, 1925.

Salvemini, Gaetano, "Mazzini," *Encyclopaedia of the Social Sciences*, X (New York, 1933), pp. 240–41.

Schubiger, Maria, *Giuseppe Mazzini im englischen Geistesleben*, Uznach, 1930.

The [London] *Times* on the letter-opening case of 1844:

June 15, 1844. Account of House of Commons' debate.

June 17, 1844. Leading article.

The [London] *Times* on the Greco plot against Napoleon III, and Mazzini:

March 15, 1864, p. 11.

March 16, 1864, p. 12.

March 18, 1864, pp. 7–8.

March 19, 1864, p. 11.

Toynbee, Arnold, *Lectures on the Industrial Revolution in England . . .*, London, 1884.

Venturi, Emilie Ashurst, *Joseph Mazzini: a Memoir*, London, 1875. Includes Mazzini's *Thoughts on Democracy* and *Duties of Man*.

Venturi, Emilie Ashurst, *Mazzini's Foreshadowings of the Coming Faith*, with an introduction by E. F. Richards, London, 1916.

Wallas, Graham, *Human Nature in Politics*, Boston, 1909.

ORSINI, FELICE

Orsini, F., *The Austrian Dungeons in Italy*, tr. Jessie Meriton White, later Mario, London, July 1856.

——, *Memoirs and Adventures*, tr. [H.] George Carbonel, Edinburgh, 1857.

The Annual Register for 1858, C, London, 1859.

Mill, John Stuart, *On Liberty*, London, 1859.

The [London] *Times*, January 15 to March 13, 1858.

PANIZZI, SIR ANTHONY

The Athenaeum, October 1, 1828, p. 772, on Panizzi's textbook, *Extracts from Italian Prose Writers for the Use of Students in the London University*.

Brooks, Constance, *Antonio Panizzi, Scholar and Patriot*, Manchester, 1931.

Corney, Bolton, *Comments on the Evidence of Antonio Panizzi*, London, 1860.

Fagan, Louis, *The Life and Correspondence of Sir Anthony Panizzi*, Boston and New York, 1881, 2 vols.

Garnett, Richard, "Panizzi," *The Dictionary of National Biography*, XLIII, 179–83.

"Sir Anthony Panizzi," *The Quarterly Review*, CLI, 463–501 (April 1881).

PECCHIO, GIUSEPPE

Pecchio, G., "Greece in the Spring of 1825," *The New Monthly Magazine*, XIV, 291–320, 409–27 (1825).

[Pecchio, Giuseppe?], "Adventures of a Foreigner in Greece," *The London Magazine*, August 1826, p. 462 ff.

PEPE, GUGLIELMO

Pepe, G., *A Narrative of the . . . Events . . . at Naples, in 1820 and 1821*, London, 1821.

——, *Memoirs, Comprising the principal military and political events of modern Italy*, London, 1846, 3 vols.

——, *Narrative of scenes and events in Italy; from 1847 to 1849*, London, 1850, 2 vols. Reviewed in *The Edinburgh Review*, January 1851, pp. 33–71.

The Dictionary of National Biography, XXI, 343.

PEPOLI, COUNT CARLO

Pepoli, Count C., *On the Language and Literature of Italy. An Inaugural Lecture, delivered in University College, London, on 6th November, 1838*, London, 1838.

POERIO, CARLO

Poerio, C., *Speech of Carlo Poerio, Late Minister of Public Instruction, in His Defence before the Grand Court Extraordinary at Naples*, London, 1851.

Saffi, Aurelio, *Carlo Poerio and the Neapolitan Police*, London, 1858.

G. A., *Poerio and the Neapolitan Prisoners Transported*, a prose drama, London, 1859.

Lockhart, James, *The Patriot's Grave*, an elegy in memory of Poerio, Florence, [1867].

RICCIARDI, COUNT GIUSEPPE NAPOLEONE

Ricciardi, Count G. N., *The Autobiography of an Italian Rebel*, London, 1860.

ROMEO, FRANCESCO

Romeo, F., *Mirror; Presented to His Sicilian Majesty, Great Britain, and the Allied Sovereigns . . .*, 1st edition, tr. W. P. Macdonald, London, June 1820. 2nd edition in 1822.

——, *Case of Captain Romeo, a Neapolitan gentleman; concerning the relations of Naples with England, and the Austrian and British Parties in the Two Sicilies*, [London, 1821?].

——, *Federative Constitution for Italy. Project for its Regeneration; etc.*, London, 1822.

ROSSETTI, GABRIELE

Rossetti, G., *Disquisitions on the Anti-Papal Spirit Which Produced the Reformation: Its Secret Influence, etc.*, tr. Miss Caroline Ward, London, 1834, 2 vols.

Rossetti, William Michael, *Gabriele Rossetti. A Verified Autobiography*, tr. and supplemented by W. M. Rossetti, London, 1901.

Hunt, W. Holman, *Pre-Raphaelitism and the Pre-Raphaelite Brotherhood*, London, 1905, 2 vols.

[Panizzi, Antonio], review of *La Divina Commedia di Dante Alighieri con Comento Analitico di Gabriele Rossetti*, *The Foreign Review, and Continental Miscellany*, II, 175–95 (1828).

The Foreign Quarterly Review, V, 419–49 (February 1830). Review of Gabriele Rossetti's *Comento* on Dante.

The Athenaeum on Gabriele Rossetti:

May 19, 1832, pp. 318–19.
December 22, 1832, pp. 825–27.
August 17, 1838, pp. 553–54.

Hallam, Arthur Henry, *Remains in Verse and Prose*, pp. 211–93, London, 1863.

Schlegel, A. W., "*Dante, Pétrarque et Boccace, A Propos De L'Ouvrage De M. Rossetti*," *Revue des Deux Mondes*, August 1836, pp. 400–18.

[Smythies, Mrs. Gordon], *Fitzherbert: or, Lovers and Fortune-Hunters*, London, 1838, 3 vols.

Vincent, E. R., *Gabriele Rossetti in England*, Oxford and London, 1936.

Waller, Ross Douglas, *The Rossetti Family, 1824–1854*, Manchester, 1932.

RUFFINI, GIOVANNI DOMENICO

[Ruffini, Giovanni Domenico], *Lorenzo Benoni*, Edinburgh, 1853. Reviewed in:

The North British Review, XIX, 185–208, May 1853. Anonymous review by David Masson.

Fraser's Magazine, XLVIII, 87–94 (July 1853).

The Quarterly Review, XCIII, 117–28 (July 1853).

The Dublin University Magazine, XLII, 158–73 (August 1853).

[Ruffini, Giovanni Domenico], *Doctor Antonio*, Edinburgh, 1855. Reviewed in:

Tait's Edinburgh Magazine, XXII, 683–90 (1855).

The North British Review, February 1856, pp. 537–48. Anonymous review by David Masson.

[Ruffini, Giovanni Domenico], *The Paragreens on a Visit to the Paris Universal Exhibition*, Edinburgh, 1856.

[Ruffini, Giovanni Domenico], *Lavinia*, London, 1860, 3 vols. Reviewed in *The Dublin University Magazine*, LVII, 204–08 (February 1861).

Ruffini, G. D., "A Contemporary Hobby," *Macmillan's Magazine*, III, 467–73 (April 1861).

——, *Vincenzo; or, Sunken Rocks*, London and Cambridge, 1863, 3 vols. Ran as a serial in *Macmillan's Magazine*, May 1862 to November 1863.

——, "Sanremo Revisited," *Macmillan's Magazine*, XI, 374–87 (March 1865).

[Ruffini, Giovanni Domenico], *A Quiet Nook in the Jura*, Edinburgh, 1867. Serialized in *Macmillan's Magazine*, V, February to April 1862.

SAFFI, AURELIO

[Saffi, Aurelio], "Religion in Italy," *The Westminster Review*, new series, IV, 311–41 (October 1853).

Saffi, A., "Southern Italy: Its Condition and Prospects," *Macmillan's Magazine*, VIII, 224–36 (July 1863).

——, "Italy and the Pope," *The Fortnightly Review*, VI, 802–06 (December 1, 1866); VII, 436–55 (April 1, 1867).

V

Friends of Italy

GENERAL

McCarthy, Justin, *Portraits of the Sixties*, London, 1903.

Trevelyan, George Macaulay, *Englishmen and Italians: Some Aspects of their Relations Past and Present*, London, 1919.

ARNOLD, MATTHEW

Arnold, M., *England and the Italian Question*, London, 1859.

——, *Schools and Universities on the Continent*, London, 1868.

——, *Friendship's Garland*, London, 1871.

Letters of Matthew Arnold, 1848–1888, ed. George W. E. Russell, London, 1901, 2 vols.

Lowry, Howard Foster, *The Letters of Matthew Arnold to Arthur Hugh Clough*, London and New York, 1932.

The Poems of Matthew Arnold, 1849–1867, ed. A. T. Quiller-Couch and G. St. Quintin, London, 1926.

ASHURST, WILLIAM HENRY, SENIOR

"Ashurst, William Henry, Senior," *The Dictionary of National Biography*, II, 182–83.

COWEN, JOSEPH

Jones, Evan Rowland, *The Life and Speeches of Joseph Cowen*, London, 1885.

DICKENS, CHARLES

Dickens, C., *Works*, Centenary edition, London and New York, 1910–11, 36 vols.

——, *Pictures from Italy*, London, 1846.

——, "The Italian Prisoner," *The Uncommercial Traveller*, London 1861. First appeared in *All the Year Round*, October 13, 1860.

Dickens to his Oldest Friend. The letters of a lifetime from Charles Dickens to Thomas Beard, ed. Walter Dexter, London and New York, 1932.

The Letters of Charles Dickens, ed. Georgina Hogarth and Mamie Dickens, London, 1880[79]–1882[81], 3 vols.

Forster, John, *The Life of Charles Dickens*, Memorial edition, London, 1911, 2 vols.

Leacock, Stephen B., *Charles Dickens: his life and work*, London, 1933.

GILFILLAN, GEORGE

Gilfillan, G., *A Gallery of Literary Portraits*, Everyman's Library, London, 1909.

Watson, Robert A. and Elizabeth S., *George Gilfillan: Letters and Journals, with Memoir*, London, 1892.

GLADSTONE, WILLIAM EWART

Gladstone, W. E., "Giacomo Leopardi," *Gleanings of Past Years*, 1845–76, London, 1879, II, 65–129. This article first appeared in *The Quarterly Review*, March 1850.

——, *Two Letters to the Earl of Aberdeen, on the State Prosecutions of the Neapolitan Government*, London, 1851. 11 editions in 1851; 14 by 1859.

Balleydier, Alphonse, *La Vérité sur les Affaires de Naples; Réfutation des Lettres de M. Gladstone*, Paris, 1851.

Gondon, Jules, *A Letter to . . . W. E. Gladstone in answer to his two Letters . . . on the State Prosecutions of the Neapolitan Government*, London, 1851.

MacFarlane, Charles, *The Neapolitan Government and Mr. Gladstone, etc.*, London, August 1851.

A Review of the errors and fallacies published by Mr. Gladstone in his two letters addressed to the Earl of Aberdeen, on the State Prosecutions in the Kingdom of the Two Sicilies, tr. from the Italian, London, 1851.

Risposta di un Italiano a due Lettere del Signor Gladstone a Lord Aberdeen, Genoa, 1851.

Mancini-Oliva, Laura Beatrice, *A Sir G. Gladstone: un'esule napolitana. Canzone*, Turin, 1851.

Massari, Giuseppe, *Al Sig. Guglielmo Gladstone Parole di Gratitudine*, Turin, 1851.

Massari, Giuseppe, *Il signor Gladstone ed il Governo Napolitano: raccolta di scritti intorno alla questione Napolitana*, Turin, 1851.

[Panizzi, Antonio], "Neapolitan Justice," *The Edinburgh Review*, October 1851, pp. 490–528.

Gladstone, W. E., *An Examination of the Official Reply of the Neapolitan Government*, London, 1852.

[Lushington, Henry], *A Detailed Exposure of the Apology Put Forth by the Neapolitan Government, in Reply to the Charges of Mr. Gladstone*, London, 1852.

Farini, Luigi Carlo, *The Roman State, from 1815 to 1850*, Vols. I–III tr. by W. E. Gladstone, Vol. IV tr. by a lady under his direction, London, 1851–54, 4 vols. Vols. I–II reviewed by David Masson in *The Athenaeum*, June 28, 1851, pp. 677–78.

Davies, William Watkin, *Gladstone and the Unification of Italy*, Oxford, 1918.

"Gladstone, William Ewart," *The Dictionary of National Biography, First Supplement*, Vol. II.

Farini, Luigi Carlo, *La diplomazia e la questione italiana; lettera . . . al Signor Guglielmo Gladstone*, Turin, 1856.

Guedalla, Philip, *Gladstone and Palmerston*, London, 1928.
Guedalla, Philip, *The Queen and Mr. Gladstone*, London, 1933.
"Neapolitan Prisons, Past and Present," *Macmillan's Magazine*, VIII, 50–61 (May 1863).
"More About Neapolitan Prisons," *Macmillan's Magazine*, VIII, 167–76 (June 1863).
Morley, John, *The Life of William Ewart Gladstone*, London, 1903, 3 vols.
Zumbini, Bonaventura, *W. E. Gladstone nelle sue relazione con l'Italia*, Bari, Italy, 1914.

HARRISON, FREDERIC

[Harrison, Frederic], "Cavour and Garibaldi," *The Westminster Review*, new series, XIX, 172–201 (January 1861).
Harrison, F., *Autobiographic Memoirs*, London, 1911, 2 vols.

HOLYOAKE, GEORGE JACOB

Holyoake, George Jacob, editor, *The Reasoner*, London, 1846–61, 26 vols.
Holyoake, G. J., *Sixty Years of an Agitator's Life*, 4th edition, London, 1900, 2 vols.
——, *Bygones Worth Remembering*, London, 1905, 2 vols.
"Holyoake, George Jacob," *The Dictionary of National Biography, Second Supplement*, Vol. II.
Goss, Charles W. F., *A Descriptive Bibliography of the Writings of George Jacob Holyoake with a Brief Sketch of His Life*, London, 1908.
McCabe, Joseph, *George Jacob Holyoake*, London, 1922.

LINTON, WILLIAM JAMES

Linton, W. J., *The Plaint of Freedom*, a poem, Newcastle-upon-Tyne, 1852.
——, *Claribel and Other Poems*, London, 1865.
——, *Voices of the Dead. Charlotte Corday and Marat. Mazzini and the Countess Ossoli, etc.*, verse, [London? 1879?].
——, *Prose and Verse . . . 1836–1886*, 20 volumes assembled by Linton and presented by him to the British Museum in 1895.
Hopson, William Fowler, "Side Lights on William James Linton, 1812–97," *The Papers of the Biographical Society of America*, XXVII, part 2, pp. 74–82 (1933).

MARIO, JESSIE WHITE

Mario, J. W., *The Nation*, New York, March 15, 1906, p. 218; March 22, 1906, p. 241; December 9, 1909, pp. 564–66.

MASSON, DAVID

Masson, David, editor, *Macmillan's Magazine*, Vols. I–XVII, 1859–68.
Masson, D., "Politics of the Present, Foreign and Domestic," *Macmillan's Magazine*, I, 1–10 (November 1859).

Masson, D., "Dead Men Whom I Have Known; or, Recollections of Three Cities," on Agostino Ruffini, *Macmillan's Magazine*, XI, 323–36 (February 1865).
——, *Memories of London in the 'Forties*, Edinburgh and London, 1908.
——, *Memories of Two Cities, Edinburgh and Aberdeen*, Edinburgh and London, 1911.

MILNES, RICHARD MONCKTON, FIRST BARON HOUGHTON

Milnes, R. M., *Memorials of a Residence on the Continent, and Historical Poems*, London, 1838.
——, *The Events of 1848, Especially in Their Relation to Great Britain. A Letter to the Marquis of Lansdowne*, London, 1849.
Reid, T. Wemyss, *The Life, Letters, and Friendships of Richard Monckton Milnes, First Lord Houghton*, London, 1890, 2 vols.

NICHOL, JOHN

"Nichol, John," *The Dictionary of National Biography, First Supplement*, III, 225–27.
Knight, W. A., *Memoir of John Nichol*, Glasgow, 1896.

LORD PALMERSTON

Bell, Herbert Clifford F., *Lord Palmerston*, London and New York, 1936, 2 vols.
Bulwer, Right Hon. Sir Henry Lytton, *Life of Viscount Palmerston*, Philadelphia, 1871, 2 vols.
von Ficquelmont, Count Carl Ludwig, *Lord Palmerston L'Angleterre et le Continent*, Paris, 1852, 2 vols.
Guedalla, Philip, *Palmerston*, London, 1926.

RUSKIN, JOHN

Ruskin, J., *Arrows of the Chace, etc.*, Orpington, England, 1880, 2 vols.
——, *Letters upon subjects of general interest . . . to various correspondents*, London, 1892.
——, *Works*, Library edition, ed. E. T. Cook and Alexander Wedderburn, London, 1903–12, 39 vols.
Collingwood, W. G., *The Life of John Ruskin*, London, 1900.
Cook, E. T., *The Life of John Ruskin*, London, 1911, 2 vols.
Harrison, Frederic, *John Ruskin*, English Men of Letters, London, 1902.
Larg, David G., *John Ruskin*, Edinburgh, 1932.
Roe, Frederick William, *The Social Philosophy of Carlyle and Ruskin*, London, 1922.
Shaw, George Bernard, *Ruskin's Politics*, [Oxford], 1921.
Wilenski, Reginald H., *John Ruskin: an Introduction to Further Study of his Life and Work*, London, 1933.
Wise, Thomas J.; and Smart, James P., *A Complete Bibliography of the Writings . . . of John Ruskin*, London, 1889–93.

RUSSELL, LORD JOHN

Russell, Lord J., *Italy, Corrected report of the Speeches of . . . Lord John Russell delivered in the House of Commons . . . February 5, and . . . 6, 1861*, London, 1861.

Russell, John (Earl), *Recollections and Suggestions, 1813–1873*, London, 1875.

Early Correspondence of Lord John Russell, 1805–1840, ed. Rollo Russell, London, 1913, 2 vols.

The Later Correspondence of Lord John Russell, 1840–1878, ed. G. P. Gooch, London, 1925, 2 vols.

Comandini, Alfredo, "*Lord John Russel* [*sic*] *e l'Italia*," *Rassegna Italo-Britannica*, Milan, October, 1918, pp. 11–25.

McCarthy, Desmond; and Russell, Lady Mary Agatha, *Lady John Russell. A Memoir . . .*, London, 1910.

Farini, Luigi Carlo, *Mémoire Sur Les Affaires D'Italie adressé à la diplomatie européenne*, Paris and Brussels, 1859.

Farini, Luigi Carlo, *Lettres . . . à Lord John Russell*, Paris and Brussels, 1859.

Farini, Luigi Carlo, *La Quistione Italiana. Lettera del 19 febbraio 1859 di Luigi Carlo Farini a Lord John Russell*, 3rd edition, Turin, 1859.

Fyers, William Augustus, *The Crisis of Europe. A letter . . . to . . . Lord John Russell*, London, 1859.

Walpole, Sir Spencer, *The Life of Lord John Russell*, London, 1889, 2 vols.

SHAEN, WILLIAM

Shaen, Margaret Josephine, *Memorials of Two Sisters, Susanna and Catherine Winkworth*, London, 1908.

Shaen, Margaret Josephine, *William Shaen: a brief sketch*, London, 1912.

THE SOCIETY OF THE FRIENDS OF ITALY

Address of the Society of the Friends of Italy, 5th thousand, London, 1851. Printed by George Jacob Holyoake.

Tract No. II of The Society of the Friends of Italy, *The Charge of Terrorism in Rome, during the Government of the Republic, Refuted by Facts and Documents. The Documents Furnished by Mr. Mazzini*, London, 1851.

Tract No. V of The Society of the Friends of Italy, *The Place and Duty of England in Europe*, a lecture delivered April 28, 1852, by Professor F. W. Newman, London, 1852.

STANSFELD, JAMES

Stansfeld, J., *The Italian Movement and Italian Parties*, London, [1862].

"Stansfeld, James," *The Dictionary of National Biography. First Supplement*, III, 352–54.

Hammond, J. L. and Barbara, *James Stansfeld: a Victorian Champion of Sex Equality*, London, 1932.

VI

The More Important Writers of Fiction

COLLINS, WILKIE

Collins, W., *The Woman in White*, London, 1860, 3 vols.
Ellis, Stewart M., *Wilkie Collins, Le Fanu, and others*, London, 1931.
Phillips, Walter C., *Dickens, Reade, and Collins: Sensation Novelists*, New York, 1919.
Sehlbach, Hans, *Untersuchungen über die Romankunst von Wilkie Collins*, Jena, Germany, 1931.

DISRAELI, BENJAMIN, EARL OF BEACONSFIELD

Disraeli, B., *Novels and Tales*, Hughenden edition, London, 1881, 11 vols.
[Disraeli, Benjamin], *Contarini Fleming, a Psychological Autobiography*, London, 1832, 4 vols.
——, *Lothair*, London, 1870, 3 vols.
Maurois, André, *Disraeli. A Picture of the Victorian Age*, London, 1927.
Monypenny, William Flavelle; and Buckle, George Earle, *The Life of Benjamin Disraeli, Earl of Beaconsfield*, London, 1910–20, 6 vols.
Speare, Morris Edmund, *The Political Novel: Its Development in England and in America*, New York, 1924.
Ward, Sir A. W., "The Political and Social Novel," Vol. XIII, Chap. XI, *The Cambridge History of English Literature.*

ELIOT, GEORGE

Eliot, G., *Daniel Deronda*, New York, 1877, 2 vols. First published in London, 1876.
Cross, John Walter, *George Eliot's Life as Related in Her Letters and Journals*, London, 1885, 3 vols.
Kitchel, Anna Theresa, *George Lewes and George Eliot, A Review of Records*, New York, 1933.

MRS. GASKELL

Mrs. Gaskell, *Round the Sofa*, London, 1859, 2 vols.
Letters of Mrs. Gaskell and Charles Eliot Norton, 1855–1865, ed. Jane Whitehill, London, 1932.
Haldane, Elizabeth, *Mrs. Gaskell and Her Friends*, London, 1930.
Sanders, Gerald De Witt, *Elizabeth Gaskell*, New Haven, 1929

Waller, Ross D., "Letters Addressed to Mrs. Gaskell by Celebrated Contemporaries," *Bulletin of The John Rylands Library*, Manchester, XIX, 102–69 (1935).

Whitfield, A. Stanton, *Mrs. Gaskell: Her Life and Work*, London, 1929.

KINGSLEY, HENRY

Kingsley, H., *Silcote of Silcotes*, London, 1867, 3 vols.

Ellis, S. M., *Henry Kingsley, 1830–1876. Toward a Vindication*, London, 1931

LEVER, CHARLES

Lever, C., *Novels*, ed. Julia Kate Neville, London, 1897–99, 37 vols.:
The Daltons or Three Roads in Life, first published in 1852.
The Dodd Family Abroad, first published in 1854.
The Fortunes of Glencore, first published in 1857.
Tony Butler, first published in 1865.

Lever, C., Articles in *The Dublin University Magazine*, 1852:
"Lord Palmerston and our Policy in the Mediterranean," March, pp. 329–38.
"Great Britain and Italy," July, pp. 85–92.
Letter to the editor, December, pp. 748–52.

——, Articles in *Blackwood's Edinburgh Magazine:*
"Italian Brigandage," May 1863, pp. 576–85.
"Garibaldi," May 1864, pp. 614–18. Signed "Cornelius O'Dowd."
"Garibaldi's Last," November 1867, pp. 609–12. Signed "Cornelius O'Dowd."

Downey, Edmund, *Charles Lever: His Life in His Letters*, London, 1906, 2 vols.

Fitzpatrick, William John, *The Life of Charles Lever*, revised and new edition, London, 1884.

BULWER-LYTTON, EDWARD GEORGE EARLE LYTTON, BARON LYTTON

Bulwer-Lytton, E., *The Last Days of Pompeii*, "The New Household Edition," Boston, 1891. First published in 1834.

——, *Ernest Maltravers*, London, 1837, 3 vols.

——, *Alice or the Mysteries*, London, 1838, 3 vols.

——, *My Novel*, Edinburgh, 1853, 4 vols.

Lytton, Victor Alexander George Robert, Second Earl of Lytton, *The Life of Edward Bulwer, First Lord Lytton*, London, 1913, 2 vols.

Sadleir, Michael, *Bulwer and His Wife: a Panorama*, 1803–1836, London, 1933.

MEREDITH, GEORGE

Meredith, G., *The Letters of George Meredith*, ed. William Maxse Meredith, London, 1912, 2 vols.

——, *Poetical Works*, ed. G. M. Trevelyan, London, 1912.

Meredith, G., *Works*, The Memorial Edition, London, 1909–11, 27 vols.:
The Ordeal of Richard Feverel. A History of a Father and Son, first published in 1859.
Sandra Belloni, first published as *Emilia in England* in 1864.
Vittoria, first published in 1867.
Correspondence from the Seat of War in Italy, first published in 1866 in *The Morning Post.*

Meredith, George, reviews of *Emilia in England:*
The Reader, April 23, 1864, pp. 514–15. By Richard Garnett.
The Athenaeum, April 30, 1864, pp. 609–10.
The Saturday Review, May 28, 1864, pp. 660–61. By Mrs. William Hardman.
The Westminster Review, July 1864, pp. 253–54.
The Examiner, July 23, 1864, pp. 468–69.
Time, March 1886, pp. 379–80. By Arthur Symons.
The Pall Mall Gazette, June 14, 1886, pp. 5–6.

McCarthy, Justin, on *Emilia in England*, "Novels with a Purpose," "*Con Amore*"*; or, Critical Chapters*, London, 1868, pp. 24–49.

Meredith, George, reviews of *Vittoria:*
The Spectator, February 3, 1866, pp. 136–37; and February 9, 1867, pp. 161–63.
The Pall Mall Gazette, January 25, 1867, pp. 10–11; and June 14, 1886, pp. 5–6.
The Saturday Review, February 2, 1867, pp. 149–50; and *October* 16, 1915, pp. 373–75.
The Athenaeum, February 23, 1867, pp. 248–49. By Geraldine Jewsbury.
Revue des Deux Mondes, June 15, 1867, p. 1023. By E.-D. Forgues.
Vanity Fair, June 26, 1886, p. 360.
Time, August 1886, pp. 253–54.
The London Quarterly Review, July 1912, pp. 84–98. By Dora M. Jones.

Forman, Maurice, Buxton, *George Meredith: Some Early Appreciations*, London, 1909.

Bailey, Elmer James, *The Novels of George Meredith: a Study*, New York, 1910.

Ellis, Stewart Marsh, *George Meredith: his life and friends in relation to his work*, London, 1919.

Forman, Maurice Buxton, *A Bibliography of the Writings in Prose and Verse of George Meredith*, Edinburgh, 1922.

Forman, Maurice Buxton, *Meredithiana, being a Supplement to The Bibliography of Meredith*, Edinburgh, 1924.

Galland, René, *George Meredith, les cinquante premières années* (1828–1878), Paris, 1923.

Henderson, May Sturge, *George Meredith, novelist, poet, reformer*, London, 1907.

Moffatt, James, *George Meredith. A Primer to the Novels*, London, 1909.

Sencourt, Robert Esmonde, *The Life of George Meredith*, London, 1929.

Priestley, John Boynton, *George Meredith*, English Men of Letters, London, 1926.
Trevelyan, George Macaulay, *The Poetry and Philosophy of George Meredith*, London, 1906.
Watson, Mrs. Amy Foster, *Meredith and Italy*, London, 1919.

TROLLOPE, THOMAS ADOLPHUS

Trollope, T. A., *Impressions of a Wanderer in Italy, Switzerland, France, and Spain*, London, 1850.
——, *Tuscany in 1849 and 1859*, London, 1859. Valuable as background for Mrs. Browning's *Casa Guidi Windows*.
——, *A Lenten Journey in Umbria and the Marches*, London, 1862.
——, *Marietta*, London, 1862, 2 vols.
——, *Giulio Malatesta*, London, 1863, 3 vols.
——, *Beppo the Conscript*, London, 1864, 2 vols.
——, *The Dream Numbers*, London, 1868, 3 vols.
——, *Leonora Casaloni*, London, 1868.
——, *Diamond Cut Diamond . . . and Other Stories*, London, 1875, 2 vols.
——, *The Story of the Life of Pius the Ninth*, London, 1877, 2 vols.
——, *What I Remember*, London, 1887–89, 3 vols.

WARD, MRS. HUMPHRY

Ward, Mrs. H., *Eleanor*, London, 1900.
Trevelyan, Janet Penrose, *The Life of Mrs. Humphry Ward*, London, 1923.

WHITE, WILLIAM HALE

White, William Hale ("Mark Rutherford"), *Clara Hopgood*, London, 1896.
Taylor, A. E., "The Novels of Mark Rutherford," *Essays and Studies by Members of the English Association*, V, 51–74 (Oxford, 1914).

VII

Lesser Fiction

[Phipps, Constantine Henry, First Marquess of Normanby], *The English in Italy*, London, 1825, 3 vols. Reviewed in *The Westminster Review*, October, 1826, pp. 325–41.

[Phipps, Constantine Henry, First Marquess of Normanby], *Matilda; a Tale of the Day*, London, 1825.

[Easton, Charlotte A.], *Vittoria Colonna: a Tale of Rome, in the Nineteenth Century*, Edinburgh, 1827, 3 vols.

[Geale, Hamilton], *Ernesto di Ripalta: a tale of the Italian Revolution*, London, 1849, 3 vols.

Angelo. A Romance of Modern Rome, London, 1854, 2 vols.

Beste, John Richard Digby, *Modern Society in Rome. A Novel*, London, 1856, 3 vols.

St. John, Bayle, *Maretimo. A Story of Adventure*, London, [1856]. 2nd edition in 1884.

H[amilton], [Mrs.] C[harles] G., *The Exiles of Italy*, Edinburgh, 1857.

[Chorley, Henry Fothergill] ("Paul Bell"), *Roccabella: a Tale of a Woman's Life*, London, [1859], 2 vols.

Montemerli, Countess Marie, *La Bella Balia*, London, 1859. In French.

Webb, Mrs. Annie, *Marco Griffi, the Italian Patriot*, London, 1859.

Angelo Sanmartino: A Tale of Lombardy in 1859, Edinburgh, 1860.

Crichton, Kate, *Before the Dawn. A Tale of Italy*, London, 1860, 2 vols.

[Roberts, Miss Margaret], *Mademoiselle Mori: a tale of modern Rome*, London, 1860, 2 vols.

Alfio Balzani: or, Extracts from the Diary of a Proscribed Sicilian, London and New York, 1861.

Blagden, Isabella, *Agnes Tremorne*, London, 1861, 2 vols.

Bresciani, Antonio, *The Jew of Verona: an Historical Tale of the Italian Revolutions of 1846–9*, London, 1861. First published in U.S.A. in 1854.

Brooke, William B., *Out with Garibaldi; or, From Melazzo to Capua*, London, [1861].

[Jenkin, Mrs. C.], "*Who Breaks—Pays*," London, 1861, 2 vols.

Niccolo Marini; or, the Mystery Solved: a Tale of Naples Life, London, 1862, 2 vols.

Edwards, Amelia Blandford, *Half a Million of Money. A Novel*, London, 1865. Reviewed in *The Fortnightly Review*, III, 654–55 (January 15, 1866).

Capes, John Moore, *The Mosaic-Worker's Daughter*, London, 1868, 3 vols.

Montemerli, Countess Marie, *The Florintines. A Story of Home-Life in Italy*, London, 1870, 3 vols.

Comyn, L. N., *Elena, an Italian Tale*, London, 1873, 2 vols.
[de la Ramée Louise] ("Ouida"), *Pascarèl. Only a Story*, London, 1873, 3 vols.
[White, Linda] ("M. Dalin"), *Courtship and a Campaign. A Milanese Tale of '66*, London, 1873, 2 vols.
Hopkins, Tighe, *For Freedom*, London, 1888, 2 vols. 2nd edition in 1899.
Voynich, Mrs. Ethel Lillian, *The Gadfly*, London, 1897.
Henty, George Alfred, *Out with Garibaldi: a Story of the Liberation of Italy*, London, 1901 [1900].
Hayens, Herbert, *One of the Red Shirts: a Story of Garibaldi's Men*, London, 1901.
Spender, Miss Emily, *A Soldier for a Day*, London, 1901.
Hood, Hon. Alexander Nelson, *Adria: a Tale of Venice*, London, 1904.
Black, Ladbroke; and Lynd, Robert, *The Mantle of the Emperor: Being the Adventures and Observations of Richard Blennerhasset in the Following of the Third Napoleon*, London, 1906.
Hartley, M., *Beyond Man's Strength*, London, 1909.
Deeping, Warwick, *The Lame Englishman*, London, 1910.
Voynich, Mrs. Ethel Lillian, *An Interrupted Friendship*, London, 1910. A sequel to *The Gadfly*.
Gregg, Hilda Caroline ("Sydney Carlyon Grier"), *One Crowded Hour*, Edinburgh and London, 1912.

The More Important Poets

BROWNING, ELIZABETH BARRETT

Browning, E. B., *Elizabeth Barrett Browning: Letters to her Sister, 1846–1859*, ed. Leonard Huxley, London, 1929.
——, *Letters*, ed. Frederic G. Kenyon, London, 1897, 2 vols.
——, *Letters to Robert Browning and Other Correspondents*, ed. Thomas James Wise, London, 1916.
——, *Poetical Works*, ed. Frederic G. Kenyon, London, 1897.
——, *Poetical Works*, Oxford Complete Edition, London, 1904.
——, *Casa Guidi Windows*, London, 1851.
Reviews of *Casa Guidi Windows*:
The Athenaeum, June 7, 1851, pp. 597–98.
The Edinburgh Review, CXIV, 531 (October 1861).
——, *Poems Before Congress*, London, 1860.
Reviews of *Poems Before Congress*:
The Athenaeum, March 17, 1860, p. 371.
The Edinburgh Review, CXIV, 532 (October 1861).
——, *Last Poems*, London, 1862.
Reviews of *Last Poems*:
The Athenaeum, March 29, 1862, p. 422.
Wilson, A., "English Poets in Italy: Mrs. Browning's Last Poems," *Macmillan's Magazine*, VI, 79–87 (May 1862).
——, *Hitherto Unpublished Poems and Stories with an Inedited Autobiography*, Boston, 1914.
D., E., " Elizabeth Barrett Browning," a defence, *Macmillan's Magazine*, IV, 402–4 (September 1861).
Phelps, Ruth Shepard, *Italian Silhouettes*, New York, 1924.
Whiting, Lilian, *A Study of Elizabeth Barrett Browning*, London, 1899.

MR. AND MRS. BROWNING

Benét, William Rose, *From Robert and Elizabeth Browning*, London, 1936.
The Letters of Robert Browning and Elizabeth Barrett Browning, 1845–1846, London, 1899, 2 vols.
New Poems by Robert Browning and Elizabeth Barrett Browning, ed. Sir Frederic G. Kenyon, London, 1914.
Twenty-two Unpublished Letters of Elizabeth Barrett Browning and Robert Browning Addressed to Henrietta and Arabella Moulton Barrett, New York, 1935.

The Evening Post, New York, February 2 and 7, 1859. On Mme. Jessie White Mario and the Brownings.

The Athenaeum, March 5, 1859, p. 322; March 12, 1859, pp. 357–58. On Mme. Jessie White Mario and the Brownings.

Burdett, Osbert, *The Brownings*, revised and new edition, London, 1933.

Elton, Oliver, *The Brownings*, London, 1924.

BROWNING, ROBERT

Browning, R., *Letters . . . Collected by Thomas J. Wise*, ed. Thurman L. Hood, London, 1933.

Letters of Robert Browning to Miss Isa Blagden, ed. A. J. Armstrong, Waco, Texas, 1923.

——, *Letters . . . to various Correspondents*, ed. Thomas J. Wise, London, 1895–96, 1907–8, 4 vols.

——, *Complete Poetic and Dramatic Works*, Cambridge Edition, Boston and New York, 1895.

——, *Poetical Works*, ed. Augustine Birrell, London, 1898, 2 vols.

——, *Works*, Centenary edition, ed. Sir F. G. Kenyon, London, 1912, 10 vols.

——, *Prince Hohenstiel-Schwangau, Saviour of Society*, London, 1871. Reviewed in *The Edinburgh Review*, CXXXV, 222 (January 1872).

The Browning Society's Papers, London, 1881–90, 3 vols.

Chesterton, Gilbert Keith, *Robert Browning*, English Men of Letters, London, 1903.

Clarke, Helen Archibald, *Browning's Italy: a study of Italian life and art in Browning*, New York, 1907.

De Vane, William Clyde, *A Browning Handbook*, New York, 1935.

Dowden, Edward, *The Life of Robert Browning*, Everyman's Library, London, 1915.

Griffin, W. Hall; and Minchin, Harry Christopher, *The Life of Robert Browning*, London, 1910.

Orr, Mrs. Sutherland, *A Handbook to the Works of Robert Browning*, London, 1902.

Orr, Mrs. Sutherland, *Life and Letters of Robert Browning*, revised by Frederic G. Kenyon, London, 1908.

Phelps, William Lyon, *Robert Browning*, new edition, Indianapolis, 1932.

Symons, Arthur, *An Introduction to the Study of Browning*, enlarged edition, London, 1906.

BYRON, GEORGE GORDON, SIXTH BARON BYRON

Lord Byron, *Complete Poetical Works*, Student's Cambridge Edition, Cambridge, Massachusetts, 1905.

——, *Works*, ed. E. H. Coleridge and R. E. Prothero, London, 1905–24, 13 vols.

Lord Byron, *Works, Letters and Journals,* ed. R. E. Prothero, London, 1898–1901, 6 vols.
——, *Works. Poetry,* ed. E. H. Coleridge, London, 1898–1904, 7 vols.
Lord Byron's Correspondence chiefly with Lady Melbourne, Mr. Hobhouse, the Hon. Douglas Kinnaird, and P. B. Shelley, ed. John Murray, London, 1922, 2 vols.
Elze, Karl, *Lord Byron, a Biography . . .,* London, 1872.
Fuess, Claude M., *Lord Byron as a Satirist in Verse,* New York, 1912.
Guiccioli, Countess, *My Recollections of Lord Byron and Those of Eye-Witnesses of His Life,* London, 1869.
Hunt, Leigh, *Lord Byron and Some of His Contemporaries . . .,* Paris, 1828, 3 vols.
Medwin, Thomas, *Conversations of Lord Byron: noted during a residence with his Lordship at Pisa, in the Years 1821 and 1822,* 2nd edition, London, 1824.
Moore, Thomas, *Letters and Journals of Lord Byron: with Notices of his Life,* [London], 1830, 2 vols.
Muoni, Guido, *La Fama del Byron e il Byronismo in Italia,* Milan, 1903.
Muoni, Guido, *La Leggenda del Byron in Italia,* Milan, 1907.
Nichol, John, *Byron,* English Men of Letters, London, 1880.
Raymond, Dora Neill, *The Political Career of Lord Byron,* New York, 1924.
Trelawny, Edward John, *Records of Shelley, Byron, and the Author,* London, 1878, 2 vols.
Zacchetti, Corrado, *Lord Byron e l'Italia,* Palermo, 1919.

CLOUGH, ARTHUR HUGH

Clough, A. H., *Letters and Remains,* London, 1865.
——, *Poems,* 6th edition, ed. Charles Whibley, London, 1913.
——, *Poems and Prose Remains,* ed. by his wife, London, 1869, 2 vols.
Masson, David, "The Poems of Arthur Hugh Clough," *Macmillan's Magazine,* VI, 318–31 (August 1862).
Osborne, James Insley, *Arthur Hugh Clough,* London, 1920.

DE VERE, AUBREY

De Vere, A., *Poetical Works,* London, 1884–97, 6 vols.
——, *St. Peter's Chains; or, Rome and the Italian Revolution,* a sonnet sequence, London, [1888].
Ward, Wilfrid, *Aubrey de Vere: a memoir based on his unpublished diaries and correspondence,* London, 1904.

DOBELL, SYDNEY

Dobell, S., *Poetical Works,* with a memoir by John Nichol, London, 1875, 2 vols.
Smith, Alexander; and Dobell, Sydney, *Sonnets on the War,* London, 1855.
Jolly, Emily, *The Life and Letters of Sydney Dobell,* London, 1878, 2 vols.

HUNT, LEIGH

Hunt, L., *Autobiography*, ed. Roger Ingpen, New York, 1903, 2 vols.
——, *Correspondence*, ed. T. I. Hunt, London, 1862, 2 vols.
——, *Poetical Works*, ed. H. S. Milford, London, [1922].
Blunden, Edmund, *Leigh Hunt: A Biography*, London, 1930.
Johnson, R. Brimley, *Shelley—Leigh Hunt*, 2nd edition, London, 1929.
Mitchell, Alexander, *A Bibliography of the Writings of Leigh Hunt With Critical Notes*, London, 1931.

KING, MRS. HAMILTON

[King, Mrs. Hamilton, then Harriet Eleanor Baillie Hamilton], *The Execution of Felice Orsini, March 13th, 1858*, a poem, [London? 1860?].
King, H., *Aspromonte and Other poems*, London, 1869.
——, *The Disciples*, London, 1873.

LANDOR, WALTER SAVAGE

Landor, W. S., *Complete Works*, ed. T. Earle Welby and Stephen Wheeler, London, 1927–36, 16 vols.
——, *Works*, ed. C. G. Crump, London, 1891–93, 10 vols.
——, *Poche Osservazioni sullo Stato Attuale di Que' Popoli, Che Vogliono Governarsi per Mezzo delle Rappresentanze*, [Naples?], 1821.
——, *Imaginary Conversation of King Carlo-Alberto and the Duchess Belgioioso, on the Affairs and Prospects of Italy*, London, 1848. A shilling pamphlet, the profits of which were to go "to the sufferers at Messina."
——, *The Italics*, London, 1848.
——, *The Last Fruit Off an Old Tree*, dedicated to D'Azeglio, London, 1853. Includes *Ten Letters Addressed to His Eminence the Cardinal Wiseman by a True Believer*.
——, *Letters of an American, Mainly on Russia and Revolution*, dedicated to Gladstone, London, 1854.
——, *Dry Sticks, Fagoted*, dedicated to Kossuth, Edinburgh, 1858.
——, *The Hellenics*, new and enlarged edition, Edinburgh, 1859.
——, *Heroic Idyls, with Additional Poems*, London, 1863.
——, *Garibaldi and the President of the Sicilian Senate* (*an Imaginary Conversation*), London, 1917.
——, *To Elizabeth Barrett Browning and other verses*, London, 1917.
——, *Letters and Other Unpublished Writings*, ed. Stephen Wheeler, London, 1897.
——, *Letters . . . Private and Public*, ed. Stephen Wheeler, London, 1899.
——, Letter to *The Atlas*, March 31, 1855, p. 205.
——, Letters to *The Examiner*:
September 22, 1849, p. 597.
August 3, 1850, p. 493.
February 17, 1855, p. 100.
July 12, 1856, p. 435.
July 26, 1856, p. 471.

Landor, W. S., Letters, concerning Kossuth and Garibaldi, to *The London Review*, August 11, 1860, pp. 124–25.
——, Letters to *The* [London] *Times*:
August 21, 1856, p. 6.
March 17, 1858, p. 9.
November 29, 1859, p. 10.
December 27, 1859, p. 5.
March 17, 1860, p. 9.
Colvin, Sidney, *Landor*, English Men of Letters, London, 1881.
Elkin, Felice, *Walter Savage Landor's Studies of Italian Life and Literature*, Philadelphia, 1934.
Fornelli, Guido, *W. S. Landor e l'Italia*, Forlì, 1931.
Forster, John, *The Works and Life of Walter Savage Landor*, London, 1876, 8 vols.
Holyoake, Maltus Questell, "The Last Writings of Landor," *The Gentleman's Magazine*, CCLXXXVI, 6–16 (January 1899).
Minchin, H. C., *Walter Savage Landor. Last days, letters and conversations*, London, 1934.
Wheeler, Stephen, "Landor and Pius IX," letter to *The* [London] *Times Literary Supplement*, September 22, 1921, p. 612.
Wise, Thomas James; and Wheeler, Stephen, *A Bibliography of the Writings in Prose and Verse of W. S. Landor*, London, 1919.

MASSEY, GERALD

Massey, G., *My Lyrical Life: Poems Old and New*, 2nd series, London, 1889.
Collins, John Churton, *Studies in Poetry and Criticism*, London, 1905, pp. 142–66.

MOORE, THOMAS

Moore, T., *Poetical Works*, ed. A. D. Godley, London, 1910.
[Moore, Thomas] ("Thomas Brown, the Younger"), *Fables for the Holy Alliance, Rhymes on the Road, etc.*, London, 1823.
Moore, T., *Memoirs, Journal, and Correspondence*, ed. Lord John Russell, London, 1853–56, 8 vols.
Gwynn, Stephen L., *Thomas Moore*, English Men of Letters, London, 1905.

ROGERS, SAMUEL

Rogers, S., *Poetical Works*, with a memoir by Edward Bell, Aldine edition, London, 1875[74].
[Rogers, Samuel], *Italy, a Poem. Part the First*, London, 1822.
Rogers, S., *Italy, a Poem. Part the Second*, London, 1828.
Roberts, Richard Ellis, *Samuel Rogers and His Circle*, London, 1910.

ROSSETTI, CHRISTINA GEORGINA

Rossetti, C. G., *Family Letters . . .*, ed. W. M. Rossetti, London, 1908.
——, *Poetical Works*, ed. W. M. Rossetti, London, 1904.

Stuart, Dorothy Margaret, *Christina Rossetti*, English Men of Letters, London, 1930.

Thomas, Eleanor Walter, *Christina Georgina Rossetti*, New York, 1931.

ROSSETTI, DANTE GABRIEL

Rossetti, D. G., *Letters . . . to William Allingham, 1854–1870*, ed. G. B. Hill, London, 1897.

—— *Works*, ed. W. M. Rossetti, London, 1911.

Benson, Arthur C., *Rossetti*, English Men of Letters, London, 1904.

Caine, Sir T. Hall, *Recollections of Dante Gabriel Rossetti*, London, 1882.

Dupré, Henri, *Un Italien d'Angleterre*, Paris, 1921.

Rossetti, William Michael, *Bibliography of the Works of Dante Gabriel Rossetti*, London, 1905.

Rossetti, William Michael, *Dante Gabriel Rossetti. Classified Lists of His Writings with the Dates*, London, 1906.

Rossetti, William Michael, *Dante Gabriel Rossetti: His Family-Letters . . .*, London, 1895, 2 vols.

Rossetti, William Michael, "Some Early Correspondence of Dante Gabriel Rossetti, 1835–54," in *Pre-Raphaelite Diaries and Letters*, London, 1900.

Winwar, Frances, *Poor Splendid Wings. The Rossettis and Their Circle*, Boston, 1933.

ROSSETTI, WILLIAM MICHAEL

Rossetti, W. M., *Rossetti Papers, 1862 to 1870*, London, 1903.

——, *Some Reminiscences of William Michael Rossetti*, London, 1906, 2 vols.

——, *Democratic Sonnets*, London, 1907, 2 vols.

SHELLEY, PERCY BYSSHE

Shelley, P. B., *Complete Works*, Julian edition, ed. Roger Ingpen and Walter E. Peck, London, 1926–30, 10 vols.

Angeli, Helen Rossetti, *Shelley and His Friends in Italy*, London, 1911.

de Courten, Maria Luisa Giartosio, *Percy Bysshe Shelley e l'Italia*, Milan, 1923.

Dowden, Edward, *The Life of Percy Bysshe Shelley*, London, 1886, 2 vols.

Hill, R. H., *The Shelley Correspondence in the Bodleian Library*, Oxford, 1926.

Peck, Walter Edwin, *Shelley: his Life and Work*, Boston and New York, 1927.

Wolfe, Humbert (editor), *The Life of Percy Bysshe Shelley*, an omnibus anthology of the accounts of Hogg, Trelawny, and Peacock, London, New York, and Toronto, 1933, 2 vols.

SWINBURNE, ALGERNON CHARLES

Swinburne, A. C., *Collected Poetical Works*, London, 1927, 2 vols.

——, *Complete Works*, the Bonchurch edition, ed. Sir Edmund Gosse and Thomas James Wise, London, 1925–27, 20 vols.

Swinburne, A. C., *Ode to Mazzini*, with a preface by Edmund Gosse, London, 1909.
——, *The Italian Mother and Other Poems*, ed. T. J. Wise, London, 1918.
——, *The Ride from Milan and Other Poems*, ed. T. J. Wise, London, 1918.
Chew, Samuel C., *Swinburne*, Boston, 1929.
Galimberti, Alice, *L'Aedo d'Italia: Algernon Charles Swinburne*, Palermo, 1925.
Hake, Thomas; and Compton-Rickett, Arthur, *Letters of Algernon Charles Swinburne. With Some Personal Recollections*, London, 1918.
Henderson, W. Brooks Drayton, *Swinburne and Landor*, London, 1918.
Hyder, Clyde Kenneth, *Swinburne's Literary Career and Fame*, Durham, North Carolina, 1933.
Lafourcade, Georges, *La Jeunesse de Swinburne (1837–1867)*, Paris, 1928, 2 vols.
Lafourcade, Georges, *Swinburne: A Literary Biography*, London, 1932.
Leith, Mrs. Disney, *The Boyhood of Algernon Charles Swinburne. Personal Recollections . . . With Extracts from Some of his Private Letters*, London, 1917.
Meyerstein, E. H. W., "Two Scenes from a Tragedy by Algernon Charles Swinburne," *The London Mercury and Bookman*, No. 220, February 1938, pp. 415–23.
Nicolson, Harold, *Swinburne*, English Men of Letters, London, 1926.
Richter, Ludwig, *Swinburne's Verhältnis zu Frankreich und Italien*, Leipzig, 1911.
Swinburne and Saffi:
John Purves, letter in *The* [London] *Times Literary Supplement*, September 24, 1931, pp. 729–30.
Alice Galimberti, letter in *The* [London] *Times Literary Supplement*, November 5, 1931, p. 866.
Vaughan, Charles E., *Bibliographies of Swinburne, Morris, and Rossetti*, London, 1914.
Welby, Thomas Earle, *A Study of Swinburne*, London, 1926.

TENNYSON, ALFRED, FIRST BARON TENNYSON

Tennyson, A., *Poetic and Dramatic Works*, Cambridge edition, ed. W. J. Rolfe, Boston and New York, 1898.
Fausset, Hugh L'Anson, *Tennyson: a Modern Portrait*, London, 1923.
Lang, Andrew, *Alfred Tennyson*, Modern English Writers, Edinburgh and London, 1901.
Lyall, Sir Alfred C., *Tennyson*, English Men of Letters, London, 1902.
Nicolson, Harold G., *Tennyson: Aspects of His Life, Character, and Poetry*, London, 1923.
Ritchie, Mrs. Anne Thackeray, *Records of Tennyson, Ruskin and Browning*, London, 1892.
Tennyson, Hallam, Second Baron Tennyson, *Alfred Lord Tennyson: a Memoir*, London, 1897, 2 vols.

Tennyson, Hallam, Second Baron Tennyson, *Tennyson and His Friends*, London, 1911.

Wise, Thomas James, *A Bibliography of the Writings of Alfred, Lord Tennyson*, London, 1908, 2 vols.

Wolfe, Humbert, *Tennyson*, London, 1930.

WILDE, OSCAR FINGALL O'FLAHERTIE

Wilde, O., *Poems*, ed. Robert Ross, London, 1909.

WORDSWORTH, WILLIAM

Wordsworth, W., *Complete Poetical Works*, Cambridge edition, ed. A. J. George, Boston and New York, 1904.

——, *Poetical Works*, ed. William Knight, London, 1896, 8 vols.

——, *Prose Works*, ed. William Knight, London, 1896, 2 vols.

——, *Concerning . . . the Convention of Cintra*, with an appendix by Thomas de Quincey, London, 1890.

Batho, Edith C., *The Later Wordsworth*, Cambridge, England, 1933.

Bickersteth, Geoffrey L., *Leopardi and Wordsworth*, London, [1927].

Dicey, Albert V., *The Statesmanship of Wordsworth: an Essay*, Oxford, 1917.

Dicey, A. V., *Wordsworth's Tract on the Convention of Cintra [Published 1809] with Two Letters . . . Written in the Year 1811, Now Republished*, London, 1915.

Elton, Oliver, *Wordsworth*, London, 1924.

Güttler, Felix, *Wordsworth's politische Entwicklung*, Stuttgart, 1914.

Harper, George McLean, *William Wordsworth: His Life, Works, and Influence*, 3rd edition, London, 1929.

Wells, John Edwin, "The Story of Wordsworth's *Cintra*," *Studies in Philology*, XVIII, 15–76 (Chapel Hill, North Carolina, January 1, 1921).

Wise, Thomas James, *A Bibliography of the Writings in Prose and Verse of William Wordsworth*, London, 1916.

The Letters of William and Dorothy Wordsworth: The Middle Years, ed. Ernest de Selincourt, Oxford, 1937, 2 vols.

Minor Verse

Milman, Henry Hart, *Fazio, a Tragedy*, Oxford, 1815, pp. 27–29.

Hemans, Felicia Dorothea, *Poetical Works*, Oxford edition, London, 1914. Poems, 1816–34, sympathetic with Italian cause.

Hare, Augustus William and Julius Charles, "Ode to Italy," written 1818 by A. W. Hare, in *Guesses at Truth*, 3rd edition, London, 1847, pp. 563–64.

Sotheby, William, *Farewell to Italy, and Occasional Poems*, London, 1818.

"The Briton's Lament for Italy," *The New Monthly Magazine*, II, 17 (1821).

"The Heroes of Naples. A New Ballad," *The London Magazine*, July 1821, pp. 17–18.

[Chaloner, J.], *Rome; a Poem. In Two Parts*, London, 1821. *Cf.* Byron's *Childe Harold* or Rogers's *Italy*.

Browne, Thomas, *Italian Tales and Other Poems*, London, 1829.

Beste, John Richard Digby, *Satires and the Beggar's Coin; a Poem*, 2nd edition, London, 1831.

Beattie, William, *The Heliotrope; or, Pilgrim in Pursuit of Health*, London, 1833. 2nd edition published as *The Pilgrim in Italy*, London, [1845?]. *Cf.* Byron and Rogers.

Sharp, Richard ["Conversation"], *Letters and Essays in Prose and Verse*, 2nd edition, London, 1834.

Rhymes from Italy, in a Series of Letters, to a Friend in England, London, 1836.

[Shannon, Edward N.], "Volpi, Odoardo," *Arnaldo; Gaddo; and Other Poems; Unacknowledged by Lord Byron*, London, 1836.

Reade, John Edmund, *Italy: a Poem*, London, 1838. 2nd edition in 1845. *Cf.* Rogers and Byron.

Reade, John Edmund, *Poetical Works*, 4th edition, London, 1865, 3 vols.

Kemble, Frances Anne, "Farewell to Italy," in *Poems*, Philadelphia, 1844, pp. 23–24.

Taylor, Sir Henry, *Autobiography*, London, 1885, 2 vols. "Lago Lugano," a poem, II, 14–16 (1844).

Charles, Mrs. Elizabeth Rundle, "Italy. 1848," in *Songs Old and New*, London, 1894, pp. 337–40. This poem Tennyson liked.

Burbidge, Thomas; and Clough, Arthur Hugh, *Ambarvalia*, London, 1849.

For Rome: Ora e Sempre, [London? 1850?].

The Lays of Modern Rome, London, 1853.

Darby, Eleanor, *Lays of Love and Heroism, Legends, Lyrics, and Other Poems*, London, 1855.

Lushington, Franklin and Henry, *La Nation Boutiquière and other poems chiefly political*, Cambridge, England, 1855.

O'Brien, James Bronterre, *Ode to Lord Palmerston*, London, 1856.

Ashford, John, *Italy's Hope; a Tale of Florence*, London, 1857.

[Wilde, Lady Jane Francesca Speranza], "Speranza," *Ugo Bassi: a Tale of the Italian Revolution*, London, 1857.

"B," "Italy, 1859–60," *The Athenaeum*, March 31, 1860, p. 442.

Barlow, Henry C., *Rome from Monte Mario, with Other Way-Side Sketches*, London, 1860.

Fullom, Stephen Watson, *The Exile's Daughter. A Story of the Italian War*, London, 1860.

Italian Lyrics, and other Poems, London, 1860.

L., H., *Italy: Past—Present—and Future*, London, 1860.

MacIlwaine, Rev. William, *A Vision of Italy*, London, 1861.

Mackay, Francis Alexander, *Lays and Poems on Italy*, London, 1862.

Phillipson, Mrs. Caroline Giffard, *Songs on Italy; and Other Poems*, dedicated to Garibaldi, London, 1862.

Waters, John, *The Refugees, and Other Poems*, London, 1862.

Swann, Thomas, *Modern Italy: a Poem*, London, 1863.

Darby, Eleanor, *Ruggiero Vivaldi, and other lays of Italy* . . ., dedicated "to the Italian liberator, the hero of the age, the immortal Giuseppe Garibaldi," London, 1865.

W[heler], C[harlotte] T[heresa], *Occasional Poems, Fables, and Translations from "Filicaja," and Other Italian Poets*, London, 1865.

Irby, F. W., *Italy: Original Poems and Translations*, London, 1868.

Darby, Eleanor, *Legends of Many Lands; Sonnets, Songs, and Other Poems*, London, 1870.

Palgrave, Francis Turner, *Lyrical Poems*, London, 1871.

A Rhymester's Run through Italy, London, 1871. *Cf.* Rogers's *Italy*.

[Mudie, Charles Edward], *Stray Leaves*, 2nd edition, [London?], 1872.

Austin, Alfred, *Rome or Death!*, Edinburgh, 1873.

Austin, Alfred, *The Autobiography of Alfred Austin, Poet Laureate, 1835–1910*, London, 1911, 2 vols.

Blagden, Isabella, *Poems*, with a memoir by Alfred Austin, Edinburgh and London, 1873.

Thornbury, George Walter, *Historical and Legendary Ballads and Songs*, illustrated by Whistler, Tenniel, etc., London, 1876 [1875].

Myers, Ernest, *The Defence of Rome and other Poems*, London and Oxford, 1880.

X

Some Translated Italian Writers

ALFIERI, VITTORIO

Alfieri, V., *Tragedies*, tr. Charles Lloyd, London, 1815, 3 vols. 2nd edition, London, 1821, 4 vols.

Megaro, Gaudence, *Vittorio Alfieri: Forerunner of Italian Nationalism*, New York, 1930.

AZEGLIO, MASSIMO TAPARELLI D'

Azeglio, M. T. d', *Hector Fieramosca*, tr. [M. H. Rankin], London, 1835.

——, *The Maid of Florence*, tr. W. Felgate, London, 1853, 3 vols. Called in Italian *Niccolò de' Lapi*.

CARDUCCI, GIOSUÈ

Bailey, John C., *Carducci*, the Taylorian Lecture, Oxford, 1926.

Bickersteth, G. L., *Carducci: A Selection of his Poems, with Verse Translations, Notes, and Three Introductory Essays*, London, 1913.

Holland, Maud, *Poems by Giosuè Carducci*, London, 1907.

Rendel, Romilda, *From the Poems of Giosuè Carducci, 1835–1907*, London, 1929.

Ranzi, Giuseppe, *Il risorgimento politico italiano nella poesia di Giosuè Carducci*, Ravenna, 1906.

Williams, Orlo, *Giosuè Carducci*, London, 1914.

Zanichelli, Domenico, *Le Poesie politiche di Giosuè Carducci*, Bologna, 1931.

CASTI, GIOVANNI BATTISTA

Casti, G. B., *The Court of Beasts*, tr. [William Stewart Rose], London, 1816. The second edition, *The Court and Parliament of Beasts*, London, 1819, was signed by Rose.

DALL' ONGARO, FRANCESCO

Dall' Ongaro, F., *The Athenaeum*, March 3, 1860, pp. 293–96. By [Theodosia Garrow Trollope(?)].

FILICAIA, VINCENZO DA

Filicaia, V. da, Sonnet to Italy translated in *The London Magazine*, September 1820, p. 276.

Filicaia, V. da, Sonnet to Italy translated in
The London Magazine, September 1823, p. 252. By C. S.
Macmillan's Magazine, VII, 240 (January 1863). By Sir John Kingston James.

GIUSTI, GIUSEPPE

Lushington, Henry, translations of Giusti's "The Boot" and others of his poems, *British Quarterly Review*, February 1853, pp. 54–95.
[Trollope, Theodosia Garrow(?)], "Giusti," *The Athenaeum*, April 5, 1856, pp. 417–19.
Lushington, Henry, *The Italian War, 1848–9, and the last Italian Poet*, London, 1859.
Giusti, G., "The Boot," translated in *Macmillan's Magazine*, II, 244–48 (July 1860).
——, "Sant' Ambrogio," translated in *Macmillan's Magazine*, IV, 39–41 (May 1861).
Horner, Susan, *The Tuscan Poet Giuseppe Giusti and His Times*, London, 1864.

GUIDICCIONI, GIOVANNI

S., "Translation of Guidiccioni's Sonnet to Italy," *The New Monthly Magazine*, X, 222 (1824).

NICCOLINI, G. B.

Niccolini, G. B., *Arnold of Brescia*, tr. Theodosia Garrow, later wife of Thomas Adolphus Trollope, London, 1846.

PELLICO, SILVIO

Pellico, S., *My Imprisonments*, tr. Thomas Roscoe, London, 1833. Other translations were published: Edinburgh, 1838; London, 1850; London and Edinburgh, 1859.
——, *The Duties of Men*, tr. Thomas Roscoe, London, 1834. There were other translations in 1837 and 1869.
[Roscoe, Thomas(?)] on Silvio Pellico and Maroncelli, *The Athenaeum*, 1833:
January 19th, pp. 37–38.
February 2nd, pp. 67–69.
February 16th, pp. 102–3.
March 2nd, p. 134.
May 18th, p. 312.
October 19th, pp. 691–92.
November 30th, pp. 807–8.
Italian Scenes and Stories, London, 1872. Chapter 12 tells the story of Silvio Pellico and Maroncelli.

INDEX